BULLS IN THE CHINA SHOP

ALSO BY THE AUTHOR:

The Stubborn Earth: American Agriculturalists on Chinese Soil, 1898–1937

Edited by Randall E. Stross:

Technology and Society in Twentieth-Century America

BULLS IN THE CHINA SHOP

and Other Sino-American Business Encounters

RANDALL E. STROSS

PANTHEON BOOKS • NEW YORK

To Maureen, Rebecca, and Martin

 Published in the United States by Pantheon Books, a division of Random House, Inc., New York, and simultaneously in Canada by Random House of Canada Limited, Toronto.

Library of Congress Cataloging-in-Publication Data
Stross, Randall E.
Bulls in the China shop and other Sino-American business encounters / by Randall E. Stross.
p. cm.
Includes bibliographical references and index.
ISBN 0-394-58292-6
1. Corporations, American—China. I. Title.
HD2910.S77 1991
338.8'8973051—dc20 90-52523

Calligraphy by Henry Sene Yee
Book design by Stephanie Bart-Horvath

Manufactured in the United States of America
First Edition

CONTENTS

ACKNOWLEDGMENTS

I owe thanks to many for assistance. In Ann Arbor I was able to consult the newly opened papers of the National Council for U.S.–China Trade (now the U.S.–China Business Council) with the aid of a travel grant from the Gerald R. Ford Foundation. The Center for Chinese Studies at the University of Michigan provided additional financial support that enabled me to use the University's Chinese periodicals collection and the Americans In China materials at the Bentley Historical Library. I was fortunate also to find cheerful assistance at the East Asia Collection at the Hoover Institution and the Jackson Library at Stanford's Graduate School of Business; the Baker Library at Harvard's Business School; the U.S.–China Business Council library in Washington, D.C.; and the Center for Chinese Studies at the University of California, Berkeley.

A research trip to China in 1988 was supported by a summer research grant from the San Jose State University School of Business. In Beijing, I was the guest of Antonio Zamora, the general manager of the Great Wall Sheraton, who gave me the run of the hotel and made the entire expatriate and Chinese staff available to me for private interviews. I also wish to thank in particular Karen van Druten and Goh Siong Huat for their special efforts in making interview arrangements and helping me to use my month at the hotel fruitfully.

I learned much during my Beijing visit from several dozen business people who took time to speak with me about their experiences in China; I promised anonymity to all, and here can only thank them collectively. I was astounded and delighted by the changes that I discovered at the Beijing Library, which might be called China's equivalent to our Library of Congress, and also at the main library of Beijing University. Years earlier, between 1979 and 1981 when I lived in China, I had had many misadventures at both libraries. The librarians then worked by the dictum that patrons and library materials should not be allowed to make each other's acquaintance. But when I returned in 1988, I found that not only had the Beijing Library moved into a splendid new home, its staff was much more hospitable to foreign and Chinese scholars alike. The librarians at Beijing University had also undergone a similar transformation. The subsequent sad events of 1989, however, overshadow these welcome, but comparatively minor, developments.

During 1988–89, I was a National Fellow at the Hoover Institution at Stanford, where I prepared the first draft of the book. I would like to thank the Institution for generously supporting the project while allowing me to follow my own idiosyncratic bent; I am particularly indebted to Ramon Myers, who prodded and encouraged the project from conception through completion.

Over the course of several years, presentations given at Stanford; the University of California, Berkeley; the University of British Columbia; and an annual meeting of the Academy of Management provided opportunities to test portions of the work while in progress. The *China Quarterly* kindly gave me permission to use material in Chapter Ten that first appeared in that journal.

I am especially grateful to three individuals, Frank Hawke, Gail Hershatter, and Dan Kelliher, for extremely detailed—and painfully stringent—criticism of the rough manuscript from top to bottom. I was glad also to have additional comments about all or parts of the manuscript from Susan Champagne, Carl Crook, Tom Hofstedt, Emily Honig, M. D. Kwan, Judith and Stanley Lubman, Ramon Myers, Rick Pollay, Steve McGurk, and Neil Sieling. I count myself among the bulls mentioned in the book's title, and though these early readers helped me correct many deficiencies, I was too bullheaded to accept all of their suggestions. In the end, the book's shortcomings remain my own responsibility.

The final draft of the book was prepared during the 1989–90 school year, when I was assisted by released time from San Jose State University and by visiting scholar appointments at Stanford's Graduate School of Business and the Center for East Asian Studies.

Through all, my family gave much to make this work possible. To them the book is dedicated.

R. S.

Stanford, California
August 31, 1990

INTRODUCTION:

SALESMAN IN BEIJING

America's most famous salesman, Willy Loman, appeared on a Chinese stage for the first time in May 1983. His debut in the first Chinese production of Arthur Miller's *Death of a Salesman* was watched closely by reporters from both Chinese and American newspapers who gathered to see how Willy, the best-known dramatic representative of American capitalism and of the American dream ("riding a smile and a shoeshine"), would go over in Beijing.

Willy was played by Ying Ruocheng, heading a distinguished Chinese cast, and Arthur Miller himself had been recruited as director of the production. Miller's participation was unusual. Ying, who with the playwright Cao Yu had begun to discuss the proposal with Miller a few years earlier, could not resist boasting to Chinese reporters that China had scored a major coup, as Miller had never directed *Salesman* anywhere else abroad. For Miller, the invitation to go to China was attractive because of the challenges of adapting this particular play, about American capitalism, for an audience in a socialist China. Other plays of his had already been staged in China—*The Crucible* had played in Shanghai, and Miller had heard that audiences had been moved to tears by the memories that the depiction of the Salem witch-hunts had evoked of the suffering during the Cultural Revolution. And *Death of a Salesman* had been staged in other socialist countries, such as the Soviet Union, without his personal participation; in those cases, the play had been reduced to a morality tale about the evils of capitalism. But in 1983 the Chinese were clearly in the midst of ideological change, and their interpretation of *Salesman* seemed likely to be original. The unpredictability of the outcome and the symmetry of paired opposites—socialist Chinese actors staging a play about capitalist America—was intriguing to Miller, and to the wider world as well.[1]

In the journal that he kept during the two months of rehearsals in Beijing, Miller privately confessed that he was dubious about the chances for a successful adaptation. *Death of a Salesman* seemed more culture-bound than his other plays. He wrote: "Willy Loman had sprung out of a world of business ambition, a society infected with the success fever." The Chinese, on the other hand, had been taught "proletarian socialist values," the very antithesis of those Willy strives for. Yet Miller had been to China twice previously and was encouraged on this visit by how the Chinese seemed to approach *Salesman* without any ideological agenda.[2]

Ironies abounded in the production. *Death of a Salesman* had originally opened in New York in 1949, coincidentally the year that the Chinese Communist Party came to power and the United States broke off diplomatic contacts with mainland China. When Miller returned to China in the 1980s, he discovered that the theater costume department was best at doing clothes and hairstyles of the 1940s. It was not hard for them to re-create the world that had existed in the late 1940s when Miller had conceived *Salesman.*[3]

Other ironies concerned the changing ideological temperatures in both countries. Many years before, in the early 1950s, Columbia Pictures had filmed *Salesman,* but the studio's publicity department asked if Miller would sign an anti-communist pledge for the American Legion before *Salesman* was released, lest it be picketed. Miller, a lifetime *anti-*anti-Communist, refused. Thirty years later, however, when he got the chance to introduce this putatively anti-capitalist play in a socialist country, he discovered that the Chinese actors were not interested in the ideological aspects that had been so sensitive in the United States. Looking back, Miller regarded his experiences during the McCarthy reign in the 1950s as useful preparation for understanding what artists had gone through in China during the Cultural Revolution. "It is both strange and somehow logical," he wrote in his Beijing journal, "that I should be directing this same play in a room where more than a hundred actors spent years whiling away their blacklisted time." Miller and his Chinese ensemble had two months of preparation time before the opening night. Would Willy Loman, the American salesman, come alive before a Chinese audience?[4]

Before the curtain rose in Beijing, the Chinese principals debated whether their audience would know what a salesman was. Less than a year earlier, Ying Ruocheng had told Miller that a Chinese audience would have a difficult time understanding the play, but Ying had changed his own mind in the interim. Miller noticed the rapidity of the changes in China too. He told inquiring reporters:

> I thought we'd have to write a big essay explaining what salesmen are and put it in the program, but Willy explains in the course of the play what a salesman does. In 1983, [the Chinese] know all about that. There are now people selling stuff on commission. There are now traveling buyers going from place to place trying to buy materials. . . . It may not have been a known profession, but it sure as hell is now.[5]

Miller was angered when *Newsweek* asserted that Chinese audiences would find it hard to appreciate the play because "there isn't a salesman the length or breadth of China." Regarding salespeople as characteristic figures in a capitalist tableau was wrong, Miller felt. He wanted to show how Americans and Chinese stood on shared ground, and he would not permit Willy Loman's profession to be identified with the ideology of capitalism. While in Beijing, he said: "You go out on the street here on a Sunday and you see hawkers and pushcart peddlers and it reminds you of the Lower East Side [of Manhattan] 40 years ago." Miller was an unlikely candidate to argue that a sales impulse can reside innately in a culture, but in his eagerness to show that salespeople are found everywhere, he perpetuated an old Western view of the Chinese as a people with uncanny commercial skills. "They invented what we call commerce," Miller said of the Chinese. "These are the guys who were sitting here 800 years ago, buying low and selling high." Commercial acumen was shared by both Chinese and American cultures, and if it had not been visible in China in the most recent several decades, then it had been merely dormant, awaiting an opportunity such as the present moment to reappear.[6]

How curious this was: Arthur Miller, no eulogist of American capitalism, had come to rhapsodize about Willy Loman as a global Everyman. Instead of a parable about the unfeeling callousness of the capitalist system, the play in Beijing came to be seen in Miller's own mind as ideologically neutral; the emphasis was to be placed on the family and the failed hopes of a father for his sons. Ying Ruocheng concurred. Although the play could be read as a statement of the false values and inhumanity of capitalist society, the way it uses people such as Willy Loman and then discards them, the criticism applied just as appropriately to socialist societies. Ying said, "Every society has its version of that problem. Certainly, China does, and this is how we hope people will relate to the play, in their own terms."[7]

By the end of the two months of rehearsal, director and cast had talked often of universal bonds transcending national boundaries—Miller had told his cast that "at the deeper levels where this play lives we are joined in a unity that is perhaps biological." But the claims were untested until the play's premiere before a Chinese audience. On the night of the preview, Miller sat in the audience, intently watching their reactions to the performance. When the play opened, the high noise level from conversations, squalling children, and banging wooden seats diminished, but did not cease. Miller did not expect silence; in fact, he was pleased to see that a young couple beside him, who continued to talk during the play "at pretty much the same vocal level they would use in their own living rooms," at least did not turn away from the stage despite their continuing discussion. But then pandemonium broke out: The entire audience was on its feet, waving arms, laughing, jabbing one another—they had never seen the stage trick in which the two Loman sons, men in their thirties, disappear from the upstairs bedroom on stage and reappear in a moment as teenagers carrying a football and a punching bag. Miller was aghast at the audience reaction and later confided to his journal: This was "total, irretrievable absence of comprehension." At the end of the performance, the audience arose, applauded, slammed closed their wooden seats, and rushed off to catch their buses home.[8]

This inauspicious debut, Miller later learned, had been staged before the vegetable and meat suppliers of the theater's canteen, who had been given the tickets to ensure that the theater would get the freshest and choicest supplies. Ying Ruocheng assured Miller that, given their educational background and the infrequency of their attendance of plays, the audience had actually been "captivated."[9]

Two nights later, the play officially opened before a more visibly appreciative audience, which included diplomatic notables and foreign residents. Miller appeared on stage for the final curtain and received a standing ovation; a joyful party followed. But this otherwise triumphant moment was tinged with a lingering doubt that the cultural chasm had not been bridged. Miller said: "At some point in our milling around for our last farewells, for what reason I have no idea, I felt a kind of despair; maybe it was a fear that when all was said, I could not know what I suppose I had come here to find out—what my play really sounded like to the Chinese, and what in their heart of hearts these actors had made of it. In a word, the old opacity of 'China' was once again descending over my vision."[10] This is no Kipling-quoting neo-colonialist ("East is East, West is West . . .") speaking, this is Arthur Miller, the sympathetic "old friend" of China. Yet even he was occasionally troubled by doubts that the two cultures could ever fully understand each other.

After *Salesman* opened in Beijing, the official press had some minor criticisms. The reviewer for the *People's Daily,* Liu Housheng, praised the complexity of a character such as Willy Loman, who evokes, during the course of the play, a variety of emotions, from sympathy to loathing, from approval to disapproval. But the pacing of the play, Liu said, was too fast, like the pace of life in American society, and not appropriate for a Chinese audience. Liu also ventured a critical opinion about Ying Ruocheng's portrayal of Willy, who often seemed to avoid looking directly at the other actors on stage. Showing a canny understanding of a salesperson's style, Liu argued that salespeople develop a habit of looking directly into the eyes of potential buyers, always searching the face of prospects. Although on stage Willy Loman was not at work and did not actually need to lock eyes with others, Liu felt the play would have had more verisimilitude if Ying Ruocheng's Willy Loman had shown more evidence of the salesman's habits at home.[11]

Other Chinese newspapers interpreted the play in a more political manner. The official Xinhua News Agency, for example, described Willy Loman as a loyal victim of the corporation. A youth newspaper described Willy's suicide as "the inevitable result of the contradictions of capitalism," and presented the play as a cautionary tale—young Chinese should not be seduced by the bright lights of the West. The ideological message about capitalism that Miller took out of the play was precisely the message the Chinese authorities tried to put back in.[12]

But individual Chinese had their own interpretations. To many, *Salesman* was a play about a man who has to reconcile his dreams with the disappointing reality of his life, and worse, with that of his sons, who failed to live up to their father's expectation that they become "dragons"—a traditional Chinese term referring to the ambitious and successful. Observing the friction between Willy and his sons, and the inability of Linda Loman to prevent her husband from taking his own life, the Chinese saw a maelstrom of powerful emotions within the family. One Chinese woman tearfully exclaimed, "It's the same situation."[13] The Chinese audience also saw a different message about American materialism from that seen by American audiences. Willy Loman owned a house with two bedrooms, a refrigerator, and a telephone—the modest trappings of a middle-class American family in 1949. But in the eyes of the Chinese, hungry for information about standards of living in the capitalist West, the Lomans seemed to enjoy heavenly plentitude. Miller anticipated, half-jokingly, that the Chinese would see the material possessions of Willy Loman and ask, "He's got trouble?"; and this was precisely the question that was asked quite seriously by the Chinese audience.

When working with the Chinese cast, Miller described Willy's sons as narcissists who could not delay gratifying whatever urges they felt. The director, however, hit a raw nerve in the actors. From their reaction, he wrote in his journal, he saw that it was too early "to identify a common enthusiasm for life-improving goods and inventions with narcissism." Miller said that he could never have guessed when he wrote the play that it would eventually be read by Chinese in 1983 as a call for individualism and acquisitiveness. A young Chinese student told a CBS interviewer in the theater lobby, "We are moved by it because we also want to be number one, and to be rich and successful."[14]

Willy Loman had been preceded by hundreds, and would later be followed by thousands, of American salespeople coming to the People's Republic of China to do business. They were also accompanied by other businesspeople, such as engineers and technicians, office and factory managers, accountants and support staff, who took with them to China business ideas and practices that appeared foreign. The same fascination that drew Miller to China to explore apparent differences, in quest of shared common ground, also drew many in this small army of representatives of American capitalism. We usually do not treat businesspeople as merchants of ideas, but in the case of the United States and China, we find American businesspeople and their Chinese counterparts meeting at the intersection of culture and ideology, forced amid the everyday hurly-burly of business to confront larger questions about the self-evident differences between themselves and those on the other side. Some participants quietly assumed the role of amateur ideologues, not in the pejorative sense of propagandists, but in the neutral sense of those who articulate firmly held beliefs about an ideal socioeconomic system. And in their observations of cultural differences and adjustments required in the course of working with their foreign counterparts, they also took on the role of amateur anthropologists.

The Beijing production of *Death of a Salesman* captured in microcosm many of the elements of the business encounters that took place outside the world of the theater. Viewed from Olympian heights, it represented the encounter of impersonal systems, the socialist and the capitalist; viewed from the level of the floorboards, it was the encounter of Arthur Miller and Ying Ruocheng and other individuals whose thoughts and behavior were not mechanically determined from on high. The same was true of the encounters between American and Chinese businesspeople: at once representative of large forces, and at the same time deserving of attention to their human particularity and frequent unpredictability.

The 1983 arrival of *Salesman* in Beijing marks about one-third of the way through a remarkable decade of great change that China experienced between 1979 and 1989. I was on hand to witness the beginnings, when I lived for two years in Nanjing between 1979 and 1981 doing graduate research in Chinese studies. It was then that I first began to explore how American businesspeople saw their encounters with the Chinese, and how strikingly different that was from the way Chinese saw their encounters with Americans. As the decade progressed, I continued to watch with interest, but I also liked to station myself a few paces off to the side so that I had a vantage point from which to observe how each group thought about the people on the other side of the Pacific. As the end of the 1980s neared, I began to collect materials for a book about these Sino-American business encounters—concentrating not on trade statistics, but on the human drama of how Americans and Chinese, in the course of negotiating, selling, buying, hiring, training, socializing, and arguing, gave considerable thought to larger issues concerning their own identities and beliefs. A decade seemed a manageable, if artificial, period to examine. My plan was to begin in 1979, at the start of the normalization of diplomatic relations, and end in 1989, at the tenth anniversary.

All did not go as planned, however. As I worked on the project I discovered that I had to give attention to events in the earlier 1970s, in order to make sense of what followed. At the other end of the selected decade, the year 1989, what I had originally thought would be a contrived end to an era, turned out to be a historically real divider. After the massacre in Beijing in early June 1989, the crackdown on democracy protests in other cities, the mass arrests, and the reappearance of propaganda techniques last used in the Cultural Revolution, a new era in United States–China relations began. The business relationships remained, for the most part, intact, but 1989 marked an end to the sentimentalism of Americans, the idealism of Chinese, and the optimism of both that had charged the atmosphere in the 1980s and fueled the rapid development of business ties. Before 1989, Americans had grand hopes and expectations that China was on its way toward becoming more like America with every passing day. After the 1989 crackdown on China's democracy movement, however, Americans were forced to confront not just a Chinese government that was opposed to principles that Americans held dear, but also their own illusions about the short-term likelihood of China remaking itself into a fundamentally different society modeled on the capitalist West. Business between the two countries would go on; martial law in Beijing was lifted in January 1990; but the American business people who returned to China after the June evacuation returned with a changed outlook: no longer did they accord China the giddy special regard of the earlier years.

I anticipated neither the rapid growth of the student protests in the spring of 1989 nor the brutality of the government's suppression of them. But I was not surprised by the high level of emotional involvement Americans displayed as they witnessed the unfolding Democracy Spring and its violent end. The emotional investment Americans had made in China had begun long before that spring. One important component of it was the evolving business ties between China and the United States. I hope that this book about business relationships can throw light on the way in which the two countries' futures came to be seen by many on both sides as intertwined.

Much of the interest in the earlier encounters between American and Chinese businesspeople originated in the pairing of apparent opposites. We define who we are by determining who we are not, and Americans have long used the Chinese as an opposite people, different in every conceivable way: appearance, language, diet, customs. Located imaginatively on the opposite side of the earth, at the antipodes, the Chinese have served as an upside-down image that has provided Americans with a sense of distinct self-identity. The more extreme the difference, the more Americans have felt culturally unique, and with uniqueness, an accompanying sense of superiority has never been far behind. This habit of seizing upon apparent opposites in pursuit of a national identity is not particularly American. The Chinese themselves have a tradition, beginning several thousand years ago, which has sorted the world into a strictly bipolar scheme, Self and Other, and which has always been explicit about which of the two was regarded as superior.

In the modern era, both American and Chinese traditions were strengthened when the People's Republic of China was established in 1949. Now, added to extreme cultural difference was extreme ideological difference. In the Manichean terms of the Cold War, the Other (whether "Red China" or "the imperialist United States") was not merely different, or even inferior; it was evil incarnate. This mixture of exaggerated Otherness and normative judgment provided psychological comfort to both sides shortly thereafter, when American and Chinese troops engaged in fighting on the Korean peninsula.

After the Korean war, armed fighting ended, but the two countries remained incommunicado. Each grew accustomed to thinking of the other in the same way, as a blurry opposite image, defined as everything that oneself was not. When capitalist America looked across the Pacific to socialist China, it saw a country that was unfree, controlled by a powerful Communist Party, with an economy run by a state plan and organized in the countryside by an institution—the commune—that remained incomprehensible. The upside-down mirror image of the United States for the Chinese was one of no less sinister components, of American cities rendered all but uninhabitable by crime, of an economy run by a handful of capitalists who also held behind-the-scenes power in Washington.

In the early 1970s China and the United States began to open up lines of communication, and then for ten years, between 1979 and 1989, China, this country that had so recently defined itself as our diametric opposite in ideology, reversed some Cultural Revolution policies, then partially restored them, then reversed direction again and ventured further, repeating a cycle of taking two steps toward us and one step back. For brief periods, China appeared willing to try almost anything, regardless of earlier ideological orthodoxy. Americans were fascinated, yet periodically reminded of the original chasm of differences. Just as Arthur Miller had been troubled even at the moment of apparent triumph in Beijing, so too were American businesspeople and other China watchers troubled by lingering doubts about the possibility of ever understanding the Other.

The importance of the economic relationship between the two countries is usually measured by the volume of trade and investment flows.

But it also extends into the realm of ideas, imagination, and ideology, and in this realm the United States exerted considerable, if often overlooked, influence on China. The basic question—what happened when the world's largest socialist country began to do business with the world's largest capitalist country—can only be answered by building a collection of the experiences of the Americans and Chinese who have been participants.

I do not pretend to offer a comprehensive history of Sino-American business ties. The task I set myself is the more modest one of presenting vignettes and essays chosen for their power to express the curious interplay among business, culture, ideology, and personality. Readers will find three kinds of subjects examined simultaneously here: at the most basic level, the details of the encounters between Americans and Chinese; at an intermediate level, the interpretation of these encounters at the time, as revealed by what participants said and thought about their experiences; and at a more detached level, my own ruminations about it all. I jump back and forth across the cultural and ideological divide, interested not in an ideological agenda (I like to think), but rather in the reflections of the participants themselves. The most thoughtful and reflective contemporaries on both sides are the heroes. The guiding principle of my discussions of businesspeople is that it is not just philosophers who should be concerned about the unexamined life.

I begin the book by surveying the 1970s, the important formative period in which China and the United States became reacquainted, when Mao Zedong was still at the helm and Sino-American diplomatic relations had not yet been restored, and well before *Death of a Salesman* arrived. After looking at business interactions in the restrictive years of the late Cultural Revolution (1971–76) I then address how business was done (or not done) in the years that followed China's opening in the late 1970s. Next I explore management issues that emerged in the course of establishing joint ventures and in Sino-American consultations about management education. I close with a discussion of advertising and consumerism in China.

As an American talking about other Americans, I run the risk of exaggerating the importance of my compatriots in the much larger story of China's own economic reforms and later political upheaval. But I hope that I am successful in showing that the various encounters between individual Americans and their Chinese counterparts, when collected and viewed as a whole, possess a certain gravity and cumulatively influenced China and the United States in significant ways. Through these experiences, Americans and Chinese continually reshaped their understanding of what makes their respective cultural and ideological identities distinct. The mirror is an overworked metaphor in the historiography of Sino-American relations, but it is difficult to avoid noticing once again that Americans and Chinese continue to be important to one another, above all, as reflecting surfaces, useful as referents in the continuous process of national self-definition. The stories have the human drama intrinsic when individuals from different ideological systems and cultures come together and work in close proximity. They also have a tragic quality, as we look back with the burden of knowing that June 1989 lay ahead, exacting a heavy price from those Chinese who were most influenced by American people and ideas.

Knowing retrospectively of the breathtaking changes that lay ahead for Eastern Europe in the remaining months of 1989 and the spread of independent movements among the Soviet republics in 1990 also gives a resonant poignancy to China's reforms in the 1980s and the presence of American and other Western cheerleaders. As if a Law of Asynchrony governed the geography of socialist reforms, in the 1980s China had been bold when the Warsaw Pact countries had remained locked in seemingly unbreakable stasis. Then, in 1989, just as China's own commitment to the course of reform was cast into question and China froze, Eastern Europe melted. No sooner had the Berlin Wall and long-closed borders been opened than American companies rushed to Eastern Europe to take advantage of the new governments' encouragement of private foreign investment. Americans talked excitedly of Europe supplanting Asia as the economically dynamic region of the future. The very speed of the collapse of the Communist monopoly in Poland, Hungary, East Germany, Czechoslovakia, Bulgaria, and Romania suggested an ineluctable force, yet a force channeled by its own peculiar geographic dictates. In the eyes of Americans, China, which had so recently appeared to be the harbinger of the same ineluctable force, became the self-crippled laggard, unable to keep step with the march of history. In the excitement of discovery of new business opportunities in Eastern Europe, and in the rush to attend seminars, hire consultants, and establish joint ventures, few Americans paused to note the eerie similarity between this gold rush mentality and that of only a few years earlier in China. Both American capitalists and Eastern European ex-Communists might wish to pause and take stock of what can be learned from America's earlier business experiences in reformist China.

Ying Ruocheng, the actor who played Willy in China's *Salesman,* may be remembered by American television viewers as the actor who played the Mongol emperor Kublai Khan in the otherwise forgettable 1982 television movie *Marco Polo.* American viewers had no way of knowing that Ying was one of China's most respected living actors, whose voice has carried a great deal of weight in China's cultural affairs. At the time of the *Salesman* production in Beijing, Ying wrote about Miller in an essay published in a Beijing newspaper. The essay was didactic, as "personal" essays addressed to the public tend to be in China, and Ying was defensive about the desirability of staging plays from the West. To address criticism that apparently was in the air, and to make the case that art should not be contained by national boundaries, Ying told Chinese readers that Miller had spent his free time between rehearsals reading a translated volume of Yuan verse. These poems, Ying said, belong not to China alone, but to the world.[15]

Ying couched his appeal for tolerance of *Death of a Salesman* in an explicit disavowal that he was guilty of worshipping things foreign. To bolster his claim that he was not a cultural traitor, he used the traditional aphorism that said, in essence, use others to make oneself better: "Stones from other hills may serve to polish the jade of this one." Ying called upon other Chinese to emulate Miller. Foreign culture is good not as an end, but as a means—to make China stronger, as a tool to polish already precious Chinese "jade."

We come back to the strong sense of self of many Chinese and the defensiveness about appearing to be inferior to others. Perhaps it is this feature of modern China that sets it so apart from the other poor countries of the Third World—the historical consciousness of its past and an inchoate belief that time will bring a return of the wealth and power that once gave China a commanding position over the known world. When one looks at China from the outside, it is hard to tell where healthy national pride ends and overweening chauvinism begins (or whether the two can ever be distinguished). When Americans—who have never been known for national modesty in the international community either—met Chinese in recent years and tried to work out business deals that were in the mutual interests of both parties, both parties were sensitive to the larger verdicts being rendered about superiority and inferiority. It should not surprise us that American and Chinese participants in this story found their experiences to be emotionally charged, alternately exhilarating and exhausting, frustrating and deeply satisfying.

I

GETTING REACQUAINTED

1.

THE CANTON FAIR

When the U.S. table tennis team accepted a Chinese invitation to visit in early 1971, the Americans had to cross the *cordon sanitaire* the United States government had placed around "Red China." Travel by Americans to China was forbidden, as were almost all commercial relations. The People's Republic was not even permitted to use American dollars in international trade, and American oil companies could not fuel ships or aircraft proceeding to or from China. For twenty years, America had treated China officially as an area of contagion. Then, in April 1971, during the visit of the American "ping-pong diplomats," Richard Nixon lifted the curbs on bilateral contacts and trade. Just as it had taken a white president from the American South to successfully sponsor the Civil Rights Act of 1964, here too it took an unlikely sponsor of major change: a man whose anti-communist convictions had propelled his entire political career, and who in the 1960 presidential campaign had criticized any move that would lend "respectability" to the Beijing government. In 1971, when he reversed his stance toward China, the new position was spared criticism from the right because of the anti-communist career that had preceded the change.[1]

With the lifting of the trade embargo Americans could begin negotiating business deals with China, but the time and place for such discussions were closely restricted by the Chinese, who had long placed their own *cordon sanitaire* around foreign businesspeople. Americans, like other foreigners, were permitted to conduct business only at a trade fair held twice a year in the southern city of Canton (Guangzhou). The emphasis was on Chinese exports, and participation was by invitation only. Originally held downtown, the fair was moved in the early 1970s to a new exhibition hall directly facing the cavernous, Soviet-style Dong Fang Hotel that housed many of the foreign participants. It was a convenient arrangement—the foreign visitor merely had to cross the street to go from fair to hotel, but it also struck visitors as eerily reminiscent of the practices of imperial China, when Western traders were restricted to a small compound—also in Canton—and could go nowhere else and at no other time than the stipulated biannual trading seasons.[2]

In spring 1972, when the first contingent of twenty or so American invitees arrived at their first Canton Trade Fair, their number was dwarfed by 21,000 other participants. Most of the attendees were ethnic Chinese from Hong Kong and Southeast Asia, but there were also perhaps a thousand or so Europeans, many of whom had been making the trek to Canton since the first trade fair was held in 1957. The old China hands did not welcome the American newcomers, who they feared would bid up prices and be given red carpet treatment that the Europeans never received. The fear about prices proved well-founded. And Americans were so eager to find evidence that the Chinese were indeed according them special privileges that they reported home that the Dong Fang Hotel had added apple pie to welcome the Americans, though in fact it had been on the menu long before and was an established favorite of the German guests. The Europeans also resented the American arrivals for not having passed through the "bad old days," when, as one Englishman recalled, "there was indoctrination every night. People would come to your room and read to you from the Red Book incessantly." Americans had arrived too late; by the early 1970s, the Chinese hosts left their guests in peace at night.[3]

Ignoring the attitudes of the more experienced Europeans, the Americans were enthralled by the exoticism of the locale. When Robert Hoffman, a vice-president for Marshall Field, left his hotel in Hong Kong for the train that would take him to the trade fair, he savored his "last taste of western world luxury" as he rode in the hotel's Rolls Royce. In Canton, he found the streets to be beautiful in an "other-worldly sort of way," lined with lovely shade trees and largely free of automobiles. A group of buyers from New York returned from the fair so excited about their experiences that a fashion columnist said, "They sound more like children suddenly let loose in Santa's workshop" than sophisticated executives. The representative for Alexander's (who described her store to the Chinese as "the people's store") had told the Chinese with whom she negotiated: "Now we will start to walk together, but like children we will trip many times." Described on their return as latter-day Marco Polos, these American buyers brought back trunkloads of robes, silk shirts and pajamas, gold and jade jewelry, and other items; "a treasure trove."[4]

They also tended to assume that their trip to China was an epochal moment in the annals of modern commerce. But this fiction necessitated that Americans pretend that others had not established trade ties many years earlier. The discovery of the People's Republic thus required that the American Marco Polos and their admirers wear blinders. One sees an American hand in this scene: the stage held only actors of two nationalities, American and Chinese, the geometrically neat binary pairing, Us and Them; anyone else belonged to the audience, witness to the "historic" resumption of Sino-American trade ties. European or ethnic Chinese or Arab or African traders simply disappeared from the stage.

By their second fair, in the fall of 1972, the Americans' initial excitement had worn off somewhat. Along with the other foreign business representatives, they found many Chinese goods to be high priced with low availability for export. At the first fair in the spring, the volume of sales to American buyers had been a modest $5 million; at the second, it was a still modest $8 million. A significant increase in Sino-American trade did not seem likely. Still, the number of American participants climbed. Some hoped their businesses would stand apart from the pack; others went as commercial tourists, with spouses and children in tow. Many tried to arrange for a visa that would permit an excursion to Beijing and were disappointed. One American lamented afterward, "It was like being in Purgatory and trying to argue your way into Heaven." By the spring of 1975, Americans looked back nostalgically on the first fair attended in 1972, only three years earlier, when the Chinese had seemed to pay special attention and had provided appointments at an instant's notice and other little touches. Wrote one American to his home office: "Now we are just like other Europeans, suffering the same slings and arrows of defeat, frustration, and occasional triumph."[5]

A very small number of the Americans who went to Canton had had some previous personal acquaintance with mainland China, either before the Revolution, as children of missionaries or businesspeople there, or as American servicemen in the China-Burma-India theater during World War II. Many of the importers who attended the Canton Fair had done business previously in Hong Kong and Taiwan. But other

Americans arrived in Canton without any previous personal experience with China or the Chinese. One must wonder how Hollywood stereotypes of Asians, combined with the guarded manner of the People's Republic negotiators, who themselves were meeting Americans face-to-face for the first time, contributed to an impression of the Chinese as the inscrutable Orientals. The *Wall Street Journal,* without any hint of self-mockery, referred blandly in 1972 to the Chinese as "inscrutable hosts."[6]

To be sure, the Chinese trade officials who extended the first rounds of invitations to Americans and who conducted the negotiations committed many blunders from inexperience that reinforced the stereotype. For example, some Americans were invited to the fair and arrived only to discover that the Chinese were not interested in their line of business. Why, then, the Americans demanded to know, had they been invited? When the Chinese did not answer that a mistake had been made, the Americans supplied their own answer: The Chinese were simply the unfathomable people one expected to find at the end of the earth. James Lanigan, a representative for GTE Sylvania who had learned Chinese during the war, told other American representatives: "You talk and talk, and all they do is nod. You don't know if you're getting anywhere or not and think maybe you should go home. But then they'll call you at 1 A.M. to set up another appointment." The Chinese were unpredictable, unknowable.[7]

Americans prized directness. They did not like the way the Chinese traders deflected difficult questions with offerings of cups of tea. To American eyes this Chinese politeness, which was meant to spare the Americans from hearing disagreeable news, was interpreted as evasiveness. The American fondness for directness was also linked to a visible fondness, at least as an ideal, for what we might call "transparency": guilelessly putting one's best position on the bargaining table, without hiding critical information. But the transparent style works only if the other side adopts the same style. It was disconcerting for Americans, who were used to knowing the identity and status of business associates, not to know who was in charge when Chinese trade officials skipped over titles during introductions and disguised rank with the same blue or green outfits that everyone wore. As one American sales agent complained, "You don't know if the guy sitting across the table from you is top brass or a flunky." In the American mind, one was either transparent or inscrutable; there was no room for delicate shadings between the two extremes.[8]

Americans ascribed this inability to understand Chinese behavior to the ideological gap separating the two countries. American traders discovered that although they had been invited to China and were treated cordially, the government continued to denounce American capitalists and imperialism. American representatives were surprised when in the opera *On the Dock,* staged after a banquet during the fall 1975 trade fair, the United States was criticized for causing hardship and suffering to the Chinese people before Liberation ("When the stars & stripes flew over these docks and Yankees oppressed Chinese workers . . ."). Some took no offense and were amused; others walked out.[9]

For the most part, the foreign business visitors were kept insulated from the Cultural Revolution slogans that pervaded public places in China. If Americans and other foreign traders from capitalist countries had been able to read Chinese, they would have noticed many incongruous sights, such as the large red banners that greeted the arriving guests at the Dong Fang Hotel at the beginning of the spring 1976 fair. The inscription—in Chinese but not in English—called upon everyone to "warmly uphold the resolution of the Party Central Committee dismissing Deng Xiaoping from all his posts." Deng was the person most closely identified with the nascent liberalization of China's trade policy. Although the foreign traders were sheltered from the political hurricanes that raged about them, the Chinese interpreters and trade officials were not so fortunate. As the Chinese who had direct contact with foreigners, they themselves were in a politically suspect position and under constant Party scrutiny for signs of "unhealthy" political ideas.[10]

The political vocabulary of the Chinese, when rendered in English, was a source of amusement for Americans who had never heard the word "propaganda" used in the unapologetic way the Chinese seemed to use it. The Chinese, for example, would tell American visitors that they should do more "propaganda work" at the fair on behalf of their American companies and provide information for Chinese to study. Americans quickly learned to use certain terms and to avoid others such as "profits." When the representative from Hallmark was asked by his Chinese hosts "Why did you come?" he was ready with a well-rehearsed answer: "Not to place orders but to take the first step in establishing a relationship."[11]

To the Americans, the Chinese seemed surprisingly unpolitical at some times, and overly sensitive at others. In the spring of 1972 the first contingent of Americans arrived at about the time of the American mining of Vietnam's Haiphong harbor, yet the Chinese rarely brought up the Vietnam war. The political topic the Chinese discussed most often was American electoral politics; the Chinese quizzed each American about voting plans in the impending November election. Americans who went to China discovered that the diciest political issues were encountered later, when other Americans greeted them upon their return. Stanley Marcus of Neiman-Marcus, for example, experienced the greatest political difficulty related to his China trip on the homebound journey, when he passed through U.S. immigration in Honolulu. It took a half hour and many phone calls before the U.S. immigration officials could be convinced that it was perfectly legal again for a U.S. citizen to visit the People's Republic of China.[12]

Several years later, in 1975, American visitors saw indirect signs within China of new political campaigns and calls for "self-reliance." One American, who had seen Chinese bank employees using Japanese calculators on an earlier visit, now saw only abacuses being used. Yet the Chinese did not directly mention the campaign to the Americans and did not discuss Chinese politics. The Chinese also resisted announcing the Communist triumph when Saigon was taken in April 1975; American businesspeople in Beijing at the time got the news from newly arrived visitors and outside radio broadcasts, not from the Chinese. Americans were impressed by what they called the "business is business" attitude of the Chinese—the trade fair was open as usual even on May Day, 1975.[13]

This was as it should be, in the American view. By self-selection, the Americans in China were a group who believed strongly that international business belonged outside politics. Those who mixed politics and business and who were opposed in principle to business dealings with a Communist country stayed home. The Americans had heard of the politically charged atmosphere in China, and were pleased as well as surprised when they arrived in Canton to discover that the Chinese were "businesslike" and kept politics out of the meeting rooms. But politics were not banished completely. In practice, the Chinese policy of trade "based on equality and mutual benefit" meant balanced bilateral trade. When Americans sold far more to China than they bought in 1973 and 1974, Chinese authorities instructed their own trading agencies to supply China's import needs from countries other than the United States. Americans were also dismayed to learn that the Chinese apparently used a sliding scale in their pricing: goods sold to a First World country like the United States could be much more expensive than those sold to Third World countries.[14]

As relative newcomers, American traders were at a disadvantage whenever the Chinese gave special consideration to "old friends" such as the Europeans, some of whom had been to thirty Canton fairs by the time the Americans were first invited. "Old friends" were accorded better prices and commissions, and when desirable Chinese exports were in short supply, as they often were, the Chinese did not allow prices to be set by the market and allocation to be determined by the highest bidding. Instead, they allocated small quantities to all foreign customers. One American businessman said: "This is an intelligent way to sell because they are saying nobody is more important as a customer than anyone else. But it may come back to haunt them because the big buyers tend to get discouraged." This proved to be the case. Large American buyers were angry and frustrated because China's older customers were allowed to order before the trade fair began. When Americans inquired about supply problems, the Chinese replied candidly that they had many established customers from other parts of the world too, and "we don't forget our old friends."[15]

Veteran traders smirked when they saw inexperienced American newcomers trying to memorize selections from "Quotations of Chairman Mao." The Chinese did not expect foreigners to become Chinese. But Americans were gullible and the butt of various pranks staged by more experienced Europeans, who must have had difficulty keeping a straight face when advising Americans that it was best when dealing with the Chinese to be reserved and stiff. In 1972, one American newcomer asked an English veteran of the fair how to tell who in an identically dressed group of Chinese had the highest rank and was told the most important individuals wore white socks. The American spent the rest of the fair peeking under the table.[16]

Americans felt their way as they went, working in the darkness of inexperience, and were concerned, perhaps overly so, about the cultural differences in negotiating with the Chinese. Americans were not accustomed to the ritual followed by the Chinese in each negotiating session. This would open with lots of small talk and tea. One American reviewed a typical opening: "Everybody asks about my wife. We talk about the heat in the room. We then review the failure of communications between America and China for twenty-three years. We have a conversation about mutual benefit." More amenities, more tea. Then the mood and the subject would suddenly change, and the Chinese would turn to business negotiations, and then "it is all work."[17]

Americans were disconcerted by the way in which the Chinese "home team called all the shots," firmly directing the proceedings, buying or selling, and leaving little choice but to follow their lead and most often to accept their terms. Many discussions took place at tables on the exhibit floor, within the view and earshot of fellow competitors. The Chinese could appear inscrutable and omniscient simultaneously, as mysteriously all-knowing as they were unknowable themselves, at least in the eyes of the Americans who were ready to attribute fantastic powers to their hosts. At a time when very little information officially flowed between the countries, a Hallmark representative said, "We're a privately held company, but I'd say they knew more than most Americans do about Hallmark."[18]

During the course of the fair, the Chinese also had access to the latest information about fluctuations in world commodity markets, information that they kept to themselves and did not permit the foreign traders in Canton to obtain. This provided the Chinese with a certain advantage in negotiations which they did not hesitate to use. Business negotiations in other countries would bring buyer and seller closer together, but not in China, reported the Sylvania representative who went to Canton to purchase metals. He said that the Chinese price quote "started out at a figure higher than we would have had to pay anywhere else in the world, and after a week of negotiating it went even higher." This required some adjustment of expectations on the part of the Americans.[19]

A good sense of humor about these unfamiliar business practices was helpful, and in December 1974 a group of American traders held the inaugural meeting of a club whose founding charter mocked Cultural Revolution edicts:

> Within the ever present guidelines of equality and mutual benefit this organization is intended to be completely frivolous and non-business-like. Large quantities of booze should be consumed to achieve this end.
>
> Since it will obviously be necessary to adopt strict disciplinary by-laws to keep the proletarian rabble in line, you are hereby instructed to give immediate thought to rules which should be enacted in this regard. In doing so, you are naturally obligated to ensure that all undemocratic principles are fully maintained and even further developed. . . .
>
> Finally, we wish one and all a happy and healthy 1975 (a prosperous one in this trade is most unlikely) and now . . . . GUM BAY [Bottoms Up].[20]

This would seem to be a distinctively American form of humor, without an equivalent on the Chinese side. But some observers felt that Americans and Chinese shared a similar sense of humor. Harned Hoose, a trade advisor, claimed that Chinese humor "perfectly matches" American. It turns out that the "perfect match" was in the genre of sexist humor. A picture of a product with a suggestive shape would likely evoke a ribald remark from a Chinese negotiator, Hoose told American readers of *Industry Week* in 1973. He recounted a moment during negotiations when "a well-endowed blonde" suddenly entered the room, looking for her husband. Discussion was broken off while directions were given. After she left, "the senior negotiator offered me a cigarette and a moment of rest 'to rearrange my thoughts along business lines' before we resumed." Hoose's tale ended with the coda ". . . after that he was all business," which seems intended to show Americans that the Chinese male negotiators whom the Americans would meet were not so different, first for the reference to sex, then for the reference to no-nonsense business. The antipodean Chinese man was thus transformed into a locker-room chum.[21]

The few trade fair attendees who were invited to Beijing flew China's national airline, CAAC. It did not enjoy a good reputation among its foreign passengers (who would later explain the acronym as "China Airlines, Always Canceled"). Among its many shortcomings was the meager snack—an apple or a piece of hard candy—that it provided its passengers. But in 1975, Americans discovered that the airline now offered an enormous luncheon to each passenger. The tray consisted of a large thick slice of bread, two salted dried fish, four slices of dried beef, two chunks of duck meat, one hardboiled egg, two shrimp ball pastries, one pineapple slice, a macaroon, a raisin cupcake, a rice cake, tea, and orange soda. It marked a big change for the airline, yet it was still worlds apart (for better or for worse) from the culinary conventions of foreign airlines. If the Chinese had made a conscious decision to break with international convention and devise their own distinctive flight menu, then proper credit should be given for Chinese originality. But appearances suggest that CAAC had not consciously avoided the standards of others; it simply had no idea what was served on airlines outside China. In this and other matters, the Chinese remained almost completely unfamiliar with the practices and customs of the outside world.[22]

The Chinese displayed naiveté at their early 1970s trade fairs in the wide variety of products offered for sale, ranging from the technically sophisticated (electron microscopes) to the commercially dubious (1960s Mod clothing and goatskins dyed to look like panda). Americans could not understand how the Chinese were so foolish as to promote frozen rabbit as an export (and the Chinese, in turn, must have been puzzled at why the Americans were so uninterested because other Western buyers, such as the French, bought rabbit in large quantities). The Chinese government agencies, called foreign trade corporations, which handled all import and export arrangements, learned slowly and indirectly that the American consumer market was volatile. Hanging baskets, for example, which had sold well to Americans one season, went unsold the next.[23]

To help Chinese trade officials better understand the American market, a delegation from the Arts and Crafts Division of one of China's foreign trade corporations came to the United States in September 1975 and met with various importers and retailers. Many of the visits were to old customers and acquainted the Chinese with the fine art of American retail display (Lord & Taylor lectured the delegation about coordinating different bath accessories) and self-service. For Chinese basketry to sell in an American supermarket, the Chinese were told, the baskets needed to be packed loose in a box, from which, when opened, the baskets would be ready to sell. All of this was new to the visitors. The delegation registered the greatest surprise when told the cost of one minute of advertising on American television.[24]

The distinction between wholesale and retail also was not easily grasped. In China, the state handled all distribution, and there was no attempt to track the costs of distribution, let alone profits. Here the differences in economic system left the Chinese poorly prepared to observe a distinction that Americans expected. American wholesale importers were upset because the Chinese sold directly to retailers at prices identical to those offered wholesalers and did not compensate wholesalers for promotional efforts aimed at building a market for Chinese goods. The Chinese arts and crafts officials used the opportunity of the 1975 visit to ask many questions about wholesale operations and profits. Back in China, Americans were also asked to advise the Chinese about dropping the existing open-door policy, as they called it, of charging wholesalers and retailers the same price, and instituting a two-tiered system. The Chinese listened to an American suggestion that the Chinese provide quantity discounts and acted as if they had never heard of the concept before (the Chinese regularly provided such discounts to other customers, but played the role of the innocent whenever it suited them). American businesspeople saw themselves as beginning to build a marketing mentality among their Chinese counterparts.[25]

As long as there was novelty to be found when the early delegations of Chinese came to the United States or when Americans made their first trips to Canton, the encounter was an adventure in cross-cultural learning. But when the novelty wore off, frustrations about the way the other side wanted to do business were exposed. We know more about the American frustrations because Americans here, as elsewhere, were more vociferous, but the Chinese had their own complaints. The frustrations stand as testimony to the gulf that separated not just two cultures, but also two economic systems, capitalist America and socialist China. When doing business with the other side, Americans and Chinese were forced, as individuals, to try to bridge the gap. It was often a painful process, and not necessarily seen as worth the trouble.

Americans were concerned about saving time, and going to Canton for a slow-paced trade fair did not seem a wise expenditure of a scarce resource. For all the trouble of getting to Canton, the Americans still were unable to visit the factories or even meet with factory representatives at the fair. All negotiations were carried out through the intervening buffer of foreign trade corporation officials.

In between the semi-annual fairs, when American importers tried to cable or write Chinese offices, they often received no response. The Chinese would send out samples of goods to American importers, the Americans would cable back asking about the price, and when no answer was forthcoming, would send out additional cables, running up thousands of dollars of expenses—and still no reply from China. American importers routinely did business with many different nations, including other Third World countries, and in their informal comparisons of Chinese business practices with those of others, the Chinese stood out as being the most uncommunicative. One American importer complained directly to a visiting Chinese delegation: "I have sent samples and sketches to Peking and not heard a word. When I send samples to Thailand, I receive a cable saying 'your sample arrived, etc.' But I don't even get a cable from China saying something has arrived." In 1977 one American spoke for many when he said: "Correspondence in the PRC appears to be a lost art. If they have responded to any letter of mine, I have not seen it, nor do I have an acknowledgment of my letter of credit." For Americans who had an image of China as a supremely literate society, these problems were a puzzle.[26]

The centralized control over all foreign trade in China undoubtedly contributed to the breakdowns in communication. Moving a message between Beijing offices and outlying bureaus and the various factories was not logistically easy when each person whose desk it crossed had many political and bureaucratic reasons to shirk a clear decision on the matter at hand. (In the late 1980s the problem would persist; even routine letters of business correspondence would be sent out from China only after getting the protective "chop," or stamp, of an appropriately high official in the office.) In the 1970s European traders could correspond with provincial-level branch offices of the foreign trade corporations, which were that much closer to the factories that produced the goods. But Americans had to correspond exclusively with the head offices of the foreign trade corporations in Beijing, which only exacerbated the problem of getting messages to and from factories that were at the other end of this long hierarchical chain.

Americans interpreted the frustrating silence as a reflection of China's ambivalence about the desirability of doing business with the West. It maddened Americans, as a matter of principle as well as self-interest, to see Chinese passing up business opportunities. An American window-blind company, for example, saw an irony in the fact that China, the leading grower of bamboo, could not assemble the simple technology to make a workable bamboo window curtain. Another American approached the Chinese for an order for straw hot pads to fit under casserole dishes. The item was simple, no special technology was required. Yet the Chinese passed up the opportunity. To the Americans, the Chinese needed to be less ambivalent, more aggressive; they needed to make up their mind that they did indeed want to expand exports to the United States. In a 1978 survey of American importers who had done business with China, one American suggested that as soon as the Chinese decided they wanted to expand their U.S. market, the solutions to all their problems would be "easy."[27]

The Chinese government held Chinese business representatives, like all other Chinese, to strict standards of maintaining a politically correct "attitude." American businesspeople in the 1970s also looked to Chinese business representatives for evidence of a proper "attitude" toward doing business, which meant displaying eagerness. In the eyes of Americans, it was an attitude conspicuously absent among the Chinese. Unfortunately, the Chinese who were engaged in foreign trade arrangements were caught in the middle. On one side were the Americans, asking that the Chinese show a capitalist interest in doing business, and on the other side were the Party officials who had come to power during the Cultural Revolution, closely scrutinizing subordinates for dangerous signs of precisely the sort of attitude the Americans hoped to see. The result of this unstated push and pull of competing ideologies often was paralysis.

American importers who attended the trade fair were told by the Chinese, and reminded each other over and over again, that doing business with China required patience. It was a platitude that provided limited solace in the face of enormous time pressure. Orders successfully placed at one fair often were still unfilled by the next. Once loaded on a Chinese vessel in Shanghai, the goods would take three months to reach the American East Coast—a long time when shipments from Japan or Hong Kong took only thirty days. One American importer tried to explain to the Chinese that after it placed a large order in the fall for straw handbags and then had begun advertising the bags, demand was "stimulated" and thousands of women would be irate if the bags did not arrive in time for the spring season. The next April, when the bags still had not arrived, the firm had to charter a plane to go pick up the bags, which had gotten only as far as Hong Kong.[28]

The willingness of Americans to endure such frustration testifies to the special hold China had on them. Would American importers have endured the same extreme aggravations in delivery with any other country? Would they have quiescently accepted letter-of-credit terms that would have been unacceptable elsewhere? At a predeparture briefing in New York for first-time attendees headed for the trade fair, an experienced China hand warned: "Sometimes there is a very frightening gap when you have lost control of your goods and control of your money." It was allowed that "this is unusual compared to dealing with any other countries." The only way to explain the bewitching allure of the China market, and the willingness of otherwise tough, unsentimental importers to suspend customary rules of business, is to focus on the subsurface emotionalism. Although rarely examined in the full light of day, the emotional tug—that included novelty, exoticism, the challenge of doing business with opposites, and the excitement of gaining entrée to sources closed to Americans for more than twenty years—must have been a powerful one, because importers were tolerant of exceptions in their business dealings with China that they would not have allowed anyone else.[29]

Their patience was tested again when the goods finally arrived. The problems American importers had with the Chinese extended far beyond familiar ones of mixed-up orders. Americans complained that the Chinese paid no attention to proper marking and packaging. Cartons arrived without numbers, or with two conflicting numbers. Once opened, they were discovered to contain twice as many of whatever—shoes, silk flowers, bags—as the box was intended to hold. Importers had to break down the shipments and repack for distribution if the goods were still salable (once crushed, the silk flowers did not return to "good health"). The Americans railed about the waste of labor spent on opening, for example, 200 cartons to ascertain the contents of each and then repack, but it must have seemed a minor concern to the Chinese, whose state enterprises were notoriously overstaffed. The last thing they would be familiar with was a shortage of labor. The American complaint to the Chinese, that this needless unpacking and repacking meant "shrinking profit margins," would not have been understood either.[30]

Some problems seemed perfectly preventable to American importers, such as the porcelain that was apparently dirty when it was packed at the factory, or pieces flawed by bubbles or other visible imperfections not caught by inspection. Other problems stemmed from the prevailing low quality standards in China. One American importer, for example, reported to the Chinese that in the case of breakable items, such as glassware, breakage rates in transit ran 90 percent, with no insurance protection available to cover the losses. He said that the packing was satisfactory; the breakage was caused by the weakness of the stem attached to the cup.[31]

One complaint that was sounded over and over again was that Chinese companies did not understand the importance of providing attractive packaging for their products. Goods arrived in plain brown wrappers. Expensive goods were packed as tightly into boxes as less expensive ones. These were transgressions of the basic law of the American market—style over content. Americans told Chinese trade officials: put the better items in a fancier box, and use packaging to attract the U.S. buyer. One importer bluntly told a visiting delegation from the People's Republic that Hong Kong and Taiwan were able to print beautiful boxes, but not the PRC. Partly, these were problems created when one country, utterly lacking a marketing sensibility, sent goods to a country completely saturated by such a sensibility. Partly also these were problems to be expected from a developing country—much poorer than the countries to which it was being invidiously compared—lacking the plastics and special printing materials needed to meet American expectations. The Chinese had to import many of the packaging materials foreign buyers demanded they use; the cost was high and often exceeded the value of the Chinese-produced goods that were being wrapped. But the Chinese, embarrassed and reluctant to admit their supply problems, did not explain this to the Americans, who were left with the impression that the problem was simply one of China "waking up" and doing a more careful job. As long as contacts in person were restricted to the semi-annual American pilgrimages to Canton for the trade fair, communication between the two sides would remain poor.[32]

The Chinese had their own complaints about the Americans, beginning with the unreliability of some American firms that did not live up to agreements signed at the trade fair. The Chinese were angered when American traders attended the fair, placed orders, returned home, and then apparently decided that the market was not as promising as had been assumed earlier and canceled. The Chinese had seen that Germans and other Europeans were scrupulous about carrying out promises; Americans, however, were not. Given the relatively small number of American firms that participated in the trade fairs in the early 1970s, and given the newness of the acquaintance, it did not take many such incidents for the Chinese to draw generalizations about the reliability of Americans. American traders did not like to be sorted into pigeonholes of nationality, but they saw that the Chinese were always interested in tracking the nationality of the firms with which they did business. No matter how Americans tried to turn attention to the business at hand, an introductory conversation with Chinese trade officials could not advance until the foreigner had answered the insistent question, What is your nationality? One American wrote back to his home office, "Do they fix the price afterwards?"[33]

The Americans who attended the fair undoubtedly liked to think of themselves as unique individuals, whose trustworthiness should not have been affected by the inconsiderate practices of a few other U.S. citizens. But the Chinese viewed the matter somewhat differently because they held themselves to very high standards when they traveled abroad. Any Chinese delegation that visited the United States, for example, felt a heavy responsibility to do well in its mission and to avoid any dishonor not merely for the sake of the home unit, but also for the good name of their country. A Chinese abroad was an unofficial ambassador for a nation of one billion; an American abroad was an ambassador for no entity other than the immediate employer.

The freewheeling and unscrupulous business style of a few American firms, which created an unfavorable image for all American businesses, was a concern of the National Council for U.S.–China Trade, a new trade promotion organization the American business community established in 1973 in Washington, DC. Its first major task was to provide useful information to American firms about how to do business with China. Toward that end, it established a library devoted entirely to materials related to trade with China; began a bimonthly magazine and published reports and handbooks; and offered members consulting and translation services. The trade fairs in Canton were an important concern. The council helped American firms secure invitations and sent council representatives to the fairs to provide support services. It was a private organization, funded by its American membership, yet it also had a quasi-official status in the eyes of the Chinese, who knew the U.S. State Department had suggested its formation. The Chinese government, moreover, had designated the council as the American counterpart of its own China Council for the Promotion of International Trade.

The Chinese looked to the National Council for supervision of the American firms with which the Chinese did business. In fact, the council did not have the authority the Chinese assumed it had; it had no power over American firms that were not members. Still, some staff members were sympathetic to the Chinese desire to have the council provide more assistance in checking up on American firms. "I really think we should help the Chinese screen some of the Fair goers," wrote a council representative in Canton back to the office in Washington. She thought the council could run credit checks and gather other background information on companies they were recommending that the Chinese invite. In a way, the Americans in the council were unconsciously assuming something of a Chinese role, based on the traditional Chinese concept of always requiring a guarantor.[34]

The National Council for U.S.–China Trade politely conveyed complaints from its members to its Chinese contacts, and it in turn received complaints from the Chinese about American firms and regulations. Unfavorable tariff treatment hurt Chinese exports to the United States, and in 1974 China pressed hard for the council to secure most-favored-nation status for China, which would significantly reduce the tariffs. However, the change had to be passed through Congress and the White House. The council tried to explain the political difficulties that it faced in mobilizing support for such a bill, when union opposition and protectionist sentiment was increasing because of the U.S. recession. Chinese counterparts in the China Council for the Promotion of International Trade would hear none of it; these were "internal matters" of no concern to China. The Chinese told the council, "This is your problem." The

Chinese were not very understanding, but they were at least consistent. This was how Chinese officials would view problems brought to their attention that were within their own jurisdiction. They would not trouble the foreigners with the details of the difficulties; those would be "internal matters." The same principle was simply applied to Americans in getting their own house in order.[35]

The Chinese also had complaints about American customs inspection of Chinese goods and Food and Drug Administration regulation of food products, which were stricter than those of other countries with whom the Chinese had done business. Lead levels were a sore point. Federal regulations limited the lead content in porcelain to seven parts per million, but some porcelain from China contained twenty parts. The Chinese also did not like federal labeling requirements for canned foods; nor did they cooperate with the FDA in registering low-acid canned foods as required. All these problems were related to sticky issues of nationalism. When council representatives met in 1975 with representatives of the Chinese foodstuffs corporation, the Chinese complained that the regulations discriminated against China. They did not, the Americans replied; they applied to domestic producers as well. But we have our own inspectors, the Chinese said, and have a long history of exporting fruit, vegetables, and meat to Europe without receiving complaints. The U.S. FDA was meddling in China's "internal affairs." One of the Americans suggested diplomatically that the FDA pay a "friendly visit" to the Chinese factories, just as European buyers and food inspectors had paid "friendly visits" in the past. This suggestion was well received because it avoided mention of an official "inspection."[36]

Mindful of the humiliation of the nineteenth century, when China lost control over its own customs bureau, Zhang Ming, director of China's Commodities Inspection Bureau, was emphatic that his bureau was the sole authority for inspection of goods, both incoming and outgoing. Inspection certificates issued abroad were not accepted. (The Chinese implied that Americans should not assume an air of superiority—Chinese inspection had turned up more than one mouse in U.S. wheat shipments.) The bureau was not infallible, he allowed, but "the superiority of the socialist system ensures that our problems and mistakes will be gradually reduced." American traders, however, felt that the one-sidedness of the Chinese position—insisting that inspection in China be deemed final and conclusive for both incoming and outgoing goods—did not seem consistent with the oft-repeated principle of "equality and mutual benefit" in China's foreign trade.[37]

From the Chinese perspective, the American market was only one of 150, and attention could not be devoted exclusively to American requirements. When European importers bought Chinese goods, they did not ask the Chinese to put on country-of-origin labels in a Western language. In fact, they often expressly wanted to avoid having the People's Republic identified as the manufacturer, which simplified matters for the Chinese packagers. As soon as the Americans arrived, however, the Chinese felt pressured about labeling. The Americans insisted that English-language country-of-origin labels had to be put on everything. When the Chinese were slow to comply with this requirement, American buyers at the trade fair simply viewed the Chinese as unwilling to adapt to the needs of customers. The Europeans might have tolerated this, the Americans thought, but we will not. Americans saw the matter as one of national temperament—their self-image was one of "can-do" activists, wholly different from submissive Europeans. Representatives for U.S. chemical companies, for instance, resented what they perceived as the Chinese expectation that Americans would be as docile as the Europeans, accepting the product, packaging, and delivery dates as is, without trying to alter details. Americans demanded special packaging and delivery dates that suited their own timetable. But the Americans exaggerated the supposed differences between Americans and Europeans and failed to see that the European traders were comparatively meek because they had just weathered the worst years of the Cultural Revolution, when it had been very easy to offend the Chinese and be sent home, never to be asked back again. From the viewpoint of the Europeans, the Americans waltzed in late, without bothering to learn much about the experiences of the Europeans, or about the political conditions in the mid-1970s that still made it extremely difficult for Chinese factories to recover from the disruptions of the Cultural Revolution and the abysmal productivity levels that had resulted. More experienced traders marveled at the impatience of "can-do" Americans like some disappointed buyers of craft and furniture lines, who wrongly assumed that supply in China should be able to keep up with demand, given China's "seemingly unlimited manpower."[38]

In choosing their own approach to the Chinese at the trade fairs, the Americans soon heard how Europeans mocked them. In 1973, a European machinery salesman in Canton—with obvious glee—told an American reporter: "Americans are learning what many of us found out years ago—you have to be patient in dealing with the Chinese. Some American sellers barged in here thinking an invitation to the fair was tantamount to a sale. But it's not." This same brashness in the first wave of American traders was also seen in subsequent waves of Americans, and was scorned not only by the Europeans, but also by the more experienced American representatives at the fair. American "oldtimers" (some of whom assumed the title at their second fair) were upset at the behavior of the newcomers, who undermined the solidarity of the veterans who were pressing the Chinese to change production or packaging details. The newcomers, in their innocence, would go to Canton so grateful for the invitation that they felt they were obliged to make a major purchase, regardless of real interest. When the goods arrived in the United States, the novice trader would dump them on the market at prices below cost just to be rid of them, and by so doing would depress the market for other traders who depended on sales of similar goods for their livelihood.[39]

Americans in Canton competed among themselves, against the Europeans, and portentously, against the Japanese. At the fall 1972 trade fair, only the second one in which Americans participated, the Japanese arrived by the thousands when the Americans numbered only in the dozens. To the Americans, the Japanese seemed willing to pay almost any price for Chinese goods, and Japanese stickers indicating purchase were soon seen on most of the goods displayed in the antiquities exhibits at the fair. One American thought the Japanese invasion of the fair was symbolically captured in the rush to the elevators at the beginning of an afternoon session, when he was "neatly thrust aside by an elderly Japanese businessman who possessed not only a fierce competitive urge but an expertly wielded umbrella as well."[40]

Americans were not used to being pushed around like this. But an overwhelming Japanese presence—the largest foreign contingent from any country—was found at subsequent fairs. Non-Japanese foreigners found comfort in whatever they could, such as in the gossip about alleged underhanded Japanese business practices. A Hong Kong representative told the National Council: "The Americans, you see, are honest and inflexible. If the Chinese buy 30 hp motors at an [unprofitable price for the Japanese seller], then the Japanese will substitute second-grade-quality parts, etc., since there can never be enough detail on the contract to cover every part in a motor." Although Americans and other foreigners told themselves they would not stoop to Japanese methods, they were attentive students nevertheless, and were tempted to adopt some Japanese techniques. Everyone noticed, for example, that the Japanese gave the Chinese small gifts—pens and pocket diaries and such—when they distributed their product catalogs. Everyone in an office got the same gift. It was a small touch the Americans had not thought of, and yet it seemed to work effectively for the Japanese.[41]

The trade fairs in the 1970s were an opportunity for Americans to learn about Chinese business practices and about international business practices as well. The Canton fairs offered snapshots, twice a year, of the relative competitiveness of business contingents from the United States, Japan, and Europe, and the strengths and weaknesses of each group were visible to those who took the time to observe them. Americans could have learned from these experiences, but one of the weaknesses that could be seen among American companies was complacency and a failure to appreciate the superior determination and preparation of their competitors in China. Americans began attending the trade fairs at a time of extreme self-confidence, just before the first energy crisis of 1973 and before the stagflation of the 1970s and the onslaught of Japanese automobile and consumer electronics exports that would shake that confidence to the core. One of the few voices of concern at the time was that of Stanley Lubman, an American lawyer who had studied Chinese and was a participant in the earliest American contingents attending the trade fairs. In 1972, in the *New York Times,* Lubman wrote prophetically: "There are other reasons why the Chinese have not been rushing to buy from American corporations, even though they are willing to court companies whose products and technology are unusual. Many American industries are simply not competitive with those of Europe and Japan."[42]

For the most part, American businesspeople in the early 1970s did not see the signs of the impending decline in global competitiveness. At the end of the 1970s, however, they would see their own place in the global political economy in a more realistic light. And just when chastened Americans felt the need for some cheer, changes within China that opened the doors of the country still wider offered tantalizing visions of new commercial vistas. The timing was propitious.

OPENING WIDER

When the American press reported on Deng Xiaoping during the late 1970s and 1980s, it resisted treating Deng with much complexity. Three characteristics of the person, and only three, were noted: Deng was short in stature, a chain-smoker, and a "pragmatist." As self-styled pragmatists ourselves, Americans threw an affectionate arm around his shoulders as soon as the press decided that here was a militantly unideological Communist whose most famous aphorism expressed his lack of interest in Marxist theory. He did not care about the color of the cat, "so long as it caught the mouse." Years after the press first affectionately adopted this "panda bear" of a leader, in the aftermath of the Tiananmen Square massacre in June 1989, Americans were horrified that this same "pragmatic" man publicly claimed credit for ordering the People's Liberation Army to suppress the protests at whatever cost in human lives. But the sense of betrayal Americans felt in addition to revulsion came less from Deng's actions than from the "pragmatist" label that Americans earlier had pinned on Deng for the sake of convenience. Another consequence of the benevolent focus on Deng was the personalization of the economic reform program. By regarding Deng as sanely pragmatic, Americans looked back upon Mao Zedong as the opposite, insanely impractical, and thus an explanation for China's dramatic reforms in the late 1970s and 1980s seemed so evident as to require no comment. Mao died, Deng came to power. Simple.

It was not a sturdy explanation, however, because too much evidence from the early 1970s suggested that important changes in China's foreign trade policy began as the decade opened, well before the death of Mao. The narrow focus on Deng and on the rise and fall and rise again of his political fortunes distracted us from seeing a much wider consensus shared among the Chinese leadership about the need to expand economic ties with capitalist countries. Deng was denounced as the Number Two Capitalist Roader and lost all his posts at the beginning of the Cultural Revolution, but the autarky of the 1960s was undergoing serious modification even before Deng returned to positions of power. In 1971 the fall of Lin Biao, Mao's anointed successor, brought an end to the militant opposition to both the Soviet Union and the United States. At about the same time, the ascendant power of the outward-looking Ministry of Fuel and Chemical Industries and related ministries pushed through the "4-3 program," an integrated plan of importing US $4.3 billion worth of equipment and whole "turnkey" (completely set up and ready for operation) plants, which was approved by the State Council in the fall of 1972. The invitations that brought Americans to the Canton Trade Fair beginning in 1972 were one indication of this change, and the way in which the American participants were insulated from Chinese debates about foreign economic policies also showed a high-level commitment to protecting these expanded ties, a commitment that cannot be explained simply as being that of Deng and his faction. Deng was still officially in disgrace during all the developments that signaled the opening to the capitalist world.[1]

The trade figures for China also show a subterranean change. Between 1970 and 1975, China's total foreign trade increased more than 250 percent, and exports rose to 5 percent of national output, the highest level in the history of the People's Republic. After the death of Mao, during the Hua Guofeng interregnum (1976–78)—still before Deng Xiaoping had the opportunity to exercise full political power—trade surged beyond these watermarks, passing $20 billion in 1978, some 40 percent higher than the level of three years earlier. This expansion of trade between 1971 and 1979 proceeded steadily, with only one year of downturn—the turbulent year of 1976. Again, more than Deng must have supported this change.[2]

Most telling of all was the Chinese purchase of foreign technology, which included some $2 billion in the "turnkey" plants ordered between 1972 and 1974. In 1975, when imports were cut back to reduce the 1974 trade deficit, large-scale imports of foreign plant and technology continued. While the Cultural Revolution was still officially in progress, China accepted some 3,000 foreign technicians to supervise the construction and initial operation of the plants; at the same time some 1,000 Chinese technicians were sent abroad for training.[3]

At a time in which the domestic airwaves in China were filled with denunciations of imperialism, and billboards in cities and on farm buildings even in remote villages were plastered with the slogan "Self-reliance," these expensive purchases of whole plants from the capitalist camp represented a major change in policy. But they were not regarded as such by the Chinese leadership because they saw the technology imports as inert tools that did not affect the nature of Chinese society or pose a danger to its socialist organization. In 1975 Deng reasoned: "We should introduce new technology and equipment from other countries and expand imports and exports. Foreign countries all attach great significance to the introduction of new technology and equipment from abroad. Take their products apart, and you'll find that many parts or components are also made abroad." If others borrowed eclectically from the technology developed in other countries, there was no harm in China doing the same.[4]

Many observers inside and outside China have pointed out the similarity between westernizing Chinese in the 1980s and the Confucian westernizers of a century earlier, the Self-Strengtheners, from Lin Zexu (1785–1850) to Zhang Zhidong (1837–1909), who also called for technology imports from the West. They believed that the technology was of practical use, but was not essential. Zhang's formulation, "Chinese learning for the essential things, and Western learning for practical things," satisfied those who needed to believe that Chinese superiority was still unchallenged. It was a convenient rationalization, in the words of Joseph Levenson, "whereby something of western culture could have a place in China and yet be kept in its place." Westernizing Chinese leaders in the 1970s again seemed confident that technical imports would not affect anything of essential value in China, but unlike the Self-Strengtheners of a century earlier, contemporary leaders were confident not of the superiority of Chinese culture so much as of Chinese socialism, which they viewed as more advanced than both the capitalist system and the revisionist Soviet system. As long as the *essence* of the Chinese socialist system remained unchanged in character, it could safely accommodate the practical usefulness of Western technology.[5]

In the mid-1970s, not all Chinese leaders agreed with Deng. In early 1976, the group that would later be known as the Gang of Four and their cohorts launched critical attacks which led to the second purge of Deng, five months before Mao died. The assaults on his domestic and foreign policy ideas often centered on the issue of technology imports. In the eyes of the critics, Deng sought to depend upon foreign technology, and by so doing "put the Chinese people under the yoke of imperialist slavery." The Ministry of Foreign Trade was also singled out for "national betrayal and capitulationism," for it was said to have imported without restraint products that China could produce itself.[6]

One of the longer articles published during the anti-Deng campaign in the *Guangming Daily* drew direct and unflattering parallels between Deng and Zhang Zhidong, the nineteenth-century Self-Strengthener. Zhang was accused of regarding foreign machines as "divine," and therefore becoming dependent upon foreign blueprints, materials, and engineers for his Hanyang Iron Works and other enterprises. The author of the attack, Jing Shi, observed a real problem of Zhang's that obviously was recurring in the present: Dependency on imported plans, parts, "even bricks," often caused interruptions in construction. Jing asked sardonically: "How was [such dependency] going to result in China's 'self-strengthening'?"[7]

The heart of the criticism directed at Zhang and his modern acolyte Deng Xiaoping, however, concerned control over technology, and not the importance of technology or the superiority of socialism. Deng and his enemies paradoxically shared an abiding faith in technological deliverance from underdevelopment, though each would have been loath to admit such convictions to their political rivals. They all invested technology with redemptive power, and envisioned China as a modernized techno-topia in the twenty-first century. It was only the means to reach the ultimate end that they could not agree upon—would it be best to rely immediately upon imported or upon home-grown technology?

The Gang of Four radicals won the battle—Deng Xiaoping was purged in 1976—but in the end they lost the war when they themselves were purged later that year and Deng returned to power shortly thereafter. We can speculate that Deng won at least partly because the dispute was such a narrow one concerning how best to develop the nation's technological resources rapidly. Every bit of information about the outside world that slipped beneath the wall of isolation suggested a tremendous disparity between the science and technology of Cultural Revolution China and the advanced countries of Japan and the West; such evidence progressively eroded the idea that indigenous technological development in China, relying on a holy trinity of "workers, peasants, soldiers," was catching up. The concept of "self-reliance" needed to be refashioned, expanded to the point where it lost any real meaning. Deng found a way to do this in a speech presented to the United Nations in 1974, when he declared that self-reliance "in no way means 'self-exclusion.'" It was "beneficial and necessary" that countries exchange "needed goods to make up for each other's deficiencies." By restating his allegiance to the concept of self-reliance, Deng avoided an open break. But his new definition not only accommodated the idea of trade with all countries, regardless of ideology, but also included the then heretical idea that China would accept foreign aid. One change, technology imports, was leading to another.[8]

Even during the campaign against him in 1976, Deng enjoyed clandestine support within the bureaucracy that had the most contact with the outside world, the Ministry of Foreign Trade, which made good on its promise to foreigners that the anti-Deng rhetoric in the Chinese press would not affect trade policy.[9] The dramatic expansion of imports and exports through the decade suggests the power of currents that cannot be attributed to the influence of a single person, especially one who was not in power when China's trade began to expand. Deng's ascent in the 1970s was less the cause of China's opening outward than itself an expression of the deeper change in the thinking of a broad segment of the higher leadership, which was increasingly attracted to the technology of the West.

In January 1972 the Chinese contracted with RCA to install a $3 million satellite communications earth station. It was apparently the first contract between the People's Republic and a large American company, and its format was unconventional for the legalistic Americans: Disputes were to be settled simply through "friendly consultation." To install the thirty-three-foot parabolic antenna at a station near Shanghai in time to provide communications for President Nixon's impending visit to China, RCA brought in twenty-three engineers and technicians. The job was completed in a record for RCA of thirty days, and one wonders if this early successful experience emboldened Chinese officials to import more American technology.[10]

Publicly, RCA gave due credit to the Chinese for the excellent support and cooperation that it received for the project, but privately, individual members of the RCA group were struck by the difference in attitudes toward work. The Americans saw themselves racing against the clock, trying to install the equipment in time for Nixon's visit. The Chinese staff members, however, merely watched the clock, and were reluctant to stay at work for a full shift. An RCA engineer in early 1972 explained it as the result of the Chinese workers not being paid for overtime, a subtly ideological explanation that had an unstated prescription for the ailment.[11]

The Chinese at this early date certainly were not interested in hearing suggestions from Americans about how China should run its affairs, and the Americans were discreet and did not directly push the issue. The transactions were for the transfer of specific equipment and technology; ancillary management suggestions were neither part of the deal nor welcome. Petroleum and seismic equipment from Baker Trading and from Geospace, power shovels from Bucyrus-Erie, pipelayers from Caterpillar, mining trucks from Wabco, and more communications equipment from RCA were among the purchases that China made in the mid-1970s, and each project required the presence of a few Americans on-site to oversee delivery and training. Sensing the possibility of unwanted and subversive influence upon those Chinese with whom the Americans came in contact, Chinese authorities sought to minimize the amount of time that Americans stayed.

Caterpillar discovered that initially the Chinese did not even want to have the company provide a training program; the Chinese wanted the machinery and nothing else. Only after the Chinese had an opportunity to tour the United States as guests of the company and see after-sales services provided to American customers did they become receptive to the idea. Wabco, a manufacturer of enormous trucks used in mining operations, had to run preliminary training operations for Chinese mechanics in a classroom in Beijing, far from the mine site, using pictures as a replacement for the 120,000 pound behemoths themselves. It was frustrating for the Wabco representatives ("We've always taught by doing, not showing"), but the Chinese authorities did everything possible to minimize their own vulnerability to future political charges that the foreigners had been given too much latitude.[12]

By far the largest contingent from the United States was from Pullman Kellogg, which built eight ammonia fertilizer plants between 1974 and 1978 at sites scattered around China. Over 140 Pullman employees were living in China at the peak of the project, though they were widely dispersed, with no more than 25 at any one site. They were housed in apartment guesthouses, furnished with rugs, ovens, refrigerators, Western bathrooms, and in the southern sites, air conditioners imported from the United States. In a reminiscence about the experience, Walter Buryn, a Pullman Kellogg vice-president who was project manager for the eight sites, praised the Chinese for allowing Americans to visit nearby towns and to shop in Chinese stores. The only apparent restriction was the inconvenience of being surrounded by large crowds of rural Chinese attracted by the novel presence of foreigners. On a few occasions, Buryn said, "store managers emptied their premises of Chinese customers in deference to their unexpected and unusual visitors. But after a while, they were able to relax from such formalities."

The freedom to shop or go on excursions, however, meant little more than an occasional opportunity to intermingle physically. The isolating effect of a different language, housing accommodations within a walled compound, meals provided in a separate dining room, even at the work site, and the simple fact of their crowd-attracting foreignness combined to keep the first wave of American corporate representatives in the People's Republic sealed off from opportunities to have substantive contacts with Chinese on their own, away from the official interpreter.[13]

The Chinese received technical training from American companies in the United States too, and when the Chinese and Americans reversed positions and the Chinese found themselves in the role of guest, many of the circumstances that had created an isolating experience for Americans in China were absent. The Chinese were not kept in compounds for foreigners; they were not required to eat their meals separately from their American hosts; they were free to come and go as they pleased without the worry of drawing a crowd of several hundred bystanders and of children chanting "Foreigners!" Language difficulties, of course, remained. But more importantly, the Chinese visitors were kept within the bounds of a strict self-imposed isolation, which distressed their American hosts. Between 1973 and 1977, some 400 technical personnel from the PRC stayed for training visits as short as several weeks and as long as over a year in places such as Seattle, Peoria, Houston, and Trenton. They shunned mention in the American press, and even their own American hosts, who knew them best, were most struck by their reticence, their keeping to the tight ranks of their group, and their attachment to preparing their own meals.[14]

Since all their expenses while in the United States were paid by their own Chinese work unit, the visitors never had the money or the time for much sightseeing that was not related directly to their training program. Deng Xiaoping, perhaps after hearing too many tales about Chinese visits to the popular Disneyland, announced in 1975 that the time devoted to sightseeing or recreation during such technical training visits abroad should be reduced or eliminated, which only served to further insulate the visitors. This frustrated Americans who wanted, in the words of one corporate host, "to show them as much of our way of life as possible." Some Chinese were still able to go on tourist visits to the Houston Astrodome or to Niagara Falls; some attended hockey and baseball games and were introduced to miniature golf. Others, however, declined invitations to what seemed to the Americans to be innocuous visits to a local high school or a country music concert: The Chinese did not offer explanations, so Americans speculated that "perhaps they were afraid of student violence at the school and bourgeois decadence at the concert." Out of consideration for the sensibilities of their guests, the American hosts at Stewart & Stevenson in Houston cut short a plan to invite visiting Chinese to a local movie: "We couldn't find one without sex or violence in it."[15]

What seemed to Americans to be so unusual in their Chinese guests—such as their stubborn attachment to their native cuisine—could also have been observed in the behavior of the American trainers who had gone to stay in China at the same time. Though their stints in China were short, the Americans wasted no time in re-creating the domestic life of home. An industrious example was Annie Taber, wife of one of Wabco's technical representatives assigned to the Benxi Iron and Steel Works, in Liaoning Province. Taber, a fireball of energy, spent most of her three months in China during the summer of 1976 repainting and redecorating the family's Benxi apartment, using paint, wall-to-wall carpeting, and drapes ordered from the United States. At her request, the company sent food packages—instant potatoes, powdered milk, peanut butter, and cake mixes—to supplement Chinese food. No oven was available, so she used a pressure cooker to "bake" the cakes. Dissatisfied with the laundering of the family's clothes and the high prices charged by the local laundry, she washed them by hand herself. With evident good cheer, she succeeded at creating a familiarly comfortable home for herself, her husband, and their eleven-year-old son. But it was an enormous expenditure of effort for results that could not be enjoyed for long. By the time the apartment was furnished and arranged, the Wabco project was completed and the family returned home to Peoria.[16]

What impression the Tabers and other Americans left behind is impossible to determine. But the reverence for Mao Zedong that dominated public discourse in China at the time was so powerful that the sojourning Americans grew fond of the old man. When Annie Taber heard the news of Mao's death, after her return to Peoria, she broke out crying and thought of the sadness of her Chinese friends. The episode captures a moment, one of the last, in which the mourning Chinese seemed to be still under the spell of the charismatic Founder, and Americans who had stayed in China could empathetically share in the last days of the revolutionary *zeitgeist,* even as their very presence in China indicated, and surely hastened, the passing of the era.[17]

If we look back not only to the American training programs but also to changes observed by American visitors to the Canton trade fairs during the mid-1970s, we can trace the course of Chinese experimentation with a new outlook toward foreign businesspeople. The National Council for U.S.–China Trade continuously evaluated Chinese business practices during this period, and kept, in effect, a report card that assessed changes. The council's report on the spring 1975 fair, for example, said that the Chinese had achieved "mixed" results in coming to a better understanding of foreign markets. Among the new products was a Shanghai tractor, boasting a brilliant red paint job and tricked out with chrome everywhere—gear shift, bolts, trim. This "achievement" was offset, however, by the display of a home sewing machine intended for the American market but bearing in large letters the unpromising English brand name of Typical.[18]

In the mid-1970s, American traders were discouraged by what they felt was a decline in the more cordial, relaxed atmosphere of the fairs of a few years earlier. By the fall of 1975, American attendees were already mourning the passing of the way of the past, in which business had been discussed in a leisurely manner over tea, and the Americans had had time to call their home offices and discuss the prices offered by the Chinese. Now they dealt with young negotiators fresh out of foreign language institutes who did not know the product, who demanded of each trader what the current world price was, or what the trader had last paid for the same item outside China. The Chinese official then set the price accordingly and gave a next-day deadline for a reply, which meant the American had to spend the evening camped in the telex office, desperately trying to get timely guidance from the home office. Yet if we do not adopt the partisan perspective of the American traders, we can observe that the Chinese were merely beginning to employ practices, such as monitoring world prices for the commodities and products that they sold, which would have seemed perfectly "businesslike" elsewhere.[19]

Chinese sophistication about pricing grew visibly during the 1970s. In the early years of the decade, when Americans first began trading, the

Chinese seemed to have literally no idea what they should charge. In 1973, when Robert Hoffman, the buyer from Marshall Field's, first went to the fair and rejected items on the basis of the prices being "out of line," the Chinese asked him what he thought the prices should be. He reported: "In every case where we restated a price, they accepted it, and we bought the item." But this easygoing pliability in the Chinese attitude toward their own prices gave way to an understanding of the potential relationship between high demand and high prices. Soon the Chinese boosted prices on the goods sold at the fair, in some cases by 300 percent. Ideological differences among their foreign business partners were then put aside, and Yugoslav traders joined with the Americans in complaining about the changes. True, the foreigners granted, the Chinese raised their prices because they had seen what their products were bringing on the retail market in the United States. But the Yugoslavs felt that this had misled the Chinese, because the artificially high prices in the United States would fall when the novelty of Chinese things faded. Most vexing of all, the Yugoslavs griped, was the Chinese audacity in now charging wholesalers the same prices American retailers were getting from their customers. This showed that the Chinese did not "understand" the Western marketing system.[20]

The Chinese pressed too hard in some cases. In 1975 American toy buyers found that toys bought in Hong Kong and shipped to Boston cost less than those bought in the PRC; American pharmaceutical buyers saw that the Chinese charged about the same as U.S. producers. So why, they reasoned, should they buy from the Chinese, when the purchase entailed worries about timely deliveries and FDA approvals? Buyers of frozen shrimp were also put off by prices well above prevailing prices in the United States, but the Chinese were encouraged by substantial orders placed by the Japanese. A Japanese official tried to explain: "This is the Oriental way of doing business. The shrimp buyers will suffer serious losses in order to keep their allocations for the future."[21]

This was not consoling. Americans did not want to see "outrageous" price setting on the part of novice Chinese traders rewarded. But the Chinese increasingly displayed a sense of the immutable "law" of supply and demand so often invoked in the United States as the capitalist foundation of a rational market. When first applied in China, it worked to the clear disadvantage of American buyers. During the fall 1975 fair, for example, Chinese officials admitted that some items that otherwise would have been available were being withheld in the expectation that their prices would go up. Earlier, at the spring fair, after Chinese trade officials discovered that feathers and down were in short supply in the global marketplace, the Chinese set prices ruthlessly according to whatever their American buyers would bear. In this transitional period the Chinese did not apply these laws of supply and demand as vigorously when dealing with European buyers, who were given a lower price. As a matter of policy, the Japanese were given the lowest prices of all for the scarce supplies. Still, prices were much, much higher than they had been. One buyer noted that seemingly bottomless demand had set off "sky-rocketing prices." He moaned, "The Chinese have cornered worldwide supply—the stuff is like gold."[22]

The Chinese pushed their advantage further and tied foreign purchases of raw feathers and down to the importer's willingness to import finished products from China, such as ski jackets, which earned higher profit margins (a concept that was intuited in the People's Republic, even if it was not yet politically acceptable to discuss openly). A European buyer in the midst of "feather fever" placed a sizable order for pillows just to rip them open and pull out their valuable stuffing. In such a frenzy, it was actually difficult for the Chinese to see much relationship between price and demand. A senior Chinese trade official said: "It doesn't seem to matter how much we raise the price, the buyers shout 'more, more'; if we raise it 50 percent or even 100 percent, it's still 'more, more'."[23]

A secondary market sprang up. Foreign brokers stood outside the negotiation rooms of the fair, and supplies obtained by one buyer were promptly resold to another at a 30 percent markup. The Europeans made an instant profit whenever they resold their allocations to the Americans. The Chinese, however, sought to eliminate such practices, but instead of setting a universal price that ignored nationality, they simply prohibited resale of their feathers and down and in 1977 inserted a clause in all European contracts that forbade reexport to the United States. Subsequently, the worst of the "feather frenzy" for Americans passed; supplies caught up with demand, American buyers built up their inventories, and the Chinese lifted their earlier restrictions on European reexports to the United States. When prices were adjusted favorably for American buyers, American traders declared that the Chinese had "matured," and a hopeful report about the spring 1978 fair was titled "New Flexibility, New Era?"[24]

Americans were happy to see some flexibility, beginning especially in fall 1977, when small changes seemed to portend more significant ones. The music of Mozart and Beethoven could be heard on the loudspeakers; hotels were noticeably cleaner; and the service in the restaurants improved. Christmas decorations were offered for export for the first time since the Cultural Revolution, and American porcelain buyers were surprised by the willingness of the Chinese to provide styrofoam packing to reduce breakage and see-through containers designed for retail sale. In the words of one American, China's state corporations had adopted a "down-to-business" attitude.[25]

Change gathered more speed in 1978. The veteran fair attendee would not have recognized the place: air and hovercraft service to Canton; a new "coffee shop" with hamburgers at the Dong Fang Hotel. For the first time, representatives of the Chinese producers, who until then had remained in the shadows, were permitted to participate actively in business talks with foreign firms. China's foreign trade corporations, the mediating buffer placed between Chinese producers and foreign buyers, began to compete actively among themselves for foreign business, offering lower prices, faster delivery, and better packaging. Americans applauded the return of material bonuses in the Chinese foreign trade bureaucracy, which had reintroduced material incentives to spur staff members to work harder and more effectively. Sino-American trade at the fall 1978 fair jumped to $142 million, 80 percent above the previous record. Shortly afterward, the two countries jointly announced that diplomatic relations would be restored on January 1, 1979.[26]

These events, so heady for American businesspeople and seemingly so inexplicable, were merely the culmination of changes that had been launched at the beginning of the decade. While the changes were not inevitable, one can at least say that they appear to be the result of an underlying centrifugal force that had begun building well before the end of the Cultural Revolution. Knowing something of the momentum of that force helps us make better sense of the restoration of diplomatic relations with the United States and the single incident that most dramatized the openly commercial receptiveness of the Chinese leadership: the 1979 visit to the United States of Deng Xiaoping.

To prepare the Chinese public for the visit Deng was to make, the Chinese media had to revise its standard depiction of the United States. It did so abruptly. As late as the summer of 1978, *People's Daily* published stories that followed the timeworn formulas. A story about New York, for example, began by mentioning the glittering modernity of Manhattan, with its tall skyscrapers, then launched a predictable exposé of what lay in the shadows: tawdry Times Square and Forty-Second

Street, with bars, adult bookstores, and "live naked models." A short drive away was the separate world of Harlem, filled with garbage and despair, prostitutes and drunks and unemployed youth. Another article, no more flattering, reported condescendingly that capitalist societies were caught in a "gambling frenzy." In the United States, it said, Atlantic City had decided to use casinos to increase government revenue and forty-four states permitted some form of legalized gambling. In these stories the facts were unimpeachable, but the slant was heavily didactic: Comrades, do not harbor any illusions that capitalist societies are anything but loathsome places to live.[27]

Suddenly, however, at the end of 1978, the *People's Daily* abandoned these conventions and ran a new series of stories about the United States that included unpredictable points of admiration as well as criticism. Based on a trip that Chinese journalists had recently made to nine American cities, from Los Angeles to New York, the series was full of unalloyed awe, beginning with the delegation's first impression of the country—the "beautiful" sight of the Los Angeles landscape glimpsed from the airplane window, extending as far as one could see—and continuing with a recitation of flattering statistical data. The description of the meal at the World Trade Center in New York, for example, reeled off only impressive numbers ("the elevator ride to the 107th floor only takes one minute"; "20,000 persons can be accommodated in the Center's restaurants at one time"; "80,000 tourists visit daily") in just the same way that Chinese tourist guides extolled the extraordinary dimensions of the Great Hall of the People on Tiananmen Square.[28]

Automation in the United States especially interested the visitors. "Automatic lights" at street intersections kept traffic orderly, without the presence of police. Newspapers, subway tickets, Coca-Cola, and coffee that came from automatic vending machines also impressed the Chinese. Yet the wondrous machines found everywhere had not softened American workers, who seemed to be extremely hard-working. When the Chinese delegation trooped through newspaper offices, television stations, and factories, employees raised their heads briefly, greeted the visitors, then returned to work. If the old formula had applied, this would have been interpreted as a sign of the slave-like conditions under which Americans were forced to work. But this time it was interpreted as a salutary example of American industriousness, what one Chinese reporter called "work is work, play is play, and the two are kept entirely separate." It was cheering for Americans to be told that they were hard workers. Summarizing the Chinese stories for American readers, a *Los*

Angeles Times reporter noted: "Many Americans, especially those past middle age, could swear that the old-fashioned work ethic is in its death throes. But the *People's Daily* seemed to think that America's factories and offices are veritable beehives compared to slow-paced Chinese workshops, where workers have sometimes been spotted sound asleep."[29]

The stories in *People's Daily* were no less didactic in their own way than the traditional stories about capitalist society, but the message to be drawn was new: "work harder" replaced the old one of "capitalist society is rotten to the core." The cheerful, courteous service found in the hotels and restaurants visited in the United States also was noted. Granted, tipping was expected ("you have to tip even to go to the bathroom"); but as long as one could afford it, the "service was always good." Here too a message was implied about improving the quality of services at home in China. This praise was not just a change in the relative weight granted to positive and negative aspects of capitalist society. It also reflected a new way of thinking about economic performance that went beyond the gross measurement of physical quantities of metric tons of wheat or steel and looked at the qualitative nature of services, which did not lend itself to easy quantification and targets.[30]

Praise was tempered by some criticism. The problems of crime in U.S. cities drew comment, but rather than following the conventions of the past, these Chinese visitors relied (just like Americans) upon the anecdotal lore of taxicab drivers with whom they struck up conversations. The Chinese also noticed that American trains were not only inferior to those they had ridden in Europe, they also were inferior in many respects to the trains in China. As for automobiles, the Chinese seemed pleased to discover that the lagging development of automobile production in their own country placed them in an "advanced" position in the eyes of the Americans, who complained of the problems America suffered because of its dependence on cars, and which China had been fortunate to avoid: long commute times because of crowded highways, high costs of gas and insurance, parking problems, pollution, and so on. Americans often repeated a warning to their Chinese guests, "You should learn a lesson from us. Don't copy our mistakes—definitely don't expand the number of automobiles like us."[31]

Americans were not entirely serious about this putative "mistake"—our continued stubborn attachment to automobiles betrays weak conviction. But many Americans were genuinely impressed by Chinese reliance on pollution-free bicycles as the backbone of urban transportation, and other Americans, even if not so admiring, warned the Chinese about the "mistake" of relying on automobiles as a way of being polite to the visitors from the PRC. Americans' confession of regret about the dominance of automobiles in their own society helped assuage any feelings of envy their visitors may have felt.

The Chinese reporters eagerly accepted the proffered solace, and they also devised their own forms of consolation. After watching the old 1950s film *The Man with the Golden Arm* and discussing the drug problem in the United States, Wang Ruoshui, deputy editor-in-chief at the *People's Daily,* devised a set of evenly balanced dualities to describe the United States (and, by tacit inversion, the People's Republic). He mused, "A materially rich society may be spiritually a very poor one; a scientifically advanced country may be a philosophically backward one." Wang's phrases bear an uncanny resemblance to the old formula of Zhang Zhidong and the idea that the Chinese could borrow the useful parts of Western material culture and retain their own philosophically superior Chinese essence. It permitted the Chinese reporters and their readers to gaze directly at the blinding sun of capitalism without injury. It helped prepare China for the visit Deng was about to make to the United States in February 1979.[32]

War is no time for idle chit-chat between protagonists, and the Cold War was no exception. Over the course of virtually its entire duration, the leaders of the United States and the Soviet Union rarely met face-to-face other than at infrequent, deadly serious summit meetings. The occasion when one leader actually toured, however briefly, the country of the reviled empire of the other was so rare that these moments always drew the intense interest of the general public in both countries. Such visits offer an occasion to watch the confrontation, at close range, of the two ideological systems and to glimpse the faces of the mystifying Other.

The pattern in the case of China and the United States was similar: for more than twenty years there were no contacts, high-level or low, between the two countries. Then came the breakthrough of the Nixon visit to China in 1972. Deng Xiaoping technically visited the United States two years later, but the occasion was a speech delivered to the United Nations, and so it was not regarded as a visit that allowed him to see and experience much of the United States. His 1979 visit, however, was surrounded by hoopla and excitement in the United States; the public viewed the willingness of Deng to undertake a four-city, coast-to-coast tour of the country as a break in the Cold War.

But amid all the anticipation, there was little reflection about equally historic visits that the heads of the United States and the Soviet Union had exchanged twenty years earlier, when the Cold War preoccupied both countries. In 1959 Richard Nixon, then vice-president, visited Moscow for a ceremonial occasion, the opening of the American National Exhibition; and then Premier Nikita Khrushchev had come for an eleven-day, multicity tour through the heartland of the United States. In the American press, these visits had been treated with an unmistakable partisanship, as if the American "way of life" were on trial and every victory for the home team needed to be chronicled.

The American National Exhibition that Nixon opened in Moscow was provided to "educate" the Soviet public about the United States. It was a self-consciously propagandistic display of American technological prowess, with hundreds of large photographs and a Ramac 305, an "electronic brain" that offered written replies in Russian to any of 3,500 questions about the United States. When Nixon and Khrushchev strolled together through the grounds, it should not have been surprising, given the ostentatious nature of such an exhibition at a time of extreme ideological tension, that the two leaders would spar openly. The boxing analogy was explicitly in the mind of Nixon, who felt that in earlier banter Khrushchev had knocked him "out of the ring," so it was important to "climb back in and fight again." When the two arrived at a model of an American kitchen, Nixon jabbed and remarked that such a kitchen could be afforded by an ordinary American steel worker. Khrushchev struck back ("American houses were built to last only twenty years" and in the Soviet Union "we build for our children and grandchildren"), and thus was launched the start of the famous "kitchen debate" about whose system was better. Within moments it degenerated into a sharp exchange in which Khrushchev and Nixon each accused the other of veiled ultimatums and nuclear bullying, all in front of the incongruous display of American kitchen appliances.[33]

Contrast Khrushchev in 1959 with Deng Xiaoping in 1979. The Soviet leader had displayed palpable pity for the United States, stuck as it was with its capitalist system. Early in the kitchen-debate exchange, Khrushchev explained: "America has been in existence for 150 years and this is the level she has reached. We have existed not quite forty-two years and in another seven years we will be on the same level as America. When we catch you up, in passing you by, we will wave to you." He was so confident of the superiority of his system that he could indulge in posed self-mockery, taking Nixon on a boat ride down the Moscow River and bantering with the swimmers in the river, "Are you captives? Are you slaves?," then nudging Nixon in the ribs and shouting, "See how our slaves live!" When Khrushchev visited the United States, he brought with him this same armored sense of the superiority of socialism, so the sights and sounds of his trip were merely an entertainment, nothing more. The compliments he gave his American hosts were both sincere and condescending. At a Des Moines meat packing plant, for example, Khrushchev sampled his first American hot dog, an event that was covered as closely by American newspapers as if the Soviet leader were discovering the very essence of the superiority of American culture. "We have beaten you to the moon, but you have beaten us in sausage-making," declared Khrushchev semi-jovially, praising the hot dog but at the same time needling Americans about their inferiority in more important arenas of competition.[34]

Deng Xiaoping was not given to such an obstreperous style, but even setting aside the obvious differences in personality, Deng experienced his visit to the United States in 1979 in quite a different frame of mind than had Khrushchev. He too had faith in the superiority of socialism, but it was more a faith in the *ultimate* superiority of socialism. For the moment, there was much assistance that could be rendered by an advanced capitalist country. Unlike Khrushchev, who asked for nothing from the United States, Deng in 1979 openly asked for American technology and investment. This was unprecedented, not just for the People's Republic but also for any Communist country at any time other than during World War II. Perhaps Americans sensed the historic nature of the occasion, for as Deng went from Washington, to Atlanta, to Houston, then to Seattle, taking his message to business and civic groups, he was feted royally.

When Khrushchev had arrived in the United States, demonstrators in New York, chanting "Khrushchev is a murderer," had clashed violently with police. But when Deng arrived, the few demonstrators were merely a curiosity, and most of the coverage was given to the welcoming receptions and the scarcity of invitations for the hottest social event of the season. The National Council for U.S.–China Trade, which sponsored a gala and a reception in Deng's honor, enjoyed a surge in membership and inquiries as companies joined in the belief that membership brought entitlement to the much-sought tickets (unfortunately the tickets had already been distributed to the older members of the council and to the White House). In Atlanta, some 1,400 guests packed into a welcoming luncheon, where even power brokers such as Burt Lance had to stand in line to gain admission. A professor at Emory declared Deng's arrival to be the "biggest thing since the Sugar Bowl between Alabama and Penn State," an only-in-America kind of tribute that the guest may not have appreciated fully.[35]

An itinerary that swung through the American South, a traditional bastion of anti-communist sentiment, would have been unthinkable for Khrushchev. Deng was greeted with some coolness, especially in Houston, where radio talk shows and letters to the editors of Texas newspapers called Deng a "Red murderer" and referred to China as a "captive Red nation." The two Texan senators, John Tower and Lloyd Bentsen, stayed away in a bipartisan show of fear of anti-communist criticism. But the interests of big business in the state helped surmount the hostility Deng would otherwise have encountered. Some twenty-one Houston companies already had contracts with China, including Pullman Kellogg, the firm that had built the eight ammonia fertilizer plants. Governor William Clements, who owned an oil-drilling company whose specialty was of interest to the Chinese, was criticized by other Republicans for having welcomed Deng to the state, but Clements had stated before Deng's arrival his intention to present a "normal show of Texas hospitality." Clements expressed the view of other businesspeople who put ideological objections aside when they threatened to interfere with business: "Whether we agree with him politically, philosophically or whether we like chop suey or not, is beside the point."[36]

Whereas Khrushchev was known for his bluff directness, Deng kept his impressions of the United States to himself. Although his stock speech mentioned interest in learning from the United States, it did not reflect any particular change from what he had said before his trip, that technology from the United States and the West should be used in China's modernization drive. He rarely departed from his prepared remarks, which praised the United States in general terms and denounced the Soviet Union (Americans relished having this unlikely ally, a Communist, within the anti-Soviet camp). His interest in the United States was strictly selective; he spent almost all of his visit making his pitch directly to the American business community.

Deng seemed to treat the United States as a simple source of technology and trade opportunities; he showed no interest in learning anything about the United States not related to business. There were no tours of schools, homes, museums, shopping centers. Atlanta city officials were scandalized to learn that the Chinese who handled arrangements for Deng had not been interested in the suggestion that a visit be included to the grave of Martin Luther King, Jr. Only after the suggestion was pressed again after Deng had arrived in Atlanta was this arranged, a perfunctory tribute squeezed in before the stop that really interested the Chinese, a visit to a Ford assembly line.[37]

Americans wanted to know what impressions their country was making upon Deng and his accompanying delegation. The Chinese reporters were asked constantly by their American counterparts of impressions of things American—television, expressways, architectural marvels. The apparent absence of awe, even of much interest, was shocking to behold. On the press bus, Chinese journalists did not have their noses pressed to the window, greedily observing the spectacle that passed before them, as Americans had expected. Instead, many dozed and occupied themselves in other ways. One American reporter, Joseph Lelyveld, was alert to how this insistent American curiosity about Chinese reactions led to ethnocentric questions on the part of Americans, and ethnocentric replies on the part of the Chinese. He described a scene at the seventy-three-story Peachtree Plaza, the world's tallest hotel, in which a Chinese broadcaster was standing by an enclosed lagoon where a fountain was splashing. The Chinese had been asked by several Americans about his thoughts regarding the hotel and he asked in reply, "Is there anything special about it?" Lelyveld wrote, "The Americans, who tend to assume that the Chinese will want Peachtree Plazas of their own once they taste the forbidden fruit of modernization, are surprised by his response. 'You don't like it?' one asks. 'I don't know,' he replies. 'There is nothing like it in China to which I can compare it.' "[38]

The silence of the visiting Chinese left American reporters free to inscribe whatever they wished upon the bland smiles of the visitors. Take two examples: the tour of the Hapville Ford plant near Atlanta and, later, the much-commented-upon visit to a barbecue near Houston. Even before Deng had arrived in Atlanta, the Ford stop was already being viewed as a wonderful showcase of American capitalism that should get a significant rise out of the Chinese. A member of the White House staff described it in advance as likely to be the "sexiest" stop during the Atlanta visit, and when the Chinese delegation arrived, the Ford workers appreciated the novelty of seeing ten golf carts filled with Chinese Communists cruising through their assembly plant. "Hey, ChiComs," called out one worker, using the military shorthand of an earlier era when the Chinese were the faceless enemy.[39]

Deng had visited Japan a few months earlier and had delighted the Japanese press with approving remarks about the "bullet train," and at a tour of a Nissan car plant had declared, "Now I realize what modernization is like." But in Atlanta Deng remained impassive and did not show much interest in how the large Ford LTDs were put together, unlike his display of interest in the assembly of the smaller Nissan cars in Japan. So American reporters stepped in and called attention to this tableau of American productivity that Deng had not offered comment upon. The Ford plant produced an average of 83 cars per year for each worker, a rate which the *Los Angeles Times* could not resist contrasting with China's output of one vehicle per worker annually. Orville Schell, whose articles and books narrated in close detail—often disapprovingly—the changes taking place in the wake of reforms in post-Mao China, was among the press contingent at the Ford plant, and he attributed symbolic significance to a gesture that Deng made when he patted "admiringly" the hood of a shiny, yellow sedan, "dolled up with imitation leather roof, wire wheels, automatic transmission, push-button windows, air conditioning." For Schell, the pat on the hood before Chinese television cameras was intended by Deng to signify his personal approval and send "a clear signal to his people back home."[40]

Deng did not need to add anything; the images seemed to speak for themselves. Each evening, the national television network in China broadcast shots of Deng's tour relayed via satellite. The feature stories in the Chinese newspapers and magazines about the United States that had preceded Deng's visit had not been sufficient to prepare the public for the wealth that they saw displayed on the television screen each evening. Even senior Party officials were shaken. On the evening when scenes from the Ford plant and the glass towers of the Peachtree Plaza were broadcast, one group of high-ranking officials and army officers in Beijing had gathered before the television set in a celebratory mood after attending a banquet. But as they watched the footage on the news, the mood turned somber. One of the officials turned to the others. "What have we done?" he asked. "Have we wasted thirty years?"[41]

Deng Xiaoping's attendance at a barbecue and rodeo show near Houston a few days later was also a major highlight of his visit, at least in the eyes of the American observers. Again, Deng was silent, and again, Americans supplied their own interpretations. Orville Schell described Deng's willingness to don a new Stetson cowboy hat as a gesture of surrender to the West, a genuflection at "a temple of the American way of life" that reversed several centuries of "China's historic resistance to the West." Made at the time, this assessment arguably was too severe. But it demonstrates nicely the eagerness of American observers to read in Deng's gestures a portent of historic change and an embracing of

American ways. All the American reporters were struck by the incongruity of "the leader of revolutionary China" riding in a stagecoach, waving his new cowboy hat at the crowd. Roundup Rodeo, where Deng and his delegation had been taken, was aimed at East Coast natives transplanted to Houston who wanted a "Western" experience on Saturday nights. But the rodeo's faded sign "Where the East Meets The West" took on a new meaning when the Chinese and the accompanying journalists arrived.[42]

The Texans themselves were not as excitable as the reporters. The "cowgirl" hostesses who worked at the rodeo, when asked, did not draw a connection between communism and the identity of their Chinese guests. Other Texan guests had given the matter more thought. One member of the Houston Chamber of Commerce, which presented the Chinese with the Stetsons, said to a reporter, "Sure they're Communists . . . But what do you give a dog to vaccinate him against rabies? You give him a little rabies, don't you? I don't think this guy Ping is a Communist anyway." This offhand assessment of Deng Xiaoping showed the persistence of the biological metaphor of communism as a contagion, which unknowingly mirrored the Communist Party's portrayal of capitalism in strikingly similar biological terms. (One even sees the same notion of ideological "inoculation" in Mao Zedong's 1957 statement that Marxists welcomed criticism: "Fighting against wrong ideas is like being vaccinated—a person develops greater immunity from disease after the vaccine takes effect.") Yet another, newer idea was seen in the American attitude toward the visitor, the idea that Deng Xiaoping was not one of Them, but one of Us. It was a thought that was never possible when Khrushchev had visited in 1959, and it colored American perceptions of Deng's gestures and his silence. If Khrushchev had toured Texas and had been taken to the Rodeo Roundup, his reactions would have been just as attentively monitored, but in the absence of explicit comments by the visitor (a supposition that in the case of Khrushchev is rather fanciful), the American press would not have attributed such portentous meaning to each gesture. In 1979, Americans were ready to see Deng in a particular light, and Deng's silence during his trip was for him a master stroke, because it permitted Americans to believe whatever they wanted about his impressions during the visit.[43]

Deng returned to China riding a triumphant wave of favorable American publicity. Vice-President Walter Mondale told Deng it was a good thing for American politicians that Deng was not an American citizen "because you could be elected to any office you sought." Praising Deng for giving "real meaning to the word 'pragmatism,' " the *New York Times* observed on the editorial page that Deng would not let ideology obstruct China's modernization. Paraphrasing Lincoln Steffens's famous statement when he visited Russia after the Bolshevik Revolution, the *Times* said: "One is tempted to think that [Deng], soon after his return to Peking, will tell his comrades on the Politburo, 'I have seen the future, and it works.' "[44]

This was an American conceit, yet it may have turned out to be apt in a way that the editors of the *Times* did not appreciate. Though what Deng told the Politburo upon his return is not known, we can speculate that he did deliver a positive report. But it would have been a positive report no matter what had taken place. Deng Xiaoping's trip was too short, his interest in the details of the scenes visited too scant, for it to have been a substantive experience of gathering new ideas. Deng had already made the key decision to increase reliance upon Japan and the West; otherwise the trips would not have taken place. Just as Lincoln Steffens's line was said by William Bullitt, his traveling companion, to have been made up before Steffens even got to Russia and to have existed in various forms until it was finally polished into its final, well-known form, so too, we can guess, did Deng Xiaoping have an equivalent line about the United States (and Japan) representing the future that was in mind even before he began his visit.

The very brevity of the trip is likely to have made it paradoxically more influential than a more extended one would have been, because it was too short for anything but the most superficial kind of confirmation of preconceived ideas that linked modernity to an idealized America. Deng did not need a sophisticated grasp of economic and social realities in the United States to be captivated (one could argue that the more sophisticated his knowledge, the less captivated he would have been). He simply wanted to collect confirming sights of America's material splendor and take his pitch directly to the American business community. His interpretation of what America had to offer China undoubtedly was his own, not that of his eager American hosts. In a fashion, Deng joined a list of other Chinese leaders—Hong Xiuquan, leader of the millenarian Taiping Revolution in the mid-nineteenth century, and of course Mao Zedong, in the early twentieth—who took a sketchy knowledge of foreign ideas and applied them in China with momentous consequences.

Hong's understanding of Christianity was based on the reading of a few pamphlets; Mao's declaration in 1920 that he was a Marxist occurred years before he would have the time to actually study the Marxist classics in depth. But in both cases superficial knowledge was more than sufficient to crystallize inchoate preconceived ideas. Deng Xiaoping did not learn much from his trip to the United States, at least visibly, but it appears that the visit served a similar catalytic function, crystallizing the idea that China would benefit greatly by increased interaction with the United States, Japan, and other capitalist countries. The details of implementation were not worked out then; Deng and his lieutenants simply improvised as they went along, which itself might be read as a lesson learned: quiet abandonment of reliance on the lumbering apparatus of Five-Year Plans and a willingness to make policy decisions as events unfolded and without *a priori* assumptions. It was a style that might be described as one of optimistic extemporaneity, but whether Americans can rightfully claim to have helped shape it is impossible to say.

3.

CHINA CHIC

Americans were not merely pleased about establishing ties with the People's Republic, they were at times almost ecstatically happy. Beginning with the February 1972 visit to Beijing of Nixon and Kissinger, and then, in a second burst of excitement at the time of formal normalization of diplomatic relations and of Deng Xiaoping's visit in early 1979, Americans regarded all things Chinese as attractive, alluring, hot. The shift in mood was possible only because the official Chinese view of the United States had softened so dramatically. As late as 1971, the Chinese had declined the New York City Center of Music and Drama's invitation to host a Peking Opera Troupe visit to the United States (the Chinese reply said in part: "Our model dramas are specially prepared for the appreciation of our working people, not for our enemy and money-scented capitalists like you.") But a few months later, in early 1972, the Chinese rolled out a welcoming red carpet for the American president and his entourage, and China became the rage. Chinese restaurants in American cities enjoyed a new vogue; enrollment in Chinese language classes in American universities bulged; Chinese-inspired fashions suddenly became haute couture. In a gown described as "opulent chinoiserie for grand evenings," the First Lady, Pat Nixon, was featured on the cover of *Ladies Home Journal* and gave the White House imprimatur to the fashion.[1]

The exotic allure of China was heightened by the inaccessibility of the country to ordinary tourists. From the summer of 1971 until the summer of 1978, the number of American sightseers permitted to visit

China was exceedingly small, restricted to group tours organized by politically sympathetic organizations or special interest groups such as doctors, teachers, or union members. The Committee of Concerned Asian Scholars led off with a tour in June 1971, and was granted an interview with Premier Zhou Enlai, hardly an ordinary stop on a tourist circuit. The book the group subsequently published had a breathlessness visible even in the exclamatory title—*China! Inside the People's Republic*—and launched what was to become a wave of sympathetic books about China based on three-week group tours of a selected set of communes and museums and factories and kindergartens. In 1974 Americans established the U.S.–China People's Friendship Association, which was dedicated to further "people-to-people" contacts but which became the *de facto* gatekeeper: as the organizer of "study tours" of China for members, the Friendship Association was the primary organization that obtained visas for interested Americans.[2]

The system of receiving invited delegations of what German critic Hans Enzensberger calls "radical tourists" was not a new one. The Soviet Union had invented the system in the early 1920s. But while Enzensberger describes the system as an unfortunate defensive outgrowth of the isolation imposed on the socialist world by its capitalist enemies, Paul Hollander, in *Political Pilgrims,* has heaped criticism on the foreign visitors themselves for their gullibility and blindness to socialist shortcomings. As Jonathan Mirsky, one of the members of the first 1972 "friendship tour" to China recounts, when he revisited China many years later, well after the end of the Cultural Revolution, and met the guide who had shown them a Chinese version of Potemkin villages, the guide said, "We wanted to deceive you, but you wanted to be deceived." Hollander places the radical tourists who went to China in a larger story of utopia-seeking Western leftist intellectuals who, as visitors to the Soviet Union and also to revolutionary Cuba, saw only what their hosts allowed them and what the visitors themselves wished to see. He is mercilessly thorough in collecting embarrassing examples of naive utterances about the People's Republic by visiting intellectuals, and the term that he coins, "the techniques of hospitality," well describes the methods by which the hosts in China, the Soviet Union, and Cuba smothered their privileged guests with kind attention and influenced their perceptions and judgments.[3]

The visitors' fervid interest in China and suspension of customary critical faculties (my own too, as I was among them) cannot be explained as simply as Hollander insists as the product of leftist ideology. Actually, gullibility turned out to be a phenomenon seen in other Americans who were politically much less sympathetic. For every leftist Hollywood celebrity like Shirley MacLaine who traveled to China and returned gushing praise, one can easily find a matching counterpart from within the inner sanctum of Wall Street who went to China and said essentially the same thing. To cite one example: "The social experiment in China under Chairman Mao's leadership is one of the most important and successful in human history" are words spoken not by John Kenneth Galbraith, but by David Rockefeller. Aside from a few stalwart defenders of Chiang Kai-shek's Nationalist government on Taiwan, Americans all along the political spectrum were equally susceptible to "China Fever."[4]

In the summer of 1978, China began to issue visas for ordinary commercial tours in significant numbers. By the end of the year, China had played host to some 100,000 foreign tourists, exclusive of Hong Kong residents and other overseas Chinese, a number that represented about as many visitors as had been accommodated in the preceding twenty years. Aside from helping to increase "mutual understanding and friendship," which had been the rationale in the past, an openly pecuniary reason was now added: to earn money "for the grand plan of our Four Modernizations." The visas permitted travel only in a group and offered itineraries of limited choice, but the opening to tourism meant that wealthy Americans who took pride in having gone "everywhere" could go to the one place from which they had been barred. As word spread, travel agents in the United States discovered that eager tourists would seemingly pay any price. "It's a great country club statement today to say you've just returned from China," observed a travel agent in a story that reported the various furtive means the agents employed to secure one of the scarce visas for clients.[5]

China was not prepared for the onslaught. What was called the "great China tour craze" created tremendous logistical problems for hotels and transportation systems that were not equipped to handle the deluge. Unlike the tourists of the revolution in the early 1970s, whose numbers were smaller and who went to China with a sense of adventure and a tolerance for inconvenience, the new wave were "a different breed altogether," noted John Fraser in the *Christian Science Monitor.* Fraser said: "When it gets down to a crunch, their passion is hitched somewhat more to the availability of plentiful hot water in a hotel room than a vision of the Ming tombs."[6]

Yet despite complaints about hotel service or poor hygiene or other problems on their trips, these early American tourists softened on the plane ride back, and upon their return to the United States had cheery reports that stoked the envy of those who had not yet made the trip. These reports from America's most privileged class were an inviting target for lampooning:

> Where did you get that simply divine little Mao hat? Oh, in Peking? How passé! We've been there twice! And we're going again in October. If Harold's dreadful board can bear being out of touch. Aren't the Chinese simply jewels! So respectful—and egalitarian! And, would you believe it, they bicycle to work—just like my broker![7]

When actual conversations came to resemble the fictional ones of satire, Marilyn Bender, a contributing editor of *Esquire,* observed that not only was China now chic, but the greatest ardor came from the right, not the left. On her own trip to China that summer of 1978, she noted the ironic declarations of her traveling companions: a woman who spent half of each year in Palm Beach, the other half traveling around the world, said: "Look, I'm to the right of Attila the Hun. But when you see everyone in clean, white shirts, peddling on their bicycles, going somewhere, seeming to have a purpose, you have to be impressed." Ideological convictions were disarmed upon arrival. "I don't think they could have managed this under capitalism," said a corporate executive who at home believed that all of America's troubles began with the presidential defeat of Barry Goldwater.[8]

The ideology of left and right was completely reversed in this season of "China chic." With the right singing the praises of the People's Republic, it fell to the liberal *New Republic* to issue a lacerating criticism of China and its blinded American friends. The object of its ire was the Sichuan Garden, arguably the best Chinese restaurant in Washington, staffed by chefs sent from China by special arrangement with China's Sichuan provincial government. The restaurant attracted celebrities and cabinet heads in the Reagan administration, like Caspar Weinberger and Raymond Donovan, and had become a symbol of what the *New Republic* called official Washington's current "love affair with China." The problem with the Sichuan Garden was that its seventeen chefs worked twelve-hour days, were kept secluded in a house near the restaurant on their off-hours, and were not paid with "a bourgeois trifle like money, since they don't really live in America, except geographically." The *New Republic* turned even more sarcastic: "We have a quaint folk custom in this country, too. It's called freedom." If this custom could not be extended to foreign embassy personnel, this was regrettable, since diplomatic relations did need to be maintained. "But we don't need Chinese food. International business and cultural dealings ought to begin with a clear understanding that when people are in the United States, wherever from and whatever for, they are free. And if certain governments find this intolerable, they can take their vinegars and spices and go home."[9]

It was a rousing commentary that might have been expected in the pages of the conservative *National Review.* But the blooming of China chic on the right, as well as on the left and in the middle, meant that ideology was a poor predictor of reactions to the People's Republic, and a bipartisan ideological free-for-all ensued. What is striking in the season of China chic is the absence of moderate statements. When Americans talked about China it was with strong words and few qualifiers, telltale signs of the emotionalism that lay at the heart of the American relationship with China. No other country could excite Americans, or excite their reactions, like the People's Republic.

Andy Warhol once called Bloomingdale's a museum for the people. In the deadpan manner that was Warhol's, the statement confounded common sense—this posh department store was only for certain people, the affluent and the trendy, not the unwashed masses. But the statement also harbored the quite reasonable idea that Bloomingdale's merchandise could be treated like artifacts, enjoyed as a display, inspiring admiration (or covetousness), and serving as a window on the times. With the normalization of relations with China in 1979 and with China chic the rage, Bloomingdale's museum for the people was transformed in the fall of 1980 into a museum for the People's Republic of China.

The "Come to China At Bloomingdale's" promotion, as it was called, was not the first modern adaptation of a Chinese motif to American fashions. One can reach back to the early days of the Nixon administration, when Bloomingdale's opened a "China Passage" shop on the day in 1971 that the United Nations voted a seat for the People's Republic. Or one can recall, at about the time of Nixon's visit to China in 1972, the alacrity with which a Beverly Hills fashion show domesticated the exotica of the Chinese revolution, with waiters dressed in Mao suits and the little red books of Chairman Mao's *Quotations* provided as precious decoration. But the scale of the 1980 Bloomingdale's show set it apart from the past: on display were hundreds of examples of Chinese merchandise, said to be worth $10 million, ranging from antique furniture to thirty-seven varieties of tea. The flagship New York store had thirty separate in-store boutiques on eight floors devoted to the China theme; even the hair salon offered new styles (without photographs, we can only imagine what a style named "China Then/Now" must have looked like). A collection of imperial ceremonial robes and a reproduction of a Suzhou garden house were added attractions. The China exhibit followed the single-country promotional theme that Bloomingdale's had used previously for Israel and India (the Indian display had been named in a paroxysm of hyperbole "India—the Ultimate Fantasy," which, strictly speaking, left no room for sequels or contenders), but was the size of those two promotions combined.[10]

Bloomingdale's buyers had made some 130 trips to China since the early 1970s, and it seems that they took with them a proclivity to mythologize the Chinese as a kind of pure tribe of craftspeople living in a world untouched by the corrupting influences of capitalism. Carl Levine, a Bloomingdale's vice-president, said: "The workmanship is excellent, probably because they haven't yet learned the sloppiness of the Western world." And yet Americans could not resist introducing the Chinese to their own world and watching for Chinese reactions to Western concupiscence. The Bloomingdale's lingerie fashion coordinator showed some female Chinese clothing designers a copy of "Sighs and Whispers," the store's lingerie catalog. "They were amazed and finally, I think, enchanted," she said. The Chinese then designed a nightgown for the store that retailed for half of what such a garment would have sold if produced in Europe. Bloomingdale's buyers took this as confirmation of the perfection of Chinese craftsmanship, adaptable even to the risqué designs of American lingerie.[11]

Among its various in-store Chinese boutiques, Bloomingdale's set up its own China-inspired "People's Store," which was intended to re-create the "authentic worker" look, featuring the utilitarian greens and blues that Chinese then used in their work clothes adapted to such items as jogging outfits. Fashion designers, in their ceaseless search for novelty, smoothly incorporated these drab Chinese color schemes to provide a proletarian *frisson* for a bourgeois clientele. An even more preposterous adaptation was Bloomingdale's modish rendering of Chinese-influenced "designer spaces." In one, described by one art critic as "what a Chinese SoHo loft would look like if China had any," sculptured sofas covered in black gabardine faced each other, separated by a black calfskin rug, and illuminated by a flickering twenty-foot-long mural made of aluminum paillettes and printed with a huge dragon. This was "the ultimate China disco accessory." In another room, a new collection of furniture from Baker, Knapp & Tubbs, ostensibly "inspired" by sixteenth-century Ming designs, featured a marital bed made of walnut and ash burl veneers which sold for $3,295, and a curio cabinet at $1,550, described as "the étagère of the 80's." Clearly, these "inspirations" had no connection to any "People's Store" in real-life China, either conceptually or financially. They were fantastic (and costly) figments, worlds away from Chinese realities. Americans used China for their own purposes in ways that the Chinese themselves would have had difficulty recognizing.[12]

The romanticism of China chic fits easily within the professional world of fashion. But the larger business world would not seem to be easily influenced by such passing fancies. The self-image of the American businessperson includes seriousness, wariness, a steady focus on the "bottom line." Yet China chic raged as wildly through industrial America as it did through Bloomingdale's, exposing an often emotional side to American business decision-making that does not jibe with the model of cool, rational objectivity. What had captured the imagination of hundreds of American firms during the early and middle 1970s, when the Canton Trade Fair was the primary point of contact, subsequently captured the imagination of thousands of firms at the end of the 1970s and on into the 1980s as trade and investment opportunities expanded. The more China talk in the air, the more hard-nosed American businesspeople were drawn to the mysteries of this world of the Other.

The hold that China had over the imagination of the American business community was uniquely strong, and it can be partly explained for the usual reasons—the size of the potential market, the long period of commercial and diplomatic seclusion. But let us add an additional reason: the ritual declarations of friendship. Americans, unused to the formalities of business ritual, gamely played along with the Chinese in the routine of polite declarations of the importance of building long-term relationships, of establishing trust. Aside from the hazards of too many toasts with potent *maotai* liquor, these conventions were innocuous enough. The problem was that by dint of sheer repetition, the ritual turned out to have a real effect, inculcating the idea that the business relationship between the two countries could not be measured in the usual terms of generally accepted accounting principles, but belonged in a special, protected realm, that of *friends.* The effusive declarations of friendship softened Americans who in other countries would take pride in remaining unsentimental about business affairs.

The key to opening the door to business with China, the Chinese told the Americans, and the Americans then solemnly repeated, was "friendship." Granted, it appeared a silly banality, but it must be true, the reasoning went, because the Chinese seemed to emphasize it so much. "It sounds trite and corny," the 3M director of China affairs said in 1980, "but they really do mean it." The *Wall Street Journal* dutifully summed up the imparted wisdom with this subheadline about the importance of friendship in the China trade: "Without It, Business Can't Go Anywhere; With It, Trade May Expand Everywhere." This statement shows the remarkable degree to which Americans seemed willing to accept Chinese terms of defining the business relationship.[13]

It was the Chinese who insisted on choreographing the ritual, but Americans were more than willing to play their assigned roles not only then, when China chic was in the air, but much later, when contacts were more routine and the novelty of the encounter had worn off. Take, for example, the Chinese press coverage in June 1988 of an interview with Malcolm Stamper, vice-chairman of Boeing, and his sixteen-year-old grandson, who had come to Beijing for a trade and investment conference. The senior Stamper knew what the ritual called for when he faced the gathered Chinese journalists: "This is the third generation. I brought him along so the friendship between Boeing and China can continue from generation to generation." A Chinese reporter praised this wise "strategic" thinking, then turned to the grandson, who seems to have known intuitively what the reporter was searching for. What were the boy's impressions of Beijing? "Much more modern than I had imagined." How is the hotel in which he was staying? "The service is wonderful, and the food is better than even what my mom cooks!" And so on. Alone, the scene is insignificant, but when one considers its replication on thousands of occasions, one sees that the ritual incantations had a momentum of their own. Their significance can be confirmed with a simple test: Where else in the world have American businesspeople been so caught up in such friendly, treacly effusion? China got Americans to say things that would have been unseemly anywhere else.[14]

State and local government officials in the United States played a contributing role in the production that spotlighted the magical market of China. In late 1978, President Jimmy Carter asked attendees at a National Governors' Association meeting to court the Chinese. The response was a pell-mell rush in the next few years as states staked out special relationships with what they called their "sister" provinces. Ohio and Hubei were the first pairing, and by 1984 eleven other states had set up similar relationships with Chinese provinces, and many more had sent high-level trade delegations to China (Governor George Wallace of Alabama was sighted among the ranks of governors who trooped off to China accompanied by local business figures). Individual American cities also matched up with Chinese counterparts: St. Louis and Nanjing in 1979, then New York and Beijing, San Francisco and Shanghai, Los Angeles and Canton. The scramble led to some states "sharing" a single province, an arrangement that the first arrival did not like. Michigan, for example, objected to the way that "two-timing" Sichuan Province had signed agreements with Michigan and also with Washington State, each separately calling for "preferential" treatment. In a curious way, the scramble for exclusive "sister relations" with Chinese provinces faintly resembled the imperialist scramble for spheres of influence in China in the last days of the nineteenth century. Unlike in the past, however, this competition was welcomed by the Chinese hosts, who remained firmly in control.[15]

The race to set up relationships with the most promising Chinese candidates brought out local boosterism among competing American states and localities that outdid anything George Babbitt ever said about his dear Zenith. Washington State gave itself the title of "America's natural gateway to China." Illinois, "America's number one export state," was thus well-matched with Guangdong, home of the Canton Trade Fair. Ohio, which wanted to distinguish itself, could only come up with the fact that it had "more cities of over 100,000 than any other state."[16]

Each state competed especially to impress the Chinese with its interest in close trade ties. Illinois sent a delegation of 160 on a 1985 trade mission; the group boasted that "never before have so many people come to China on a trade mission from the United States." Maryland was more subtle and tried to remind the Chinese of the historical ties the state had with the China trade. When Governor Harry Hughes of Maryland welcomed Wan Li, then governor of Anhui Province, on a visit to the United States, Hughes sent his Chinese guests to the fully restored mansion of William Paca to recover from jet lag. Paca, like other colonial leaders, had been a Sinophile (ours is not the first age when China has been chic), and the Paca home included two acres of Chinese gardens and a stairwell of Chinese design. To help remind the guests of Maryland's past connection to China in the age of the clipper ships, they were served a Chinese breakfast on Paca's original blue-patterned Chinese plates (one is tempted to say "served on China china").[17]

It is a wonder that the plates, there and elsewhere, did not crack from the heavy hyperbole about the bright prospects for Sino-American trade. When Boston's Mayor Kevin White returned in 1982 from a trade mission to China, he said: "I've come back from China a different person. The only other time that I've significantly changed with that abruptness was the night after Martin Luther King was shot." The details of the transformation were not spelled out; it seemed to mean a new bundle of inchoate feelings. For White, the unstated syllogism seemed to be that "the future" was "international trade," and China was a part of international trade, therefore China *was* the future.[18]

Others added their voices. Governor John Spellman, at what American reporters called a "moving occasion," declared that the friendship agreement between his Washington State and Sichuan could well turn out to be "the most important thing I've achieved." The politicians spun out wild dreams—Illinois's Thompson was so excited at the opening of a permanent trade office in Shenyang that he began talking of Illinois state trade offices in each of China's twenty-two provinces. Aides on such trips stoked the dreams with announcements of hundreds of millions of dollars of trade agreements "under discussion," or tens of millions' worth signed in "letters of intent," which home-state newspapers often reported without delving into the nonbinding nature of such documents. Businesspeople were also caught up in the stampede to a bright future. Henry Strauss, a Colorado businessman who had played an active role in establishing a friendship association with Hunan, articulated what many thought: "This thing could ultimately be worth billions if developed on an ongoing basis."[19]

Promoting sister relationships and taking trade missions to China was as politically risky as it was costly. For governors and mayors who used the public purse to pay for their trips, it was a matter of political necessity that they return with optimistic news of lots of business signed up. Otherwise, their critics could attack with the charge that the trips had been nothing but junkets financed by the taxpayers, or that foreign glamour was being used to avoid domestic problems. Boston's Mayor White tried to explain the importance of looking beyond local problems in Boston, outward, upward, to China: "Racism and potholes and schools are important, but they should not be so blinding that you don't see this other potential for other generations coming behind." San Francisco's mayor, Dianne Feinstein, responded to criticism that reached her while her 1979 mission was still in Beijing by arguing that San Francisco needed to keep up with the Joneses, the other cities who had already sent trade delegations. "We could have stayed home and everything would have gone to New Orleans or Long Beach or Seattle."[20]

Both the Chinese hosts and their American guests had ulterior motives in talking up Sino-American trade relations, in addition to the publicly stated ones. For the Chinese, promotion of friendship agreements with American states and cities helped serve as a counterweight to the Japanese. In China's Northeast, where the Japanese presence was largest, a warm welcome extended to the delegation from Illinois was apparently intended to show, in the words of an American delegation member, that the Japanese don't "have a lock on the business here." For the American side, an adroit governor not only worked to avoid home-state criticism, but also tried to generate positive political capital. Many tried to bring along a television reporter so that the "historic" nature of their mission would receive proper coverage back home. The trips also gave the governors a chance to cement ties with the home-state business representatives who accompanied them and who were potential campaign contributors. On some occasions American politicians got so excited about the publicity being generated that they momentarily forgot that the Chinese were not voting constituents. When Governor Thompson of Illinois, for example, met Party Secretary Zhao Ziyang and other high-ranking Chinese officials at a St. Patrick's Day reception in 1985, Thompson could not resist pinning shamrocks on their lapels and exclaiming, "When you're hot, you're hot." This was intended to mean that his delegation's trade mission to China was a success, but the unfortunate Chinese translator, who had never heard the expression, was left unaided to stammer a speculative interpretation.[21]

It was hard to remain detached with Chinese authorities lofting estimates of their future purchases of Western equipment and technology that ran into the billions, and with American politicians and businesspeople lending credence to these extravagant estimates with their own testimonials—Ohio trade officials claimed, for example, that Ohio and Hubei had transacted about $300 million worth of business between 1979 and 1982, and added that the sister relationship deserved the credit. Some skeptics argued that the sister relationships did not seem to lead to increased trade or sustained contacts as claimed, but such doubts could always be answered with the response that Governor Spellman gave when needled by a reporter about another charge, that he was dealing with Communists. Spellman snapped, "They're one-quarter of the world's population. It's in our interest and in the interest of world peace that we know and have relations with them. We can't ignore them, can't isolate them, in a rational world." His words were true—in a rational world, it indeed made no sense to ignore or isolate the People's Republic. But the receptions, the boosterism and political grandstanding, the talk of instantaneous deep friendship that accompanied the establishment of sisterly relationships, these are not the stuff of which a "rational" world is made either.[22]

With normalization of diplomatic relations and Deng Xiaoping's visit to the United States in early 1979, and talk of new sister relations with Chinese provinces and cities filling the local newspapers, corporate America began to take serious notice of the People's Republic. How representatives of the largest companies went about exploring business opportunities and deciding to commit personnel and funds to develop business ties with China cannot be fully understood without reference to the emotionalism that colored Sino-American relations. When American businesspeople went to China in increasing numbers, especially from 1979 on, they were surprised to find that the Chinese were, on a personal basis, unexpectedly likable. Upon returning to the United States, a vice-president of American Hoist & Derrick expressed typical American reactions: "The people were the most friendly, cordial, courteous and hospitable people I have ever met." One could even joke with them. "You couldn't meet nicer people." Such effusive praise deserves a second look, however, because it reveals the inherited legacy of Chinese seen as the opposite people, of the land of Fu Manchu, of evil and inscrutability, beyond the pale of Christianity and capitalism. When Americans went to China for the first time they were prepared for the worst, and were flooded with feelings of relief and pleasure (and perhaps also a touch of guilty remorse) when the stereotypes proved to be so obviously wrong. Ironically, the Chinese in the People's Republic who discussed business with the Americans were the beneficiaries of previous racist American stereotyping: Americans emotionally embraced these flesh-and-blood Chinese, who turned out to be so much "nicer" than expected.[23]

Americans also romanticized the probity of the Chinese, at least initially, in a fashion that can be explained only by the notion of China being located at the imaginary antipodes. Americans regarded the Chinese as constitutionally averse to corruption. A Pullman Kellogg official, for example, told the American business community in 1979 that the one thing which never came up during extensive negotiations with the Chinese was any mention of a bribe. His explanation: "The Chinese aren't made that way." For veterans of business dealings in the more corrupt parts of the Third World, the People's Republic appeared otherworldly, a business Shangri-La. No corruption. An almost limitless supply of potential customers and cheap workers, ruled by an honest (albeit Communist) government. As the *Wall Street Journal* put it, "the first thing foreign investors and traders did was drool."[24]

When the Chinese raised prices and seemed to overcharge foreigners, the foreigners would joke about the "good old days" in the Philippines or Indonesia, where a little grease helped get bureaucratic wheels turning. China's worst problem seemed to be that it was *too* honest, which was really the best kind of "problem" to confront.

But if it seemed too good to be true, it was. The Chinese "character" proved just as susceptible to the temptations of corruption as that of anyone else. Americans seemed hurt to see the spread of foreign gift-giving to Chinese officials as they came into more frequent contact with foreigners. To some Americans, China soon "descended" to the level of other developing countries, "catching on to such Third World tricks as special taxes and petty bribery." Initially discovered in an uncorrupted state of purity, having been protectively shrouded by the isolation of the Cultural Revolution years, China soon lost its innocence in the eyes of these Americans. Anecdotes that would have been regarded as a commonplace elsewhere—such as the story of a Chinese official who in 1984 offered to set up high-level business contacts for a foreign company in exchange for a retainer to be dropped in a U.S. bank account—were given considerable attention in the American business community and recounted with sadness, as if such stories revealed Paradise Lost.[25]

Yet their loss of puritanism was counterbalanced by the exciting arrival of the Chinese at the doorstep of our own world of consumer hedonism. China watchers had thought that the Chinese would be interested only in large industrial items—heavy machinery, steel mills, fertilizer factories—but when China announced in 1978 that it had signed with Coca-Cola, this showed, according to one American newspaper, that "the Chinese could have fun, too." Afterward a State Department spokesman said: "Since then, I've been wary of saying what they wouldn't be interested in. I wouldn't discourage anyone." Anything now seemed possible, and this served to ignite the optimistic imaginations of American companies large (such as Coca-Cola—see Chapter 11) and small (such as Nostalgia Lane Records, which thought that there might be an oldies-but-goodies market in China).[26]

The American business community was also attracted to China at the time of diplomatic normalization by the feeling that this was a strategically rare opportunity. Deng Xiaoping was aging; China could reverse its course and return to the isolationism of the past. The moment had to be seized. One American trade advisor put the matter in picturesque form: "Everyone should get all the hay in the barn as quickly as possible before it starts to sprinkle." Others were more concerned about getting in quickly not before the door closed, but before one's competitors got in. "If you don't get through the gate," warned a vice-chairman of Gould, Inc., a manufacturer of industrial computers, "you'll be locked out."[27]

Hard sales figures were less important than a place among the rank of pioneers, the privileged group who would get to open what another spokesman for Gould called "virgin territory," a phrase that the radical Gang of Four, if they had heard it, might have taken as a sinister announcement of intended rape. In fact, Americans were plotting a strategy for China that was in some ways quite similar to what the radicals in China had feared if China were to be opened to expanded foreign trade and investment. "Companies realize that they can make the Chinese 'dependent' on their technologies, their own way of doing things, and their spare parts," an American lawyer told readers of *Fortune* in 1979. "If businessmen do things right, it will make the Chinese long-term customers." This kind of dependency was precisely what the Gang of Four had worried about. Even though the American lawyer was quick to disavow the idea that foreign companies wanted to "enslave the Chinese," the idea of creating technological dependence clearly seems to have been an element in the strategic thinking of some of the first companies that went to China.[28]

One observer at the time noticed that Americans who played the role of "business pioneers" in China enjoyed "psychological compensation." The adrenalin generated by going where no other American had been is seen in the reminiscences of Armand Hammer, the octogenarian chairman of Occidental Petroleum who had long derived pleasure in playing the role of the bad boy in American capitalism by doing business with the Soviet Union from the time of Lenin. Now, with China opening to commerce with the capitalist world, Hammer had another outlaw country with which to do business and shock the ideologically prim American establishment.[29]

Publicly, Hammer emphasized that he was simply practicing solid business principles, going wherever opportunities appeared; good business transcended ideology. He also said that trade could serve to reduce tension between the superpowers and help promote peace. But privately, it appears that Hammer was also strongly attracted to the romantic aspects of doing business with exotic Asia. In 1932 he wrote, "Business is business but Russia is romance." When China opened, he affixed an addendum, "The same goes for China today."[30]

His autobiography, published in 1987, is much more revealing than Hammer probably intended. When relating how he came to gain entrée to the People's Republic, he shows us not a sober businessperson, or even a solemn advocate of world peace through trade, but rather a boyish adolescent, preoccupied with his own personal conquests, delighting in breaking rules and relishing the sense of being first. His first contact with Deng Xiaoping, he tells us, was made when he impishly lied his way past Secret Service men and White House officials and crashed the rodeo dinner for Deng and his entourage in Simonton, Texas. Hammer not only enjoyed his talk with Deng, who asked Hammer about his meetings with Lenin and his experiences with Lenin's New Economic Policy, he also enjoyed "the look of surprise" on the faces of the Texan oilmen who saw an "invader from California in their midst."[31]

The involvement with China seems to have been immediately satisfying to Hammer personally. He was asked by Deng to come "help us," given special permission to fly his own jet to Beijing, and fetched every day from his hotel by a fleet of immense black limousines, which Hammer regarded with the delight not of an adult millionaire, but of a teenager on prom night. Apparently wealthy capitalists were no more resistant to the "techniques of hospitality" than the leftist intellectuals that Paul Hollander mocked. In one week in Beijing, Hammer signed four preliminary agreements, for oil exploration, coal mining, and two other projects, but they seemed less important than the opportunity to confer with some of the world's most powerful figures.[32]

Wall Street did not particularly care for the Hammer style of flaunting close ties with the enemy. The fact that many of Occidental's agreements with the Soviet Union and Eastern Europe had fallen far short of their announced goals was loudly repeated by critics, skeptical that much would come of the new agreements signed with China. Hammer offended the prevailing orthodoxy not merely by arguing that corporations should do business with Communist countries, but also by trumpeting the message in a passionate crusade. The conservative establishment began a vigil and waited eagerly for this maverick to fall flat on his face.[33]

It was unfair for critics to single out Armand Hammer's Occidental for its quixotic interest in China when all the major petroleum companies were also scrambling to gain entry. Unlike Oxy, these companies did not expose themselves to the reproaches of Wall Street with messianic rhetoric about building world peace. But they were no less captured by a fever of optimism and a growing conviction that China was sitting on staggering reserves of untapped oil. The longer foreign oil companies had been denied an opportunity to explore China's petroleum resources for themselves, the larger the resources loomed in their imaginations. When China was still closed to foreign investment, *Newsweek* reported in 1975 that "the only sure thing is that China's oil riches are vast." In this version China threatened to rival all of OPEC, possessing "more oil than is contained in the North Sea and Alaska's North Slope combined."[34]

The Chinese leadership did not lightly decide to undertake joint cooperation with foreign companies to develop its petroleum resources. The Chinese were especially sensitive to any appearance of losing to other countries the benefits of developing their own natural resources. On this point, China's political factions agreed. But the decision to import foreign steel technology in the early 1970s had led China to the reluctant decision that it would have to export large quantities of oil to pay for the steel program. The success of OPEC's tough stance in staring down the wealthiest developed countries was encouraging. Then, in the late 1970s, as an alliance formed between the Soviet Union and Vietnam, the ancient territorial disputes between Vietnam and China in the South China Sea led to new strategic considerations about drawing Americans into South China Sea oil exploration. The American oil majors, for their part, desperately wanted to diversify their sources, especially as the Iranian revolution unfolded in 1979. They were also interested in China for the old-fashioned reason that they wanted to make a lot of money in a short amount of time. The Americans thought the price of oil would go up to $50 a barrel within two years. A vice-president for a Houston oil services firm later said, "Everyone thought they'd go in, hit oil immediately, and get rich."[35]

Risk is always present in the "oil patch," and undertaking a high risk project in China does not itself reveal the romantic tug of China chic. But the way in which the American oil companies went about deciding to enter the China market, and the terms of unprecedented severity that they accepted from the Chinese, show a special emotionalism that can be distinguished from the ordinary acceptance of extraordinary risks. The initiative to go to China in many cases was launched not by exploration units or other functional groups deep within the company. Rather, in several cases in addition to Occidental, it was the political activities of a single powerful person at the top—a company chairman, chief executive officer, or director—who developed contacts with Deng Xiaoping or other Chinese notables and made the commitment to invest. Competition with rivals was also very much on the minds of oil company executives. One chief executive officer, for example, remained uninterested in China, despite the impassioned importuning of an underling. But when the CEO read a front page story that Exxon, Penzoil, and other companies had decided to go to China, he changed his mind.[36]

So began the involvement of American oil companies, joining other foreign companies in a self-admitted blind rush to China. Together, the oil companies spent $1.7 billion between 1979 and 1985 for petroleum exploration in the South China Sea. The psychological aspects of this adventure are noteworthy especially because the Chinese sensed the fever of the foreign oil companies and skillfully used it to their own advantage. To begin with, China kept its own geological logs to itself and required foreign oil companies to undertake one of the most extensive seismic surveys ever completed anywhere. It cost an estimated $200 million and produced data that had to be turned over to the Chinese government before the Chinese would decide which offshore tracts would be made available for exploratory drilling. Other foreign countries, such as Norway and various African countries, had organized speculative seismic surveys such as this, but they had purchased the surveys as a service contract, and had not been as brazen as the Chinese were in requiring that foreign companies underwrite the costs as a show of goodwill.[37]

Between 1979 and 1982, the Chinese digested the seismic data and drafted a tough model contract for oil development ventures. It was sharpened with helpful advice provided by American oil companies, who individually thought that the Chinese had favored their company with special confidence and trust and who gladly explained the details of production sharing arrangements and risk contracts to what seemed to be an attentive "student." At the same time that the Chinese presented themselves to Americans as innocents in the world of petroleum development, they also sought advice from Norway and other governments that had negotiated with multinational oil companies.[38]

The Chinese settled upon a contract form that demanded much of foreign partners, who were required to bear all exploration expenses and drill a minimum number of wells in a designated area, using Chinese support services at prices the Chinese set as they wished. The oil companies grumbled that the Chinese were going to make a lot of money even if no one found any oil. Helicopter service charges, for example, were so high that they paid the price of a new helicopter in just a few months. Companies realized that each exploratory well would cost $8 to $10 million to drill, double the outlay in U.S. waters. Yet when the Chinese issued the model contract in 1982 and invited bids—just to tender an offer each firm had to pay $40,000 for each South China Sea block—the foreign companies did not hesitate. Later, a European oil executive explained that emotion had supplanted reason and the Chinese were able to impose inflexible contract terms because "we all wanted acreage."[39]

The one company that stood apart from the rest in the frenzy was Mobil, which did not sign a contract in the first round of bidding and which closed its Beijing office between 1984 and 1987 after spending an estimated $20 million on its unsuccessful approach to China. At the time, in 1984, competitors granted Mobil credit for having "more guts than most to tell the Chinese they wouldn't put up with the terms." But it was still too early to know whether the withdrawal was wise or not. Neither Chinese nor foreign geologists could really know with any certainty what would be found.[40]

Time soon proved, however, that estimates had been far too high. By 1985, after forty-nine wells had been drilled, only seven had any oil or gas flow, and of these, the only notable find had been the unexpected one of gas, not oil, which Arco discovered near Hainan Island. One drilling manager told of new assessments: "Rather than Prudhoe Bay-sized discoveries [10 billion barrels], we're talking about 50 to 100 million barrels of recoverable oil at best." Some oil industry representatives tried to maintain a chipper outlook. "Nobody ever said it was going to be cheap," said a consultant at China Energy Ventures, Inc., an American firm which had a vested interest in keeping U.S. oil companies active in China. Others sought hope in the history of oil exploration elsewhere—in the North Sea, Alaska, Libya, and Angola—where major discoveries were made only after many more exploratory wells had been sunk. But for the most part, gloom replaced the earlier elation, reflecting the movement of the emotional roller coaster that seemed to dominate business with China. The president of Penzoil's exploration unit said, "At this point, we are very discouraged. We rolled our dice and we seem to have gotten snake eyes." Arco, which had discovered the huge gas field and appeared to be the one winner, was in a difficult position because falling oil prices made the Chinese reluctant to invest in developing the field. In 1986 Beijing pressed Arco to make major concessions as a condition for developing the project. With more than $100 million invested in exploration, money that could not be recovered if the project were allowed to collapse, Arco had little choice other than to accept new terms set by the Chinese, who knew Arco was too heavily invested to withdraw.[41]

The American oil-patch representatives had two advantages that helped them absorb the disappointment: first, much similar experience elsewhere, and second, the self-conscious gambling ethos that survived from the rough-and-tumble culture of Texas wildcatters. (To help the Chinese better understand Texas, a seismic exploration company, Geosource, presented them with mementos of Texan culture: four armadillos shipped to Beijing, with enough Ken-L Rations to last a month and instructions that the West Texan critters also liked to eat scrambled eggs and dirt.) In the aftermath of the dry wells, both foreigners and Chinese pointed at the other as being responsible, but the foreigners did not have much to say other than to accuse the Chinese of being overly optimistic. The Chinese, however, did not have the experience of the foreign oil companies and did not have same philosophical equanimity the foreigners had learned to call upon. Chinese officials were bitter and felt that the foreigners had not given the exploratory drilling their best efforts. Chinese officials even accused one firm of failing to use the latest technology and suggested that the use of outdated equipment was responsible for the failure to find oil (a charge that would have had more plausibility if the oil companies had been hired on a fee-for-service basis instead of risk contracts that required millions of dollars of their own capital to be invested in these ventures).[42]

The disappointing results from the first round of drilling, the foreign anger at Chinese prices for services, and the gradual erosion of world oil prices between 1983 and 1985 meant that time did not work in China's favor. For the foreign oil companies China fever had passed, and in the second round of invited bidding that began in late 1985, foreign companies brought a sober sensibility to the negotiations. *Fortune* read a morality lesson in these experiences, observing with satisfaction that foreign reluctance to invest in further oil exploration in China was the result of Chinese "boondoggling" and overpriced services. Now the Chinese would finally reap what they had sown. But this assessment failed to note that the oil companies were merely the pioneers, and hundreds of companies were more than willing to follow in their footsteps in a headlong rush to China. The initially bubbly enthusiasm about

China in the U.S. oil industry was replicated throughout the wider business community. Each portion had its own separate encounter with China; each company insisted on having its own giddy fling.[43]

The oil companies had one immediately natural reason to have been intrigued by China, whose unsurveyed territories along the continental shelf truly had been one of the last such large, geologically unexplored terrains in the world. Other American companies went to China with commercial hopes that had a less plausible rationale. Much China chic in the business community was a socially created phenomenon of the moment, not the outcome of thoughtful analysis. The aura of mystery surrounding the China market seemed at times to be consciously nurtured by the Chinese, who some Americans thought had purposely limited foreign visits so that outsiders would continue to perceive the country as mysterious and exotic. (One U.S. executive corresponded for years with a Chinese official who signed his letters simply "M 903," which the Americans described as "*Get Smart*-style," calling to mind the 1960s television spoof of spy thrillers.) Whether the mystification was intended or not, American businesspeople were captivated. One banker observed, "Even the most hard-bitten businessman has this bug, this bagful of 'I was in China' anecdotes."[44]

As early as the mid-1970s, a number of trade publications and newsletters, all specializing in the China trade, sprang up in the United States and other Western countries. By 1977, no other country in the world had as many trade publications devoted exclusively to one country as China had, a startling phenomenon for a noncapitalist country whose share of world trade was all but insignificant. The newsletters had low circulation and high subscription fees, but businesspeople were willing to pay for subscriptions to many at the same time, figuring that one might contain a few nuggets of information that could lead to the big payoff, an echo on a more modest scale of the gamble undertaken by the oil companies.[45]

The bimonthly magazine *China Business Review,* which was published by the National Council for U.S.–China Trade, was the best of the China-trade publications and contained a great deal of concrete information that served to reduce the mystery that clung to China in the popular American imagination. Yet the council's purpose was to promote trade between the two countries, and its magazine, not surprisingly, did not generally print information that undermined that aim. For example, the story that the *China Business Review* published about the experiences of the Pullman Kellogg employees and their families told readers that relations between Kellogg and the Chinese had been smooth. It did not mention the many conflicts at the various sites between Americans and Chinese officials, apparently because the company did not want to offend the Chinese and had insisted that the article be rewritten several times and approved before publication. In such cases, the council could not take an independent stand for the greater glory of journalistic integrity. Though a nonprofit, ostensibly independent organization, it had to be careful of offending its U.S. members, whose dues were the primary source of funds. In the course of their work, staff members came to know of many problems that plagued U.S.–China trade, but for practical reasons they could divulge little. Consequently, the *China Business Review* was just another voice in the choir of boosters for China trade.[46]

China was promoted not merely as another new market opened to Americans; it stood apart in a special realm in the imagination, impossibly large and evaluated not with the cold calculus of ordinary business, but in the softer vocabulary that the Chinese themselves offered, of friendship and assistance in the country's modernization. It was one large cuddly human-interest story for Americans, an opportunity to combine business with pleasure. The story of Norman Dong, an eighteen-year-old "businessman" and goodwill ambassador who lived in Bergenfield, New Jersey, is instructive. Dong was a native New Yorker of Chinese and Danish descent, and while a high school student in the early 1980s he had decided he was tired of "backyard barbecues" and the banality of New Jersey suburban life and wanted to do something to bring China and the United States closer together. He spoke not a word of Chinese and had no prior business experience, but he peppered Chinese trade officials with letters, asking if there were any business project with which he could become involved.

His letters were passed on through the trade bureaucracy until one of them reached the Tianjin Bicycle Industrial Corporation, which expressed an interest in talking further. Dong, accompanied by a thirty-one-year-old brother who did speak Chinese, flew to Tianjin and signed an agreement that set up bicycle exports to the American market. All that was missing was an American distributor. Here matters stood when the *New York Times* lionized young Mr. Dong as a "gutsy" teenager, a "rebel with a cause," and published a long, flattering feature with an accompanying photograph of the entrepreneur. A happy conclusion to the story was never written—Dong was not able to find an interested

American partner—but the concrete facts of business actually completed were far less important than the imaginative appeal of the story. Anyone could reach out and "do business" with the Chinese in a happy marriage of self-interest and altruism, business and diplomacy. The ordinary conventions of commerce and journalism were suspended; the scheme alone, regardless of its realization, was sufficient to be newsworthy.[47]

The press was merely reflecting the same idea that had captured the business community, that China stood apart from all other markets, *sui generis.* The immensity and exoticism of China were overwhelming. In 1979 one trading firm, Roth International, tried to interest American exporters in Latin American markets, with which the United States carried on trade several orders of magnitude greater than the bilateral trade with the People's Republic, but which did not excite the interest of large U.S. industrial firms the way China did. Roth argued that it was much easier to do business with Mexico ("Try dialing Mexico City. It's as easy as dialing Minneapolis. Then try calling Beijing."), yet this was not appreciated because of the "euphoria of selling to the most populous market in the world," which, Roth said, was distracting top managers from realizing that "there's more gold in enchiladas than in fortune cookies." China so dominated the business imagination that Frank Weil, an assistant secretary in the U.S. Department of Commerce, pleaded in 1979 with American businesspeople who joined trade missions to the People's Republic that they consider other markets in Asia, such as Japan, Taiwan, or South Korea. Weil said: "When they stop for refueling in Tokyo, I want to take them out and say, 'Look at the market you've got here.' " That Japan would need to be put on the map is a telling statement about the preoccupation with China.[48]

When China began in 1979 to offer investment opportunities in addition to trade, China chic was not just a matter of fashion but an influence in costly business decisions, as the oil companies first discovered and others would learn for themselves. "Companies should weigh the decision to invest in the China market just as harshly as when they're going into Nigeria, Brazil, or India," advised an international consulting firm. It was sensible advice that would not have been needed elsewhere, for only China had the combination of emotional lures that pulled so hard at the American imagination.[49]

II

DOING BUSINESS

BUMPS

During the Cultural Revolution and before, when the Chinese enjoyed a feeling of ideological certitude that is now long lost, they often used a wonderfully emphatic phrase—"irresistible historical trend"—that referred to various events, especially those they cheered, such as the wars of national liberation in the Third World. The Chinese dropped the phrase in the 1980s, but if they had still used it, one wonders if they (or we) would have been tempted to say that the growth of trade and other economic ties between the People's Republic and the United States was also an "irresistible historical trend." Until June 1989, it seemed to many to be inexorable. Two-way trade started at a paltry level of $5 million, climbed to one hundred times this figure, $500 million, by 1978, doubled immediately in 1979 upon normalization of diplomatic relations, then soared further until it exceeded $14 billion in 1988. It appeared destined for much higher levels in 1989, until the suppression of the Beijing demonstrations. During the same time period, U.S. direct investment in the PRC rose from virtually zero to about $3.5 billion. These gross figures create the impression that the trend was a smooth ascent.

Beneficial changes in trade policies on both sides, which had started in the early 1970s with American and Chinese gestures of conciliation, indeed continued in the 1980s. The United States granted China most favored nation status, reducing tariffs and moving China to special categories that permitted comparatively relaxed controls on military-related exports. The Chinese, on their part, decentralized foreign trade administration and decision-making to a degree that was hard to imagine even at the time of Deng Xiaoping's visit to the United States in 1979. State enterprises and newly reorganized foreign trade companies were made more responsible for their own profits and losses, and were given freedom to retain a certain portion of foreign exchange. These reforms set the organizations off in pursuit of dollars and yen, often at the peril of undermining the interests of one another and the state. In the midst of this internecine competition for business with foreigners, the Chinese were especially keen on working with Americans. Though the People's Republic was only thirteenth on the list of America's most important trading partners in 1988, America consistently was one of China's most important foreign trading partners, second only to Japan if we exclude the special case of Hong Kong.[1]

The growth of trade ties between socialist China and capitalist America between 1971 and 1989 was not as irresistible, however, as a listing of progressive trade reforms or a schematic charting of beginning and ending trade figures suggests. The overall trend hides a pattern of wide swings, both economic and emotional, that characterized the China business well before the shocks of 1989. Surges of Chinese imports were often followed by jolting retrenchment. The pattern can be seen in the 1970s, when two-way trade jumped 740 percent from 1972 to 1973, then a more modest 16 percent between 1973 and 1974, and then dropped by 51 percent between 1974 and 1975. In 1978, China signed $7 billion in contracts with American and other foreign partners (some $3 billion worth were signed in ten hectic days at the end of December), then abruptly suspended or canceled the agreements as part of a retrenchment. Boom-and-bust continued in 1985, when Chinese imports jumped 54 percent compared to the previous year, then were slashed the next when foreign exchange reserves were drawn down from the shopping spree. In late 1988, a central tightening of credits left many Chinese enterprises hard pressed to meet contractual obligations with foreign business suppliers, creating a gloomy business outlook even before the political crisis of mid-1989. One year, a Chinese enterprise would be flush with an allocation to make foreign purchases, which it had to spend that year or lose entirely; the next year, it would have no allocation at all. This was unsettling to Americans who became accustomed in other developing countries to predictable, steady increases in sales. Each Chinese retrenchment set off cries of complaint, even betrayal.[2]

Foreign businesspeople themselves helped create the financial crises and subsequent import cuts about which they complained so loudly. In 1978, for example, some 57 banking delegations descended on China offering a total of $27 billion in immediate loans. A Japanese banker observed, "It's crazy. How are [the Chinese] going to pay for it all?" Heedless, the Chinese and their foreign partners signed agreements for deals worth billions, including a $1 billion iron-ore mining project with U.S. Steel (at the signing called the largest project to be undertaken abroad by the company), another billion-dollar hotel deal with Hyatt International, and a $100 million mining proposal with Bethlehem Steel. Chase Manhattan bragged that it had bested the Japanese and other rivals in securing official Chinese support for its place as the lead bank in financing a $250 million world trade center in Beijing. When the retrenchment of 1980 hit and the Chinese announced that these deals were off, the Americans were taken by surprise. As one attorney observed, "Americans have been thrust into a cold shower."[3]

Americans were actually spared the coldest shower; it was the Japanese and Germans who experienced the biggest shock because they had earlier contracted their own strains of "China fever" and had many more contracts for large-scale projects. "This is one of the occasions it has been an advantage to be behind the pack," gloated a U.S. trade official. The hardest news for the Japanese and Germans was the halting of the construction of the Baoshan steel mill, the $1.4 billion project outside Shanghai which had gotten underway in 1977 and was dependent primarily on Japanese and West German contracts. The Chinese offered to pay the stipulated cancellation penalties and did not understand the symbolic impact that cancellation of Baoshan—the flagship project of the Four Modernizations campaign—would have on the financial plans of the individual foreign firms that had been their partners, nor the psychological impact the announcement would have on the larger business community. In the negotiations between the Chinese and Japanese about the terms of the plant cancellations, Gu Mu, a vice-premier, innocently asked a Japanese official, "This is a minor problem for the giant Japanese economy, isn't it?"[4]

For many American companies that had only just begun to explore the possibility of doing business with the People's Republic and had felt far outdistanced by the Japanese and the Europeans, the "readjustment," as the Chinese euphemistically described the retrenchment of 1980 and 1981, was not such a bad thing. Roger Sullivan, then vice-president of the National Council for U.S.–China Trade, put it philosophically: "We were lucky that readjustment came along because it gave us a chance to catch up. As our chairman of the board once said, it's like when the yellow flag goes down at Indianapolis—you can't pass anybody, but you can't fall behind either." But some Americans did not view the retrenchment so dispassionately. The euphoria about China business was replaced quickly by gloom. Seminars in the United States about doing business with China were canceled because of a drop in interest. Businesspeople in other industries started to pay closer attention to the experiences of the foreign oil company executives, and disheartening rumors spread, such as the one about an oil company chief executive whose thirty-two trips to China had failed to close one deal.[5]

The Chinese could not understand why Americans and other foreigners were so easily discouraged. In 1979, China's government agencies took under active consideration some 800 joint venture proposals, but by 1980 only some 13 or so had moved into operation or were under construction. Foreign businesspeople interpreted this small number of projects realized as a bad sign, and criticized the Chinese "bureaucratic morass" and "chronic indecision." Chinese decision-makers, however, viewed the few approvals as a praiseworthy display of self-restraint, following the realization that their country's infrastructure was simply incapable of supporting anything other than a few pilot projects. As one Chinese economist tried to explain to an apparently disbelieving audience of foreign businesspeople: "We have limited resources, and some of these proposals, even if potentially profitable, would take too much of our capital to match the foreign investment or too many of our skilled managers or engineers away from other projects with a higher priority." The Chinese thought that they would be praised for prudence, and not encouraged to approve projects they knew had a high likelihood of failure. The tabling of the Chase Manhattan–sponsored world trade center that had been proposed for Beijing, for example, stood in the American mind as a symbol of Chinese unreliability. Americans were incensed about the "broken deal" and were not sympathetic to the explanation offered by a Chinese trade official, who argued that Americans "should be encouraged, in fact, by our willingness to take a hard look at a project, even when half the design work is done, and cancel it if it then appears to be unprofitable." The official added a sharp ideological coda: "You can't preach to us about making economically rational decisions and then object when we do so."[6]

The trade center project, unfortunately, was not an ideal case for the Chinese to claim as an example of purely rational decision-making. It was common knowledge in Beijing that the project had been at the center of acrimonious feuding between the Ministry of Foreign Trade and the Beijing municipal government, which controlled all land and construction and wanted a bigger share of the profits. (When the city did not get its way, it retaliated by assigning a plot for the project that was a third of the size the ministry had requested, and at a site far from the center of the city.) The project also depended on a financing scheme that was unconventional by foreign standards: prospective foreign tenants were to pay five years' rent in advance, at $100,000 a year. This proved to be an unattractive offer. Furthermore, Chinese representatives to the National People's Congress—until this time known only as a somnambulant rubber-stamp assembly—directly criticized the proposed trade center as an extravagant white elephant, an embarrassment at a time when the state budget had an $11 billion deficit.

It was this last criticism that apparently killed the project. But it was also the very criticism that most concerned foreigner observers, for it suggested that business decisions had been inappropriately politicized in China. "A broken deal, however legal by the contract, does not inspire confidence," said one American contractor in 1980. The Chinese, it seemed, had torn up the deal for their own domestic political reasons. "It could happen to any of us," the American concluded glumly. In canceling the trade center China, still so opaque to American businesspeople, gave new life to the worst stereotypes of the insensibly political Communist and the unfathomably inscrutable Oriental.[7]

Yet the Americans recovered their optimism in a remarkably short time. In early 1981, "you'd have to spend the first half-hour of each meeting with important U.S. executives trying to explain Baoshan," said Jerome Alan Cohen, an American lawyer who was a China specialist. But by late 1981, skittish American investors were buoyant once again; trade increased, joint ventures were started, and American expectations again soared far higher than circumstances justified, setting up the next turn of the cycle and bitter disappointment. On the eve of President Reagan's trip to China in 1984, American interest in China business followed the same course of overheated optimism, then disillusion. In the trough of disappointment, Americans revealed how much they had treated China as a special case, and so regarded its failure to realize their hopes as a kind of betrayal of trust. *Fortune,* in a 1987 article that carried the title "The China Bubble Bursts," heaped scorn upon China, saying it was "still little more than an ambitious Third World country: backward, bureaucratic, and greedy." But the characterization is less telling of China, which had yet to claim that it was anything but a part of the developing Third World, than it is revealing of Americans and their earlier feeling that China belonged in a class by itself.[8]

Compared to relations in the early 1970s, business between the People's Republic and the United States in the decade following China's wider opening in the 1980s was relatively free of obstruction from ideological differences between the two partners. But ideology remained much on the minds of all participants: On one side, China fitfully dismantled, then partially restored, Marxist orthodoxy; and on the other, Americans cheered with partisan gusto for capitalist orthodoxy in its stead. Both sides hurled criticism at the other when differences of outlook interfered with business.

When Chinese reporters visited the United States on the eve of Deng Xiaoping's visit, the reports they presented to Chinese readers were full of praise for the United States as a nation of hard workers and impressive technology. But soon after normalization and Deng's visit, the Chinese authorities decided that too much praise was being given to the United States; the Chinese people were forming improper ideas about capitalism. A wave of negative reports about America were published in 1980 to serve as a salutary corrective. As a group, these reports returned to the gloomy depictions of the past, describing American consumption as erected not on the strong shoulders of diligent workers, but rather on the rickety structure of installment credit. True, wages were high, but so were the prices of goods and taxes. One Chinese author, who had taught in the United States in the 1940s, reported he was aghast to find when he returned for a visit thirty years later that the haircut which used to cost 50 cents now cost $5, a tenfold increase (an increase made all the more dramatic by his neglecting to mention any increase in nominal wages for the same period).[9]

The sharpest attacks on the United States were made by an American-trained vice-president of Qinghua University, Zhang Guangdou, whose vitriolic denunciation of American society in early 1980 was distributed as a limited circulation document for Chinese Communist Youth League members. Two years before, the *People's Daily* had praised Americans for their willingness to study other countries and had used as an example the employment of German scientists after the fall of the Third Reich. The same example, however, was used by Zhang to show the criminality of the Americans, whose scientific and technical achievements were the result of plundering the expertise of other countries. Zhang described Americans as bestial: "After our victory over Japan, the Americans came in. American soldiers pushed their way around, doing whatever they pleased, raping women. They did every bad thing possible." Acknowledging that 20,000 PRC citizens had emigrated in the first year since diplomatic relations were restored and that an untold number apparently wanted to follow, Zhang told his Chinese audience: "Capitalism has great unemployment, so how are you going to get along if you go abroad? You only know how to do simple labor, so if you go, you will be a slave—entering the ranks of the unemployed." Zhang's speech was not intended for foreign ears, but once Western reporters got hold of the transcript, they publicized its contents. The *Wall Street Journal* was delighted, for Zhang's remarks showed that Americans were as "inscrutable" to the Chinese as Chinese were to Americans. The *Journal* repeated, with relish, a bizarre anecdote told by Zhang: "In the American social system, there are family problems. If a son goes to his mother's home to eat, he must pay money. If the mother goes to [her] son's house to eat, she must also give money. I'm not joking in the least. I'll give you an example. A family invited me to eat dinner. Four of them invited me, and after eating, and in front of me, they took out a calculator and calculated who owed what."[10]

This harsh look at the United States was part of a two-track policy. Publicly, Chinese authorities encouraged the growth of trade and investment ties with the United States, and privately they explained the ties as a tactical expedient and redoubled the traditional denunciations of capitalism to check any erosion in ideological faith. Chinese trade officials, however, had understandable difficulty in calibrating the proper degree of welcome in their encounters with capitalist representatives. The message they heard from the state media was that profits were, by definition, exploitative, and that China had to allow exploitation to a certain degree as the price of modernization. Sun Ru, deputy director of the Guangdong Provincial Institute of Philosophy and Social Science, explained: "What [foreign] investors need is profit, what we need is modernized socialist construction. Well, each takes what he needs." Foreign observers were dismayed to hear authorities explain in this fashion what was elsewhere publicly called "mutual benefit": The Chinese were telling themselves that what was of benefit to foreigners exploited China, while what was of benefit to China remained morally untainted.[11]

China was not able to expand exports and attract investment as quickly as Deng Xiaoping and other leaders had hoped. Some factions within the state were committed to expanding foreign economic ties, but others remained obdurately opposed and slowed business with campaigns aimed at ideological prophylaxis. As Xu Shiwei, the secretary general of the newly formed China International Trade Association, explained, many Chinese trade officials believed that trade was not in China's best interests. Xu, who himself felt strongly otherwise, summed up the philosophy of the others: "The more you export, the more you allow yourself to be exploited." It was a philosophy that some portions of the state bolstered, even as other portions tried to counteract it by publicizing the more liberal message of people like Xu. Confusion and its natural adjunct, a conservative reluctance to take positive action, were the result.[12]

In China, the harsh characterization of American capitalists was credible because virtually no one was a specialist in "America-watching." The United States had a small army of "China watchers," researchers in and out of the U.S. government who were dedicated to the study of some aspect of Chinese politics and society. The few America experts in China were mostly people in their sixties or seventies who had studied in the United States forty or fifty years before. China's Institute of World Politics was not established until 1979, and its American section had only eight researchers, of whom only one had been to the United States, and that in 1950. The Chinese authorities established the American section to catch up with individual Chinese who were far ahead in learning about new developments in the United States. So many influential Chinese had gone to the United States during China's reopening in the 1970s, including officials, trade negotiators, scientists, and students, that they were able to form judgments of the United States independently, without reliance on the simple critical formula the authorities had provided in the past.[13]

The head of the American section, Hu Zhengqing, had been in the United States during World War II, and had been sent to a submarine base in Florida for training. In 1980, when interviewed by an American reporter, he noted that Americans and Chinese held ideologically incompatible viewpoints. "It's impossible for Americans to look at China from a Marxist-Leninist viewpoint. We use the Marxist-Leninist viewpoint to study the U.S." Hu added, "Events will prove who is right," which was precisely the sentiment felt by American capitalists, who also saw in the Sino-American business dealings a showdown of fundamentally opposed ideological systems, and who, no less than Hu, were confident the outcome would favor their side.[14]

The American business community helped highlight the ideological and cultural differences by lobbying Chinese authorities to grant permission for Bob Hope and an appropriately diverse American entourage to come to China. In 1979, on the first Fourth of July after normalization, Hope presented his show in Beijing, along with Mikhail Baryshnikov, *Sesame Street*'s Big Bird, and Peaches and Herb, a soul-singing duo whose female member performed in a notoriously scanty outfit. One reporter, Jay Mathews, said at the time: "Chairman Mao liked to talk about contradictions, but he never saw anything like this." This was spectacle, with Americans entertaining themselves by watching the Chinese watching the Americans. The outcome was predictable enough (Baryshnikov was a hit; Hope's one-liners were a flop; Peaches' skimpy disco outfit was received with stony silence), but the significance of the event was not that the Chinese were given an opportunity to learn much about Americans, but that the Americans, the instigators, derived so much pleasure from the juxtaposition of perceived differences between American and Chinese societies.[15]

In the earlier encounters when Americans were first attending the Canton Trade Fair or were training Chinese at a site in the hinterland, Americans instinctively kept an informal ideological balance sheet and granted credits when the Chinese were discovered to have institutions or policies that were unexpected and deemed praiseworthy. The chairman of John Deere, William Hewitt, for example, was surprised during a trip in 1973 when the Chinese told him that savings deposits earned interest and were inheritable. These and other facts seemed to Hewitt to be at variance with what was "prescribed" by Marxism. In other cases in the early years, Americans informally debited the Chinese balance sheet when problems appeared behind the official façade. In the early 1970s, American technicians noted that there were locks everywhere they looked in China, even in the Peking Hotel. If Americans suffered from crime, it was a comfort to learn that so too, apparently, did the Chinese.

But these comparative judgments of Chinese society did not constitute much more than scattershot remarks. The Chinese seemed stolid, self-confident. Edward Gorman, chairman of Joseph Magnin's, wrote in his China trip notes: "They seem to say, here is what we are doing, here is where we are heading, please come to see it if you want, but, whether or not you like it, this is it." When China opened wider at the end of the 1970s, the apparent ideological ferment within China's own leadership showed that China was not so self-confident after all, and the much loosened restrictions on travel to and from China created an atmosphere in which both Americans and Chinese were not only aware of ideological, cultural, political, and other differences, but also of the state of flux in China. Americans saw an opportunity to pull the Chinese away from the Marxist-Leninist encampment.[16]

Americans began with compliments and praised the Chinese for being different from the Russians in just the right sorts of ways. In the tourist wave of 1978, one Wall Street executive drew a typically invidious comparison between the Soviet Union, which he had visited ten years earlier, and the People's Republic. In the Soviet Union, "the tourist guides were downright insulting, the food unbearably monotonous. In China, there are no drunks, no black marketeers importuning the tourist to change money or sell blue jeans. No dissidents clamoring to go to Israel. There don't seem to be any dissidents in China." The same comparison would be made again and again, always to the disadvantage of the Soviets. Luiz Themodo, a trade show impresario described by the *San Francisco Chronicle* as "a capitalist fox in the socialist hen house," said: "I have dealt with both the Russians and the Chinese. The Chinese are nicer to deal with—but not easier. They are very good businesspeople. We don't want to take advantage of them. But we couldn't if we wanted to." As testimony to the mythical business acumen that Americans saw as part of the genetic makeup of Chinese, Richard Nixon would remark later, in 1989, "How many Russian laundries do you know in New York?" Amid these effusions, American whites sometimes drew an invidious comparison between American blacks and Chinese. Edward Gorman said that when a crowd of curious Chinese surrounded his car, he had no feeling of menace, but "in a similar situation in or near Harlem we would have felt downright frightened."[17]

In their zeal to offer encouraging praise of the Chinese, Americans could be extremely self-deprecating. An RCA engineer credited the Chinese with having a highly developed civilization "when my ancestors were still painting their faces blue." Other Americans extended similar courtesies. When New York Mayor Edward Koch visited Beijing, he said in a speech that while he was proud of the United States, the people of China also had every right to be proud of their country. It was unexceptional politesse, but it reflected magnanimity that could not be matched by the less powerful and confident partner. Frank Ching, a *Wall Street Journal* reporter, observed in 1980 that after Koch's compliments, as after the many similar speeches given by Americans, Chinese officials never paid reciprocal homage to the achievements of the Americans in their presence, and stuck to reiterating the superiority of socialism. This rankled. But it was interpreted as a sign of Chinese weakness. If the Chinese economy could perform well, Ching wrote, the Chinese would not have to reiterate their own superiority, and "a confident, purposeful China could let facts speak for themselves."[18]

Having thrown down the gauntlet, challenging visiting Western businesspeople to see which system, socialism or capitalism, was best, China found itself in a difficult position, less sure over time of the outcome. By the end of the 1980s, reformist officials and journalists were much less interested in such old-fashioned ideological contests than at the beginning, yet the government was unable to admit publicly that it wanted to pick the gauntlet back up and end the competition. The more public confidence in the superiority of socialism eroded, the more conservative authorities felt compelled to launch defensive ideological campaigns—the "antispiritual-pollution campaign" of 1983–84 being only the best known of the group—which built up the self-image of Chinese socialism by tearing down Western capitalism. The progress of Sino-Western business ties was interrupted by these outbursts, which should be understood as rearguard salvos in an ideological battle the Chinese themselves had confidently joined but had difficulty sustaining.

Americans and other Western businesspeople in China watched uneasily when Chinese self-praise shifted to xenophobia, as it so often did. The authorities were everything but consistent: At times, they sponsored campaigns in which foreign influences were denounced as pernicious and corrupting, and published articles that extolled Chinese heroes of the past who had ably controlled Western "barbarians." Yet at other times, and even at the same time as these campaigns, the same authorities were concerned that foreign businesspeople would take offense and leave, and hastened to offer individual assurances to potential investors and traders that their business would continue to be welcome. Occasionally, the Chinese state was not so much inconsistent as it was powerless, as when in May 1985 a riot broke out in Beijing after China's soccer team lost to Hong Kong in a World Cup qualifying competition. Rioters outside the stadium threw rocks and bottles at cars, attacked a number of people, and left four police officers seriously injured. Although at first glance it may have seemed similar to riots that had followed soccer games in Europe and Latin America, it was different in one important respect, one that understandably concerned the foreign community in Beijing: It was foreigners who were singled out for attack.[19]

In the coverage of the riot in the *Los Angeles Times,* questions were raised about whether foreign business executives might be subjected to harassment in China and about the implications for foreign companies that were thinking of starting operations in China. These were precisely the sorts of concerns that the Chinese authorities, anxious to attract foreign investment, wanted to allay. In the wake of the riot, a large and conspicuous contingent of Chinese police stood outside a Pierre Cardin fashion show in Beijing. The state-owned People's Insurance Company quickly paid off claims of damage to foreigners' cars. And China's Olympic stars urged the Chinese people to show "good sportsmanship" toward foreigners. Applying a salve of cheery sportsmanship to the growing problem of popular resentment of foreign special privileges, the state did the best it could. The paradox exposed by such an outburst as the soccer riot was that capitalism could not gain ground in China without running the risk of tripping a violent reaction.[20]

No one issue got Americans and other Westerners so speechlessly angry as Chinese prices for hotel rooms, offices, meals, and other business services, what, in the American view, was more accurately described as out-and-out gouging. The complaints started early, in the days of the Canton Trade Fair, when Americans noticed prices charged to foreigners for meals and excursions going up. In retrospect, when the Chinese charged Americans the equivalent of $1 for a glass of orange juice, and one American wrote home in 1975 about the "ripoff," it was quite premature. Later, when China opened wider and Americans flocked to Beijing to talk business, prices for services hit heights that would make those of the 1970s seem like bargains. One wave of price increases came in 1980. Foreign companies were suddenly charged $2,800 to install a telex machine when the fee previously had only been $100. Overnight, the charge for installing a telephone went from $20 to $1,400. Shortages of office space forced some foreigners to pay up to $400 a day, sometimes ending up with a small room at the back of a restaurant, the only space available. "Prices have gone cuckoo," said one American trader who had done business in China since 1973.[21]

The "China fever" that brought Americans to China kept their enthusiasm from wilting, and they proved willing to pay almost anything to obtain a room in Beijing. An extreme example was the case of a group of a dozen executives from three American companies who wanted rooms together for a one-week stay in Beijing. No ordinary hotel had rooms together, so the group decided to stay in the only place where they could be accommodated, the Diaoyutai state guest house. The basic group rate was $3,850 a night, and the total bill for the week's stay, including meals and transportation, was $36,000.[22]

Foreigners from less affluent countries were also hit by the increases;

the Chinese eliminated the favored pricing they had sometimes granted in the past. The American lament about prices was taken up by Third World representatives in Beijing, like the diplomat whose rent nearly tripled in 1980 and who said: "I have been assigned to posts in New York, Washington, Geneva, Manila, Hong Kong and Tokyo, so I speak from experience when I say that Beijing's new rates are in a class by themselves. This is absolute extortion." The diplomat directed his ire at the Chinese, but others undoubtedly directed their anger at the eager newcomers, the Americans, whose arrival on the scene in large numbers coincided with the Chinese decision to increase prices.[23]

More increases were to come. In 1984, the main hotels increased their room rates over 100 percent with no improvement in what guests complained was "appalling" service. By 1985 it cost a foreign company a minimum of $65,000 a year to have "one room, a typewriter, and a teapot." Larger operations cost more than $200,000 a year. The representative for Cummins Engine who was posted to Beijing was glad to get an apartment for his family for only $72,000 a year in the new Lido complex in north Beijing because he had been paying $125,000 a year in a hotel, where monthly laundry bills alone ran up to $400. For the new apartment, the Cummins representative had to pay a full year's rent in advance and give a security deposit of three months' rent, but he did so gladly because there were no cheaper alternatives. By 1987, an American lamented (without too much exaggeration) that "Peking is the only city I know of that's more expensive than Tokyo."[24]

In Beijing, where entertainment that appealed to resident foreigners was scarce, intramural discussion of the gouging was transformed into gallows humor and itself became a grim form of entertainment. Stories were told of recent misfortunes visited upon hapless foreigners: the residents of the infamous Peking Hotel who had to pay a surcharge if they brought in an extra chair or table (the hotel management explained that the room stewards had more dusting to do, and the residents countered that no dusting was done in any case). Or the old China hand who returned to China in 1980 and arranged for a ten-person luncheon at the same Peking Hotel, and was told it would be $120. Although it was a much higher price than he remembered from the mid-1970s, he went ahead with his plans, and was lucky to discover before the event took place that the quoted price he had thought was $120 for the table of ten was actually $120 per person. (He canceled the reservation, which still cost him $300). Or the woman in Beijing who had to pay a $30 tariff on a baby sweater that had been handmade and sent to her by her mother. Or the man who was asked by local authorities to pay daily rental charges for a Jeep Cherokee that he personally owned.[25]

Perhaps most galling to foreigners was the two-tiered pricing system in which foreigners paid much more than Chinese for air and rail tickets, hotels, and restaurant meals. The policy led to unusual applications, such as when an American woman, married to a Chinese-American man who was entitled to the lower prices charged locals, discovered that in their hotel she had to pay triple what her husband paid for her side of the bed. In a country in which "friendship" stores served exclusively foreign guests, and where "friendship" was toasted at every banquet, Americans and other Westerners began to refer derisively to "friendship prices."[26]

Borrowing the term the Chinese frequently invoked, foreigners complained that they themselves were the ones being "exploited," but they used the word in a different way. The exploitation came not from high prices per se, but from what foreigners called "the principle of the thing," which was the conviction that everyone should set prices in some fashion according to their own costs. This basic principle was ignored in China, where the prices the foreigners were charged seemed, in the words of one, "fixed at levels designed to relieve him of his money rather than related to any real costs in the Chinese system." If the local costs of doing business in another country happened to be high, and all businesspeople, local and foreign, had to pay the same prices, foreigners would not be happy about the situation, but they would accept it. But in China, knowing that local costs were not so high and that the Chinese system sorted customers into the two separate groups—locals and foreigners—with separate prices for each, foreigners were left with what an Australian described as a "sour taste" in the mouth.[27]

At every point that the Chinese raised prices for services, foreigners muttered that if things got any worse, they would have to fold their tents and return home. Such noises were made at the beginning of the 1980s and they were still being made at the end of the decade, before the student protests and the violent suppression that followed changed immediate concerns from prices to the more elemental one of personal safety. It was the military that sent foreigners fleeing briefly in 1989, not the cost of doing business. Looking back on the 1980s, one can see how the exodus the foreigners said always loomed appeared less and less threatening to the Chinese as the years passed and the foreign business supplicants continued to arrive. When a European diplomat suggested in 1984 to one of Beijing's vice-mayors that prices were exorbitant, the Chinese replied nimbly, "How many people have left?" One response, though not offered to the vice-mayor, was the standing joke of the cynical members of the Beijing expatriate community, the saying of an imaginary P. T. Wang: "There's a foreigner born every minute." But the wisecracks and grumbling of the unhappy foreign veterans were mostly confined to the bars of the foreign hotels, and were expressed directly to the Chinese only by the fearless. Doing business in China was too dependent upon maintaining goodwill to permit frank airing of complaints. One American trade consultant, whose own timidity was underlined by his refusal to be mentioned by name in the newspaper article that quoted him, explained that "no one wants to take a chance on offending the Chinese, so no one sounds off." The American said that "the Chinese have a way of letting you know that if you won't agree to their terms, then someone else will." And the Chinese were right.[28]

Foreign businesspeople retorted by saying that high prices on services hurt the interests of the Chinese as well as those of the foreigners because ultimately the gouging of foreigners prevented China from obtaining foreign goods at the most attractive prices. But this was not a convincing argument, for it provided no reason why China should not try to capture the "discount" for itself earlier, by setting hotel and meal charges at stratospheric levels, rather than waiting for a vaguely promised "most attractive price" at some point later, if and when it decided on a purchase. China went for the sure thing: the wallets of the armies of salespeople that came calling. A less dramatic but a sounder foreign argument, however, was that high prices hurt China's interests because the gouging frightened off small- and medium-sized firms. In some fields it was the smaller firms that were technical leaders and could offer technology that China needed and could not obtain from the large multinational companies. Americans wagged their fingers and admonished the Chinese for endangering the foreign goose that could lay many golden eggs.[29]

Chinese authorities, however, remained unmoved. Somehow they had picked up the idea that two-tiered pricing systems were "a common practice abroad," so they did not feel their policy merited a fuss. They also argued that the higher prices charged to foreigners were necessary because the government provided subsidies for food and travel to Chinese citizens and had no obligation to extend the same subsidies to visitors. This explanation did not seem cogent to the visitors, however, who observed that the Chinese government seemed to have no idea of the actual operating expenses for a banquet or a rail trip. Scott Seligman, then on the staff of the National Council for U.S.–China Trade, pointed out in 1982 that arbitrary setting of prices was not a nefarious tactic used to strip foreigners of their valuables, but was simply standard practice in a nonmarket economy. When cost accounting did not exist, prices for anyone—Chinese and foreigner alike—could be set by whim.[30]

The best argument made by Chinese hotels and other providers of services in defense of prices was devastating because it used the foreigners' own vocabulary: Foreign businesspeople were not coerced into coming to China, nor did they come out of altruistic motives. They came for reasons of self-interest. Therefore, the Chinese authorities said, if the financial arithmetic was displeasing, foreigners were free to return home. As long as they decided to remain, however, they were fair game. Where this line of thinking led is revealed in a story told in 1985 of a Chinese policeman who held an American woman "ten percent responsible" when a bicyclist plowed into the side of her car while she was stopped at an intersection. Baffled at being held responsible at all, she explained to the policeman that she had been sitting in a stopped car. "Yes," the policeman replied politely, "but if you hadn't been in China, this never would have happened."[31]

When confronted with the argument that high prices or no, it still must have been in their interest to remain, some Americans denied that they were making money. "They should take a look at my balance sheet if they think operating in China is so all-fired profitable. China has been a cost center for my company for the last three years," said one businessperson quoted in a newspaper story in 1982. We might describe the money-losers as the China-chic contingent. But other Americans who complained also occasionally confessed *sotto voce* that they indeed were making money. The Cummins representative who signed the $72,000-a-year lease for a new apartment said: "You've got to realize we do make money in China. We wouldn't be here if we weren't making money." Such disclosures, even if the circumstances were atypical, still served to weaken a show of unanimous protest on the American side.[32]

Americans interpreted the hard line that the Chinese took as, in part, a flexing of nationalistic muscles, letting outsiders know who was in command. It was also seen as a manifestation of that culturally innate business acumen that made the Chinese and Americans ideological soulmates. "My theory is that the Chinese, despite thirty years of communism, are still capitalists at heart," said an American oil executive in 1980. "They are charging us whatever the market will bear. This is just plain, old-fashioned supply-and-demand economics." Even as the gouging of foreigners made doing business in China extremely painful, Americans found solace in seeing their hard-hearted hosts as long-lost cousins in the family of free enterprise.[33]

The escalating costs of doing business in China brought together exporters of all nationalities into a confederacy of grumblers, but they still remained mutual competitors, each group fighting fiercely with the others for a piece of an alternately expanding and contracting China market. Americans did not do particularly well in the competition. If one takes a close look in any given year at the total value of American exports to China, for example, and breaks out the sale to China of a few large-ticket items, such as Boeing aircraft, or of agricultural commodities and raw materials that were purchased by China for political or strategic reasons as much as any other, then the residual export deals do not look so impressive. This is especially so when one thinks of the money, time, and energy expended in the pursuit of these deals. Just as American importers had been outclassed by Japanese and Western competitors in Canton during the initial period of reacquaintance in the 1970s, American exporters were outclassed by their commercial rivals in the broadening of trade relationships in the 1980s. It was not a matter of being unpopular with the Chinese. American directness, lack of guile and, implicitly, the association with American power, wealth, and technological prowess—all these made the Chinese interested in listening to American sales proposals. We prefer your technology and indeed would most like to work with you, the Chinese told Americans, but you just do not know how to do business.[34]

It seems both sides liked to lecture the other on how business ought to be done. In Chinese eyes, the Americans should have demonstrated their commitment to the bilateral trade relationship by lifting the remaining restrictions on high-technology exports and speeding up the first stage of the permit process in Washington. The often equally slow second stage of review that was administered by CoCom, the Paris-based international agency established by a number of industrialized countries in the West to oversee militarily sensitive exports to socialist countries, was also an impediment. American companies that were affected by the frustrations of export applications and rejections—and there were many such companies, especially in the computer industry—did their best in lobbying Washington for further relaxation of controls, and were moderately successful. Between 1971, when the trade embargo was lifted, and 1981, China was placed in what the United States called country group Y, which meant that the restrictions were those placed on exports to the

Warsaw Pact countries of the Soviet Union and Eastern Europe, but were more relaxed than if China had been placed in country group Z, with Cuba and North Korea. In 1981, China was placed in its very own category in which restrictions were liberalized further, though its standing was not yet equal to that of the NATO allies. Corporate America was eager to declare the Cold War over, but interests in the Pentagon were much slower to call off hostilities completely.[35]

Access to cheap credit was another demand of the Chinese that American businesspeople were unable to meet. While the Japanese Export-Import Bank and its counterparts in Europe and Canada provided China with access to the equivalent of billions of U.S. dollars in credits to facilitate Chinese purchases of goods from their respective countries, American companies had no similar government support. The U.S. Ex-Im credits available for exports to China were too little, too late, and not competitive. U.S. banks, eager to offer commercial credit to the Chinese in the absence of U.S. government programs, discovered that the Chinese were not much interested in paying commercial rates of 8 percent if the Japanese or Europeans were offering government-subsidized rates of 7, or 5, or even 2 percent. During the Reagan administration, U.S. government policy in the area of export credits was set by the same ideological principles that had altered domestic policy and led to the privatization of some government services. Private firms in the international marketplace were to compete as best they could on their own, without the "artificial" prop of government export credits. The U.S. government urged the export-import banks in other capitalist countries to follow its lead and reduce or eliminate their subsidies, but the other countries failed to comply. Corporate American representatives found themselves without a protective financial shield. It was ironic that just as Americans acclaimed the imminence of the victory of capitalism in the People's Republic, the Reagan administration's reaffirmation of the tenets of *laissez faire* hobbled the competitiveness of America's own companies against business-government alliances on the part of capitalist brethren who were not such fundamentalist zealots.[36]

If the Chinese were unhappy about U.S. government policies, then American exporters were unhappy about the same policies. If the Chinese were disgruntled about delays in export approvals or credit terms, American exporters served as their proxy in taking these complaints to those in authority in the U.S. government. And if the Chinese were unhappy about restrictions placed on Chinese exports to the United States—textiles being the category of most contention—then American exporters took up the matter as a concern of their own. They knew the Chinese tied economic relations with each country into a giant bundle of interlinked connections, and when the United States did not resolve the issue of textile protectionism, China retaliated in 1983 by refusing to purchase American cotton, soybeans, wheat, and synthetic fibers. This sort of retaliation made American exporters concerned with abstruse matters of U.S. import policy that would otherwise have not been of much direct interest. On the other side of these disputes, however, the American industries that felt threatened by new imports from the People's Republic lobbied hard to raise tariff walls and other protection. Fighting the larger and more numerous business interests that wanted to expand business with China, worried domestic industries like textiles tried to paint a picture of an impending inundation of imports from China, an apocalyptic flood that would destroy the American Way of Life. "There is no way for the free-enterprise world to challenge $20-a-month wages," wrote Ranan Lurie in 1985. Lurie argued that American workers were going to discover that competing with "Communist wages" would be more destructive than competing with robots. This kind of concern about Chinese exports, though a minority voice, was sufficient to produce a schism in the American business community. The Chinese were vociferously upset with any manifestation of protectionist measures in the United States, but they held the United States to a wholly different standard of proper trade policies than those applied to their own country, which was one of the most protected markets in the world. They also should have noticed that capitalism was not the monolith that had been taught in Chinese classrooms, no more than communism was the monolith that had been taught in American classrooms.[37]

The U.S. government was often besieged by warring parties among the business community, one group urging improved trade ties with the People's Republic, with the aid of eased U.S. and CoCom export controls and more government-assisted export financing, while the other group demanded attenuated ties and increased vigilance against a future tide of Chinese imports. Neither group got all that it wanted—if anything, the protectionist lobby probably did the better of the two, despite its smaller size—and neither seemed satisfied. American business representatives in Beijing who were struggling against their better-financed, less-regulated Japanese and European rivals continued to complain about lack of government support from Washington. In 1983, when Secretary of State George Shultz passed through town, he was treated to a jeremiad of pent-up frustration from the resident Americans, who may have thought Shultz, formerly president of Bechtel Group, the giant construction firm, would lend a sympathetic ear. On this occasion, however, Shultz did not make the polite noises of support the petitioners wanted to hear; in fact, he lost his temper with the complainers. When asked by a businessman, "Why is it that we cannot get a license out of the U.S. government when the Japanese and West European competition can get an equivalent license in a relatively short time?" Shultz snapped, "Maybe they are just better. Why don't you move to Japan or Western Europe?" He had his own complaint to make that some U.S. businesses signed deals with the Chinese even though they knew the technology could not be exported, then when the application for an export license was turned down, they complained to the government that a commitment had been made and had to be honored. Shultz said, "Buddy, that's your problem when you do that. Don't complain to the government." Another person asked about steps that the U.S. government might take to help persuade the Chinese to make more living and working space available to U.S. businesspeople. He responded by saying almost exactly what the Chinese also told American businesspeople: One assumes that the Americans benefited from doing business in China or they would not still be there.[38]

This was not an encouraging reply, and worse, the presumption that Americans must be profiting or they would not remain in China served only to legitimize business conditions that in many cases made it impossible for American companies to break even. Propelled by China chic, they had gone to Beijing with naive enthusiasm, then discovered the high prices that made doing business there an extremely expensive proposition. The representative offices of American banks were the best-known group of notorious money losers in town, but there were many others who also bravely wore a pained smile in public while they internally hemorrhaged copious amounts of money in the course of trying to make a go of China. Those who were in China were trying to do what they had been urged to do by countless numbers of American business books and newspaper editorials and economists and politicians—to look beyond the short term of the fiscal quarter to horizons of ten or twenty years away, and to look beyond the familiar terrain of the domestic and European markets to a Pacific region that seemed bursting with future promise. China appeared to be the perfect place to implement what these hopeful Americans referred to as a "long haul" strategy. But in the immediate present the costs were killing; the home office accountants were not so stout of heart and pressed for word of operational profits.

On top of all this, the Chinese government—and then the U.S. government—complacently overrode the complaints of the Americans with the disheartening assertion that their continued presence showed that they must be making money.

The boom-and-bust cycle in the China market not only influenced American evaluations of future prospects, it also influenced toleration of the high costs of doing business. When prospects seemed bright, the costs were an irritation that could be overlooked; when prospects dimmed, the costs had the power to enrage. In either case, business conditions in China, though themselves objective facts, were seen through the mediating screen of emotions, which played such an important role in getting Americans to China in the first place and continued to be important in the experiences that followed.

Over time, the Chinese took care of the worst of the housing problems that had aggravated Americans at the beginning of the 1980s. The addition of apartment complexes such as that of the Lido helped; so did the opening of several office towers and many hotels that served to break at long last the hated monopoly of the Peking Hotel. The prices of course were incredible—office rents in the new Noble Tower were $45 a month per square meter, compared to $25 to $35 a month for office space in Hong Kong's most prestigious office block—but at least now there were a few choices. More business services became available. A new direct-dial phone system connecting some of the office buildings and hotels was a great help (in the early days, in 1979, American businesspeople staying at the Peking Hotel had been known to phone New York just to be able to get the room number of bankers who were staying under the same roof and which the hotel staff could not retrieve).[39]

The improvements made life in Beijing more comfortable and less vexing. Yet foreign complaints about doing business got worse. Stephen FitzGerald, a former ambassador to China from Australia in the 1970s, offers a possible explanation for the paradox when he suggests that the more that China succeeded in providing business conditions that seemed to foreigners in some respects "normal," the more expectations were raised, and consequently the more frustrated people felt when difficulties remained. By the late 1980s, the foreign businessperson who arrived in Beijing for the first time could remain immersed in the world of the foreigner—the sights, sounds, and tastes of the interchangeable hotel and restaurant environment known to the business traveler of corporate America.[40]

In Beijing, the new hotels and their Western restaurants and coffee shops and bakeries and gyms, and the foreign office towers with their digital-display elevators and Western interior designs and desktop computers and photocopy machines, could impress a newcomer because they were such a surprising transplant and did not look Chinese at all, aside from the nationality of the staff. The look and feel of the tiny enclosed bubble within which the short-term business traveler stayed was beguilingly familiar and, as FitzGerald points out, it confused the visitor and raised expectations. Foreigners were tempted to believe that the Chinese had created their own branch extension of the international commercial world and were ready for business. But they were not ready. The physical infrastructure was built much more quickly than the necessary social infrastructure—the legal protection and work habits and reliable supplies and a host of other matters. The disjunction between the rapid transformation of the hotel world in Beijing in the early 1980s and the much slower pace of change in the society that lay beyond the light cast by the new rooftop restaurants created tremendous frustration.

In some ways, at least, it was better in the 1970s when Western hotel and office environments had yet to be built and American visitors were reminded virtually every waking moment that they were not in Los Angeles or Cleveland or Atlanta, but at the other side of the world. The hotels were uncomfortable, the food was bad, and nothing looked familiar. Even the prosaic business of going to the bathroom (in China, as in the rest of Asia, the fixtures were designed for squatting, not sitting) had been a reminder that one had left home. In the 1980s, conducting business in China became harder to do at the same time that the Western-style living conditions for guests made cultural differences and inherited systemic problems momentarily disappear. When the remaining problems were soon discovered not to have vanished at all, Americans were impatient: The Chinese had made improvements in one sphere, why not in the others? The evidence before their eyes—the new hotels and office buildings and apartment towers—were the symbols of China's new membership in the international world. These had been unimaginable a few years before, and yet there they were, suggesting to Americans that anything was possible. No obstacles stood in the way of China's modernization, if only China willed it to be so.

5.

NEGOTIATIONS

Within the English-speaking world, Americans take a casual approach to the mundane civilities of greeting and introduction, with our unceremonious *how are ya*'s and *gladtomeetcha*'s. Tocqueville commented long ago upon the distinctiveness of American informality, so unlike the case of aristocratic England. He attributed the American manner ("natural, frank, and open") to the democratic character of U.S. society, in which social position and rank are supposedly irrelevant. If two Englishmen who were traveling abroad happened to meet by chance at what Tocqueville called "the antipodes," surrounded by strangers whose language and manners they hardly understood, the expatriate Englishmen still would avoid one another, being too anxious about relative status differences. But Americans in the same circumstances, he wrote, would see one another as friends for the simple reason that they were both Americans.[1]

In his hypothetical example, Tocqueville was interested in juxtaposing American gregariousness and English reserve; he did not explore the question of how the American manner may have contrasted with that of the unnamed antipodean people encountered abroad. But in the contemporary era, as business opportunities beckoned Americans to China and Chinese to America, this question came to the fore. Individual American businesspeople were afflicted not by status anxiety so much as what we might call *culture anxiety,* which made even the simple mechanics of greeting a foreign counterpart a worrisome matter. When the antipodean people is met in the flesh, the usually invisible motions of hello and good-bye suddenly become visible. Nothing seems insignificant, and everything seems tricky.

Americans who went to China confronted formal receptions upon arrival at the Beijing airport and ended their visits with banqueting and ceremonial sendoffs. American business culture, with its informality and practicality—the "shirtsleeves" style that disdains time-consuming ritual—was not adapted for these circumstances. In China, the top officials of the hosting ministry or organization would extend courtesies rare in the United States, such as personally going to the airport on the arrival or departure of foreign guests instead of dispatching subordinates or an impersonal taxi. When Chinese representatives came to the United States to pay business calls on the same companies that had sent representatives to China, the problem of reciprocity arose. Although some American corporate heads did try to repay the Chinese with an equal measure of personal attention, the more common American practice was to heed uneasily the advice of Americans familiar with Chinese customs that visiting Chinese did not expect foreign executives to make special trips to the airport when it was not their usual practice, though it would be much appreciated.

The contrast between Chinese emphasis on and American obliviousness to cosseting guests was so great that Americans who were sensitive to the difference felt embarrassed by the behavior of other Americans toward the Chinese. In May 1988, for example, a Chinese vice-premier visited Minneapolis on a trade visit and was hosted by the Minnesota World Trade Center. At a dinner provided to honor the visitor, local business figures and politicians gathered at the Minneapolis Club, but Rick Nolan, the president of the World Trade Center, was conspicuously absent. When the local newspaper later tracked Nolan down, he explained: "A man has to set priorities," by which he meant that he had been fishing with his family. A Minneapolis columnist seemed uncertain whether to laugh or cry: "Shouldn't the $70,000-a-year president of the Minnesota World Trade Center be talking trade to the vice premier of China instead of fishing with fuzzy grubs?"[2]

Americans generally were unsure about the line separating informality from rudeness. Some worried about the apparent *faux pas* committed by their insensitive compatriots, such as the absent Minnesotan host, who embarrassed them on these occasions or during visits to China. As guests in China, Americans stepped as tentatively as if walking through a minefield, anxious about the polite small talk that preceded serious business discussions and the much feared banqueting that tested the skills and constitutions of the most intrepid and seemed to be governed by its own special code of etiquette. To help negotiate a way around these cultural obstacles, Americans offered coaching and advice to their colleagues.

Be prepared, the China-bound were told, to spend considerable time discussing pleasantries at the beginning of a meeting with the Chinese: the weather, how long one had been in China, and other cities in China one had visited, a subject for which, in the words of one American observer, the Chinese had "a never-ending and inexplicable fascination." Do not wear suits and ties and embarrass your hosts, another American advised in 1979, when the Chinese themselves still wore the tieless jackets that had come to be known in the West as Mao jackets. Oh, on the contrary, the Chinese were most impressed when Western businessmen wore dark, pin-striped suits, said other Americans, who on this and other matters dispensed advice that was often contradictory. One American would counsel businesspeople to avoid any attempts at humor; the next would advise the opposite, claiming that Chinese negotiators enjoy a hearty laugh.[3]

Guidance extended to the details of how to politely avoid the sea slugs, fish stomachs, and duck brains served at the banquets. It is not polite to refuse a dish altogether, Scott Seligman told readers of the *China Business Review.* But one need not feel compelled to eat all of what was served (Seligman confided that the equivalent effect of having hazarded a bite or two could be achieved by the artful pushing of the food around in the dish). The Chinese continued to serve dishes that were costly delicacies yet clearly met with a tepid reception from Western guests. This, Seligman commented, merely showed that the banquets were as much for the Chinese, who enjoyed the opportunity to eat these dishes, as they were for the guests.[4]

Uneasiness about how best to comport oneself when meeting with the Other was mirrored on the Chinese side. As was the case with the Americans, Chinese gave other Chinese advice about avoiding *faux pas,* and the same preoccupation with the most minute details can be seen: When you meet foreigners, do not ask how much money they make, and do not casually ask how much their clothes and belongings cost. When you enter a meeting room with foreign guests, you must take off your hat. When you walk, step as lightly as possible, and when you talk, do not be too loud. If you meet foreigners on the street, you should greet them and shake hands, but do not ask foreign guests, "Where are you going?" or "Have you eaten?" When you see people who have fallen or have had other kinds of unfortunate accidents, you should immediately step forward and offer assistance. Do not stand by and laugh at them. When you go to the bathroom, fasten your belt and button your fly before coming out.[5]

The Americans were not the only ones who were anxious about their behavior at banquets; the Chinese had their own set of concerns. The Chinese were advised to follow Western conventions. One should sit straight and not put one's arms and elbows on the table, they were told. When eating, make sure the knife and fork do not make a banging sound on the plate. Do not use the knife to bring food to the mouth. When hosting foreigners, dispense with the traditional formalities of starting the meal with a declaration that the food was going to be terrible and an apology for the poor hospitality.[6]

The Chinese were advised by their own side, just as Americans were advised by theirs, to avoid political issues, but the Chinese were also told repeatedly to protect "the country's secrets," which was a category of capacious dimension. Chinese representatives were further given special advice concerning proper behavior when hosting foreign women. Foreign female guests were to receive "respect and consideration," which translated into the male chivalry that women in American society had succeeded by and large in extirpating. Apparently oblivious to the change, Chinese in the 1980s were told to follow rules that were remembered from visits to the United States in the 1940s: When walking or going up stairs, or getting on an elevator or a bus, a male should always let the female guest go first, and so on. The prosaic matter of shaking hands apparently provoked complex considerations in the case of Chinese men and foreign women. China's *Worker's Daily* advised its readers in 1981: "When meeting a female guest, one should not take the initiative to shake her hand if she does not first extend her hand. A nod of the head is sufficient."[7]

This twin cacophony of advice and warnings concerning cultural pratfalls, some of which was internally contradictory, only served to make natural culture anxiety worse. On the American side, seminars on "Doing Business With China" drew attendees who were worried about inadvertently committing gaffes when they went to the People's Republic, but in many cases the advice provided by China experts only heightened the anxiety. One American said, "I know that the professors and government officials were trying to be helpful, but by the time we were through listening to them I was worried as to whether I could ever learn how to operate in China. When I finally got to Beijing, I was just putty in the hands of my hosts, afraid to express any views for fear that I would make a mistake."[8]

Eager to please and also exhilarated by the novelty and by what one described as the "electric atmosphere" of competing delegations coming and going, Americans who entered business negotiations with the Chinese in Beijing during the 1980s did not begin in a neutral stance. Their very presence in China—and tolerance of the high prices paid for the privilege—showed a certain predisposition toward accommodation that facilitated agreement. Using one of the sports metaphors that fill the business lexicon, Americans spoke of the "home court advantage" that they cheerfully ceded to the Chinese. Although Chinese delegations came to the United States to tour the facilities of prospective vendors, no decisions could be made before the Americans went to China and made the pitch there. Lucian Pye, foremost American chronicler of these business negotiations, has said that the home court advantage enjoyed by the Chinese was significant because it helped to create an atmosphere in which the Americans seemed to need the business more than the Chinese did.[9]

If we were to extend the sports metaphor, we could say that the negotiations in China were a game in which the home team had many more players on the field, set the kickoff time, called all the timeouts, and controlled all the other rules. The Chinese team often numbered more than two dozen members whose individual specialties included every imaginable domain: the pertinent technical fields, finance, law, raw material procurement, factory construction, translation, and all under a designated leader, the "responsible person." At the beginning of the 1980s, American observers noted that trade with foreign partners had grown too quickly for the Chinese trade bureaucracy to train a corps of confident negotiators. Consequently, many Chinese negotiators seemed poorly educated and were extremely cautious in making concessions; they did not want to be accused in a future political campaign of having been taken advantage of. Pye criticizes them for mistaking "hypercautiousness" for prudence.[10]

Americans should have been careful about wishing for a change in players on the Chinese side, because they soon got their wish: the replacements were even more tenacious and unyielding than the starters had been. Sensing that their lack of in-house international experience put them at a disadvantage in negotiations with Western multinationals, Chinese enterprises began hiring professional Chinese negotiators from newly formed trade consultancies. These outside professionals, Americans soon discovered, had a poor technical understanding of the products or technology under discussion and tended to be singlemindedly inflexible about the price offered, regardless of revised terms or technical specifications, because their own performances as negotiators were measured by the simple yardstick of prices. Then, by the latter years of the decade, still another kind of negotiator appeared on the Chinese team: the American-trained MBA who had returned to China. One American who had encountered one of these MBAs said that the Chinese had "really shredded" the American's proposed numbers: "He knew just where to look, and he cut the profit right out of the deal." For the Chinese side, however, it must have seemed poetically sweet to have these returned students on their own side of the table, using American techniques on the Americans themselves.[11]

The Americans in Beijing who conducted substantive business negotiations often operated with an irate coach on their own side—the chief executive of the company who had been captured by China chic, had gone to China for a whirlwind visit, and had acceded to the Chinese preference for agreement on general principles first, leaving discussion of details for later. Such easily arranged general agreements allowed the executive to display publicly a concern with being culturally sensitive, as well as business savvy. Look at me, the executive would exult: I have succeeded quickly where other foreigners have gotten caught in the bog of Chinese bureaucracy. The details were deemed a simple technical matter, left for the subordinates who followed. So it was they who were stuck with the difficult task of making an otherwise meaningless statement of polite generalities into a satisfactory agreement, and it was they who found that the home office did not want to hear about difficulties encountered in the course of negotiating with the Chinese. The chief had not had any problems working with the Chinese, so the fault must lie with the underlings.

One American negotiator, whose company president and board chairman had returned from their trips to China with memories of enjoyable encounters with the Chinese, said that "with respect to any other part of the world they defer to the specialized knowledge of the man in the field, but not in China. When I report problems in the negotiations, I sense that they are impatient with me rather than with the Chinese." It was a situation that showed once again the uniquely personal stake that the uppermost echelons of American business placed in the China market. It was left to their minions to work out the particulars, and they had to do so cautiously. A junior American assigned to the negotiations felt "I have to bend over backward not to offend the Chinese," lest they complain over his head directly to his home office in New York and bring down the wrath of the boss.[12]

American negotiators feared criticism from their own side, and so did the Chinese negotiators from theirs. In this, the two representatives potentially could have shared a sense of embattled solidarity, but the mechanics of forming bonds of friendship interfered. The Chinese seemed to stress friendship in the earliest stages of the talks; the Americans later, after serious negotiations began. But by then the Chinese tended to withdraw into the web of bureaucratic consultations that took place in the background. Americans observed how personally reserved the Chinese were, and contrasted it to their own backslapping style. The individuals who were best able to overcome cultural differences were the engineers on both sides, who quickly established a professional rapport that transcended business and nationality.[13]

Americans and Chinese shared a desire to please one another by adopting the other's vocabulary or political position. What a curious reversal we witness when the mayor of Shanghai reassured a group of American businesspeople in carefully memorized English that "I don't care how much money foreign business makes in Shanghai" (a crowd-pleasing declaration greeted by smiles and applause), while American companies, which had heretofore espoused a militantly apolitical line in their operations abroad, dramatically ended operations in Taiwan (which was well-intentioned but was not necessarily what the People's Republic wished). Each side tried to please the other, and in the case of the Americans unrealistic promises were sometimes made to the Chinese in their zeal to show their worthiness to receive Chinese hospitality. These gestures, however, could also create a sense of credit due, then disappointment, when the other side did not seem properly appreciative. Consequently, negotiations became entangled not just with financial and logistical details, but with emotional ones as well.[14]

From the Chinese perspective, vigilance was the watchword when negotiating with foreigners. This was not just an anachronism from pre-Liberation historical memory or from the sloganeering of the Cultural Revolution; it was also a manifestation of more recent encounters with Western charlatans who promised more than they delivered. Not all Americans fit the collective self-image of straightforward innocents who were easy game for stereotypically crafty Chinese negotiators. When

China opened wider in the late 1970s, the pioneering American firms that descended upon Beijing included a disproportionate number of aggressive entrepreneurs and mountebanks who escorted the Chinese into negotiations that in many cases came to unhappy endings for them. As Owen Nee, a China-trade attorney, reminds us, "The street of broken dreams in the Peking Hotel had more American flimflam men than a Kansas county fair." Early negotiations were made unpleasant by foreigners whose antics in some instances were grotesque. What were the Chinese to think when a European, for example, rose from the negotiating table where discussions had stalled over price and announced: "You've had everything I can offer you except the shirt off my back, and you can have that now." He unbuttoned and took off his sweaty shirt, tossed it on the table, and stalked out of the room. Whatever the Chinese thought, they were restrained in what they said and merely suggested that the company not come back again.[15]

Even though Americans and other Westerners were fond of saying that the Chinese knew more about their companies than they themselves did, in fact the Chinese often did not know much about their potential business partners when negotiations began. The Chinese felt most comfortable with the largest multinational companies (an irony considering the fierceness of earlier Marxist denunciations of the operations of multinationals in the Third World). In a handbook prepared for their own negotiators, the Chinese said that the largest foreign companies did not need to be investigated—their financial resources and the sophistication of their technology were not in question—but thorough preliminary research into the solidity of middle- and small-sized firms was a necessity. A salutary story was told of negotiations for a joint venture that had proceeded for more than a year before the Chinese discovered that the foreign company had come to China capitalized by only a few thousand dollars and lacking a reputation for creditworthiness. The negotiations in this case were terminated; in others, disillusioning discoveries only came later. Referring to losses suffered in such instances, one Chinese official described them as the "tuition fees we had to pay" to learn how to deal with dishonest investors.[16]

Visiting business school professors from the West confirmed the worst fears of the Chinese and encouraged them to be vigilant against ill-intentioned foreign investors. N. T. Wang, from Columbia University, and a Canadian colleague visited Guangdong in 1983 and warned of traps that could ensnare the unwary Chinese, such as project loans whose interest rates could float dangerously ("if rates continue to rise, then the Chinese people will really be taken advantage of"). The North American visitors also advised the Chinese to investigate the motivation of companies that proposed investment in China when they had already invested in similar projects in export processing zones elsewhere in Asia. The American advisors suggested that such companies went to China because conditions there were superior, which was precisely the suspicion the Chinese already had. Hearing foreigners confirm it only hardened the Chinese conviction that there was little need for concessions. If China was not so desirable, their reasoning went, there would not be an endless parade of business suitors marching through Beijing. The Chinese were not completely misled in gauging foreign business interest by the hordes of supplicants that came to them, but looking merely at the number of business visitors obscured an important distinction that should have been made between the interest of exporters (very high) and that of potential investors (less interested than warily curious). The Chinese hosts mistook the inquiries and negotiations as evidence that China was in a position of uncontested advantage.[17]

The Chinese pressed their advantage by playing the various business representatives against one another, taking a leaf deliberately from Wei Yuan (1794–1856), one of the most cynical of the earlier Westernizing Self-Strengtheners, who had written of "using barbarians to control barbarians." The authorities told individual Chinese enterprises to solicit multiple bids for imports and invite several prospective investors for each joint venture project, and always report back to the higher authorities the details of their negotiations with foreigners. This was a matter of national interest, it was explained. China was too large a country for a Chinese enterprise that was negotiating with a foreign partner in one place to know the details about similar negotiations elsewhere. Without centralized coordination, small domestic variations from one locality to another in wages or licensing fees for technology transfer might give foreign investors "a hole to sneak through" (an often used phrase that brought to mind images of rodents, not humans). Having two or three foreign firms compete for any given contract seemed ideal. If fewer, the advantages of choice would be lost; if more than three, however, prospective foreign bidders would look at the long odds and lose interest.[18]

During negotiations, the Chinese used control of information to keep the foreign representatives constantly off balance. The Chinese insisted that the prospective vendors reveal their interests and proposals first, a style Lucian Pye describes as "the classic pose of bazaar bargaining," stifling expression of their own interest in order to keep prices low. As talks proceeded, the imbalance was not much changed—foreigners had to disclose far more than the Chinese did. Chinese negotiators often told their foreign counterparts that domestic regulations or policy guidelines dictated certain terms and prohibited others, but these were classified secret documents and could not be shown. Yet the Chinese seemed to feel that nothing the foreigners said, even when alone in their hotel rooms or talking long distance with their home offices, was beyond their right to know. Although it is hard to sort out afterward which stories were embellished, many businesspeople told of experiences similar to that of an American commodities trader in Canton who telephoned his home office for instructions. When he went to the bargaining table the next day with what he insisted was his company's lowest offer, the Chinese negotiator smiled and countered, "No, it isn't."[19]

The Chinese, who encouraged timely exchange of business intelligence among themselves, were not happy if foreign companies did the same. Pullman Kellogg, for example, was told after contracts were successfully signed that it would be "unfair" and an act of unfriendliness if its negotiators were to tell other foreign companies about their experiences. Even the simple announcement of a seemingly innocuous deal could set off Chinese alarms, as when an American paper company announced a $20 million purchase from China in 1980—the largest single order in the company's history, and understandably a sale of great importance. But the Chinese, apparently anxious about signaling strong interest in paper products in foreign markets and driving up the price it had to pay, told this and other paper companies from which it was making purchases that it did not want the details of the sales to be revealed. Even in the global marketplace, the Chinese insisted on maintaining a façade of bazaar reserve. But the Chinese overestimated the propensity of foreign companies to share notes during the course of negotiations, especially in the hyperexcited rush to China in the late 1970s and early 1980s. The Beijing hotels were filled with foreign businesspeople who dawdled after their dinners, having little else to do, yet each company group did not talk with another. One American described the scene in 1979 in this fashion: "You sit there surrounded by Westerners all whispering about their deals, but you never find out what they are up to—nor do you tell anybody who you are or why you are in Peking."[20]

Self-imposed reticence is not surprising in circumstances in which the hosts fanned mutual competition and drove up the value of scraps of information by restricting their circulation. But the system, whose bias was toward silence, worked too well in restricting information; negotiations were often hobbled because the Chinese negotiators were just as much in the dark as their foreign counterparts. The Chinese delayed talks again and again, partly as a tactic, partly as a way for negotiators to show their superiors what shrewd bargainers they were, but also partly because the Chinese at the lower levels were required always to seek instructions. The problem was more than one of overly centralized authority; one can discern a separate problem of overly centralized information control. In a system in which all information was automatically assumed to be confidential and released outside an office only on a case-by-case determination of need-to-know, it was difficult for Chinese negotiators to learn the details of higher-level plans, specifications, and priorities. This reduced the advantage for the Chinese side that the system was supposed to provide.

If some point under negotiation seemed otherwise lost, the Chinese resorted to an extremely effective defensive tactic and said, "Ah, but you do not understand China." Knowing that no foreigner felt qualified to assert otherwise, it was the coup de grace to any troublesome contention. It was invoked so often, however, that its ostensible purpose—to call the attention of the foreign party to cultural or ideological differences—was overshadowed by its actual use as a multipurpose club against foreign negotiators. If Chinese said they could not accept foreign terms because of unspecified "internal rules and regulations" and the foreigners asked to see the rules themselves, the Chinese patiently told the foreigners that they did not understand how things worked in China. And if the foreign company had a China expert as a consultant, a person acquainted with Chinese laws and regulations who questioned the invocation of undisclosed rules that were at variance with previously disclosed regulations and precedents, Chinese negotiators took the foreign clients aside and told them that they did not need a consultant. From the Chinese perspective not only did foreigners not understand China, but also it was best that this remain so.[21]

The Chinese also undermined their credibility when they selectively used a screen of cultural differences to protect interests in setting up contract terms for joint ventures. Their negotiators, for example, learned to insist on late-shipment penalties in their import contracts but not in their export deals. Foreign business partners that tried to negotiate terms which protected their own interests were told that "old friends" should not cavil about what the Chinese described as "small details." If the foreigner insisted, the Chinese response was the final one that ended discussion: "This is not the way it's done in China."[22]

The differences in commercial legal practices had not been so troublesome in the 1970s, when China was just beginning to reenter the world economy and had little in the way of a legal system that had survived the Cultural Revolution. At that time, some Americans; including legal scholars, were impressed with the absence of a legal apparatus. In 1977, for example, Victor Li, one of the leading authorities on Chinese law in the United States, wrote a book titled significantly *Law Without Lawyers,* in which he suggested that the lack of familiar Western laws in China was an expression of an alternative legal model, different from a Western model because it served a different society, after all. The Chinese had their system, we had ours, and Li warned that we should be careful in making critical value judgments about theirs.[23]

In some cases, the early American business pioneers were charmed by the system. In 1971, when RCA Globcom signed the agreement with the Chinese for sale of the satellite station, the document that was drafted by the Chinese, and accepted by RCA, was only one-and-a-half pages long. For the Americans, it seemed a quaint throwback to an (undoubtedly romanticized) earlier age in American business when deals had been sealed with little more than a handshake; the contract with the Chinese was the shortest one RCA had signed in several decades. The prevailing standard in the United States was suggested by the length of a sales contract between Boeing and the Chinese at about the same time. The Boeing agreement, which was drafted by the American side and ultimately accepted by the Chinese despite objections, was over 100 pages.[24]

RCA and other companies were amenable to using a Chinese format for contracts in the 1970s because the Chinese were seen as scrupulously honest and consistent about upholding the same high standards of ethical conduct on their own side as those expected of the foreign partner. Protection of foreign business interests did not need much legal elaboration, and what was included in the brief contract form favored by the Chinese was followed so closely to the letter that foreigners were reassured that additional clauses were not necessary. Just as American tourists who went to China for the first time in the 1970s came back with fables along the lines of you-can't-even-throw-a-Kleenex-away-without-the-Chinese-returning-it, so too were American businesspeople impressed with the honesty of Chinese customers who returned anything sent to them that was not literally included in the contract. If the contract said the Chinese were entitled to 192 spare bolts, the Chinese would count them, and if there were 193, would write a letter to the United States asking what should be done with the extra one. Even more extreme was the tale told by a Wabco representative who provided Chinese with wrenches in a plastic vinyl case. The Chinese refused to accept them because the contract had not referred to any case as part of the deal. Such stories reinforced the American impression that Chinese negotiators were tough, but also supernaturally honest.[25]

Americans did not see the Chinese in the same light in the 1980s, however. The Chinese insistence on their own standard of minimal legal formality did not seem nearly as endearing after the earlier reputation of honesty was tarnished, then destroyed, by Chinese behavior that seemed too cravenly self-interested to be explained away as mere cultural differences in approaches to legal agreements. Like other foreign businesspeople in China, Americans were dismayed when the Chinese did not disclose full costs, such as wages, utility hookups, land use fees, licenses, and "facilitation" fees, until late in the negotiations for joint ventures or even not until the contract was signed. The Chinese also insisted on renegotiating so frequently that foreigners came to feel an agreement was never settled with any finality, and that the Chinese regarded a final contract as a working draft subject to an infinite number of revisions as the project progressed. The foreigners were not exaggerating; the Chinese government confirmed the existence of the problem in 1984 when it had to instruct its own negotiators to regard a signed contract as settled. The only exception was to be in cases in which both parties agreed to a change, "and the side that enjoys an advantage naturally is not going to lightly give away its advantage."[26]

The Chinese negotiators paid little heed. If they did not explicitly demand renegotiation of signed contracts, they achieved the same end by announcing that higher-level authorities had demanded certain changes, which happened to be major ones and invariably favored the Chinese. Even after the approval of higher authorities was secured and a joint venture begun, a change of mind on the part of the Chinese partner could still lead to additional renegotiations because the Chinese wielded a powerful sanction: footdragging in implementation that could take any of dozens of forms, all of which were paralyzing. If the foreign party objected and invoked the arbitration clause that was in the original contract, the Chinese would use the ever handy mention of cultural differences and say that using outside arbitration was an "unfriendly act." In one case involving a small American company which had sent a representative to Beijing for talks after what seemed to be a clear breach of contract by the Chinese side, the Chinese negotiator announced that he would not sit down at the table to talk unless the American side promised that no legal action would be taken. "Friends" did not settle their disputes that way. The Chinese remained standing, determinedly silent with a fixed frown, until his condition was met. These incidents led foreign investors to feel that their contract rights had no real protection because even if they won an arbitration battle on the neutral ground of a tribunal in Geneva or Stockholm, they would lose the war in China, where the Chinese side could obstruct implementation at will.[27]

When prospective foreign investors balked at placing their money in projects that seemed to be hostage to the vagaries of the host partner, without any substantive legal protection in sight, the Chinese pointed not only to cultural differences but also to ideological differences: Expect different rules, the Chinese told Western capitalists, when you come to a socialist country. To blunt the complaints of leery Western investors, the Chinese could cite chapter and verse of capitalist theology about the importance of risk-taking. When an American negotiator told his Chinese counterparts that it seemed excessive to expect the Americans to take on the risk of an $80 million investment with no way of recovering the investment if the Chinese government should happen to frustrate the deal, one of the Chinese officials replied with a wry smile: "Capitalists take risks. We're Socialists."[28]

The response of the foreign businesspeople was to argue that the apparatus of legal protection they sought in China should not be seen as intrinsically Western or capitalist, but rather as a purely neutral body of *international* practices that belonged to no particular culture or ideology. Stephen FitzGerald told the Chinese in 1986: "If we are to say there is an Australian way of doing business and you must do things our way, or a Chinese way and we must do it your way, that is a recipe for endless conflict and ultimate disaster. It is not accidental that international business codes and practices have emerged over the last hundred or so years or that there is an International Chamber of Commerce, which codifies such practices and provides an impartial point of reference." The Chinese, or at least some in the upper reaches of the trade bureaucracy, came to agree with FitzGerald during the course of the 1980s. American lawyers noticed a change in the traditional Chinese aversion to long contracts. At least in cases in which it seemed to be in their interest, the Chinese side began to prepare a first draft of a contract on its own initiative instead of waiting to respond to a Western draft, and what would have been a seven-page draft a few years earlier for a complex project of technology-transfer was now seventy pages. In other cases in which it seemed to their advantage not to sign a detailed contract, the Chinese still relied upon an appeal to the "Chinese" way of doing things, relying on the trust of friends and a simple handshake, not lengthy contracts.[29]

The cultural defense of a tradition that did not place much importance on legal protection for business was seriously eroded not so much by pressure from American and other businesspeople from the West, but by increased contacts between Chinese of the PRC and ethnic Chinese partners from Hong Kong, brought together most frequently in the Shenzhen Special Economic Zone. Initially, the PRC officials had prevailed upon the Hong Kong representatives to accept the "Chinese" way. We're all Chinese, they said, so we do not need to write things down in a Western form. What little that was committed to paper was often written so ambiguously that it was easy for the two parties to draw reasonable but radically differing interpretations of what had been agreed upon. Unlike the case of PRC officials lecturing Americans that foreigners did not understand Chinese business customs, here Chinese worked with other Chinese and could not use the same lecture when unanticipated problems and disputes mushroomed. American lawyers regarded these intramural Chinese problems as an indirect vindication of the legal profession's longstanding contention that legal codification of agreements was a universal imperative that obeyed no cultural boundary. In 1987, Jerome Alan Cohen noted the increased receptiveness of PRC officials to more elaborate contracts and legal provisions after the officials had experienced frustrations attempting to do business without them in Shenzhen and elsewhere in China. Cohen drew this conclusion: "Experience has taught them that if you don't write things down carefully, you do get disagreements." One might say that however unevenly the change in attitude toward the law was in China, and however incomplete the construction of protective legal structures for foreign investors, still an important ideological shift had taken place. Law schools were reestablished in China; private lawyers hung up their shingles advertising their availability as trade consultants. Americans began to praise the Chinese for "linear" negotiations. These developments marked the apparent end to the Chinese socialist experiment that had attempted to avoid the high costs paid by the litigious West. The costs of doing business without law had proven to be higher still. There would be no more talk of Law Without Lawyers.[30]

American negotiators impressed the Chinese as experienced and knowledgeable, candid and forthcoming, concrete and practical. Americans were also seen as being inordinately proud to the point of arrogance about their economic accomplishments. The Chinese saw the Germans in a different light: extremely thorough in preparation (a compliment not paid to the Americans) and comparatively stubborn about prices, which once offered were rarely changed. The Japanese were seen as unwilling to compromise, and especially sly. Chinese negotiators believed that it was not wise to be very candid with the Japanese; frankness was repaid with their taking advantage.[31]

The Chinese trade officials and professors not only sorted negotiating styles of foreigners by nationality, they also favored some styles over others, such as the American style over the Japanese. Americans, for their part, thought that U.S.–based multinationals enjoyed an advantage in negotiations with the People's Republic that they did not have elsewhere in the Third World because their total exclusion in the previous decades meant that they began in China with a fresh start, without facing an accumulated backlog of grievances. Nevertheless, Americans were grouped with the West Germans for representing what one Chinese writer, Dong Hongqi, called the Western style of negotiating, which was legalistic to an extreme. What was called an Eastern style was exemplified by the Japanese, whom the Chinese viewed as unforthcoming and unwilling to say what they thought, even if they were in complete agreement. Japanese vendors also offered prices that were inflated 20 percent or even 50 percent by what the Chinese derisively called "high water content," which the Japanese would allow to be squeezed out in the course of bargaining; they would then claim generosity in granting concessions.[32]

In sorting different negotiating styles along an Eastern-Western dichotomy, Dong placed Hong Kong businesspeople in the Eastern group, but noted an important difference that set them apart from the Japanese. Although the Hong Kong negotiators also padded initial offers with a high water content, they were "more familiar with the way things are in China" and more flexible. Perhaps best liked of all nationalities, however, were not the Hong Kong compatriots, nor the candid Americans, but the West Europeans, defined as the British, French, Canadians, Italians, and Australians, and excluding the Germans. The negotiating style of these Europeans seemed to Dong to be a good intermediate blending of the best of East and West: The negotiators offered prices with low water content, yet they worked hard to make sure a deal succeeded and were not overly worried about problems with particular clauses. Such a blend avoided what the Chinese deemed to be the worst aspects of dealing with the Japanese, with their inflated prices which had to be whittled down, and the Americans and West Germans, with their obsessive concern with each individual clause in a contract.[33]

Americans advised their colleagues not to give in too early, to be ready with a "walk-away point" in negotiations with the Chinese. One company that sold the Chinese electrical equipment told others that it had lasted longer than another which had "run for cover after a few weeks" and had dropped the contract into the lap of the Chinese at overly generous terms. Trade consultants warned less experienced Americans that the Chinese would "expose you to long-winded things until your time runs out and you're ripe for the plucking." One of the Pullman Kellogg negotiators told readers in *Fortune* about the secrets of his success, secrets which also revealed concern about the physical fortitude of the Americans: "You can't sit around there like a weenie or give in because you're tired." Furthermore, Americans told others in preparation for meeting the Chinese that vendors should not underprice their offerings as "loss leaders" just to get in the door, assuming that future sales could be made at a profitable higher price. Experienced American traders warned that the Chinese later would say that a precedent had been established with the first sale and no more could be paid subsequently.[34]

The Chinese were indeed just as tough and formidable in practice as Americans perceived them to be. But this was so because of a different Chinese conception of the negotiating process, which viewed negotiation as a zero-sum game. Chinese negotiators equated foreign gains as Chinese losses and resisted with full force. The negotiators who represented China's foreign trade corporations and other agencies empowered to work out the details of contracts with foreigners were so forceful and effective that the Chinese authorities in the upper reaches of the central government who were responsible for China's overall foreign trade had to explain to them that they were too unyielding with the foreigners, that negotiations should *not* be seen in zero-sum terms, that foreigners and Chinese could derive advantages simultaneously. Americans could take some small comfort in the observation that their perception of Chinese negotiators as fiercely tenacious was thus well-founded.[35]

Tenacity, however, was not a unique characteristic. Americans encountered without undue worry equally determined adversaries in negotiations around the world. China was an exception, and the advice Americans gave their own side inadvertently reveals the special treatment American businesspeople accorded the Chinese. If Americans were headed for a European or Middle Eastern or African destination, they took with them the armored toughness that is simply taken for granted in the unsentimental realm of international business. To remind them on the eve of their departure of the need to have a "walk-away point" in negotiations would be unnecessary, if not insulting. But strangely this was not the case for Americans headed for China, who needed a review of the most elementary principles used universally in the business. The banality of much of the advice Americans had to dispense is telling testimony to the disorientation of China's Otherness. Without help, Americans lacked a sense of the appropriate application of either the subtle or the heavyhanded.

Help was often not welcomed, either. Americans operated as individuals, separated from one another not just by industries, or companies, but also by divisions and departments within a single firm. In many cases, each individual who went to China was determined to succeed on his or her own, without stopping to do much research or gathering the experiences of others. At the same time that Chinese were telling their own negotiators to exploit every possible free source of information about foreign firms by contacting their own embassies and Bank of China offices abroad, Americans preferred to rely on a seat-of-the-pants approach that was elevated to the level of a business philosophy. Americans would improvise when they got there. For preparation, all that was needed was some reading on the plane ride over.

Trade experts in America tried vainly to combat such thinking by sounding an unchanging chant: "learn the territory, study the customers." One might wonder why there was a need to have these bromides repeated, but one writer, David Lyman, insisted in 1984 that his observations of Americans during his seventeen years of experience in Asia showed that it still bore repeating. Indeed, he was right. John Frankenstein, an American management professor, discovered in a 1984 survey of company representatives in Beijing that 40 percent of his sample openly admitted their own firm had not investigated China's economic plans and objectives to decide how their product or service might fit China's needs. Much of what Americans sold to China was the result of the Chinese doing a worldwide search and determining that they wanted a particular American product or technology. American businesspeople were merely the passive, lucky beneficiaries. As an American summed it up in a letter to the *New York Times* in 1988: "Much of what we sell to China happens despite ourselves, the result of unsolicited orders. . . ."[36]

American trade consultants who were based in Beijing were the ones who saw firsthand the waves of American newcomers, each wave unaware of what had been learned by those who had come before. By the late 1980s, one could hear stories in Beijing of how individual companies had failed to pay any attention to their own experiences in China and were making the same mistakes in the third or fourth joint venture that they had made in the first. American individualism was so strong that American businesspeople went to China with the conviction that success or failure depended on their efforts and theirs alone. Reading or talking with others was a waste of time. If one wanted to do business in China, one had only to hop on a plane and do it.

The American style of negotiating should be placed against this background. An exploratory trip to China was often undertaken without much preparation, spurred by China chic; the emotional undercurrents found new channels once talks began and Americans got to know individual Chinese negotiators. A new, exciting dimension appeared: a chance to help a people that was extending a hand asking for assistance, the very hand that had so recently waved Chairman Mao's Little Red Book in mass rallies that thunderously denounced imperialism. When these same people asked American negotiators for help in the giant task of China's modernization, Americans were touched in a sentimental spot. "I've been in countries negotiating with people hostile to me because I am American. But the Chinese really want our help." It was difficult to resist these entreaties, as the Chinese of the 1980s were in a perfect position to activate a latent missionary impulse in Americans. Not only did their revolutionary past make the Chinese particularly valuable converts to the fold, but Americans also viewed them as blessed with a native intelligence that augured limitless potential for future economic development. Furthermore, the Chinese were appealingly civilized in their manner; unlike the Soviets, the Chinese were viewed as socialists who behaved with proper decorum. When invidiously comparing the polite Chinese with rowdy Russian negotiators, one American put the matter this way: "You won't see any pounding of tables in China."[37]

The altruistic impulse of assisting socialist China soon conflicted, however, with the imperatives of profit-seeking. Initially, it was gratifying to hear the Chinese negotiators talk about how backward their country was, how advanced the United States was, how badly China needed help. But the corollary of we-are-a-poor-and-backward country was that China asked for steep discounts, claiming that it was unable to pay what more developed countries could. This placed American negotiators in a difficult position: Emotionally, they wanted to give China the special consideration that was asked because they did regard China as *sui generis.* Yet rationally, Americans were troubled by the unprofitable proposals and the precedent that would be set if they were accepted. Some did grant exceptional terms for the Chinese, with the rationalization that such gestures were a strategic investment in the relationship, yet secretly worried that they were being taken advantage of. Other Americans held off, but did so with wrenching self-doubt, or less out of conscious decision than out of impulsive frustration that the talks had not proceeded quickly enough. American impatience worked both ways, resulting in premature closure of deals as well as premature withdrawal from talks.

Whether negotiations were successful or not, Americans often relied on unexamined impulses, superficial preparation, and "gut feelings." Richard Cortese, president of Alpha Microsystems, was quoted in 1986 in a trade magazine as "joking" that "something strange always happens on the flight over—instead of them investing capital in you, they want you to invest capital in them. And instead of you getting money from them, they're getting money from you." But it was not just a joke, it was very often true. In short, the most salient characteristic of the American negotiating style in China was that Americans, without a compass, constantly moved, whether forward or backward, with uncertain step.[38]

The Japanese in China seemed to possess the sure step Americans lacked. Americans themselves agreed in some ways with the Chinese, who characterized Japanese and Americans as being at opposite ends of a continuum. The Japanese were a full generation ahead of their American competitors. While Americans dispatched negotiating teams composed of people with no China-related experience, the Japanese sent people who had been "friends" with China beginning in the 1960s, and were ready to move in when the door first opened in the early 1970s. The Japanese set upon a deliberate course of building market share in China long before it was clear to others that there would ever be a domestic market for expensive imported consumer goods. Although the

Japanese had their own emotional variants of China fever, their actions at least conveyed an impression of steadiness and purpose, which by the late 1980s seemed in retrospect to have been farsighted and prescient in ways that American business could only envy. And while many of America's largest industrial companies felt that posting even one permanent representative to a Beijing office was a costly trial, by the early 1980s Japan's four largest trading companies alone stationed more than 200 employees in China, and each company maintained a still larger staff in its Tokyo offices whose sole responsibility was to provide support services for the China trade.[39]

Japanese prepared for negotiations with the Chinese with thoroughness and intramural cooperation. While the Americans did not like to do research, the Japanese relished it; moreover, they shared the fruits of their investigations with one another. American businesspeople in Beijing noticed how the Japanese, who were present in such numbers as to make non-Asian faces in many foreigner hotels seem a rarity, traded information and leads within the Japanese business community and drew up elaborate lists of procurement officials in Chinese government organizations throughout the country. Americans were dismayed to hear the other foreigners say that these Japanese lists were more complete and accurate than those published internally by the Chinese government itself.[40]

Measured on the scale of toughness that was so important in the minds of Americans who approached the negotiating table in China, the Japanese were Herculean figures who could stand up to long tours in China as negotiators or as permanent representatives. When Americans dispatched employees to one-year tours, the Japanese sent theirs for five years, and while Americans remained clustered in Beijing, the Japanese established offices in many other places as well, leaving Americans far behind, for example, in the important economic center of Shanghai. Japanese were willing to spend a considerable amount of time investigating markets in smaller cities too. Ying Price, an American commercial consul based at the U.S. consulate in Canton, told American businesspeople: "Japanese traders are willing to go out into remote parts of the country for up to three months, leave their wife and their kids and families behind, and live on salty eggs and *congi* rice soup." It would be hard, she added, to find Americans willing to make that kind of sacrifice.[41]

Americans did not have the necessary fortitude, and neither did the Europeans. They watched in wonder as the Japanese seemed to spread throughout China, demonstrating a long-term commitment to developing markets that Americans were so unsure about. Japanese companies were willing to unite to defend themselves against the Chinese ploy of playing one company off against another; the Japanese were known to decide among themselves which one should get a contract, while the others simply withdrew from the negotiations. The Japanese also seemed to know exactly what were the most promising business opportunities in China, and so were confidently *un*aggressive in the area of investing in joint ventures with the Chinese as long as investment conditions remained unattractive. But Americans, under the same pressure from the Chinese to invest but not feeling as sure of themselves, agreed to invest in ventures in numbers far exceeding the Japanese.[42]

The Chinese were angered by the refusal of Japanese companies to invest in China or license Japanese technology, and when talking with Americans, they described the Japanese as sly and ruthless, luring Chinese to purchase systems at teaser prices in order to make them dependent on expensive after-sales service. Though angry about the slowness of the Japanese to invest, the Chinese often hid their feelings when talking face to face with the Japanese; then the Chinese spoke of their common bonds as Asians. In the eyes of Westerners in China, the Japanese did seem to understand the Chinese better, to be much more adept at the little touches.

As often as Americans heard the commercial rapacity of the Japanese denounced by Chinese, from cab drivers on up to government officials, the facts seemed to reveal that the Chinese felt otherwise, or they would not continue to buy so much from Japan. American business representatives grew irritated at the apparent insincerity when the Chinese "confessed" to Americans that they did not like doing business with the Japanese. In 1984, one American told a conference of other resident Americans in Beijing: "I find that the Chinese love to come in and waste my time talking about the Japanese, getting information, but they love to sign contracts with the Japanese because [the Chinese] talk quality and buy price.[43]

In fact, the Chinese government did not act with unified purpose. One part of the government, what we might call the procurement bureaucracy, pursued China's interests by seeking the best combination of value and price for China's imports, regardless of the nationality of origin, though practically speaking it drew again and again from Japan's offerings. Another, wholly separate part of the Chinese government, the investment bureaucracy, tried to attract as much foreign capital as possible; and failing in natural attraction, used economic coercion, threatening to withhold access to China's market without investment in joint ventures. American companies listened carefully and decided in many cases to accede to Chinese pressure, considering it a necessary price to be paid for gaining market access. Japanese companies, however, took advantage of the fact that China's investment bureaucracy had no real power over the procurement bureaucracy to make good on its threat to withhold entry to the China market. Until the late 1980s, China's procurement bureaucrats purchased goods from Japan without directly tying the purchases to Japanese investment and technology transfers. This infuriated other Chinese bureaucrats and their clients, American investors, who felt that their demonstrated commitment to China went disproportionately unrewarded.

For Americans who were still adjusting to the differences of doing business on the opposite side of the world, the Japanese seemed to have an inside pan-Asian advantage, regardless of lingering Chinese memories from World War II. The Japanese knew what they were doing in China, and Americans were envious. Chinese negotiators made Americans feel worse when they told them: "Because they are Orientals, the Japanese are also more adept than Americans at doing business in China. The philosophy of Westerners is like an arrow. Very specific. Very straightforward. But the Eastern philosophy is like a cloud in the sky. We are not direct. We are a lot of 'maybe,' a lot of 'should be'. . . . The Americans do not always understand this. But the Japanese do."[44]

American negotiators had to overcome this dreadful feeling of starting off for China from the wrong side of the old East-West divide, excluded from a start on equal terms with Japan because American-Chinese cultural differences were so much greater. Lack of international business experience, especially in Asia, made many Americans vulnerable to this concern about cultural disadvantage. But it was a concern that deflected attention from an alternative explanation of comparative Japanese success in China that had nothing to do with culture and everything to do with the structure of Japanese trading companies and the much greater resources at their disposal compared to even the largest firms in America's Fortune 500.

The "big four" Japanese firms—Mitsui, Mitsubishi, Marubeni, and C. Itoh—each had a wide range of import and export interests in many different industries, which not only allowed them to deploy many more staff members in China, but also facilitated coordination between different subsidiaries—including banks—and permitted flexibility in negotiations that single American firms could never match. If negotiations on one deal stalled, the Japanese could move their negotiators to another project, so it was not as frustrating for the Japanese company as it was for a much smaller American company for whom few or no other China projects were in the works. Depicting differing philosophies between East and West as a matter of straight arrows and clouds is a poetic way of trying to explain greater Japanese patience, but a better explanation would be that Japanese trading companies had so many deals going in China at any given time that stalled negotiations on any one did not jeopardize the company's operations.

Their size also made it possible for them to be *less* aggressive in marketing their products because each trading company had so many possible candidates that it made sense to find out first what China needed, then fit Japanese products to Chinese priorities; as importers too, the trading companies could easily handle countertrade and other proposals that went beyond the narrow confines of exporting a given item to China. American firms, on the other hand, typically with product lines in a single industry, and usually with a much greater interest in exporting than importing, had fewer options and had to push harder in marketing their wares, regardless of whether they fit with Chinese plans. This made negotiations all the more difficult, but for a reason that was plainly structural, not cultural.[45]

Chinese negotiators granted Americans an initial allotment of goodwill and the presumption that America remained the preeminent world leader in technology, but American negotiators had few advantages when they sat down with the Chinese. Frustrations in breaking into the China market left Americans open to Chinese blandishments to set up joint ventures, which the Japanese successfully resisted. When joint ventures went sour, ill-will between the partners was inevitable and ended up hurting a foreign company's overall campaign in the China market. What to do? Negotiations with the Chinese revealed the emptiness of the ritual incantation of American businesspeople in China, that theirs was a commitment for the long-term future, because when talking with the Chinese about details, it was not clear what was a good investment for the future business relationship and what was not.

III

HOSTING FOREIGNERS

6.

EXPATRIATES

Beijing braced itself for a massive onslaught of Americans when diplomatic relations between the two countries were restored at the beginning of 1979. At the time, the American community in the Chinese capital consisted of only about 100 or 200 people (small though it was, there was little agreement about the exact number), and it was expected to expand to 1,800 or so by the next year. Virtually all the resident Americans were attached to one or the other government, either to the U.S. State Department or to Chinese agencies that had hired foreign experts as English teachers or translators. Some engineers and oil-equipment representatives rounded out the American community. The imminent establishment in Beijing of a permanent business community from the States represented one concrete change that was expected in the wake of formalized diplomatic ties.

Older residents worried whether the newcomers would behave themselves. A U.S. marine guard contingent had set an earlier example of regrettable conduct when the State Department had only a "liaison office" in Beijing. These Marines earned for themselves a reputation for unrestrained inebriation and enjoyed marching through Chinese parks with full battle packs on. The Chinese, not charmed by what the Marines surely regarded as just fun, finally had them ejected from the country. For the resident Americans who stayed, it was a worrisome memory. What would become of the American community in Beijing if sudden expansion brought among the newcomers hundreds of uncouth, stubborn individualists transplanted to a society in which an individual could not do whatever he or she wished?[1]

By process of self-selection, and unsurprisingly given the exotic location of their destination, many of the Americans who first went to China in the 1970s were those who were attracted to the unusual, and who in some cases themselves displayed behavior that was unconventional by any standard. (The British Victorians who roamed the globe and drew fame as the great white explorers had early established an unwritten law in this regard: the more outré the behavior, the more exotic the location sought.) Among the American China hands in the business community, the most colorful behavior of all, collectively speaking, was seen in the self-appointed business advisors who appeared on the scene as soon as trade ties were resumed in the early 1970s. The professional advisors flourished in the decade before China had opened further, when the opportunity to set up a resident office had not yet materialized.

These consulting intermediaries, upon whom American companies at first were quite dependent, were based outside the People's Republic, and in some cases flourished only because it was so difficult for companies to secure permission to post their own representatives in China. Harned Hoose was one of the successful early brokers—and a gifted showman—who exploited the insecurity of his American business clients. He was a lawyer who had been born in China to missionary parents. With his theatrical waxed moustache, Hoose was a magician who claimed special access to the Chinese. His China trade consulting practice, not inappropriately, was based in Los Angeles offices that bore a Hollywood touch: His firm occupied an old mansion that had once belonged to Greta Garbo. Hoose had filled it with Chinese knicknacks and musical instruments, and took his American clients on long, exhaustive tours. When the tour dragged on and the unsuspecting clients became fidgety, Hoose would explain that it was all part of his plan—the tour was intended to provide invaluable training in the patience that would be needed to be successful in China. For providing this and other "consulting services"—by his own admission, Hoose recognized that his primary service was that of "holding the hands" of companies awaiting replies from the Chinese to their inquiries—Hoose earned a handsome salary and flattering attention in the American business press.[2]

Hoose could legitimately claim that he knew China because he had grown up there. But many other trade consultants became experts in the twinkling of an eye, as soon as Nixon made his initial diplomatic overtures to China. In 1970, for example, Andrew Jank was merely a public relations person in Washington who had worked in the Nixon campaign. In 1971, he transformed himself into a China trade expert. Canada being the closest place to meet an official from the People's Republic, he made an appointment with the Chinese embassy in Ottawa to meet with the commercial attaché. The appointment led nowhere; the Chinese official explained that China had no business relations with the United States and could not discuss trade. But afterward, with the guiding hand of a PR professional, Jank transformed his unsuccessful visit to Canada into a highly successful one. In advertisements placed in the *Wall Street Journal* for his "Sino-American Engineering & Trading Associates," Jank told prospective clients: "Our recognition by and direct dialogue with Chinese commercial offices can provide important benefits to the clients we accept and serve."[3]

Lots of consultants like Jank were available in 1972, offering "expertise" at seminars or to individual clients. James Ryan was the head of another firm that hung out a shingle. Ryan claimed important contacts in China first established when he was a pilot in Asia during World War II. He said he had served as personal pilot to Nikita Khrushchev's brother-in-law and personally knew "most of the heads of state" in the socialist bloc. He had a plush suite of offices in the Time-Life Building in New York, fifteen employees, and, it turned out, a criminal record. The U.S. government discovered that Ryan had received large fees as a consultant on deals that swindled a string of financial institutions out of millions of dollars.[4]

It would not be fair to say that a majority of the early China brokers were charlatans. The field was a large one, and many different kinds of individuals and companies tried their hand at selling their services as brokers. All were beneficiaries of the pervasive feeling among Americans that, as one observer put it, "there were only a couple of people around who could introduce companies to the China market." If there were only a "couple of people" who actually had access to Chinese officialdom, it was difficult for American companies to sort out the genuine ones from the impostors. In 1972, an executive at Armco said he had fifteen letters from Hong Kong brokers who claimed they were first cousins of Mao Zedong and could arrange a deal in Beijing: "They're practically waiting for you at the airport when you get to Hong Kong." Given the fact that Americans had not done business with mainland China for a whole generation, it is not surprising that when business contacts were renewed, inexperienced Americans had to fend off a crowd of brokers clamoring to sell their services. What is surprising, however, is the longevity of the reliance on these brokers, whose clients invested them with extraordinary powers. In the late 1980s, almost twenty years after resumption of trade with China, a market for brokers still flourished, and in fact still drew in unlikely figures, including a moonlighting kindergarten principal in Hong Kong whose skill in wheeling and dealing in the China trade and arranging for sales of used trucks and purchases of wicker baskets and coal made her the subject of human interest stories in the business press.[5]

Charles Abrams, a New York real estate man, later dubbed the P. T. Barnum of the China trade, was another consultant who made a splash in the late 1970s. Abrams peddled influence and specialized in arranging joint ventures between relatively small American and European companies and Chinese factories. Instead of charging a commission, he demanded 20 to 50 percent of the equity of each joint venture. His reasoning: "It's better to have part of something than 100 percent of nothing." By 1980, he had set up seventeen such ventures, with his partners supplying both the operating capital and technology, while he contributed his own travel expenses and "my greatest asset—favorable relations with China." In one remarkable deal, Abrams secured a 20 percent stake in a $20 million plastics venture in which his own cash outlay was only $6,600. He exuberantly told Chinese officials at the bargaining session, "We'll make entrepreneurs out of you, too."[6]

Abrams was not only successful in signing up foreign investors for his unique business deals, he was also successful in floating a $2.5 million public stock offering in his company, despite debts of $1.4 million and a prospectus that warned investors of a self-admittedly high degree of risk. His greatest asset, he said, was the intangible one of his contacts with the Chinese. Regardless of whether the contacts were as valuable as he claimed, the perception that they were so in the eyes of his American clients, and the steep price that they paid for the privilege of investing in one of his deals, demonstrates the eagerness of Americans to look to a fixer to get them into the China market.[7]

Californian G. Y. Lin was another fixer who charmed American clients. Alex Haley, who met Lin when both worked on a television deal with Central China Television, called Lin "brilliant." Whenever the group wanted to go to a place in China where foreigners were forbidden, Lin would "flash his Buddha's smile," in Haley's phrase, and disappear. Haley said, "The next day all the papers had been stamped and we were in business." It was a performance that gained dramatic effect from Lin's studied reticence about who his contacts in the Chinese government actually were. A number of children of highly placed senior officials in China stayed at his home back in Lafayette, California, where Lin sponsored their study at local colleges, but Lin was prickly about any imputed charges that their fathers were thus indebted to him. He preferred to say that the deals he arranged in China were made with the help of "friends," but would name no names.[8]

Executives at TWA headquarters in New York were also impressed initially by Lin, who upon request quickly arranged an audience for TWA with senior Party Central Committee member Bo Yibo. Jerry Cosley, a TWA vice-president, recalled: "I remember thinking at the time that this was no Hong Kong fixer, this guy really had some juice." Delighted with their find, TWA gave Lin about $200,000 for what Cosley called "baksheesh, for all I know," money that Lin was to use "to open doors." The money disappeared, however, without Lin producing either concrete results or an accounting of where it had gone. TWA severed ties with him and fired two senior company officials, but plans to recover the $200,000 in court were dropped because TWA did not want to make the company's embarrassment public.[9]

The U.S. Departments of State and Commerce did their best to explain to the American business community that it was not necessary to depend on intermediaries. Government officials pointed out that Boeing had sold $150 million worth of aircraft to China without the help of a broker. If a fledgling China trader needed help, the U.S. government stood ready to offer counsel without charge. It also made available business information about China that went largely unnoticed. In 1972, a *Wall Street Journal* reporter polled at random attendees of China business conferences, at which the price of admission was hundreds of dollars. The reporter discovered that all the individuals with whom he talked had made no effort to read any of the free or inexpensive literature that was available, such as detailed booklets put out by the U.S. Department of Commerce and the Canadian Department of Industry, Trade, and Commerce, which cost $1 or less, and which presented information similar to that found in the commercial China trade conferences staged for profit by private organizers.[10]

Ten years later, most American businesspeople approaching China for the first time continued to be unaware of the vast amount of information that was available in English about the People's Republic—translations, government studies, articles and books by scholars. Some opportunistic books took advantage of this neglect, such as Phillip M. Perry's *China Business Directory,* which was published in 1980, ran 352 pages, cost

$55, and reassured the buyer in its subtitle that this was a *Practical Guide.* Stanley Lubman pointed out in a review of Perry's book that no fewer than 100 of its 350 pages had been lifted word for word from other publications without quotation or attribution and then passed on as the latest information available. Perry claimed his material had been "gathered up through the final months of 1979"—but in fact the uncredited sources were already several years old and had been overtaken by drastic policy changes in China in the interim. Lubman caught the author *flagrante delicto* in the act of plagiarism: "I can't resist adding that portions of the volume which the 'author' used to provide much of his chapter on negotiating with the Chinese were actually written by someone whose work on this subject I know very well, namely me."[11]

A larger question, which Lubman raised, was how anyone could have expected to get away with stealing information from others without giving due credit. The answer that Lubman suggested was that an author like Perry must have known that many American businesspeople remained unaware of the free material available from goverment and other sources. To many Americans, China remained beyond the understanding of a layperson. "Too many firms," Lubman said, "think that because China is on the other side of the world, everything is so upside down that they can't usefully find out information as they might, say, about a Western European country." This, he said, was no excuse for individuals not trying to learn more on their own. The advice could have been applied to all, whether clients of brokers or not, and whether headed to China for a short business trip or as a foreign resident.[12]

While fly-by-night purveyors of China contacts and information came and swiftly went, a second group of immensely greater integrity emerged: American brokers who stayed in the China business and were able to sustain a good reputation among their clients. They were among the first to settle into Beijing hotels and begin lives as expatriates in China. It was also they who were most visible because their consulting practices demanded that they create a public image for themselves and because many American companies used American representatives in Beijing before they set up their own offices there.

Many of the expatriate brokers in Beijing were young, fluent in Chinese, and clothed sometimes in the larger-than-life garb of myth. When we speak of the mythology of American business, we are referring to myths in a positive sense, as inspirational tales that help knit a culture together. For businesspeople in the United States, the triumph of the individual over adversity is the recurrent theme of their own mythology, exemplified by the Horatio Alger novels of the nineteenth century and by the self-promoting autobiographies of prominent people in the late twentieth. At the core of American capitalism is the belief that anyone who merits success will be able to achieve it, and the pantheon of American business mythology honors outstanding individual entrepreneurs, not the companies they built.

If the mythic figure of the Successful Entrepreneur has been important to the American business culture, it is only natural that a cousin, the Successful American Entrepreneur in China, was created in the course of developing business ties between the two countries. Virginia Kamsky was a prominent member of the new China brokers. Her story is interesting because it contains in microcosm the themes that animate the American business culture. Kamsky, who set up her own company in Beijing in 1980 and soon had many American companies as clients, would explain her success as a story of old-fashioned American pluck. Her autobiography was crafted in such a way as to enhance her public image and to help prospective clients see her company as indispensable. Critics accused her of shameless and unending self-promotion; defenders accused the critics of envy at her success. Unquestionably, Kamsky was gifted at creating an image of herself as an indefatigable yet smoothly bicultural intermediary. A tale that she liked to tell serves to introduce questions not only about cultural differences, but also about the especially visible place of American businesswomen in China.

The story begins with Kamsky in Canton, representing a Japanese company and facing the possibility of losing a $40 million machinery sale if she did not get her clients to Zhanjiang, a port city about 250 miles away, by the next night in time for a critical meeting with a Chinese agency that had set a deadline on proposals. It was raining; all flights to Zhanjiang were canceled. Unwilling to risk the chance that planes would remain grounded the next day, Kamsky rented a jeep for the twelve-hour drive. She then had to convince three separate Chinese units to provide gas cans filled with extra gasoline because there would be no roadside stations on the way. She rushed back to the hotel to pick up her Japanese clients.[13]

Here, we discover, gender presented a problem. The clients, all men, told her she could not go on such a trip—there were no suitable bathrooms for women along the way. Kamsky ignored the protests, packed the Japanese into the jeep, then set off on a trip that would make a great Jeep commercial: bumping over unimproved roads, fording rivers where the roads were washed out, using ferries where available, and working out a satisfactory system of privacy for rest stops. Kamsky said, "We'd stop along the way and I'd go behind the jeep and they'd go in front." It's a terrific story, in no way spoiled by the predictable ending: The clients got to the meeting, spent the next ten days in negotiations, and finally won the contract. In Kamsky's retelling, when the Chinese officials later asked the Japanese at a farewell banquet in Beijing what most impressed them on their first trip to China, the senior Japanese representative answered, "We learned a lot about American women."[14]

One can easily imagine the nonplussed Japanese men encountering for the first time a Kamsky or her many female American confederates in Beijing. What is of particular interest here is the way that the Kamsky story was used by reporters who helped create the mythology of the American Superwoman and Superman in Beijing, which required for dramatic effect a steep ascent between humble origins and subsequent business success. By 1985, *Forbes* told American readers in a breathless profile, Kamsky had traded her modest one-room hotel home in Beijing for a "luxurious apartment on New York's Park Avenue," which she had "bought for herself" and where she could display her "collection of fine Chinese porcelain." Without diminishing the blood, sweat, and tears that she and others like her shed in building their companies in Beijing, it can still be noted that her business of providing good contacts in China was itself helped at the start by excellent contacts in the United States. Kamsky had undergraduate and graduate degrees from Princeton; had accompanied Chase Manhattan's president Willard C. Butcher on a trip to China; and soon after had been installed as the bank's first representative in Beijing, at the age of twenty-four. This provided a secure platform from which to strike out on her own two years later. She told different versions of how she came to secure her first three clients—at one time she said that the three companies approached her, at another time she said that she had approached them—but in any case it seems that getting the three signed up and collecting $35,000 in retainer fees to set up a shop in Beijing was easily done. It is curious, however, that the only American company she mentioned by name as an early client was W. R. Grace. As a profile of Kamsky mentioned elsewhere, without drawing any connection, she happened to be the daughter of Leonard Kamsky, the chief economist for Grace.[15]

These personal details would not be germane if it were not for the myth that the China market was a land of opportunity for hardy but otherwise powerless American entrepreneurs. Both business journalists and the China traders themselves were caught up in myth creation, in their zeal to describe China as a place where an entrepreneurial American, with little more than some Chinese language skills and lots of guts, could dart agilely and successfully around giant corporations that did not know how to begin to operate. Ellen Kiam, another well-known broker, explained to reporters from *Venture* magazine that doing well in China required a personal touch, which the entrepreneur could provide and the big corporation could not. Kiam was married to Victor Kiam, who later became the head of Remington Products and well known for his line, I-liked-the-shaver-so-much-I-bought-the-company. She got into the China business unintentionally when she accompanied her husband on a trip to China in 1974 and went shopping for Christmas presents. She shipped jewelry and antiques that arrived at home too late (February) and in far too great volume to be used for Christmas gifts, so she decided to go into business. The mythic stories of Kamsky, Kiam, and others are not stories of duplicity and deception; rather, they are mythic in the benign sense of larger-than-life tales created by the American business press and addressed to an eager audience in the business community that looked to the entrepreneurial motif as inspiration.[16]

In a parallel fashion, the People's Republic extolled the virtues of the ordinary person in its own versions of proletarian mythologizing. But the actual personnel who were assigned leading roles in China's foreign trade and investment policies were multimillionaire Rong Yiren, whose pre-Liberation family fortune was made in textiles and flour milling, and the "Shanghai Mafia," including figures such as Jing Shuping and Xu Zhaolong, whom Rong gathered around him at the China International Trust and Investment Corporation (CITIC) and whose families had also accumulated enormous wealth before 1949. The anomaly of appointing a Rong Yiren as one of the most visible representatives of the People's Republic, the person charged with attracting foreign capital and technology, was not lost on foreign observers. Many stories were published in the United States describing in respectful wonder the incongruity of Rong's ostentatious wealth and his socialist home. At a time when the average Chinese worker earned only about $35 a month, Rong lived in a mansion with a staff of servants, chauffeurs, and gardeners; his favorite hobbies were collecting expensive cameras and cultivating roses.

During the Cultural Revolution, his inherited wealth had been confiscated and he had been pressed into working as a janitor, but by the late 1970s, with his fortune restored and a state appointment to head the newly created CITIC, he was the equal of any Western capitalist.

Foreigners thought that deploying Rong at CITIC was a conscious Chinese stratagem of "using an ex-capitalist to catch a capitalist." All the attention that Rong Yiren received in the Western business press was noticed, in turn, by the Chinese press, which translated profiles of him from *Fortune* and similar magazines, proudly citing them as proof that one of their own was now included in the ranks of world business leaders. When Rong visited Brazil and Chile in early 1987 to look for investment opportunities for CITIC, reporters asked him if it would not be peculiar for China to invest in Chile, whose military government had such a long and well-known history of brutally suppressing leftists. Rong paused for a long while, then blandly replied that he personally had not seen any such things on his visit. What he and the Chinese government were saying to the international business community was a blend of challenge and reassurance: At any level American capitalists wish to compete, we are ready with people who think no differently than you do.[17]

The American captains of trade and industry in China cultivated celebrity, but for the rank and file expatriates who were attracted to working in China as employees—whether as company representative, consultant, attorney, banker, public accountant, mining engineer, or other functionary—fame was only a remote possibility. The footsoldiers had to have other motivations.

One of several common motives was that of going to this remote country as a pioneer, being present at the making of history, and playing a role, however modest, in its creation. The American expatriates who settled in Beijing at the end of the 1970s exuded enthusiasm for their work. A typical testimonial at the time was that of Kenneth Morse, who worked for Chase Manhattan: "This whole job is an adventure and I love it. . . . I wouldn't trade places with anyone—not at this moment of history." China was seen by some as a frontier, though the psychological rewards were accompanied by the frustrations of its being on the furthest margins of the world of international business.[18]

Some Americans believed they were contributing directly to the modernization of China. "When you're selling something to the Chinese that is a major upgrade from anything they've ever seen before," said one young American representative based in Beijing, "and you know it's going to make a major impact in the industry that you are involved in, I think it's different from selling that thing in Birmingham, Alabama, where it's just another of the same thing." A few years later, another expatriate, Roderick Macleod, who had worked in Shanghai for four years in the early 1980s representing the accounting firm Coopers & Lybrand, wrote from an older, and somewhat chastened, perspective about the intense hopes that had made working in China extremely exciting, and the dangerous sense of hubris that it induced. In the late 1980s, Macleod wrote:

> I succumbed to the same dream. Then . . . I had to accept the fact that one man can't make a difference. The usual reward for such intense involvement in China and its future is "burnout," so that most Westerners want to leave after a few months or years. (The fact that I don't get burned out, except on those inevitable bad days, may be because I come and go a lot. . . .)[19]

The expatriates who stayed on in China did so, in many cases, for a simple reason: the financial reward. The American who one moment spoke of the satisfaction of selling equipment in Beijing at another moment confessed that he had been spoiled financially and wondered whether he would still be there if it were not for the money. Certainly by 1984 the giddiness of the initial arrival five years earlier had worn off, and another American in Beijing spoke emphatically and claimed to speak for the collective group: When they had started, the rewards had been psychic rewards of going to an exotic location, working with the Chinese, what was in retrospect self-mockingly called "the China syndrome." But as some of these attractions had worn off, the importance of the financial compensation had proportionately increased. At some point, the American asserted, "you are really doing it for the money, and if it weren't for the money you wouldn't be here."[20]

The pay was indeed generous. When multinational companies set up compensation policies for expatriate employees, they used a "balance-sheet approach," which attempted to assess which living costs were higher or lower than those at home, and to set compensation in such a way that the employee neither gained nor lost financially on an assignment overseas. But this balance-sheet approach was based on the assumption that compensation policies were primarily a matter of comparing apartment rentals or grocery store receipts; it was difficult to compare intangible differences that did not lend themselves easily to quantification, such as the perceived desirability of living in various cities abroad. For an American facing an expatriate assignment, Paris and Beijing were very different cities, different for reasons not necessarily related to cost of living. So the balance sheet had to equalize the relative attractiveness of different posts by including additional compensation like "hardship" allowances which in fact subverted the idea that employees should not gain financially. In order to attract and retain expatriates for hardship posts, companies had learned, the financial gains must be large. Thus, it was market forces, not the abstract niceties of pay equalization, that drove pay for expatriates upward.

Among hardship postings around the world, China in the early 1980s was regarded by American companies as one of the hardest assignments of all. The hardship allowances for employees in the People's Republic were usually higher than those in Saudi Arabia and the Soviet Union, and for some companies China was the only place in the world for which such allowances were offered. Most firms paid a hardship allowance of about 25 percent of base salary; this premium was usually still higher for employees assigned to cities other than Beijing and Shanghai. In Zhanjiang, in Guangdong Province, which was used by multinational petroleum companies as a supply base for offshore oil operations, the allowance was 55 percent of base pay, the highest allowance found in a worldwide survey of compensation practices. Completion bonuses were offered by many companies to retain employees. The highest paid individuals, who had the perfect set of technical and linguistic skills, were paid so well that their compensation created problems for the company. Georges Holzberger, an associate at Russell Reynolds Associates, cautioned companies that "your China employee has to fit into the company's earnings structure so he isn't earning three times as much as the guy he's reporting to."[21]

On paper, Beijing and other Chinese cities were costly places to live, especially because of the lack of inexpensive apartments. But American expatriates were personally spared most of this hardship because their employers paid for their housing, which in the early 1980s was a hotel bill that also included meals in the hotel restaurants and incidentals such as laundry. Many company representatives received a per diem in addition to their salary and other allowances. One American resident in Beijing observed, "My wife and I will sometimes go days without spending one penny of our own money." When multinationals hired outside human resources consultants for advice about refining compensation systems for expatriates in China, the consultants discovered that companies were not deducting from the employees' pay the estimated average expenses for housing that would have been spent at home, a standard practice elsewhere in the world. The consultants were appalled at the spectacle of expatriates saving a large percentage of their pay and bonuses. This was not supposed to happen with the balance-sheet approach; going abroad was not supposed to produce a financial windfall. But companies ignored the advice of the consultants to eliminate the "double compensation" that violated practices elsewhere and stuck to unusually generous compensation policies. The rationale was not voiced, but it is easily understood: In order to get employees to the most opposite of places, to struggle at the cliff face of daunting cultural and ideological differences, to work under conditions that made it difficult to retain people at any price, exceptional circumstances demanded exceptional pay.[22]

One more, extremely important, motivation of the younger Americans who went to work in China was the opportunity to hold positions of responsibility that were not available at home for junior people, especially those who lacked the formal credentials of a business degree or previous corporate experience. In Beijing in the early 1980s opportunity seemed to abound everywhere for young Chinese-speaking Americans, as companies moved from episodic talks with the Chinese to establishing permanent representative offices and joint or wholly-owned ventures on Chinese soil. American firms needed individuals who could work well at the interstices of two cultures and ideologies. The Virginia Kamsky case—heading up Chase's Beijing office at the age of twenty-four—was not exceptional at that time. Companies scrambling to establish a beachhead in China were willing to forsake traditional seniority rules. Alternatively, young people, also like Kamsky, discovered that they could strike out and succeed on their own, or be in demand by small trading and consulting companies. The U.S.–China Industrial Exchange, for example, was started in 1981 by Roberta Lipson, then twenty-six, and Elyse Silverberg, then twenty-four. As it grew, the average age of its employees remained a young twenty-six, and its Beijing offices, with rock music in the background, gave the place what one visitor in 1986 described as "a collegiate air." One reporter estimated in 1985 that about 20 percent of the U.S. business community in China was under the age of thirty.[23]

The work was often physically as well as mentally strenuous, and young people argued that youth was a critical asset when commercial battles in China were won "through sheer tenacity." Many of the young expatriates had already done stints in China for language study; these were the ideal candidates in the view of one expatriate office manager, much more attractive than people who were brought over from the United States as untested quantities. He explained: "I don't want to have to babysit this person and take care of his shattered illusions about China or whatever. I want someone who has been here and is scarred up a little bit." The young expatriates who were hired to serve as the Beijing representatives of large companies discovered that they had access to corporate heads and visiting dignitaries they would not have seen back in the States.[24]

For young women in particular, China offered exceptional opportunities, and American expatriates in Beijing noticed that in 1980 a majority of the trading businesses were run by women. Four out of five of the legal representatives were women, too. For a number of years, Kamsky hired only women, and even when the number of employees in her firm had grown to twenty-five, only two were men. She liked to compare her company to the all-woman army of fierce warriors in a famous Chinese novel, who were known as consistent victors. She noticed a dichotomy between the respect she received in China and its absence when she returned to the United States:

> When I worked for Chase in China, I found that I could sit with the minister of petroleum and talk about financing a $200 million project and no one said "Isn't it amazing that you're a woman negotiating such a transaction." . . . When I went to the South or the Midwest—I handled grain and cotton companies for Chase—there was always a comment like "It's really fascinating for us to have a female account officer!" And there would always be a real concern about letting a woman handle the account.[25]

Other American women in China agreed, saying that women in Beijing were accepted as negotiators and business partners without sexism. "It's not like being in the States," said one, "where immediately you walk into a room and these fifty-year-old men think, 'Oh, she's cute, she's studying business, isn't that nice.' [In China, the Chinese] accept you and you don't have to prove yourself first." Return visits home served to confirm the perception of different treatment. When Elyse Silverberg, for example, went back to the United States for visits and compared notes with women college friends about their varying work situations, she said: "I realize how great I have it in China."[26]

American women credited the Chinese for having a comparatively egalitarian society and more understanding of businesswomen who had children. Silverberg, who had a young son, noticed how her own behavior changed depending on the nationality of business callers who came to the Beijing hotel office that doubled as her home. With Americans, she was reluctant to even mention her son, concerned that she would appear "unprofessional." But with Chinese, she said, her guests were always interested in talking about her child as soon as they discovered his existence. If, when walking her Chinese guests to the front door, they encountered her son toddling down the hall, the Chinese wanted to hear all about him and play and talk with him. In the same situation in the United States, "I might pretend that I didn't see him and get the clients out quickly."[27]

Chinese women in China, however, would not be likely to receive the same attentive treatment from Chinese men as the American women received. Recent studies about the place of women in contemporary Chinese society, such as Margery Wolf's *Revolution Postponed* or Emily Honig and Gail Hershatter's *Personal Voices,* present incontrovertible documentation of the pervasiveness of sexism—not merely inherited prejudice from before 1949, but the product of subsequent state policies. Despite the cheery descriptions of the absence of prejudice reported by many American businesswomen in their own experiences in Beijing, the Chinese still paid close attention to gender in their encounters with and reflections about foreign businesspeople.[28]

The compliments Chinese paid to American women are revealing. When, for example, the Chinese praised an American woman for being a tenacious negotiator, the intended compliment should stand out because there was not similar commendation of individual American men. Praise of tenacity and similar words of praise offered by Chinese men unintentionally cast doubt on the acceptance of women of ability in Chinese society. We must remember that, generally speaking, the Chinese negotiating teams or the Chinese groups assembled for business banquets were composed overwhelmingly of men, usually older rather than younger. Chinese women were often completely absent. This pattern, coupled with the exclusive or almost exclusive use of women employees, who were usually younger rather than older, by American consulting and trading firms such as Kamsky Associates, WJS International, and U.S.–China Industrial Exchange, set up the starkest of imaginable contrasts in gender and age when Chinese and American business teams got together. Kamsky said that her use of female employees was a conscious decision, intended to give her firm a distinctive cachet, but she denied that there was any latent sexual cachet in the matching of American women and Chinese men. She maintained that a woman doing business in China enjoyed no particular advantages. But another Beijing expatriate, Jamie Horsely, saw that the considerable success of

American women in China was related in some measure to their sex. She had seen the same phenomenon when she lived in Taiwan and had come to believe that Western businesswomen in Asia as a whole were treated like "a third sex." She felt that this was a definite advantage: "You stand out more. You're a novelty, and people pay attention to you."[29]

The idea that American women in China were seen as a "third sex" means that the respect they received from Chinese men had nothing to do with how the men viewed the "second sex," Chinese women. In an informal study of sexual politics in international business, American men in Beijing sometimes bitterly (but privately) commented on the way Kamsky exploited sexual differences without acknowledging that she was doing so. One male expatriate claimed that when Chinese women were appointed as negotiators instead of men, the interpersonal relationships between Chinese and Americans were noticeably different than when Chinese men were negotiating with American women. "I don't think a foreign male can charm a Chinese female negotiator as much as a foreign woman can charm a Chinese male negotiator."[30]

American businesswomen in China worked exceedingly hard, and their achievements unquestionably reflected the reward due any similar effort, by anyone, regardless of gender. But their achievements in China were always framed on both sides by the sexism of the two societies. If they were exempted from the scorn Chinese men accorded Chinese women, it was because their foreignness mattered more. But their foreignness did not eliminate their gender identity; it merely changed it into the "third sex," a category that may have been freighted in the minds of some Chinese men with the sexual allure of the foreign and the forbidden. American women circumnavigated half the globe, yet as far as they traveled to escape the constricted career opportunities and patronizing attitudes in the United States, and as successful as they were in beginning business or law careers in the superficially egalitarian society of New China, they were never able to find a work environment where gender truly did not matter at all. Even at the place of opposites, some things remained stubbornly the same.

American businesspeople have not settled at all the question of whether foreign language skills are vital in an overseas assignment or not. During the 1980s, business leaders sounded boilerplate alarms on the banquet circuit, linking decreased trade competitiveness with American monolingualism and ignorance of other cultures. The expansion of business ties with the People's Republic was seen as the harbinger of a future in which

Americans would have to buckle down and learn non-European languages if they were to secure a place in an Asia-centered global economy. Walter Hoadley, the executive vice-president of Bank of America, returned from a sojourn in China in 1979 lamenting that few Americans spoke Mandarin, and "almost none are now planning to learn." The language barrier, Hoadley concluded, ranked as one of the largest obstacles to further Sino-American ties. Politicians sounded similar warnings. California Assemblyman Tom Hayden, for example, wrote an opinion piece for the *Los Angeles Times* in 1985 on the subject of the seemingly perilous imbalance between Asians studying English and Americans studying Asian languages. A young black woman who was at UCLA majoring in international economics with a minor in Chinese studies, and who worked in Hayden's district office, seemed to Hayden to embody the future, or at least what the future should be, if Asian language and area studies enrollments in the United States were not so distressingly low.[31]

Businesspeople in line positions, however, did not echo a shared consensus about the economically strategic importance of language skills. The business community, when surveyed about the general importance of foreign languages in overseas assignments, split into divergent camps: One group, the majority, believed foreign language is important but not critically so; a sizable minority, about a quarter of the sample in one large survey, believed languages skills were not critically important; and only a small minority, about 10 percent, believed languages were vital in such assignments. The range of opinion was found in microcosm among American businesses in China, and the line of division tended to be drawn between those who themselves knew Chinese and those who did not. Sixty percent of a small survey of American representatives in Beijing in 1984 declared knowledge of Chinese to be "essential," a much higher percentage than would have been found in a survey of Americans still in the United States. But the group sampled in Beijing had a lot of Chinese-language study under their collective belts, and perhaps the most remarkable thing about the survey is the evidence that pointed to a contrary conclusion. Even Chinese-speaking expatriates did not all agree that the language was critical. The portion of the sample that had usable command of Chinese—some 65 percent of the group—was actually larger than the 60 percent which declared it essential.[32]

As a matter of national pride, it was somewhat embarrassing for Americans to rely heavily on the services of Chinese interpreters, both when Americans went to China and also when Chinese came to the United States. It was also unnerving to see that Japanese companies stationed in China posted many more staff members who spoke Chinese; in one trading company, all 26 representatives in China spoke Chinese. A survey of American and Japanese companies revealed that the Japanese believed the chief representative or senior manager should be able to speak Chinese well enough for use in business, and many Japanese companies paid for language training in China. But otherwise Americans who did not themselves speak the language could not see any serious disadvantages in relying on interpreters.[33]

It was impossible to assign any concrete value to the ability to listen to intramural Chinese discussions during negotiations, or to the ability to talk directly to Chinese counterparts or employees without intermediation. These were advantages that were impossible to measure, by their nature invisible to those who could not enjoy them, and more likely to be viewed as *un*valuable than *in*valuable. The language problems in Chinese and American encounters that remained visible were vaudevillian mishaps that left no lasting damage, like this well-known bit of Beijing lore: The foreigner hops in a taxi to go to the Peking Duck restaurant, and not knowing Chinese, communicates his destination by flapping his arms like a duck. The driver nods and proceeds to the airport. Needless to say, the basis of such a story is questionable, but more important is what such apocryphal tales reveal about those who pass them on; here the message non-Chinese-speaking foreigners could draw is that language problems are comical but harmless and can always be straightened out in the end.[34]

Though usually uncredited, bilingual interpreters did play an important role in helping to soften the rougher edges of Americans and other foreigners in their dealings with Chinese. Jan Berris, a senior staff member of the National Committee for U.S.–China Relations and herself an interpreter, told an illustrative story of a visiting Western scientist who was about to give a talk to a large audience and was upset that children were still playing and talking in the aisles when he was about to speak. After waiting in vain for someone to quiet the children down, he told his interpreter, "Will you tell those little bastards to shut up!" The interpreter, in turn, quietly spoke into the microphone in Chinese, "Little friends, would you please be just a bit more quiet, if you don't mind." On other occasions, Berris said, interpreters found that translations of jokes and other forms of humor were simply impossible, and one had to do as the Doonesbury character Honey once did when she was interpreting a speech by an American and told her Chinese audience, in one frame, "I think he's about to make a joke . . ." and then in the next, "The joke has been made, and he will be expecting you to laugh at it. Go wild."[35]

Unfortunately, Americans in Beijing who were bilingual often found themselves unwillingly placed seriously in the position of Honey, forced to make explanations *sotto voce* in Chinese on behalf of their non-Chinese-speaking American peers, which in turn created distrust on the American side. One American representative who spoke Mandarin complained that in negotiations "the person you're representing, for example, can't tell whether you're translating or whether you're explaining, or whether you're making excuses for the Chinese people."[36]

Mindful of prospective clients, trade brokers who did not speak Chinese, such as Ellen Kiam and Noble Trading's Leslie Schweitzer, naturally had a vested interest in declaring publicly that the language was not needed. Schweitzer reasoned that if you knew how to speak Chinese, then "you're thinking about how you're saying things and not keeping as alert." Her reasoning was seemingly confirmed by the laments of bilingual business representatives like the one who reported: "The better your Chinese gets, the more boring your job gets." This was because you could not help noticing mistakes in translated documents and starting to take on the burdens of translator and thinking about linguistic problems. "Business people who don't speak Chinese have nothing to do but think about business problems."[37]

Indisputably, translation work reduced one's status in the group. In the hierarchy of roles in the American business enterprise (and one could add in the U.S. Foreign Service as well), language facility ironically is associated with the lowest positions on the ladder. The bilingual expatriate cannot allow herself or himself to enjoy the use of the foreign language; in some cases, the expatriate will consciously decide not to use the language, lest it affect the professional status earned by other skills and qualifications.

These concerns are not exaggerated; they reflect quite accurately the ambient values to be found in American organizations and the way in which many Americans seem most comfortable with the neat dichotomy of Self and Other and do not like to see it blurred with bilingual people who stand in the middle. Some American companies in China—the oil companies being the most notorious—turned away candidates who spoke Chinese. In the opinion of one observer, "They want a very clear separation between us and them." Bilingual business representatives were caught in the middle because the Chinese also did not like the line of separation blurred. One American who had long been a Beijing resident explained: "Sometimes it unsettles the Chinese, when you've been here for a number of years, and you come across as almost [a Beijing native], and it scares them. And sometimes it's a disadvantage, because they sometimes think this guy knows too much, or you sound like you know too much." The Chinese, like the Americans, wanted Self and Other clearly distinguished.[38]

If the system not only failed to reward but actually penalized Americans for using foreign language skills in managerial roles, then business leaders and politicians were wrong in criticizing low foreign language enrollments in American schools. Americans had translators and interpreters, but they moved out of the field as soon as they could; the Chinese experienced the same difficulty in retaining their own interpreters when alternative opportunities and paths to upward mobility developed by the middle 1980s. Still other Americans and Chinese purposely avoided becoming professional interpreters; reading the telltale signs of a mean occupation, they went elsewhere, where recognition and compensation were greater.[39]

For what proved to be a fleeting moment in historical time, in the late 1970s and early 1980s, U.S. employers in Beijing were interested in Americans who had done Chinese and related area studies. But the Sinophiles were hired because nobody else wanted to live in Beijing, and companies were anxious to get representatives in place as soon as possible. American companies, by their own admission, often hire people as if they were sending out firefighters—acting quickly, because the fire needs putting out, and sending someone who can stand the heat. But once the Beijing office was established, once the supporting infrastructure for expatriate life in Beijing expanded and made the city less of a hardship posting, and once companies got over the initial China fever and began methodically to map out a longer-term strategy, regular employees from the United States began to be posted to China.

In the mid-1980s, when the first postnormalization generation of students in Chinese studies began to flock to Beijing in search of work, they discovered that language skills were not so highly valued; the employment opportunities for these new graduates, whom Hayden had imagined to be "the future," were actually quite limited. The old expatriate Sinophiles, who had gotten their first jobs by fortuitous timing a few years before when American companies had rushed to China, saw how different a fate awaited those who now came looking for work. "It's really hard," said one established American, "because there are so many of them and they are all floating around and they all have about the same credentials."[40]

By the late 1980s, many companies had actually cut down on the size of their Beijing staffs or moved to Hong Kong, further cutting employment opportunities. By then too, an important realization had belatedly seeped in: An enormous pool of Chinese-Americans, or Hong Kong, Singaporean, or other ethnic Chinese who were native speakers and who were trained engineers, lawyers, or other professionals meant that companies did not have to choose between technical or language skills; they could hire employees who had both. Many companies discovered they had candidates for China assignments within their own organization: well-trained Chinese-Americans who were already employees. The roll of American representatives who went to China in the 1970s reveals many who had been with the companies that sent them for many years. Peter Lee, who had a Ph.D. in chemistry from Michigan State, had worked for Coca-Cola since 1972 and was its representative when the company initiated talks with the Chinese. Ming Hsu, an RCA vice-president specializing in China projects, had begun working for RCA in the 1950s. She was described in a 1981 profile as "a twenty-five-year RCA veteran who worked her way up the ladder and would be in her position even if the company didn't have anything to sell to China." At Kaiser Engineers, no fewer than seventy of its employees happened to speak Mandarin or Cantonese at the time of diplomatic normalization with the People's Republic. The company, like many others, exploited the advantage in trade negotiations and in training Chinese engineers. Over the course of the 1980s, the proportion of American representatives in China who were ethnic Chinese rose higher; by 1988, more than half of the American companies in Beijing had hired people of Chinese descent as their representatives. PRC natives who had recently emigrated to the United States also began to return to Beijing and joined other Chinese-Americans as American employees.[41]

This enormous pool of human resources was ignored when speechmakers talked about a shortage of "Americans" who spoke Chinese. American companies in Taiwan had established a pattern that American companies in the People's Republic soon repeated: relying upon Chinese-speaking ethnic Chinese as well as English-speakers in the host country. Taiwan had become one of the single most important trading partners of the United States without creating a proportionate demand for Americans who had studied Chinese. Native speakers of Chinese were always preferred over college-trained speakers; moreover, the native speakers were available in plentiful numbers. U.S. business ties with the People's Republic could grow enormously, just as in the earlier case with Taiwan, by relying upon this ready pool of candidates.

An apparent contradiction arises: Why would American companies seem to devalue the importance of foreign language facility among employees who were not of Chinese descent, in a majority of cases claiming that language was not critical to their business, yet at the same time, apparently place a high value on language capability by dispatching ethnic Chinese as their representatives in China? Here we have an anomaly that has less to do with foreign languages than it does with the persistent mystification of racial difference. For Americans who were not Chinese-Americans, the perceived gulf between Americans and Chinese, between Us and Them, was enormous, and ethnic Chinese seemed to be the only humans who could stand in the middle and remain in contact with both sides simultaneously. Ethnic Chinese emissaries thus were psychologically valuable, important for providing the mechanical service of English-Chinese interpretation, but equally important for their Other-ness, for fulfilling a symbolic function as the corporeal unity of two culturally opposite worlds. Non-Chinese-Americans thrust them into this role; some Chinese-Americans themselves also marketed their utility in this fashion, claiming a better "understanding" of the Chinese, or as Yue-Sai Kan phrased it with a nicely American touch of Spanish, "We are simpatico with the Chinese mentality."[42]

Other Americans did not question these claims too closely. They did not even always check to see if the Chinese-Americans spoke Mandarin well before sending them to Beijing. Dialect differences—Mandarin, Cantonese, and Shanghainese speakers, for example, are all mutually unintelligible—seemed less important than simply having authentic Chinese people on the scene, who would serve as guides by some innate genetic compass. Race, not language skills, was the key attribute. This can be illustrated by examining some of the silliest anecdotes other Americans told about the value of having ethnic Chinese as employees in China. In the standard anecdote, we meet an American lawyer in Shanghai about to be charged $200 a night for a suite he did not want to stay in, or a Honeywell vice-president about to go for a taxi ride, also in Shanghai, at rates that unbeknown to him had been raised a moment before in his foreign honor. Both were saved by accompanying Chinese-Americans, who came to the rescue and scolded the hotel manager and taxi driver, respectively.[43]

The variations on the theme extended to stories in which the happy ending is a multi-hundred-million-dollar deal, secured only with the timely intervention of a Chinese-American at the moment of impasse. Boeing negotiators, for example, found that the Chinese were baffled about why American jumbo jets provided so many accommodations for dogs; the puzzle originated, it turned out, from a direct translation into Chinese of industry jargon, "doghouses," for the compartments in which food trays were stored. If the story ended here, it would be an amusing one. But Americans insisted on assigning a dollar value of $160 million—that is, the value of the entire deal eventually signed—to what had been jeopardized by the temporary cross-cultural misunderstanding. Thus $160 million had been "earned" for Boeing by the Chinese-American employee who had straightened out the mistranslation. Now, as an exercise, substitute for the Chinese-American an Irish-American, or some other American who learned to speak Chinese by studying in the college classroom and during a junior year abroad in Taiwan. He or she could easily have "rescued" the situation. But anyone except a Chinese-American in the role would ruin the tacit racial punchline that was addressed to the Chinese in the People's Republic: We have one of yours on our side. On the PRC side, the Chinese brandished Rong Yiren, meeting Americans on grounds of wealth. The Americans met the Chinese on grounds of race.[44]

The Chinese in the People's Republic were no less racial in their outlook than the Americans. They embraced Chinese-Americans, of whatever post-emigration generation, as close blood relations, whose kinship ties were protected from the vicissitudes of bilateral trade. Tang Junde, a PRC official at the China Science and Technology Center, expressed the widely shared belief that Chinese-Americans were racially bonded to the People's Republic: "We know that, no matter what the problems, [Chinese-Americans] are committed to China." And many Chinese-Americans ritually declared the blood oath that was expected of them, like Honeywell's Margaret Lee, who the *New York Times* quoted in 1988 as saying, "As long as you have Chinese blood, you are Chinese." This belief in a bond—half nationality and half hematology—was sufficient to be enormously influential. PRC officials gave Chinese-Americans special entree that was not given to others, and struck deals that would not have been arranged with others. In this fashion, the bond became self-fulfilling; the more that Chinese and Chinese-Americans on both sides of the Pacific believed in and talked about a special relationship, the more successful they were in working together, and the more that they—and others who were watching—came to believe that it was an unshakable cultural law.[45]

Chinese-speaking Americans who were not ethnically Chinese saw that they were excluded from the blood nexus that tied Chinese-Americans to the motherland, and they saw that deals were lost as a result. Fred Spieler, in the course of working for a trading company affiliated with Crocker National Bank, told the story of an American customer that submitted a low bid for a contract to build a $25 million aluminum-foil plant but lost out to a British competitor who had hired the services of a Chinese-American. These and similar stories were often explained by foreigners as illustrations of the importance of *guanxi* (pronounced as if it were spelled *guan-shee*), or personal connections, in Chinese culture. But they missed an important point: personal connections and the racial rhetoric about once-a-Chinese-always-a-Chinese were not timeless verities. The concepts mattered only because they were believed in and sustained day by day with repetitive incantation. As long as Americans and Chinese continued to tell themselves and others that race mattered, it did continue to matter—but it was the belief that determined action, and not the reverse.[46]

7.

WORK AND PLAY

The American expatriate in Beijing circa 1980 inhabited a tiny, cramped world where office and home in most cases were in the same hotel room. It was a world that was no less confining socially and intellectually—a paradox in a country so large and culturally rich. Here the contrast between ideological systems was exposed as dramatically as it ever would be. A few years before 1980, the stray American businessman or woman in China either could not live as a long-term resident or was too isolated, like the Pullman Kellogg employees, to constitute a separate world of expatriates. A few years after 1980, however, Americans and other Western and Japanese representatives would be present in numbers too large, and the Chinese apparatus of ideological and social controls would be too overwhelmed, for observers to see the two different systems so clearly in neat juxtaposition. In 1979 and the early 1980s, at the moment when China first began to accept large numbers of foreign business representatives as residents, there was drama to be seen in the arrival of the capitalist phalanx in Beijing, whose center thoroughfare still was guarded by oversized portraits of Marx, Engels, Lenin, and Stalin.

Then, moving to Beijing was like moving back in time to a sheltered Hollywood back lot. Jay Mathews, the first Beijing correspondent for the *Washington Post,* wrote a self-deprecating piece in 1979 about turning the parking lot at the Peking Hotel into a baseball field for his son. Crowds of Chinese were attracted to the spectacle of "a clumsy American father chasing ground balls," while the armed People's Liberation Army (PLA) soldiers, who kept the spectators in place, were enthusiastic fans of the young American batter and his father. In retrospect, the scene has a touchingly odd combination of disparate elements—the American pastime protected, in a way, by the armed defenders of the Chinese revolution. The scene would not be possible a few years later, when the parking lot was crowded with imported automobiles, and the PLA guards had been replaced by pedicab touts and money changers, whose entrepreneurial aggressiveness provided visiting Americans with an uncomfortable reminder of a less polite form of their own capitalist heritage. Nor would it be possible ten years later, in 1989, after the PLA lost its benign image in the wake of martial law in May and the bloody street fighting in June.[1]

A mild harbinger of the violent capacity of the PLA can be seen when one looks back on the earlier period, at the beginning of the 1980s, when the capital was still unaccustomed to the presence of foreigners. Foreigners noticed that the PLA guards could display an unfriendly face, but it was reserved for Chinese visitors who sought entrance to the hotel, the Friendship Store, or the other places the authorities reserved for foreigners only. Ironically, the Chinese guards could be friendly to baseball-playing Americans, the representatives of the opposition, and most unfriendly to members of the Chinese public, who were supposed to be their protected charges. Americans were taken aback by being treated favorably in a country that had so recently denounced them. In 1979, for example, shortly after the United States switched diplomatic recognition from Taiwan to the People's Republic, an American who two weeks before in Taiwan had been ordered out of a taxicab when the driver discovered the nationality of his passenger, was pleasantly surprised in Beijing when the Capital Taxi Company provided prompt service upon being told the customer was from the United States. A longtime foreign resident recalled that this had not been the case before. "Americans used to have to wait an hour, so they would say instead that they were Albanians. Now it's the Albanians who have to wait forever."[2]

Before arriving in Beijing, Americans expected the worst imaginable living conditions; upon arrival, however, they discovered the physical accommodations were not as bad as they had anticipated. Some companies arranged for the use of special quarters. One apartment—"obscenely large" in the words of the American resident—had three bedrooms, living room, dining room, enormous kitchen, three baths, and a maid's quarters. Another company occupied an estate complete with swimming pool, tennis court, and jogging path. These were exceptions, certainly, but Americans discovered that even the Peking Hotel turned out not to be the abominable pit they had expected. It had air conditioning, television, and little touches, like motorized window curtains, that were modern and quaint at the same time, reminding visitors like James Sterba of America in the 1950s. A public relations executive, upon arrival in 1979, declared with unmistakable surprise, "This is not slumming by any means."[3]

American expatriates realized it was unseemly to complain too much about physical privations or the lack of familiar foods on the shelves of the Friendship Store. Most were acutely aware of the disparity between their accommodations and meals and those of the average Chinese family, even in Beijing, one of the richest areas in the country. One American woman whose husband worked for Beijing Jeep, a joint venture with American Motors, explained to a visiting hometown reporter from Milwaukee that living in China presented problems like locating a turkey for Thanksgiving or cinnamon for a cake. The American realized, however, that such complaints would seem petty when printed, and she tried to draw a lesson for Americans that could be learned from the Chinese: get along with less, do without. With so little in material possessions, the Chinese appeared to "get along fine." It was a lesson that left unstated the tacit dichotomy—materially rich West and spiritually rich East—that had so long dominated foreign and Chinese views of each other. But the lesson did not take. Expatriate Americans did not cheerfully greet the absence of familiar consumer goods, and the Chinese, by their frenzied attempts to prosper as quickly as the economic reforms permitted, themselves seemed to repudiate the idea that their former privation had been fine with them.[4]

Some Americans did try weakly to put a better face on the material poverty of China, which could not be erased easily, and to curb their complaints about irritating material privations. But they made no effort to put a better face on the way the Chinese authorities, in this early period around 1980, willfully isolated foreigners and made their lives in Beijing suffocatingly hermetic. Expatriates had only each other for friends, and though their social universe was often "international" in encompassing many nationalities, the Chinese hosts were missing. It was a condition that was harder to bear because it was the result of deliberate policy. The PLA guards at the front of the Peking Hotel were merely the most visible part of a security apparatus that restricted individual contacts between foreigners and Chinese and enforced psychological isolation. In no other place, well-traveled expatriates said, did they find that they had no true friends among the local people. For gregarious Americans, this was an unanticipated and biting privation.[5]

The physical segregation of foreign residents made it easy for the authorities to control informal contacts with Chinese outside of business. In the United States, anyone can enter the lobby and public areas of a major hotel, but the guest rooms are private; in China, the entire hotel compound was private—no one was permitted to pass through the gate at the perimeter without authorization—but once inside, guest rooms were no less "public" than lobbies. Rooms were secured not by locks but by floor attendants, who had a different understanding of private and public space than their American guests. They entered guest rooms frequently every day without knocking (and heedless of the consternation of the foreign guests). One crew made the bed; another cleaned the bathroom; still another barged in unannounced with the mail, and so on, throughout the day. Experienced foreign hands advised that it was best to stay fully clothed unless one stood in the security of a locked bathroom. Yet as far as an outside Chinese visitor was concerned, the guest room of a foreign acquaintance was an impossibly distant sanctum sanctorum. And as far as the American guests were concerned, the hotels, as physically comfortable as they were, served as a gilded isolation ward.[6]

Chinese acquaintances who came to the hotel compounds in which foreigners stayed had to face the humiliation of being turned away at the gate by guards. If they got as far as the hotel door, they had to register and state their business, a procedure designed to create uneasiness and leave a hint of possible future inquiries from the Public Security Bureau about improper fraternization with foreigners. The diplomats and journalists who lived in three special apartment compounds had a little more privacy than the businesspeople who stayed in hotels. Although their apartments were not under the surveillance of floor attendants on duty around the clock, their compounds were guarded just as well against even invited Chinese guests. Foreigners who wanted to invite Chinese to their homes had to smuggle them through the gates hidden in the backs of their cars.[7]

Some American expatriates speculated about other reasons why it was so hard then to make close Chinese friends. Perhaps it was also a problem of culture. Americans who had lived in Taiwan before they had gone to the People's Republic recalled that it was not easy to make close friends there either, but at least no artificial barriers stood in the way. Americans could, and did, live in Chinese homes in Taiwan. In Beijing, the opportunity to leave the foreign ghetto and live with Chinese was as romantically appealing as it was practically impossible. As long as the authorities kept such tight restrictions on contacts between foreigners and Chinese, Americans who longed to break free of the segregated hotel life did not have to confront a contradiction inherent in the two most frequent American complaints, material privations and isolation from Chinese society. One American astutely observed that if Americans in Beijing were suddenly given permission to live with Chinese families, and brought along refrigerators and washing machines and VCRs and all the other appliances they regarded as essential to making life comfortable, the sought-after "integration" would be elusive.[8]

In a political climate in which the Chinese state frowned upon overly close contacts between foreigners and Chinese, Americans also worried that incipient friendship with Chinese acquaintances could endanger the Chinese friends. Americans discovered that the Chinese they met, or rather the Chinese who sought Americans out, defined friendship in ways that made Americans, sooner or later, uncomfortable. One American businessman explained the difference by characterizing American friendships as "easy to make and superficial," and Chinese friendships as "difficult to develop and terrifically involved." Americans were dismayed when Chinese friends asked for favors that escalated without apparent end, starting with requested purchases on their behalf at the Friendship Store and moving upward to the point where the Americans felt there was no limit to what was asked, including arranging and paying for travel abroad. The Chinese, when they got to the United States, continued to expect more from their American friends than the Americans thought reasonable, and stories of unusual requests circulated among expatriates and jaundiced their views of Chinese in general. Imagine the brazenness, said one American, of the Chinese who were traveling in the United States on business, who had misbudgeted and had run low on money, and expected their American friend, and not his company, to pay personally for the remainder of their expenses.[9]

The American host in the story was also aghast that the Chinese delegation invited themselves to stay in his father's house; here the different conceptions of public and private space are revealed again. It did not take many such stories for Americans to generalize inductively that friendship with a Chinese person carried with it serious risks for the American as well, not political risks, but the frightening financial risk of being expected to pay for trips abroad, or for college education for the

Chinese friend's children. Americans often talked about the "exchange relationships" that defined Chinese friendships in Chinese society, as well as those with foreigners: the *quid pro quo* that seemed to be the basis of all social relationships; the careful calculation of reciprocated favors; the apparent absence of friendships that were free of calculation of potential personal advantage and connections for the future. Though not as self-conscious about such calculations, Americans also assumed that some rough *quid pro quo* balanced their own friendships; that is why the Chinese, by asking so much of their foreign acquaintances without apparent thought to balance, seemed so peculiar.

At the most personal level of individual Chinese and Americans who wanted to be friends—but whose respective needs and conception of what constituted friendship were so different—it was inevitable that the requests for favors would be asymmetrical, given the inescapable disparity between developed world and Third World. If other Third World countries seemed to be more fertile ground for friendships with expatriate Americans, despite the same material disparity, one might suggest that the Chinese stood out because of the bluntness of their requests. This lack of inhibition in making requests of their foreign friends in turn could be explained, as some foreigners did, as the same phenomenon seen in Chinese friendships with one another. But one could also say that the requests Chinese made of foreigners in some cases seemed edged with a distinguishing sharpness that came from an implicit sense of entitlement, a sense born from years of political teaching about the iniquities of Western capitalism.

If we were back in the United States, argued one American expatriate in Beijing, we would be too busy with work and family to maintain many close friendships there. Given that American expatriates were at least as busy in China, he reasoned, it was unrealistic to think it was the artificial barriers that were keeping foreigners from having many friends. Work in Beijing tended to displace all else: six long days a week, and ten, twelve, or more hours a day, mediating between American employers and Chinese clients, all of whom seemed equally impatient. "Everything is a crisis," summarized one exhausted staff member. The absence of basic services taken for granted in the United States changed what elsewhere would have been a minor errand into a major production. The phone system was perpetually jammed (some offices had an employee whose only job was to keep dialing numbers until a connection was made); shouting at the top of one's voice over the phone was often required. Office supplies were difficult to obtain; an American company that opened in Shanghai waited in vain to be approached by Chinese supply houses offering office equipment, lightbulbs, mops, and other supplies. The Americans were ready to buy, but the Chinese never came to sell. For Americans this was mystifying until they saw for themselves, in the course of time-consuming searches for supplies in the city, that the Chinese distribution system was unlike anything at home. Desirable goods arrived erratically and sold out immediately. The only way to secure what one needed was to shop constantly and improve the odds that one would happen to be in the right store, at the right time, when a new shipment arrived.[10]

Short of personnel, American managers in Beijing had to do much of the typing, filing, and scheduling (and American women had to suppress the feeling that the work they were doing was the gender-typed secretarial drudgery from which they had thought they had escaped). American expatriates also had to devote much time and energy to hosting visitors from the United States (sometimes bearing the most distant of connections, like a brother-in-law of a customer who happened to be touring China) and Chinese clients who came from all over China (because they were no less frustrated by the phone system than the Americans). The expatriates who lived in Beijing expected visiting Americans to be reasonably self-sufficient. One expatriate observed that American visitors "of very high stature come to China, and turn into children, and need to be taken care of twenty-four hours a day." In fact, the visitors did encounter formidable language and bureaucratic difficulties when attempting the simplest errand on their own, but the explanation that the more experienced resident put on it was that China's strangeness alone produced a "paralyzing effect."[11]

The Chinese visitors who arrived unannounced often stayed for days at a time and needed equal attention. One had to maintain a cheerful demeanor for everyone, what one American called the "smiling-good-guy-friend-of-China" look. It was a regimen that for some Americans was exhausting. The uncontrolled descent upon the office of sundry visitors and clients was also enervating because there was no place to which one could retreat. At the Peking Hotel, home and office were either adjacent or identical (Virginia Kamsky gave slide presentations to American board chairmen and Chinese ministers in the only room available, her hotel room, with the projector propped on the bed and the slides projected on the wall). There was no place to go home to, where the door could be barred. "Our hotel is a place for Chinese to work," said one American expatriate, "not for us to live in." The Peking Hotel staff even enforced parietal rules that only heightened the feeling of confinement and fish-bowl surveillance. An American businesswoman was awoken one night at 2 A.M. with a call from the front desk which informed her that they were "missing" a male guest and wanted to know if he was in her room. Eventually such bed checks were relaxed, but the hotel still posted a regulation that visitors were not allowed in rooms between 10 P.M. and 9 A.M.[12]

Given these working and living conditions, American companies thought it best to send unmarried or unaccompanied "single-status" employees who were married but whose spouses were not allowed to go under company policy. The assumption was that unemployed spouses in Beijing, not knowing Chinese and left idle in hotel rooms while their wives or husbands were preoccupied with a challenging job that demanded long hours, would be miserable. Childless couples were also favored over those with children. In a survey of American expatriates in Beijing in the early 1980s, about 40 percent were single or on single-status; and of those who did have children, a majority had left them at home or at an intermediate commuting base with their spouses.[13]

Yet the married expatriates who had families living with them in Beijing believed they could handle the challenges of China much better. "The family is a cushion," said one, whose wife, a teacher at a local school, and whose children had their own separate windows on Chinese society. In 1979, when some of the American children attended Chinese schools, instruction was in Chinese, and though they were put into classes exclusively for foreign children, they brought home a glimpse of a curriculum different from that their American parents had known. The ten-year-old son of one American expatriate returned home one day, for example, proudly announcing that he had won first place in field games at his school and had been sent to all-city competition—in the grenade throw. Parents observed that living in China made their children independent and resourceful, and envied the way they were able to get around town on their own.[14]

Only about a quarter of the accompanying spouses in Beijing were working outside the home, according to a 1984 survey. Those who did not work followed their own preferences, spending time either in relatively solitary pursuits such as sewing or reading, or in group activities such as bridge or social clubs. In either case, their lives were mostly self-contained and would not have varied much in other expatriate posts. But feelings of loneliness were pervasive. In the emotionless language of a survey instrument, "spouse adjustment" was one item that was tracked, and in the case of the 1984 survey, the adjustment was described as "poor" or "very poor" in 20 percent of the cases. For all the exoticism of its locale, life in Beijing for many Americans was simply boring. If it was any consolation, foreigners decided life in Beijing did not seem to be any less boring for the Chinese residents. Why else would young Chinese men ride around on buses in their free time for want of something more exciting to do? Why else would the minor collision of two bicyclists instantly attract a crowd of hundreds? Or why else, foreigners wondered, would the Chinese have nothing better to do than spend whole summer evenings squatting in front of the large hotels, watching the foreigners come and go?[15]

In the early 1980s, the expatriates felt they were under the watchful gaze of Chinese society all the time, and indeed they were. Travel within China provided no respite. Foreigners were still not permitted to go without special permission beyond an encircling perimeter around the city, and travel by train or plane to other Chinese cities also required the permission of the police and issuance of travel papers, the equivalent of an internal visa. Unlike the Japanese, who were more accustomed to adjusting their movements to the limits imposed by geography, Americans were used to being unfettered. It was more frustrating for them to live in China, a country whose size exceeded even that of their home country, yet to be so bound to one city. One American compared his earlier life in Abu Dhabi with that in Canton, which seemed much more claustrophobic. "Something that's very important to me is the opportunity to get away from people," he said, hastening to add that he did not see himself as an antisocial person. It was nice, however, to be able "to get in a car and drive somewhere," a luxury that had been possible even in the small sheikdom of the United Arab Emirates, but paradoxically was not possible in the immensity of China.[16]

Malcolm Forbes exemplified the Americans who hated artificial limits and pushed at them whenever possible. Although he went to China in 1982 only as a short-term visitor, he managed to slip out from the constrictions imposed upon resident Americans. The story begins with a balloon-motorcycle entourage that Forbes took with him to China. The decision to take *Forbes* magazine's sardonic subtitle *Capitalist Tool* to the People's Republic as the team name should have given the Chinese an inkling of the consciously provocative behavior that was to follow.

Forbes and the five other team members saw themselves as free-spirited motorcyclists and balloonists who would work their way from Xian to Beijing as they pleased. Their motorcycles were Harley-Davidson FXRs, which were described by a team member as consciously chosen to make a statement: "As big and bad and baroque as any motorcycles you have ever seen." What the Chinese thought they had given permission for, however, was a closely supervised tourist excursion, with many visits to temples and model communes, some motorcycling, and occasional permission to provide demonstration rides in the balloon as long as it was kept on a tether. At times, as many as forty Chinese security officials and other bureaucrats accompanied the six-person team. Free flight was a particular concern of the Chinese hosts, and Forbes spent most of his trip apparently obsessed with getting exactly what the Chinese authorities were determined to deny. At a dinner near the end of his visit, Forbes whispered in a conspiratorial tone to his American balloonist:

> Listen, what if tomorrow when we are giving rides on the tether at the sports college, what if I were to just untie the knots and take off? I mean, what could they do? Throw me out of the country? I'm leaving on Friday. Impound the balloon? I'm giving it to them as a present. Arrest me? Shoot me down?[17]

The "accident" happened just as planned, though a Chinese javelin thrower was in the basket along with Forbes when the tethers were cast loose; as the balloon ascended in free flight, the Chinese passenger gamely waved to the crowd below, in the words of an American, like "the homecoming queen in a parade." The balloon landed on the artillery range of a military base (as soldiers ran up to the descending basket, Forbes shouted identification, "We are from Am-er-i-ca," and the soldiers, he claimed, gasped to think that the foreigners had traveled so far in a balloon). Forbes, being Forbes, did not suffer any punishment for his prank.[18]

The visit of the *Capitalist Tool* team expressed perfectly the clash of American and Chinese sensibilities. For representation of the American anarchic impulses there were the Harleys for roaring across the open country, rebellion plotted at a stifling formal banquet, and most symbolically perfect of all, a balloon soaring free as the conclusion. Opposed were the enemies of free expression—the Chinese public security officials and other disapproving functionaries who sought to control the itinerary. The Americans felt their Chinese handlers were squeezing them into the mold of conventional tourists, and the Forbes entourage had the power not only to resist but to also live out the wildest and most cherished fantasies of all expatriates.

Unlike Forbes, Americans who were regular residents in Beijing could not defy Chinese restrictions with such impunity. If they broke the rules, they at least had to do so without drawing attention to themselves. American companies responded to the problems of restricted internal travel and little available Western entertainment by providing generous rest-and-recreation policies, in many cases allowing three or four R&R trips out of China each year. Some companies provided more trips to single managers than to married ones, and more trips to expatriates who were posted outside the comparatively luxurious Beijing. The restorative benefits of the excursion were regarded by some companies to be so important that they literally required their expatriate managers to leave the country periodically (though few seemed to have needed any prompting). When Jonathan Zamet, a consultant who specialized in international compensation, discovered that the average American working in China received about three leaves a year, whereas expatriates working in Saudi Arabia received an average of about half as many leaves, he was mystified. "I understand that China is a very difficult place to live in," Zamet said, "but I can't understand there being twice as many leaves as in Saudi Arabia." The reason for the generous leave policies was undoubtedly the same as that for the generous financial compensation: China was located as far from the pale marking the world of the familiar as one could conceive. Living in the Soviet Union may have been a possible analogue, but China was culturally further away. Westerners who had lived in both Moscow and Beijing reported that they found Soviet society induced more paranoia about surveillance, but life in China was more isolating, a paradox in the world's most populous country.[19]

The isolation seemed less confining after the creation of a more complete expatriate world, beginning with the opening of the first joint-venture hotels, the Jianguo (1982), the Great Wall (1983), and the Holiday Inn Lido (1984). The Lido apartment complex provided an alternative to hotel life, and a new joint-venture supermarket offered fresh croissants, Danish brie, and hothouse lettuce. Gone were the old days in which the rare arrival of cheese and butter in the Friendship Store would cause such a sensation in the expatriate community that the news upstaged, on one occasion, the visits of British Prime Minister Margaret Thatcher and Soviet Deputy Premier Ivan Arkhipov. New office buildings for foreign companies, beginning with the opening of Rong Yiren's CITIC Building, made separation of office and home possible. But the grocery stores and bakeries and discotheques and sports broadcasts from the Armed Forces network pulled in by satellite dishes, while making life in Beijing more familiar and more comfortable, did not solve the problem of isolation. They did not break down the separation of foreigner and Chinese, and that portion of the isolation that was caused by the material gap got worse, not better, over time.[20]

Foreigners were, in fact, ambivalent about their distance from the gritty, sooty Chinese reality that lay beyond the protected complexes of their hotels and offices. Like the commuting New York stockbrokers in Tom Wolfe's *Bonfire of the Vanities,* weary expatriates in China felt the urge to "insulate, insulate, insulate." Outside the sanctuary of the hotels, a simple meal in a Chinese restaurant meant an ordeal of crowds, spitting, long waits, surly service, limited menu, and stares from Chinese visiting the capital from other provinces who found the physical differences of the foreigner, the Other in the flesh, of inexhaustible interest. With the opening of modern Western hotels and restaurants, foreigners had alternatives to disagreeable brushes with *echt* China. One longtime American expatriate explained: "Life is more tolerable now because there are restaurants to go [to] where you feel you're not in China." He continued, "There are places where you can get service that doesn't make you uptight." But these places were not readily accessible to Chinese of ordinary means.[21]

The Chinese authorities joined the new growth industry of building recreational oases for Beijing expatriates. Golf courses were opened for the first time in the history of the People's Republic. The North China International Shooting Academy opened for business near Beijing in 1987, providing recreational shooting with all manner of weapons, from pistols to anti-tank rocket launchers. And in the same year the management of the Diaoyutai Guest House began to offer "club memberships" to foreign corporations that cost $40,000 and permitted two top corporate officers to use the pool and other accommodations indefinitely. The Chinese shrewdly marketed the club like a country club in the United States, emphasizing the facilities less than the fellowship of powerful figures who already belonged, like honorary members President Yang Shangkun and Prime Minister Li Peng, who did not have to pay. By 1989 sixty companies had signed up, including Occidental Petroleum, Johnson & Johnson, and AT&T.[22]

These changes made expatriate life in Beijing quite different in the late 1980s than it had been in the days of the Peking Hotel monopoly of the late 1970s. But outside of Beijing, Shanghai, and Canton, where expatriates were concentrated in the largest numbers, Americans were dispersed to posts in places that were much slower in acquiring similar bubbles of Western hotels, restaurants, and clubs. When American researchers inquired how the expatriates in the outback spent their free time, they were surprised to see that "sleeping" was frequently listed as a recreational activity, a response they had not gotten when interviewing expatriates in the major cities. Even in the capital, with all its material comforts, we see the paradox—American expatriates in China wanted to be there, yet the romantically appealing aspects of such an assignment were submerged by the dominating fact of foreignness, by the nagging ambivalence of wanting, but then again not wanting, to be a part of Chinese society. For many, the initial excitement was ground down by the isolation, the ennui, and the frustrations in battling Chinese bureaucracy in its myriad forms. The experience could produce a cumulative exhaustion that short R&R trips eventually could not overcome. When enervation and cynicism proved irreversible, one had to return home.[23]

It may be tempting to explain these problems as the symptoms of provincial Americans who simply had had little prior acquaintance with life outside the United States. It is true that American companies preferred comparatively short overseas assignments, generally two to three years, shorter than the average assignment for the Europeans (three or more years) or the Japanese (five years) and would seem to be an indication of poor preparation or comparative weakness. But if we look at those Americans whose experience and hardiness made them stand apart from the average, we see that there was little correlation, in fact, between length of prior foreign experiences and degree to which expatriates were able to settle happily into assignments in China. By the nature of their business in oil drilling, or mining equipment sales, or industrial plant engineering, or aircraft maintenance, or other industries, most of the companies that posted American expatriates to remote locations in China, with the most arduous living conditions, had had many decades of experience in handling difficult conditions around the world. Their employees and their families were in many cases people who had grown up in hardscrabble country, in Appalachia, or rural Texas, or other places in the United States where the amenities of the new luxury hotels in Beijing would have been as unknown as they were to the Chinese. Many of them regarded themselves as permanent expatriates and had lived virtually all of their adult lives outside the United States. They were no strangers to hardship. But China presented even these veterans with frustrating conditions they had never seen anywhere else. Bob Linton, a representative for General Electric, for example, who had spent twenty-eight years in a dozen different countries, and in 1989 was living in the Beijing Lido, the nicest apartment complex in the entire country, described his China assignment as one in which "everything is a struggle." His wife had found life in Beijing so vexing that she spent half of each year away. The high failure rate for expatriate assignments in China is suggested by a stray fact in a 1985 survey of sixty-six companies in China, which reported that no fewer than fifteen expatriates had returned home prematurely.[24]

One aspect of the adjustment problem, the debilitating Otherness that the foreigner was always reminded of, could be checked by looking at the experiences of Chinese-Americans or other ethnic Chinese who were sent to China by American companies. If they wished, they could shed the sense of Otherness by changing clothes and slipping out onto the street incognito. The power to become invisible at will was much envied by non-Chinese expatriates. But foreigners of Chinese descent had their own problems, because being an ethnic Chinese on Chinese soil opened troubling existential questions about identity that non-Chinese did not have to face.

The difference in the two worlds that ethnic Chinese expatriates in China inhabited is revealed in the depiction of their role on the two sides. In newspapers and popular magazines in the People's Republic, the American identity of Chinese-American businesspeople who came to China was submerged; they were described as devoted patriots, tireless contributors to the economic development of the motherland. In the standard profile of Chinese-Americans, journalistic convention demanded the mention of exactly how many hours were devoted to helping the People's Republic. *Guangming Daily* told readers in 1985, for example, that Li Huiying, an American who had started a trading company that specialized in technology trade with China, worked seven days a week and was so busy that she had no time to go to movies (Li was quoted as saying, "We do not do this work to make money. Our wish is to do our utmost for the Four Modernizations."). *Beijing Daily,* in a profile of an American television producer, Zhang Wen, followed the same pattern in its description—Zhang was said to spend four hours every day in a library, studying unspecified "science and technology of the world's advanced countries," to help China. Popular magazines were filled with inspirational stories of Chinese-Americans who had made good and were returning to do what they could for China; Wang An, founder of the Wang Laboratories computer company that bears his name, was a favorite subject of these biographies. The point was to demonstrate the fusion of Chinese-American interests and those of mainland Chinese. Here there was no Otherness associated with the accident of different citizenship; theirs was reputedly just one large happy family, newly reunited with the return of the filial sons and daughters from America.[25]

The American press, however, stressed just the opposite, emphasizing the alienation and ideological distance Chinese-Americans found when they went to China. The *New York Times,* for example, ran a long profile in 1988 on Margaret Lee, the Honeywell representative who had grown up in the People's Republic and who in 1982 went to the United States to attend Carleton College in Minnesota. Her story, as the *Times* told it, was one of drastic ideological conversion. Lee had gone from the fires of the Cultural Revolution, to Carleton, to life as a Honeywell expatriate based in Hong Kong who went to the People's Republic on business. She dressed in Christian Dior suits, lived in an expensive apartment on Hong Kong's prestigious Kennedy Road, and had her child served from an engraved silver cup. These details were all carefully noted by the American reporter. Lee's story was appealing to Americans not only for its encompassing such breathtaking change, but also for its satisfying confirmation that their system attracted others without need of proselytizing or crass ideological marketing, that it stood above the rest by virtue of its own self-evident merits.[26]

Lee's overnight self-transformation took place, it seemed, upon mere contact with the bounteous American system. When she arrived at Carleton, she was described as a tiny figure huddled in a Chinese jacket, but her self-directed remaking began immediately, when she translated her Chinese name *Hong* as Scarlet, instead of Red, discarding the revolutionary association that her parents had intended when she had been born (and acquiring in its place the name that to American minds will always be associated with the heroine of *Gone with the Wind,* who could not possibly be more antithetical to the Iron Girls of the Cultural Revolution). No American coaching was visible. The new Scarlet replaced the old Red before her American friends realized what was happening. Roy Grow, one of her Carleton professors, said: "One week I saw her in a Mao jacket and Mao pants, the next week I saw her in a white tennis outfit with a racquet over her shoulder."[27]

After graduation and induction into the ranks of Honeywell, Lee returned to China, but it was less a journey of repatriation than of expatriation from her adoptive home. Americans valued her presence, and that of other emigrants from the People's Republic now among the ranks of expatriates, for much more than business reasons. These most recently created Chinese-Americans provided reassuring confirmation that the frustrations of living in China were not a simple subjective problem of cultural difference; when Chinese from the People's Republic, like Lee, were placed in the same position in China as native-born Americans, they had the same complaints. How could it be dismissed as the whining of American provincials when Lee herself, without prompting, spoke with abhorrence of the crowds in Chinese cities, of the fighting necessary just to board a bus ("life doesn't have to be such a hard struggle"), of the lackadaisical pace in the workplace. Her full assimilation of American sensibilities was noted by her Honeywell supervisors. Lee's initiative and drive in her career received perhaps the highest praise possible when the president of Honeywell Asia-Pacific said, "She takes the ball and runs with it." The Americanization of Scarlet, *née* Red, was complete.[28]

Americans were delighted to have the chance to employ a PRC native such as Lee whose ideological alienation from her birthplace was so visible. But Americans were not comfortable appointing PRC nationals to the top positions in their China offices. Foreign representative offices in Beijing and other Chinese cities were composed of two groups: the expatriates of many different nationalities who held senior positions of responsibility, and Chinese nationals who had to be hired through FESCO, the state bureau that belonged to the Ministry of State Security and wielded monopoly control over the supply of Chinese staff until the late 1980s. The division within the office between foreigners and Chinese was quite clear. All Chinese employees disappeared for closed meetings every Saturday afternoon, when office-skill training and political study took place. Foreigners assumed that anything they said or did was likely to be reported at the Saturday meetings, and protection of business secrets was impossible. The Chinese government also did not like to see its FESCO assignees developing too close an attachment to the foreign companies; getting too close to one's foreign boss was said to be a criterion for being fired by the state. The foreigners, for their part, wanted their Chinese staff members to develop loyalty, but at the same time foreign companies were reluctant to appoint locals to jobs of top responsibility. They hesitated not just because of doubts about the sophistication of Chinese business practices and skills, but also because of lingering fears that the employees would take the side of the Chinese government in any dispute or would pass on proprietary information to the state security apparatus which, after all, was their real employer.[29]

In 1984 a Canadian bank, the Bank of Nova Scotia, blurred the line of separation between Chinese and foreign employees when it appointed Guo Bohua, a PRC citizen, to the position of chief representative in Beijing, a role otherwise occupied exclusively by expatriates. In outward appearance, Guo, who was thirty-six years old, displayed the correct style of an international businessperson: three-piece suits, digital watch, chauffeur, and able skill in wining and dining clients at expensive restaurants. He played the role so well that few people he met realized that he was a mainland Chinese. "People think that I am from Taiwan, Hong Kong, or the U.S.," he said. "When they first meet me, they always say: 'Ah, Mr. Guo, your [Mandarin] is excellent.' " Yet the expatriate community treated Guo frostily, and was scandalized when he attended the Foreign Bankers' Association's monthly meeting for the first time in October 1985. As long as Guo remained an employee of FESCO (Guo received only a small fraction of the salary that the Canadian bank paid to FESCO, which remained his nominal employer), he would be seen as Them, not Us. The personal past that included a chapter in the Cultural Revolution, which in the case of Americanized Margaret Lee was mentioned as an innocuous bit of detail to show how far she had traveled, was used in Guo's case to suggest something sinister. In the eyes of foreign bankers, he was an "ex-Red Guard," whose radical past may have been only temporarily papered over.[30]

How ironic for Guo and other Chinese, who had lived through the Cultural Revolution when Loyalty Dances honoring Chairman Mao were demanded of everyone to prove ideological fervor and purity, only to find that foreigners, twenty years later, demanded proof of ideological fervor and purity too. They required, as the Red Guards once had, a complete break with the past. The foreigners were no less ideological than the Red Guards had been; they were merely gentler and more subtle in administering their own tests of loyalty.

The Chinese public was acutely aware of the lines separating Us and Them that the government drew around the foreigner hotels, Friendship

Stores, reserved floors in restaurants and special waiting rooms in railway stations, and other places designated for the exclusive use of foreigners. College students who had returned from studies in the United States and had gotten accustomed to access to all retail establishments were among those Chinese who were most public in their denunciation of the restrictions that kept Chinese out of places in their own country. In 1986, for example, Americans watched with concern as a recent Chinese graduate of an American university ignored the sentries positioned at the door of a major hotel in Beijing and headed to the elevator, defying the guards' demands that he stop and register at the door. He managed to get on the elevator, but was intercepted by a group of attendants when he got off at his floor. Livid with anger, the young man freed himself and dared them to call the police. Such impassioned confrontations were frequent and heartrending. An American reporter who spoke Chinese told the story of witnessing an old Chinese man, wearing shabby blue clothes and a long beard, being turned away from a Friendship Store. "Why can't I go in there? All those foreigners can go in." A store clerk smiled nervously as the old man went on, "Isn't my money good enough? Damn it, this is not fair," and threw some coins in contempt at the clerk's feet. The incident put a somber pall over what had been a happy shopping excursion until then. The American brought the story about the old man to a close: "We picked up our parcels and walked past him to our waiting bus. I felt uncomfortable and a bit ashamed."[31]

The Chinese public had other reasons to feel bitter about the special privileges the state accorded foreigners. The introduction in the spring of 1980 of Foreign Exchange Certificates (soon referred to as FECs), which were scrip that foreigners were supposed to use in place of the regular currency, drew more public attention to the line between Us and Them. The hotels, restaurants, and other places that served foreigners accepted only FECs, which theoretically should not have affected the ordinary Chinese person on the street, who was denied entrance anyhow. But FECs soon were recognized by other Chinese establishments and their employees as preferable to the regular currency—with FECs, one could get hold of the forbidden fruits of the Friendship Store, for example—and ultimately the Chinese public was affected, and increasingly enraged, by the dual currency system.

The Chinese press tried to vent some of the anger, and curb the unauthorized adoption of FEC-only practices around the country, by printing letters to the editor that told of inappropriate attempts to collect FECs instead of regular currency from ordinary Chinese. A sample letter published in a Chinese business newspaper in 1987 conveys the deep resentment, and the feelings about Us and Them, stirred up by the FECs. The Chinese writer, who had recently stayed in a middling hotel for Chinese, not foreigners, had gone to a shop in the hotel on a rainy night to buy cigarettes. "FECs Only," hung a sign over the counter, even though Chinese brands, which had not been imported and presumably had no legitimate claim on foreign exchange, were on display. The writer tramped off into the rain, but before he left, he took the liberty of asking the clerk, "Now, how many guests at this hotel are going to have FECs?" The clerk ignored him, and he mused that perhaps she did not see him because he was not a foreigner but a Chinese, "with my black hair, yellow skin, and short nose." He had no objection to places that served foreign guests insisting on payment with FECs, but not other places, such as this hotel. The whole country seemed to him to be going mad over FECs. The headline of the essay was "Don't Forget The Chinese."[32]

Chinese also were angered by the preference cab drivers showed in picking up foreigners, who they knew would pay in FECs. Regular currency was increasingly rejected as acceptable legal tender. The Chinese public did not use taxis as frequently as foreigners did, of course, but when Chinese needed them, such as for a wedding reception, or for sending off visiting relatives to the train station, or other special occasions, hopping on a bicycle or taking a perpetually crowded bus would not serve well. Trips to the hospital, for anything other than the most acute medical emergency, also required use of a taxi. But the Chinese taxi drivers seemed to "cozy up to the 'Big Noses,' " said Beijing residents, and often refused point blank to accept Chinese passengers. The authorities tried to explain that the preference for foreigners, which was not denied, was not caused by a "worship of things foreign," but rather, by the imposition of monthly FEC quotas on the drivers. The explanation, however, hardly served to blunt popular anger at the sight of Chinese waving for cabs at the same time that the cabs remained idle, lined up at the hotels from which foreign passengers would eventually emerge.[33]

The larger the number of expatriates and tourists in Beijing, the more Chinese residents personally witnessed the dual system of services. In 1986, when law and economics students at Beijing University set up booths in a busy shopping district to answer questions about the dual currencies, a large crowd gathered to express righteous indignation. When someone asked why China needed two currencies when other countries had only one, the students explained that foreign exchange was needed to develop the economy. The crowd could not see, however, how an economic imperative had much connection to the humiliation of being denied service in a restaurant for lack of FECs. The foreigners, who were the beneficiaries of the favoritism the dual currency system institutionalized, were embarrassed about the privileges they enjoyed—some spoke of the system as a variant of apartheid in which Chinese were discriminated against in their own country. The controversy over FECs, they learned, could take on life-and-death significance, as when Shanghai experienced a gamma globulin shortage during a citywide hepatitis outbreak, and the available supplies were obtainable only with FECs.[34]

When the Chinese government tried to explain to foreigners, as it did to its own citizens, that the dual currency system affected only a small portion of the population, the explanation was ridiculed. "One could have said the same thing about the turn-of-the-century foreign concessions in China's coastal cities," remarked one Western reporter. History was much on the minds of the more thoughtful reporters and expatriates. The special privileges they enjoyed seemed eerily similar to those accorded to the foreigners of the "semi-colonial" era before the revolution. A Chinese-American shared with readers of the *New York Times* his last impressions of China during a trip in 1979, when he boarded the train at Kowloon, headed out to Hong Kong, and found two blond-bearded men sprawled across four chairs, drinking, laughing, oblivious of the other passengers, "enjoying themselves in the manner of colonialists of a bygone era."[35]

Foreigners were appalled to see their fellows sprawled out, figuratively speaking, throughout China, and to observe that high Chinese officials used the system of privileges for "foreign guests" for their advantage, right from the beginning.[35] In 1980, Jay Mathews noticed that loudspeakers along a busy street regularly blared: "Make way for the automobiles of foreigners and high officials"; Army officers and civilian officials of high rank could also be found in Friendship Stores. Foreigners thus had to worry about resentment not only of their own privileges, but also those of Chinese officials who took advantage of their status to obtain scarce goods for themselves under the protective banner of the foreigner. Expatriates in China grew concerned about popular resentment of a new elite in Chinese society, the employees of foreign companies or of those that catered to foreigners, whose access to special privileges and perceived air of self-importance drew additional unflattering attention to the foreign presence. Mathews returned to thoughts of the past: "Unfortunately, foreign life styles here in some ways recall the last century, which ended in 1900 with the Boxer Rebellion. In that year people probably little different than I mounted walls in Peking near where I now live and fired at mobs of rabidly antiforeign Chinese."[36]

After 1980, as the expatriate presence in Beijing grew, foreigners lived and worked, as they always had, within the hermetic world created specially for them. But as this world grew larger, it was harder to see the borders, and harder still to see beyond the surrounding insulation of foreign-oriented Chinese—the secretaries, drivers, waitresses, translators, room attendants, English-speaking Chinese acquaintances—who had a vested interest in keeping China open to foreign contacts. The number of these Chinese who personally had direct contact with Americans and other foreigners, however, was tiny, even in a city like Beijing, leaving aside the unseen 800 million or so who still lived in the countryside. Expatriates in Beijing knew that the Chinese with whom they had daily contacts had grown comfortable with their presence, but they had no way of knowing much about what lay beyond.

The Chinese state was happy to collect high rents and money from foreign firms granted the privilege of attempting to do business in China. But government authorities still preferred to think of the open-door policy as welcoming the impersonal abstractions of capital and technology, not a large number of foreign bodies who would make their homes in Beijing, Shanghai, Canton, and elsewhere. The foreign presence had always meant contagion, and postrevolutionary Chinese concern about foreign corruption of Chinese morals and introduction of sexually transmitted diseases only served to strengthen the traditional antibodies of hostility. In the mid-1980s, when China began to notice the worldwide threat of AIDS, the phenomenon described by Susan Sontag—illness as metaphor—found full expression in China. In the United States, the stigmatization of the Other fell upon the gay community; in China, it fell upon all foreigners.[37]

Even before the scourge of AIDS appeared outside China, foreigners inside China were viewed as sexually threatening. When the Communist government came to power in 1949, the authorities with much fanfare extirpated prostitution in China. Prostitution reappeared subsequently in many parts of the country, but local police ignored it. It was viewed as an intramural affair—liaisons between Chinese and Chinese—without apparent victims. But beginning in 1979, when expatriates began to arrive, both the state and the wider society had to confront

Chinese-foreign liaisons. Prostitution was an embarrassment because it exposed as false the state mythology that it had successfully ended the commercialization of sex, the shame of capitalist society. It was also sensitive for deeper political and racial reasons. The idea that Chinese women sold sex to foreigners evoked dark memories of the degraded and powerless state of China before 1949, and for many Chinese the mere thought of interracial sexual liaisons seemed improper and repulsive.

Most embarrassing of all, prostitution reappeared in the capital itself. In 1979, weekly dances that permitted Chinese and foreigners to dance together were restricted to foreigners after a short trial because Chinese prostitutes had drawn the attention of foreign reporters, and also of outraged Chinese who denounced the prostitutes in big-character posters ("Beware of Dance Fever") that were put up at the short-lived Democracy Wall. Municipal authorities arrested many Chinese women for prostitution and for a time banned all dancing between Chinese women and foreigners. Such controls proved impossible to enforce because Chinese and foreigners had too many other opportunities to meet, so the state had little recourse but to launch occasional antiprostitution campaigns and waves of arrests, the brunt of which fell upon the Chinese women, not their foreign clients.[38]

When Western businessmen were arrested for sleeping with Chinese women the foreigners faced brief detention, fines, and expulsion, though legally they could also face "re-education through labor." The threat of extreme sanctions was sobering. When a Siemens employee was expelled from China in 1987 after police burst into his hotel room in the middle of the night and found a Chinese woman in the bed, the company warned its other employees to learn a lesson from the incident. At about the same time, expatriates also read in the Chinese newspapers that a forty-three-year-old Shanghai man was sentenced to death for using pornographic videotapes "to corrupt young people."[39]

The case of the Siemens employee and other similar cases were especially troubling because they showed the dissimilarity between the Chinese system of criminal justice and familiar systems at home. In China, selling and buying sex were not formal crimes under the new criminal code; they fell only within the less formal administrative law, which was the responsibility of the Public Security Bureau, not a separate criminal judiciary. The Public Security Bureau was known for a capricious bent and appeared to have ulterior motives for prosecuting some cases and ignoring others. In the Siemens case, for example, foreigners speculated that the expulsion of the foreigner may have been retaliation for the defection of a Chinese employee of Siemens in West Germany. In other cases, the charge of consorting with a prostitute seemed to be subordinate to the more important racial issue, of keeping Chinese and foreigners sexually separated. Under the guise of fighting prostitution, the Chinese imposed punishments on foreign men and Chinese women who were dating or engaged to be married. In one Shanghai case, a couple was punished under the prostitution-related articles even though, when the police entered the foreigner's hotel room, the couple was dressed and not engaged in sex.[40]

Without the protection of extraterritoriality and separate criminal systems that foreign residents had enjoyed in the Chinese treaty ports in the nineteenth and early twentieth centuries, expatriates in post-revolutionary China feared the vagaries of a criminal system that was so different from their own. The first public trial of a Westerner in China since the Cultural Revolution was that of Richard Ondrik, an American businessman who was charged in 1985 with causing a fire in a Harbin hotel that claimed the lives of ten persons. Given the same basic circumstances—the fire appeared to have started in Ondrik's room, and he confessed that he may have fallen asleep while smoking on the night of the fire—Ondrik surely would have faced civil suits if the tragedy had occurred in the United States. But the criminality of his actions—he faced a possible sentence of seven years in jail as well as a compensatory fine of about $90,000—was not apparent. He told the Chinese court, "It is difficult to think of myself as a criminal. That is because the law of my country and that of China concerning such an accident are different."[41]

Foreign lawyers were not permitted to practice in China, so Ondrik was represented by a Chinese lawyer who performed as she was trained: that is, her statements to the court did not protest her client's innocence, but rather pleaded for leniency. Ondrik had his own counterarguments for his defense: The hotel had bought smoke detectors and exit lights but had not installed them; there were no fireproof doors or sprinkler systems; the fire extinguishers had not worked; once the fire was discovered, it had taken a half-hour for the fire brigade to arrive. In an American court, the prosecution would have stoutly resisted the attempt to place responsibility on the hotel's safety defects, but in China, the prosecution agreed that "objectively speaking," the hotel's facilities were quite wanting. This was not an important concession, however, because the point of the trial was not so much to investigate the circumstances surrounding the fire as it was to focus on individuals, not organizations or state agencies.[42]

Ondrik told the three judges who heard his case: "I am not a rich foreign tourist here to see the Great Wall, but a man who earns his salary working each day in your country." Foreign observers at the time speculated that the Chinese had prosecuted the case because of diplomatic pressure from North Korea, since five North Korean members of a government delegation had been among the ten killed. Indisputably, the Chinese judges were concerned in the trial to show that foreigners were not above the law. In the end, what seemed to matter most was that Ondrik had cooperated with the authorities during the pretrial investigation. He was fined $53,000 and given an eighteen-month jail sentence—light compared to the maximum possible of seven years—which was reduced still further to five months for good behavior.[43]

At the time of his sentencing, Ondrik predicted that his case would deter foreign businesspeople from going to China. But his experience did not deter even him. Within five months after finishing his sentence, Ondrik was back in China on business. He even went to Harbin, with no apparent hard feelings. By 1987 he had rejoined the expatriate community in China and lived in an apartment on the grounds of the Summer Palace in Beijing. He savored the change: "When I look out the window I can see a courtyard and garden. It's a lot better than looking out and seeing a guard tower and fence and people walking back and forth with submachine guns." The welcome that the Chinese extended Ondrik after his release reveals another difference between the American and Chinese criminal justice systems. In the United States, the former convict carries the lingering stigma of an undesirable. In China, Ondrik was hailed as completely rehabilitated, a walking advertisement for an effective system that reformed as well as punished. In looking back at his brush with an unfamiliar legal system, Ondrik said: "I think it was a very drastic demonstration that you're a guest in the country and that if they decide to turn on you they will."[44]

Expatriates in China were aware of their foreignness almost every moment; it was unsettling to think about the possibility, however remote, of being at the mercy of a different system of justice, with different kinds of charges and permissible evidence, a different kind of defense attorney and criteria of judgment. Foreigners risked punishment that overcompensated in severity to show that the Chinese state would not be bullied by anyone. In Ondrik's case the Chinese assumed his guilt, leaving only the degree of his contrition for judgment. But in the end they were lenient in setting his sentence, perhaps all the more so because he was a foreigner. His case left unresolved the question of where foreigners stood in the eyes of the Chinese state.

IV

IMPORTING MANAGEMENT

8.

MANAGERIALISM

The London office of the Bank of China is a curious anomaly because it has been open continuously from the late 1920s, maintaining an unobtrusive presence in a grimy building in an alley near the Bank of England. During most of the postrevolutionary period, the People's Republic and the capitalist world shared nothing but a sense of righteous ideological distaste for the other, yet China's London bankers were never recalled. They spent many of those years passing time with no known responsibilities other than watering the plants; they lived in the same offices in which they worked, and if they had any complaints about their lives, they kept them to themselves. They were all but forgotten by their Chinese employers and their British hosts.[1]

Then the 1980s arrived, and suddenly this Bank of China office was ideally located for China's move into the world of international finance. By 1984, the office was daily underwriting notes for foreign countries, snapping up Japanese government bonds, and dabbling in various debt securities. Other branch offices in Hong Kong, Singapore, New York, and Luxembourg attracted lines of foreign banking suitors. Chinese from the PRC were a puzzle to foreign observers. The Bank of China seemed so dowdy—even as its business took off, the tattered carpets of the London office remained—yet K. C. Wu, the deputy general manager, was an urbane cosmopolitan who mingled easily with the elite of London's financial circles.[2]

China, however, had very few operations with such up-to-date familiarity with capitalist practices and conventions. For the most part, China ventured out of its isolation after the Cultural Revolution on unsure legs. Chinese ministries and companies sought to expand abroad primarily to acquire the skills needed to survive in a capitalist environment, so sending Chinese expatriates to capitalist countries was more important initially than the business operations themselves. China had established about thirty companies in the United States by 1983, including some that had elegant showrooms in Manhattan, and all seemed to be well financed. They opened, however, with apparent utter lack of familiarity with American capitalism. Gong Benfang, head of one of the New York offices, confessed in 1983: "When we first came here, we were like blind men. We didn't know anyone, we had no friends or connections, and we didn't know what products would sell on the American market." Slowly, he and his compatriots learned by trial and error, though business was still not enough to pay the rent on his midtown offices. But Gong was not under the same pressure to show a quick profit in New York that many of his American counterparts felt in Beijing; Gong came prepared to lose money, he said, for five years. The losses were viewed as well-invested tuition.[3]

It was an expensive education. In 1983, the Chinese invested $2 million for a minority stake in Santec, a troubled manufacturer of computer printers based in a small town in New Hampshire, which was headed by a Chinese-American computer scientist, Jeffrey Chuan Chu, who had once told Deng Xiaoping that learning about management should have a higher priority than learning about computers, and who offered Santec as a place in which China could learn some lessons about capitalism. Unfortunately for the Chinese, the company was just emerging from Chapter 11 bankruptcy, and was struggling in a crowded market.

As the company suffered new losses, one American computer executive said: "The Chinese got talked out of some money. It's an example of the kind of mistakes they make when they don't do their homework properly." The People's Republic also paid a steep price when it ventured into investments in Hong Kong. When PRC-controlled companies invested almost $23 million to buy an interest in Conic, a manufacturer of television sets and specialty telephones, it was the first time PRC interests had bought a controlling stake in a publicly traded Hong Kong company. The new PRC investors appointed nine directors to the board, signaling their interest in playing an active part in managing a company in a capitalist system. The company they had chosen for the experiment, however, was in much poorer financial health than the

Chinese had been led to believe. Within six months, embarrassing disclosures led to suspension of trading of Conic's shares, and Alex Au, the company chairman, left town under the shadow of large, apparently irrecoverable loans that Conic had made to other companies Au owned. The Bank of China, which was the major lender, was shown to be not so savvy after all.[4]

China set up new joint ventures with foreign partners outside China—by 1982, seven joint ventures had been started with U.S. partners—but the Chinese were seen as being resistant to local ways. A Canadian executive pointed out the failure of the Chinese abroad to reciprocate the compromises Western businesspeople made when in China: "It's understood by everyone in China that you do business by Chinese customs and Chinese laws, but the Chinese have a lot of trouble accepting the corollary to that, [which is] adapting to Canadian customs and Canadian laws." In 1988, a Chinese construction company that did try to adapt to local ways when developing a residential project in Jacksonville, Florida, encountered a hostile reception.[5]

The Chinese company bought land and began to build Chinaberry Lakes, a suburban development planned to include 415 homes, a kiddie pool, a playground, and ponds stocked with fish; it had been encouraged by James Tullis, a city councilman who explained to his American constituents that "maybe by working with these people and showing them how capitalism works, we'll turn them on to it" back in China. The project got off to a bad start when the Chinese discovered that they had fallen for the classic American con—buying swampland in Florida. The Chinese had been led to believe that the property had already been "demucked"; a retired local minister said of the Chinese, "They was took, in street language." Moreover, local residents were not so interested in winning Communist converts over to capitalism. Fliers were circulated urging residents to band together and "defeat the Chinese Communists and their sympathizers." One resident said, "We've been taught to love everybody but hate the Communists ever since grade school, and now they want to build right behind us." Councilman Tullis was burned in effigy at a fund-raising barbecue held by a group of residents who opposed the project.[6]

These were some of the perils the Chinese risked when they sent representatives overseas to learn how to do business on capitalist terrain. While Americans went to China after the elusive grail of the market of One Billion, Chinese moved to the United States in quest of their own elusive grail, the managerial secrets that had made the U.S. economy the largest in the world. The Chinese quest was no less emotional than the American one. To many Chinese, *modern* management came to be equated with Western management, attracting a degree of devotion in many cases that matched that given by others to ideology or religion. One might coin a new "ism"—*managerialism*—to label this fervent belief in the transcendent power of Western management and the conviction that managerial techniques applied at the level of individual enterprises would be the salvation of modern China. The more contact that China had with capitalism, the more managerialism spread within China.

The attraction of the managerial techniques of capitalists has a long history, extending back to the early years of the Soviet Union. In the 1920s, Russians viewed Henry Ford not as a capitalist but as a revolutionary innovator; Fordson tractors shipped to the USSR promised a future free from want; mass-production techniques were widely copied, and one visitor in 1927 reported that the Russian people ascribed a "magical quality" to the very name of Ford: Communes and babies were named "Fordson." Even more remarkably, at the same time that Ford's antecedent, Frederick W. Taylor (1856–1915), the acclaimed father of "scientific management," was toasted by the bourgeoisie of the United States and Europe after World War I, he was also toasted by Lenin, Alexei Gastev, and other Soviet leaders who viewed scientific management, with its close study of efficient physical movements, its separation of planning from execution, and its piece-rate-based payment systems, as a rational way of raising productivity through "social engineering." Later, Stalin would follow; he once defined "the essence of Leninism" as "the combination of Russian revolutionary sweep with American efficiency."[7]

Much of Taylorism was in fact adapted eventually to Soviet industry, though the early praise of Taylor was later replaced in the Soviet Union by sharp criticism. It was the criticism that Taylorism was a system of "blood and sweat" that the Chinese had inherited from the Soviets during the tutelary period of the 1950s. When the Chinese began to reexamine their earlier dismissal of all things capitalist in the late 1970s and early 1980s, they had to search through early Soviet history before they discovered that Lenin himself had come around—after earlier denunciations—to viewing scientific management in a positive light. As the Chinese published cautious reappraisals of Taylor, they were careful to show that Lenin had blazed the way first. In 1981, one Chinese author said his only regret was that China had not imported Taylorism right after Liberation; decades of progress were lost because of the delay, and management standards at many Chinese factories were described as being similar to those in the United States almost a hundred years earlier, before Taylor's books were published.[8]

In China in the 1980s, one could say that any Western concept that had *science* in its name would enjoy a certain immunity from criticism. Chinese proponents of scientific management told other Chinese that "management as a branch of science" should be dated back—not surprisingly—to the birth of "scientific management" (in retrospect one can see how astute had been Taylor's choice of label for his own management principles). The simplification of Taylor's principles, and the neglect of their full consequences in undiluted application, can be seen when the *People's Daily* itself took up the cause and heaped praise on Taylor's differential piece-rate system, which paid high producers more per piece once they had exceeded an established standard—an appealing principle in the abstract but less so in practice with, as Taylor urged, a standard set so high that few workers had the physical stamina ever to exceed it. The Chinese were not interested so much in collecting case studies of Taylorism as they were in collecting ideological defenses to possible objections on theoretical grounds. In 1981, one Chinese author, Deng Zhongwen, used an argument many other Chinese would use again and again: For all purposes pertaining to management, capitalist and socialist enterprises were the same. Scientific management was a branch of science, and science obeyed no national boundaries.[9]

If Western management techniques could serve socialist enterprises just as well as capitalist, then China had only to pluck the best from around the world for its own use. Between 1979 and 1981, the Chinese began to search out foreign management knowledge in earnest: Observation delegations and students were sent abroad; foreign management experts were invited to China to lecture; study groups for Chinese managers were set up; large numbers of articles and pamphlets were published. The actual process of selection, however, was not quite so rational and smooth. Just as Eleanor Westney shows the "rational shopper" model to be inadequate in the case of Meiji Japan, so too is it inadequate in contemporary China, and for many of the same reasons. Access to information, the roles of chance and propinquity, and the prestige of the nation as much as that of a specific institution were often more influential in choices than was an idealized process of painstaking comparisons among many foreign alternatives. Moreover, the "rational shopper" model places too much emphasis on emulation and too little on the innovation necessary to adapt imported organizational forms to native conditions.[10]

Chinese in the People's Republic had an omnivorous interest in American management models and cultures. One might have guessed that Gifford Pinchot's 1985 book *Intrapreneuring* would excite interest in China; nurturing internal "entrepreneurs" within a large organization fired the imagination of the Chinese no less than it did that of executives of America's Fortune 500. In the case of China, the idea of intrapreneurs was especially appealing because it carried with it an assumption that large organizations did not need to be dismantled in order to capture the benefits of entrepreneurial energy. For a socialist economy, intrapreneuring seemed a natural. It was less predictable that other concepts would excite Chinese interest. The *One-Minute Manager,* for example, was summarized approvingly in many Chinese magazines, with its forgettable nostrums treated just as seriously as they were in the management fads reported in American magazines. Chinese authors also urged Chinese managers to Dress for Success (though in the Chinese case emphasis was placed not on the strategic importance of tie selection but on the selection of clothing colors that would stand out against the background of an auditorium). A visiting American, surprised to discover that a group of Chinese managers were unfamiliar with the concept of the supermarket, was delighted to explain the institution, but then was surprised to see that the Chinese were most intrigued by shopping carts and how they could be nested. To Americans, Chinese fascination with the American management landscape was breathtakingly undiscriminating: Everything and anything seemed to hold potential interest.[11]

Chinese proponents of foreign management theories were able to skirt direct challenges to Marxist orthodoxy by arguing that capitalism had a rich store of one hundred years of industrial experience within which was much "scientific" experience that now could be a "resource for humankind that can be used by all countries." To avoid the appearance of importing foreign management *in toto,* the Chinese author often would find some minor foreign practice, such as the under-the-table distribution of bonuses in Japan, to use as a sacrificial lamb, making a noisy show of rejection to gain acceptance for the many practices the author recommended to China. For Chinese readers who still cared, a quote from Mao Zedong could always be found for any occasion, even for blessing the study of capitalist enterprises, which on at least one occasion Mao had praised for having few employees and high productivity and for being "good at business." Mao had said: "These all ought to have principles that we can study and bring back to improve our own work." Lenin as well as Mao was often called upon to sanction the view that capitalist institutions could safely be looked upon "dialectically," which meant good as well as bad could be found in anything.[12]

Importing Western management models initially seemed shameful to some Chinese not only for ideological reasons, but for nationalistic reasons as well, for it was a reminder of China's comparative backwardness. Chinese authors, however, eased the shame by producing many articles and books about the neglected achievements of "traditional Chinese management." By rummaging in the attic of China's past for management models, the Chinese found a way of meeting the contemporary concern that too much attention was being given to the foreign models. With a bit of dusting off, the construction of the Great Wall could be used as an early example of "systems engineering"; modern information technology could be found in "embryonic" form in the smoke-signal system decreed by a Ming emperor in 1466 that alerted imperial troops to the approach of enemies. Chinese historians brightly reported that ancient China had practiced "comparatively scientific management," accomplishing what modern Western management did, and doing so far earlier.[13]

The three most often mentioned examples of Chinese management achievements were the strategic wisdom in *The Art of War,* the essence of leadership distilled in *The Romance of the Three Kingdoms,* and the stern, effective management style of Wang Xifeng, a female character in *The Dream of the Red Chamber.* The first book, *The Art of War,* was written by Sun Wu (known to Western readers as Sun-Tzu, Master Sun), who was probably a contemporary of Confucius, so the book's longevity and enduring interest were a particular source of pride. The Chinese noted that the book had been translated into English, Japanese, Russian, German, French, and many other languages, and lately had been touted by foreigners as a management guide as well as a military classic. A Chinese management delegation visiting Japan in the early 1980s, for example, was surprised—and delighted—when their Japanese hosts said they had learned all about management from their Chinese guests, and presented the Chinese with a Japanese book which turned out to be a translation of *The Art of War.* Americans used the book, too; the Chinese happily reported that it was a strategic guide for Roger Smith, the chairman of General Motors, a company described not as a venal example of oligopoly as it would have been in the past, but with adoptive pride, as "the world's largest manufacturing company." The lesson the Chinese drew was that "we should not forget that our great motherland has a long history and many precious treasures, such as *The Art of War.*"[14]

Chinese would cite a mélange of authorities and slogans, from *The Art of War* to Mao Zedong to Deng Xiaoping's call for a "Second Revolution," all in the same breath. Some became so excited about the rediscovery of Chinese treatises on management and leadership from the past that they even hailed Andrew Carnegie as an authority who showed the truth of an earlier Chinese maxim ("know one's subordinates well"). The Chinese observed that the concepts of profit-sharing and employee participation, so much in vogue in the United States, had come from Japan, and the Japanese originally had learned the ideas from China, so in the end the glories of American management were those of China too. If some Chinese got carried away and made strained claims—such as jumping from the battle plans in *Three Kingdoms* to feasibility studies today, or using *The Art of War*'s encouragement of individual soldiers to seize war booty as sanction for bonus systems in Chinese factories in the present—Western authors like the novelist James Clavell excitedly promoted translations of the Chinese classics to non-Chinese managers. A book reviewer for the *Wall Street Journal* had fun poking holes in the inflated claims that Clavell had made for *The Art of War,* which Clavell had presented as a military work with extraordinary multipurpose utility that "can equally show the way to victory in all kinds of ordinary business conflicts, boardroom battles, and in the day to day fight for survival we all endure—even in the battle of the sexes!"[15]

At first glance, one might think that the Chinese claims for the modern utility of the management principles of Wang Xifeng in the eighteenth-century classic *The Dream of the Red Chamber* were also a bit inflated, but the story of Wang truly is remarkable and modern when interpreted through a managerialist screen. The traditional view of Wang in Chinese culture has been that she was a sinister and ruthless character, but in revisionist essays by Pan Chenglie and others, Wang was presented as a tough but fair household manager who when called in to shape up the neighboring Ningguo estate set forth clear principles, assigned specific responsibilities to specific household staff members, kept close track of the household inventory, and applied the rules impartially, according to what we would now call universalistic laws, not particularistic ties. Pan argued that the strictness of Wang's rules were necessary from a "managerial viewpoint." This and similar reinterpretations of Wang were not literary exercises; they were clearly intended to send a message to contemporary policy-makers drawn from a Chinese source.[16]

With inspiration from so many sources, foreign and domestic, present and past, the managerial creed in China gathered more and more adherents. As early as 1981, some Chinese were publishing articles maintaining that virtually everything in Western management was suitable for study, including "the management of the relationship between the capitalist class and the proletariat." The Communist Party tacitly encouraged this ferment but did not take the step of giving public approval until 1984, when the Central Committee finally passed a resolution giving its imprimatur to the study of "the world's advanced methods of management, including those of capitalist countries." The Party too had come to believe that Western management was a form of pure science. The Chinese clearly did not anticipate the many ways in which the managerial school of reform, so apparently innocuous and "scientific," was ultimately subversive.[17]

Managerialism in China grew out of the conviction that management was a way of achieving modernization on the cheap. Cui Kene, a professor at Tianjin University, put the matter succinctly: Importing advanced foreign technology is very expensive; importing advanced management is not. A country such as China need only send a few people abroad, or bring foreign management professors in, and import books and journals. Cui wrote: "When studying the advanced technology of capitalist countries, one encounters patents and limits placed on classified information, but the study of management experiences is unrestricted."[18]

Deng Xiaoping agreed, and during his 1979 visit to the United States he suggested to American leaders that the transfer of managerial expertise to China would be even more useful than the transfer of new technology. The idea found favor, and in 1980 the U.S. Department of Commerce helped establish a management training center on the campus of the Dalian Institute of Technology. The long-winded name chosen for the new program, the National Center for Industrial Science and Technology Management Development, was so loaded with ideologically safe words—*industrial, science, technology, management,* and *development*—that when the *People's Daily* or other Chinese newspapers talked about the center and its mission to assimilate "American management theories and methods in industrial science and technology," conservative factions within the government would have no cause for concern about its capitalist provenance.[19]

In fact, appearances to the contrary, the National Center was not especially oriented toward technology. It offered an introduction not just to production management, but also to the same wide range of other fields that an MBA student in the United States would study: accounting, finance, organizational behavior, marketing. The initial groups of students were mid-level Chinese managers who took short courses, but in 1984 a full-fledged MBA program was started on the same Dalian campus, under the auspices of the State University of New York at Buffalo, in which Chinese students took a year and a half of classes in Dalian similar to those in an American business school, then went to the United States for a four-month internship in an American company. The program was hailed by its American sponsors as a "first," but China had had well-established MBA programs by the early 1930s. The new American-sponsored program would best be described as the reintroduction of the MBA after many decades of absence in the postrevolutionary era.[20]

The Dalian programs were joined by a profusion of management education initiatives launched by other American schools elsewhere in China. Wharton sent professors to teach at Jiaotong University in Shanghai; the School of Management at the University of Texas at Dallas built a cooperative program with Qinghua University in Beijing. Babson College, Oklahoma City University, Columbia University, UCLA, and other schools also made headlines in the United States for their China programs because Americans, unlike the Chinese, instinctively viewed management education ideologically, as the institution that taught the rules by which capitalism was played, and not as a value-free science. American management missionaries in China were hardly alone. The Canadians established their management training center in Chengdu, the Japanese in Tianjin, the West Germans in Shanghai, and the European Community in Beijing.[21]

American corporations joined in the stampede to offer management training to the Chinese, often as a goodwill gesture. In 1980, for example, when Coopers & Lybrand offered an eight-week accounting course to one hundred accountants in Shanghai, the company generously supplied everything that would be needed—instructors and twenty-five crates containing air conditioners, photocopiers, movie and overhead projectors, staplers, ballpoint pens, and erasers. Xerox made a $225,000 grant to the Chinese for a three-year management lecture series in China. A number of American companies provided management training programs in the United States for Chinese, and many more accepted Chinese MBA students for internships. Americans may have felt insecure about the relative strength of U.S. exports of manufactured goods in competitive global markets, but they all but burst from pride in sending American management insights to China. Peter Drucker, Tom Peters, and other authors of management books went to China to lecture; visiting American businesspeople on tour in China often found themselves at the lectern; and even American civic community groups set up internship programs for Chinese management students.[22]

The sponsors of these experiments, and the American management professors who participated in them, often denied any ideological significance in the management training they offered to China. "We are not teaching capitalism," said Frank Jen, one of the founders of the SUNY-Buffalo program. All that was being taught, he said, was a set of "management techniques." Trying to bend over backward not to offend ideologically, some American professors at the Dalian center had started the short courses with cases tailored specifically for managing socialist enterprises. But the Chinese told the Americans to teach them about capitalism, not socialism, which after all the Chinese knew much better than their guests. "Tell us how managers operate in the United States," the Chinese told the Americans in 1980, "and we will decide what we can use and what we cannot." This fit perfectly with the American wish to offer the training programs without the onus of force-feeding anyone.[23]

It was reassuring to Americans to hear the Chinese offer testimony to the universality of management techniques that appeared to transcend ideology. How heartening it was, for example, to hear Yu Kaicheng, the Chinese dean of the center at Dalian and the translator of the American best seller *In Search of Excellence,* say that the common ground for business people in socialism and in capitalism was that all agreed "profits are the major measure for performance." But Americans did not consistently pretend that the management training was ideologically innocent. Americans could see well enough that their invitation was evidence of a China in great flux, which meant a unique opportunity to shape the thinking of influential Chinese in the land of the ideological Other. William Dill, a professor at New York University who served as the first dean of the program established in Dalian, said in 1981: "It's up for grabs what direction China will take in the next twenty years.

They're ready to be subverted." An American diplomat in Beijing explained what one could call the "mole strategy": The Chinese graduates of the Dalian center, he said, "will have a tendency to analyze questions, address problems, and set up organizations in ways analogous to our own. And they'll get into key decision-making positions in China." Another professor returned to the theme of undermining Chinese ideology: "This may be the most subversive thing we're doing in the Communist world."[24]

It would be wrong to assume that the more exposure Chinese students had to American management teaching, the more fervid was their faith in managerialism. In fact, the students who went to the United States for management education or internships and then returned to China often were more critical of American textbooks and Western models than those who had not gone abroad. But exposure to American teachers, whether in China or in the United States, visibly stoked a managerialist faith. Richard Lee, the Commerce Department official who was the project director of the American program in Dalian, addressed the first incoming class of MBA students in what an observant reporter described as "near mystical terms," urging the new students to forge ahead and study capitalist management techniques, even when they seemed irrelevant. Lee told the students that later in their MBA studies, "Suddenly, it will all make sense." Lee and other Americans spoke about their mission in China in terms that fell just short of a religious vocabulary.[25]

The enthusiasm they took with them was contagious, and the Chinese students experienced the epiphanies the Americans had hoped for. Americans collected stories of conversions, such as that of Wan Yi, a 31-year-old MBA student who had once shouted "Down with U.S. imperialism" during the Cultural Revolution. By 1985, Wan had seen the light: "Supply and demand curves, marginal efficiency—they come closer to explaining the world than Mao [Zedong]." When a *Wall Street Journal* reporter asked Dalian students what was their favorite course, most students said it was organizational behavior. One student, Jiang Haijun, explained: "I like the course because it teaches me how to better manipulate workers." Another student quickly whispered in his ear, as the reporter put it, "less to correct Mr. Jiang's English than his ideological message." Jiang reworded his explanation: "I mean how to motivate workers." American management professors were gratified that Chinese students who in 1983 had said that study of wage structures and incentives was useless because Chinese managers would never have the power to control wages returned in 1985, after further economic reforms had freed managers to set wages and incentives, to thank their old professors. The Americans pointed to this and other examples to argue that nothing from the capitalist toolbox should be dismissed out of hand.[26]

Chinese and their American mentors waxed euphoric about the successes of the Dalian programs, and committed the sin of believing their own propaganda. By 1985, the training center boasted that nearly all 1,000 graduates of its short course had been promoted by their employers. Three graduates in particular were mentioned as exemplars of the new, modern manager: Wang Zhaoguo, who accomplished amazing successes at an automotive factory in Hubei and who by 1985 was described as the "fastest rising star" in the Communist Party and as a "possible successor" to Deng Xiaoping; Ye Qing, who became a vice-minister in China's coal ministry; and Hong Yuandong, who rose from a plastics factory to become deputy mayor of Dalian. The managerialists' own seemed to be rising to the top of a system that was meritocratic and able to recognize well-trained people after all.[27]

So boastful had both Chinese and American sponsors become that they were utterly unprepared for a bombshell of terrible publicity that exploded on the Dalian center in December 1987. Ironically, it was *China Youth News,* a paper in the country that did not protect freedom of the press, which published an exposé that embarrassed Chinese and American officials alike. The paper had dispatched a team of six reporters to track down each of the thirty-eight members of the first MBA class ten months after their return from the United States. The reporters discovered that the returned students were almost to a person unhappy because their newly acquired skills were ignored by their employers. Furthermore, the disgruntled employees could not easily leave their work units and seek work elsewhere; their original employers demanded that their Americanized employees pay the equivalent of 20,000 yuan (the equivalent of about US $5,400) or similar sums as repayment of the "training fee" the state had invested in their education if they wanted to transfer elsewhere. One MBA holder argued without success: "I myself am a part of China, so why can't I go to another place in China and work more effectively for the country?"[28]

The employing unit hoarded its human resources as zealously as it did material resources, "keeping-without-using," if for no other reason than the vague future utility of the MBA's in the inter-enterprise bargaining that was necessary for everything. Used as translators or file clerks or errand runners or unassigned ciphers with nothing to do but to sit behind a desk, the returned students were most galled when foreigners in China saw how foreign-trained Chinese managers were treated. One member of the group, who had returned to find himself used as an office boy, told of the scalding humiliation experienced one day when delivering a telegram to the foreign expert who worked at his factory and who that day called out in greeting, "Ah, here comes my dear mailman." When the Chinese explained that he had earned an MBA in the United States, the foreigner was visibly taken aback and advised, "Listen, kid, this is not the work you should be doing."[29]

The initial exposé drew national and international attention. *China Youth News* received and printed confirming letters from other foreign-trained management students who had met the same fate; foreign reporters descended on the MBA holders and printed their own exposés about the underutilization of trained managers. Acting prime minister Li Peng called a meeting of senior officials to discuss the matter, and the State Economic Commission broached the reform of the entire Party and government officialdom.[30]

Joseph Alutto, dean at SUNY-Buffalo, defended the program by arguing that the complaint that superiors were not sufficiently appreciative was the same complaint MBA graduates have in the United States. Japanese students who earned MBA degrees in the United States were also frustrated when they returned home to companies that placed a premium on seniority and were told, in effect, to wait their turn. One could also add another comparative note: MBA programs may have been ubiquitous in the United States by the 1980s, but they were still seldom found in Europe and Japan, and even in the United States they were a recent phenomenon. If it was an institution that had not spread extensively to other capitalist countries, the difficulty of its finding ready acceptance in a noncapitalist country can be imagined.[31]

Still, the plight of Chinese MBAs was fundamentally different from that of their equally ambitious and similarly frustrated American or Japanese counterparts. Chinese management students shuttled between two worlds that were the furthest apart. They went to the United States to complete their MBA programs, flushed with excitement that they were the elect. As one student woefully recalled later: "We thought we had a great future. So did our American professors." And in the United States they heard the stories about the fabled Harvard MBA, which upon conferral meant a job in a large company with an annual salary that reached $60,000. The Chinese students told *China Youth News* reporters that in the United States MBAs who often were only about thirty years old "controlled half of the U.S. economy, making giant contributions to the prosperity of the Western world." To go from a sojourn in a world such as this, where some Chinese students were often asked to stay upon graduation and offered jobs with salaries of at least $20,000, and then turn down the offers (or be forced to do so by Chinese authorities) and return home to China, where the MBA degree was literally unknown, to work for an annual salary of $250, was to return to a landscape as opposite in fundamental character as could be imagined. The homecoming of Li Xiaoyan was typical. Li had worked for a bank in Buffalo as an intern, studying computer applications for managing financial resources. When he got back to China he applied for work at many companies that turned him down. When he went to the Bank of China to try to apply for a position, the guard would not even let him in without a letter of introduction. Li remained stuck in his original job, earning $22 a month, at which he estimated he used about "10 percent" of what he had learned, and without any certainty that with the passing of time the operation of the seniority system would automatically provide him with more responsibility.[32]

Another problem that the returned MBAs had to overcome was the taint of foreign origins attached to the MBA degree. One day, for example, Wang Gongrong, a Canadian-trained Chinese MBA, admonished the operator of the office photocopier for locking up the machine an hour before lunch. Angry and reaching wildly for a defense, the operator replied: "What is it that's so terrific about you or the stuff you've learned from abroad? Foreign concepts may not be good for China." Nine months after trying to curb the unofficial siestas of the office staff, Wang had grown discouraged about implementing a job description system and office procedures not unlike those of Wang Xifeng in *Dream of the Red Chamber.* "I can't even get them to come to work during office hours," he lamented. He and other Chinese MBAs were reminded often of reasons to regret their decision to study abroad and "drink foreign ink."[33]

In the wake of the negative publicity over the *China Youth News* exposé and the spate of similar stories that soon followed, M. W. Searls, Jr., of the U.S. Department of Commerce, defended the Dalian program by pointing out that the exposé had not been of the innovative program itself, but of the Chinese organizations that employed the graduates and had failed to change. One could argue with Searls and point out that the

MBA program was guilty at least of inflating the expectations of its Chinese participants and contributing to the plunge in morale that followed graduation. But Searls was right: The criticism of the *China Youth News* exposé was directed at Chinese authorities, not the Americans. The conclusion that the six Chinese reporters drew was so scathingly critical of the status quo in China, and so outspoken in its ideological challenge, that it deserves to be quoted fully:

> We could do as before, criticizing old attitudes and calling for new ones. But in the end we realized that the waste of human resources in China is not a waste because of attitudes—it is a waste because of the structure. Without tearing down the walls of the old institutional structures that control human resources, it will be extremely difficult to fully use any new ideas.[34]

Letters printed in the following days in *China Youth News* were no less incendiary—declaring, for example, that "the problem must be solved only at the foundation of the system itself," which was to say, China needed to adopt a free market for labor: "Human talent can find its ideal place and work most effectively only in an environment of fair competition and through the adjustments of a labor market, and not by passively waiting 'to be discovered.' " Here we can see unfolding in China precisely what America's ideological warriors had hoped for—the flowering of the seeds of radical change planted in the management curriculum—and undoubtedly much sooner than they had dared hope.[35]

As small as the Dalian MBA program was—after all, the thirty-eight graduates whose postgraduation lives were chronicled in such detail were only an infinitesimal percentage of China's working population—it received the attention of the highest Chinese leaders, and the controversy in December 1987 brought some far-ranging discussion and immediate reforms. A vice-director at the State Economic Commission took up the call to allow "human talent to compete in the marketplace" and said that this reform demanded "struggle." The State Economic Commission promised the MBA graduates that after a six-month trial period with their original work units, they could change jobs if they were not assigned to appropriate tasks. Student admission policies were changed too, so that entering students in the Dalian MBA program would come principally from larger, and more export-oriented, enterprises. A year later, in follow-up investigations of the utilization of foreign-trained MBAs, little actual change was found. The episode suggests that the MBA programs and other Western-sponsored management training produced graduates that could not, even with the announced help of sympathetic central authorities, effect much change at the grassroots level.[36]

The leaders who guided the course of reform at the top subscribed to an important tenet of the managerialist faith: China could choose managerial techniques and capitalist institutions selectively, as if passing through a cafeteria, free to pick the attractive dishes and ignore the others. But the managerialists were mistaken and were slow to realize that one managerial or economic reform in China necessitated another, as each step required its own set of supporting institutions or created new problems that in turn had to be addressed with still more reforms. The Chinese may have clung to the fiction that they were proponents of reform, but if they were actually to succeed, their proposed reforms cumulatively would have to become a revolution that fundamentally changed the nature of China's socialist economy. The final form the economy would take was not likely to mirror that of America or Japan, but if the reforms continued, the result would be an economy whose core depended upon the new private sector instead of the state sector.

Americans, when claiming to be speaking about universal principles in management that transcended ideology, were actually contributing to the dismantling of the socialist status quo in China. For an example of the ideological implications of even the most innocuous-appearing management advice, consider the mild remarks given at a talk in 1986 in Shanghai by Donald Kendall, the chairman and chief executive officer of PepsiCo. He offered the Chinese some "Simple Truths of Management" that "applied to all human endeavors." The first was that complex organizations were best managed as decentralized units; Kendall was proud that a friend had once called PepsiCo "the biggest small company he had ever seen." The second principle was to hire "the best possible people," and the third was to encourage "prudent risk-taking." In citing these three, Kendall, unwittingly or not, touched upon three of the basic weaknesses in Chinese socialism: cumbersome centralism, a bureaucratized and politicized job-assignment system, and risk-averse conservatism that inhibited innovation. Just as the *China Youth News* reporters suggested that the problems encountered by the MBA graduates were less attitudinal than institutional, Kendall's principles could be implemented in China only after a thorough restructuring of the economy. At a business luncheon in the United States, Kendall's talk would not receive much attention; in a capitalist setting, his principles were clichés, and he modestly disclaimed having any "new theories or sophisticated systems" to share with the Chinese. But when delivered in the People's Republic, familiar banalities were transformed into words freighted with significance.[37]

The most radical wing of Chinese managerialists looked beyond specific organizational models in the West and enviously observed a different ethos that animated capitalist society. Americans, for example, seemed to be so unapologetically aggressive. In 1987 a Chinese student who was studying management at Tufts University in Boston compared Americans with Chinese: "The Chinese are very modest—too modest—a people. If the boss says, 'Oh, you did this very well, people here [in the United States] say 'thank you.' But in China if the boss says you did this very well, people say, 'No, no, no. I have a long way to go.' " Another Chinese, Sheng Zongshen, writing in a Chinese management journal at about the same time, blamed China's own "feudal" history for nurturing an aversion to competition. "Live in peace without competition" had been the credo in traditional society, but was no longer suited for the present. Sheng pointed to the inspirational example of Seiko in Japan, which held the dominant position in the global watch industry yet was never complacent about its position; fear of being overtaken by its competitors drove the company to strive constantly to improve. The United States was also praised for using warnings in its newspapers of eroding leadership in science and technology to challenge its people to strive harder. China, Sheng said, needed the same sense of competition and the constructive use of feelings of crisis to push people to work harder. A staff member of the Chinese Academy of Social Sciences added that if China wanted to export its products, it could not avoid encountering fierce competition. More important, Chinese factories that had no intention of producing for the foreign marketplace should also realize that they too would have to learn how to compete, or they would be unable to ward off foreign imports in the future. There would be no safe haven from the winds of competition.[38]

Western management models provoked Chinese management journals to ruminate about philosophical differences between Chinese and Western managers that seemed to hold the Chinese back. Managers and officials in China, urged one author, needed to discard their habitual "past orientation" and reluctance to try anything that did not follow precedents. Instead of seeing the country's history as a source of pride for its duration and periods of imperial glory, this author regarded it as a source of shame, an albatross that kept China from competing successfully with the likes of American managers who, comparatively speaking, had no past to be distracted by, no inherited aversion to competition, or risk, or change, to overcome.[39]

From the viewpoint of American managers, this characterization of their assumed bravura in the eyes of Chinese may seem to have been undeserved. The recurrent theme in Tom Peters's *Thriving on Chaos* (1987) and innumerable articles and newspaper columns was that American managers were too conservative, too averse to risk, too obdurate and resistant to change. But when American managers were compared to their Chinese counterparts, the Americans looked like Olympian sprinters, not the sclerotic has-beens that they had grown accustomed to seeing in the journalistic mirror.

Americans also took open pleasure in seeing socialist China adopt capitalistic institutions, as one Marxist apostasy followed the other: Legal protection of inheritance. Capital equipment leasing. Bankruptcy legislation (*Business Week:* "Free Markets and Chapter 11—Can This Really Be China?"). Pawnshops. Personal property insurance. A "Great Wall" credit card. Mergers and acquisitions which, like the rest, were read by Americans as another indication of the ultimately universal nature of capitalist principles. The arrival of the concept of hostile corporate takeovers in the People's Republic of China was reported with visible delectation in the United States. A Chinese factory official explained the concept as well as any investment banker on Wall Street: "Just as a man who is hungry has to eat, a company that wants to succeed has to expand. It's an objective law of nature." When Americans read that Chinese in the People's Republic were now saying such things, it was received as the supreme validation of the American creed.[40]

The Chinese even adopted the board game Monopoly. An American, Frank Hawke, remembered the game in 1980 while teaching a course on the American economy at Beijing University and persuaded a seven-year-old American child living in Beijing to lend him a set to take to class. When Hawke introduced his sixty-three Marxists to the mysteries of the game, Jay Mathews was on hand to report on the scene: "The brightest minds of the next Socialist generation leaned forward to hear one of the great secrets of the capitalist world: 'When you pass Go, collect $200.' " By 1985 an unauthorized copy of the game was for sale in China, virtually identical to the original except for translations of the names (for example, "Strong Hand" was substituted in Chinese for "Monopoly") and a minor rule change that forbade paying a fine to win release from jail (the authorities at the Chinese factory said they did not want to encourage lawlessness). By 1988, editorials in Chinese newspapers were praising the game, which was said to "help develop children's intelligence, judgment, and motor skills," and from which "people can learn about management and competition."[41]

For the most part, Chinese continued to hold to the fiction that the basic nature of their socialist system was not affected by piecemeal adoption of capitalist institutions, management models, incentive systems, or board games, and that at any point China could choose *not* to adopt any more. A key definition in Marxist orthodoxy was a continuing source of comfort during the reforms: The ownership of the means of production was the defining criterion of any given economic system, and measured by this, nothing fundamental had changed in the People's Republic. But at least one group of high-level Chinese advisors, of the Chinese Economic System Reform Study Group, saw quite early the revolutionary implications of seemingly harmless foreign management practices, and how few choices China actually had once it had committed itself to the path of reform. In an unsigned article that was first published in 1984, the group pointed out:

> Generally, certain foreign management methods are used with others that comprise an entire management system. Therefore, when considering whether a given method would be effective, we should not look at it alone in considering whether to use it. Rather we must look to see whether it is part of an entire system of methods that go with it. We must study all of the interconnections between the methods.[42]

As an example, the group mentioned reform of the entire financial system that was entailed in the improvement of consumer banking services. An even better example, however, was the way in which managerial reforms at the enterprise level led to changes in the decision-making powers of managers, including empowering them to hire and fire workers, but also to changes in the one area that was sacrosanct: ownership of the means of production. If it had been within their power to do so, Chinese leaders would have avoided the controversy of stock issues and stock markets, but reforms in one area, management, soon encountered hindrances in other parts of the system. Newly autonomous enterprises could no longer rely upon subsidies from the state, which meant that managers had to devise new ways of securing resources for replacing outmoded plants, for expanding into new lines, and for trying new methods. Without fresh capital they could do little, but China's state budget and financial system were strained by existing commitments. As far as the state was concerned, if enterprises wanted new capital, they were on their own and would have to seek it from employees, whose resources were limited, or from the wider public, whose resources were great but untapped. No mechanism permitted the financial resources of the public to be channeled directly into investments. Inventing a mechanism—public stock issues—required adjustment of the most sensitive part of all, ownership, the heart of the system.

When the first sale of stock took place in Beijing in 1984, it marked the first time that any Communist country permitted private individuals who did not work for an enterprise to own stock in it. At the time, the Chinese authorities were so reluctant about tinkering with new forms of ownership that stocks were permitted, but not a stock exchange. Officials explained that they did not want to do anything that would encourage "speculation" in stocks. But before long the state realized that if stock issues were to realize their potential of raising untapped capital from the public, potential purchasers needed to be assured of the opportunity to trade their shares after their initial purchase. So the state found that one compromise led inexorably to another, and small stock exchanges were established in a number of cities. By 1987, the year-old stock market in Shanghai, the city that lay claim to having had the largest stock exchange in China before 1949, had quickly regained national prominence, and more than 350,000 people owned shares issued by more than 1,000 companies. Stock markets and stock purchases expanded so fast that events took on a life of their own. State-owned companies joined in, ignoring a measure passed in 1987, during a period of ideological worry that matters had gone too far, which forbade state companies from issuing stocks.[43]

Stocks in the People's Republic were not carbon copies of those in the capitalist West, but a kind of hybrid between stocks and bonds: They had a fixed date of maturity and offered a fixed rate of return, just like a bond, but they also offered investors dividends, in addition, that were paid from the company's profits, and technically carried the notion of a share in equity and voting rights, like stocks anywhere. The first public shareholder meetings held in China bore signs of their unconventional place in a socialist economy. In 1988, for example, an official from the People's Bank of China criticized the avarice of the assembled shareholders of Hiway Electrical Company, a small computer company: "I've talked to shareholders who are interested only in how much they'll make in dividends. That's a bad attitude. You should be concerned primarily about the firm's management." One could also see stocks and bonds with "Chinese characteristics" in Shenyang, where the sale of bonds was made attractive only when the companies attached lottery tickets, so that investors had a chance of winning a television set or a refrigerator. Foreign reporters emphasized the incongruity of seeing lines of peasants who had come to Chinese cities to purchase securities, still "dressed in their Mao clothes and peasant hats."[44]

Americans followed the Chinese experiment with avid interest, for the same reason that Chinese ideologues were so leery of these reforms: Everyone, both Americans and Chinese, sensed the ideological significance of the advent of stocks in a socialist economy. Americans who taught management in China helped to push influential Chinese in the direction of stock exchanges by staging stock market games in their classes, giving students a starting "investment" in a basket of U.S. companies and having students compete to expand the value of their portfolio by buying and selling over the course of a school term. One such game was started in 1986 by Paul Thiel, an official in the U.S. Embassy's economics section, at the in-house management training school in Beijing of the People's Bank of China, China's central bank. Influencing these students meant influencing an extremely select and powerful group. In these and other management classes, the presence of American expatriates in China was contributing to deep changes in socialism, bearing out the worst fears of Chinese conservatives, who had worried about the contaminating influence of ideas from capitalism when China opened further to contacts with the West. The stock market games were the logical, and more serious, extension of the mischievous impulse to teach Chinese economics students the game of Monopoly that had started in 1980.[45]

Americans encouraged the Chinese at every step. In 1983, a year before public sales of stock were begun, the New York Stock Exchange hosted a visit by reporters from the *People's Daily,* who did not miss the symbolic significance of the Exchange. One of the Chinese reporters later wrote that the American who accompanied them as they entered the trading floor had said dramatically, "You are standing right now at the heart of the capitalist world. Now watch how the heart beats!" The Chinese watched closely. Articles, more visits, and eventually interns followed. A trio went to study the operations of the Exchange in 1988, as one American newspaper described it, "getting the jump on" Mikhail Gorbachev, whose motorcade cruised past in December 1988. China's best-known proponent of expanded use of stock issues for state-owned companies was Li Yining, a Beijing University economics professor who was dubbed "Mr. Stock Market" in the West. Li had never visited the

United States during the course of developing his proposals, but it is striking that his younger protégés, the junior economics professors who went much further than Li in their proposals for the privatization of state enterprise equity, were newly returned from the United States with graduate degrees in hand. In 1987, for example, Wang Poming, thirty-three years old, and Gao Xiqing, thirty-five years old and the first Chinese citizen to pass the New York State bar examination, returned to China after studies at Columbia and at Duke and work experiences on Wall Street to help plan a national member-owned stock exchange to be based in Beijing or Shanghai. China had sent students abroad to study practical techniques, and they had returned with a determination to change the essence of the system.[46]

In the Shenyang Exchange the furnishings were modest and the technology was simple. A blackboard served as the Big Board. But a photographic mural of the financial district in Manhattan covered one wall and showed the source of inspiration for the exchange. Chinese proponents of free capital markets went to surprising lengths to find support for their positions, such as extolling the vision of J. P. Morgan, portrayed as an embryonic "venture capitalist" who had lent critically needed "risk capital" to Thomas Alva Edison. The Ivan Boesky case was reported in 1987 not as an example of the corruption and the insider trading of Wall Street, but rather as a salutary example of someone who had broken the rules and been duly punished. The Chinese public was no better prepared for the October 1987 crash of the New York stock market than anyone else, because on the eve of the crash it had been reassured that laws and regulations in the United States had been put into place in the wake of the 1929 crash to provide protection and security. After the 1987 crash, the Chinese press was in no mood, as it would have been ten years before, to celebrate the cyclical afflictions of the capitalist system. Many Chinese provincial organizations had invested their foreign-exchange surpluses in the Hong Kong currency markets and mutual funds and had been badly hurt by the crash there. The press also knew that China in the future would be increasingly vulnerable to the vicissitudes of capital markets, so it did not gloat.[47]

Proponents of expanded reliance on stock issues in China had a ready answer to any ideological objection that came up. No, they were not tampering with the socialist system; they claimed in fact to be *expanding* socialism with stock issues, in the sense of expanding what they liked to refer to as the "publicly owned economy." (A similar argument had been made many years earlier by Peter Drucker, who claimed that "socialism" had arrived in the United States without anyone much noticing it, given the fact that union pension funds had come to own a controlling share of equity capital and legally gave American workers control over "the means of production.") In China, if competition among stock-issuing enterprises led to the stronger ones acquiring the weaker ones, such takeovers in a socialist economy were nothing to be concerned about. They indicated merely a "new combination of production factors," and the triumph of efficiency would redound to the benefit of the entire society.[48]

The Chinese progressed step by step without talking much about where these changes were headed: from American management systems without any changes in the means of ownership, then to stocks but without stock exchanges, then to stock exchanges but without stock issued by state-owned enterprises, then to unauthorized state stock issues but with a prohibition on corporate acquisitions, then to a call for more acquisitions and mergers, and so on. Each time the state built up a heavily fortified line of last defense, then found that it had to retreat further, well beyond its own ideological turf, until it had backed up halfway around the globe and was justifying its reforms with arguments put forth by the defenders of capitalism. Some residual ideological hesitancy appeared from time to time.

In one embarrassing instance in 1988, for example, the *People's Daily* published a front-page story about a scrambling crowd of eager stock buyers in a most unlikely location, the courtyard of the State Council at Zhongnanhai, the inner sanctum of state power. A few days later, in a terse retraction, the newspaper denied that the scene had ever taken place or that State Council staff members had ever purchased stock. It was a dubious denial, given the multiple layers of approval required for the first story to have been permitted to appear on the front page of the most heavily edited newspaper in the entire country. But it did indicate how certain elements of the national leadership still regarded stocks as tawdry and their purchase as unbecoming for the highest servants of a socialist state. Yet the very next week, proponents of stock issues wrested back control of the front page of the *People's Daily* and signaled the approval of the government. Party Secretary Zhao Ziyang told visiting American economist Milton Friedman (whose book *Free to Choose* had already been translated and published in China) that stock capitalization in a publicly owned economy was one of the top priorities in the economic reform program. Western observers cheered the steps, however tentative, toward expansion of this and other familiar financial institutions, but *The Economist* could not help twitting the Chinese for pretending that stock issues did not change the socialist nature of the economy: "As party doctrine holds that workers are already masters of the means of production, why should they buy shares in their own factories?"[49]

The Chinese leadership surely did not foresee that an earlier decision to "modernize" the management of Chinese enterprises would lead to significant changes in the economic infrastructure, some of which created a very difficult task of ideological explanation. But just as one management reform had led to the next, and then the next, until stock issues, of all things, were seen as necessary and perfectly acceptable, so did the introduction of stocks lead to still more reforms. As American bankers from Wall Street pointed out repeatedly to the Chinese, the introduction of financial markets required, in turn, that the public be provided with tremendous amounts of information about the economy and the major enterprises, information that in China had always been closely restricted. Loosening controls on managers and permitting them to make more decisions led to loosening controls on enterprises and freeing them to raise capital on their own, which had to lead, if the new reforms were to have a chance of succeeding, to loosening the tight control on the circulation of economic information.[50]

Logically, one reform led to the next, and economic reforms eventually led to calls for political reforms. In the spring of 1989, the politicization of Gao Xiqing, the young American-trained attorney who returned to China to devote himself to the creation of a national stock exchange, is instructive. His students at the University of International Business and Economics in Beijing were among the last to join in the student demonstrations at Tiananmen Square; among the privileged ranks of university students in Beijing, they were the most privileged of all, for they were headed for job assignments with the highest pay in trade-related posts. When they did join the student movement, Gao paid little attention. He was still throwing himself furiously into drafting China's first securities laws. One day, however, he noticed that one of his liveliest students was missing, and was told that she was on a hunger strike. Moved, Gao headed for the square himself, spending that night camped in solidarity with his students. A few days later butchery would bring an end to the demonstrations in the square. Before the army troops moved in, however, the presence of Gao and his business students at Tiananmen suggests symbolically that, sooner or later, economic and political change were naturally inseparable.[51]

9.

MASTERS OF THE HOUSE

Each of the several international hotels that opened in the early 1980s was a laboratory of a sort, where thousands of foreign guests a year were served by thousands of Chinese staff members, mostly young, inexperienced, and utterly unacquainted with the West, who in turn were supervised by varying combinations of Chinese and Western managers. Each group kept a keen eye on the performance of the other, for much rode on the outcome of the experiment. Financially, the hotels, most of which were joint ventures, were the earliest and remained the most attractive form of investment for foreign investor partners; thanks to their foreign clientele, hotels never had to worry about the foreign exchange problems that were the bane of so many other joint ventures. The hotels were also the most conspicuous foreign investments in China. They were so large—many of the early ones soared dozens of stories above the existing urban landscape—that they commanded the attention of all urban Chinese. Foreign control was a concern to some sections of the Chinese government and public. As long as these hotels harbored enclaves of foreign managers, many Chinese felt that their national sovereignty was threatened, their competence impugned, their claim to a place among the leading powers of the modern world challenged.

At the same time, however, other Chinese realized that the hotels foreign investors built were an entirely new genus of institution for which their own experience had not prepared them. While American hoteliers spoke of their own profit-minded "hospitality industry," which was driven by intense competition in providing service to customers, the

Chinese had a system of uninspiring hotels of varying quality, even the best of which were qualitatively different from foreign hotels because they were never intended to do more than provide shelter for traveling officials. The Chinese "guesthouse," as it was frequently called, was oriented toward groups of travelers who were not individual customers and who, as state employees, had little to say about where they stayed and even fewer expectations. The guesthouse provided a bed and a bottle of hot water, and little else. The guests spent their evenings as they spent their days—together. They played cards, gossiped, watched television as one noisy, self-contained group; they required no services, and guesthouses did not compete for their patronage.[1]

These circumstances gave rise to a distinctive personnel system within the guesthouses. The minimal physical exertion required to maintain what was little more than a dormitory made guesthouse jobs attractive to the children of Party cadres, whose parents got the work assignments for them. The employees' dedication to working energetically was not helped by the knowledge that their salary was guaranteed for life and that there were far more employees than would ever be required for the little real work of sweeping the rooms and changing the linen. When the work did not fill eight hours, the pace of work slowed until it did. Personal errands helped to fill the time; with a wave of the hand, an employee could leave and tend to whatever private matter seemed more interesting than work, without any penalty.[2]

The body language of the service staff telegraphed their inattentiveness. But as Liu Binyan, China's best-known muckraking journalist, pointed out in a highly critical essay published in 1986, the Chinese guesthouse represented not merely problems in the hotel industry, but also the problems that afflicted all public services in China. Most service workers were not the children of privileged parents, but the distinction between work and rest had grown fuzzy everywhere. To many foreign visitors, the phenomenon was seen as the logical extension of the entrenched noonday rest of two hours—the *xiuxi* (pronounced *shee-oh shee*)—that brought the country to an apparent standstill every day.[3]

The Chinese themselves made *xiuxi* an issue by declaring it to be one of the manifestations of "the superiority of socialism," which the socialist government even enshrined in the PRC Constitution: "The working people have a right to rest." If a foreign oil company complained that it made no sense to let an offshore oil rig stand idle merely for the noonday rest when it cost $50,000 a day to operate, the Chinese proudly pointed to the protection of their constitution. Unlike Italy, Spain,

Mexico, and other Latin countries in which workers made up for the afternoon siesta, Chinese workers did not work any later than they would have had to otherwise. The noonday break also tended to expand in both directions; foreigners complained of offices and libraries closing at 10:30 A.M. so that the staff could "get ready" for the upcoming break. By one American journalist's informal reckoning, the typical workday of the Chinese office worker was only about six hours.[4]

A "*xiuxi* spirit" could be found in seemingly every corner of China, even in urban areas and in the north where, unlike in rural China and in the south, the connection was not easily seen between the modern institution and the original desire to avoid the midday heat in a day of long hours of exhausting physical exertion. In 1980 a Western expatriate in Beijing told a humorous story about the need for *xiuxi* claimed by the state-assigned painters of an apartment the government had assigned him. He could not understand why it was taking so many weeks for the painters to complete the job, so he dropped in without notice at 10 A.M. one morning, and discovered that one painter was taking a shower and the other two were stretched out on the sofa. He asked what they were doing, and they replied in unison, "*Xiuxi.*" Five hours later he returned, and found the two still napping and the third playing with a hair dryer. In the end, it took six weeks to paint the five-room apartment, and when he complained to the government, he recalled: "I was treated as if I were a nineteenth-century imperialist oppressing the masses. The man in charge glared at me and said, 'Don't you respect the working people's right to rest?' "[5]

Ethnic Chinese from Hong Kong, Taiwan, and Singapore, who were not vulnerable to the charge of cultural ignorance and insensitivity, were no less disgusted with the constitutional enshrinement of *xiuxi.* In 1980, for example, when a Singaporean saw mainland Chinese asleep at their lathes, he said: "Life under communism has done what I would never have thought possible. The Communists have taken a naturally industrious people and made them lazy." The official Chinese response at the time would have been that the issue was one not of laziness, but of freedom. No more sweated labor for the benefit of someone else. Every worker a Master! The unofficial Chinese response of the real workers would have been still different: Yes, they knew they were supposedly the masters, but they also knew that it was the Party bureaucrats who were the real masters. The Chinese workplace was riven by class tensions that could not be officially recognized, and virtually the only weapon workers could use against the official powers was the subtle one of poor work performance. Workers and the apparatchiks of the Party-managed economy were engaged in a long struggle over whether, if to any extent, the rhetoric of Workers as Masters would be realized. This battleground in the workplace is what the foreign and Chinese managers of the first international hotels in China inherited.[6]

The Jianguo Hotel (1982) and the Great Wall Hotel (1983) were the first two joint-venture hotels to open in Beijing, and both paid a price for being early arrivals. The Jianguo got off relatively lightly: The Chinese required the inclusion of an air raid shelter in its basement, with three-foot-thick concrete walls intended to withstand a nuclear attack. This proved to be the last such The-End-Is-Near relic of the Cultural Revolution; the Chinese authorities dropped the requirement for subsequent hotel projects. Otherwise, the construction and furnishing of the hotel went smoothly because the American partner, Clement Chen, used the design of his Palo Alto Holiday Inn. So that they could see what he called "the finished product," he flew the Chinese contractors to California to live in the American model before construction began on its clone in Beijing. The Great Wall paid a higher price because it was much larger in scale—an $80 million project compared to $22 million for the Jianguo—and midway the construction responsibilities were taken over by the Chinese partner, who had no experience building a thousand-room hotel to international standards. Plumbing and electrical problems were hidden, and sloppy finishing in guest rooms had to be rectified. The bathrooms were a particular mess. "Chinese workers just had no idea what a Western bathroom looked like," said Richard Young, a Chinese-American who was one of the American principals. "To them, wallpaper is just something that covers the walls, no need to make it straight at the seams, and those sorts of niceties."[7]

One could say that Chinese construction workers had never before been expected to worry about such details; all that mattered in the state-run guesthouse had been that it have a roof, a floor, four walls, and a communal latrine that was not always inside. But in 1984, in response to the stories that had appeared about the slovenly work at the hotel, one American, Chris Urago, wrote a stirring defense of the Chinese workers in a letter to the editor of a Honolulu newspaper. Urago saw the sloppy workmanship as a consciously political statement of resentment directed at the bourgeois foreign travelers who would be coming to stay in the Great Wall Hotel. Urago wrote: "We wonder how the Chinese built a Great Wall to last centuries but cannot make a new bathroom."

The paradox is explained, he said, by the lack of interest they had in providing bathroom amenities "for the privileged while they themselves must go without." This ingenious defense of poor quality standards was similar to the Chinese state's own defense of *xiuxi.* Both claimed a higher political good for what would otherwise be indefensible.[8]

The foreign hotel builders anticipated the charge that their hotels would offend foreign architectural critics because of their un-Chinese look and feel. When Anita Zadeh, an interior designer, was called in at the last moment to work on the design of the Great Wall Hotel, she wanted the hotel to "feel like China," while the Chinese partner, she said, wanted "a twentieth-century space shuttle feel." The result, she later thought, was a balance of both, and Chinese newspapers printed fluff pieces at the time of the opening of the hotel that also talked about happy blends of East and West, old and new. But this was polite nonsense intended to protect Chinese sensitivities. Uninhibited American visitors did not talk about blends of this or that; they remarked upon how eerily identical the Great Wall seemed to the Dallas Hyatt and other American hotels, of how the Jianguo Hotel was so similar to its California parent. At the Great Wall, "Turkey in the Straw" Muzak filled the air; imported silver from Europe was at every place setting; even the hotel china, foreigners noted, was from Germany. C. B. Sung, one of the American investors in the Great Wall, defended the Western look of his hotel as being in China's immediate interest because it showed that China could meet Western standards. Clement Chen justified the architecture of his Jianguo Hotel with a similar argument. Visiting a country with an unfamiliar culture like China was fine, he said, but he had consciously designed the guest rooms as a retreat "so that once a guest gets inside, he will be able to forget where he is and feel as if he were back home."[9]

The return of the *qipao* (pronounced *chee-pow*)—the long, tight-fitting dress that has a slit from the hem to the thigh on one side—as the assigned dress of young Chinese waitresses in some of the restaurants in the new hotels also complicated matters: It was not a Western style, but it was also not the sort of indigenous Chinese symbol that postrevolutionary officials were glad to see. Government officials wrangled with Chinese managers about the proper length of the slit (if the slit went too far up, it was too revealing; if it was too low, the dress was too tight to walk in) and thought of the unsavory associations of the *qipao* and the brothels of the pre-1949 era.[10]

In the eyes of conservative Chinese authorities, the joint-venture hotels were nothing but necessary evils. They would earn badly needed foreign exchange. But unwanted influences were anticipated and dreaded. In 1981, on the eve of the opening of the first hotels, the Chinese launched a campaign in their own Peking Hotel to help the staff fend off the Western influences brought in by the guests. (Attempted seduction was given literal meaning in the salutary tale that a Beijing newspaper told of how a young male housekeeper in the hotel had to fight off the advances of a foreign female guest in her room.) "Unhealthy books and magazines" were a particular concern; all materials left behind by departing foreign guests were to be turned over immediately to Chinese authorities. At the Friendship Hotel, the sprawling complex in northwest Beijing, an educational campaign was undertaken to strengthen the "immunity" of the Chinese staff from the "pornographic" magazines and other detritus left in guest rooms.[11]

In the new hotels, however, Western influences could not be simply swept off a nightstand into a bag and dutifully turned over to the authorities; the influences inhered in the furnishings themselves, in the luxury that pervaded the workplace of the newly hired Chinese staff. Orville Schell described the Jianguo at the time of its opening as a "living advertisement for capitalism":

> Its neon signs, eternally energetic fountains, extravagant lighting and California styling make it as noticeable among the frieze of gloomy buildings which flank it as one gleaming gold tooth in a mouth of otherwise neglected dentures. Standing as it does in front of row upon row of dormitory-like housing for the families of Chinese Foreign Ministry employees (where there are usually not even any operable lights in the hallways), the Jianguo fairly sparkles with seductiveness.[12]

Fritz Sommerau, the manager of the Jianguo, wondered how his Chinese staff would respond to the ostentation they would regularly see. On New Year's Eve 1984, Sommerau said he "scratched his head" speculating how the staff "would react to the sight of resident foreigners paying 120 yuan for a bottle of imported champagne, when their own monthly income, already considerably more than the national average, is only 70 yuan or so on average. You have to think, 'What *do* they think?' "[13]

The Chinese government could not shield these hotel workers from all the pernicious influences they would encounter at their new jobs. But it could do its best in negotiations with its joint-venture partners to ensure that ventures would be "joint" for as short a time as possible so that the Chinese partner could once again be the sole Master of the House. The joint-venture agreements stipulated that full ownership and control of the hotels reverted automatically, without additional payment, to the Chinese partner after a set period of time, often only ten years. The Chinese pointed to such obviously advantageous terms and to the opportunity to learn "how to make big money," in the words of one of the Chinese negotiators who had worked on the Jianguo project, to help persuade the public that the government was acting wisely and in the national interest when it agreed to be joint partners in the hotel projects.[14]

While waiting with barely contained impatience to own the joint-venture hotels free and clear, the Chinese government wanted in the interim at least to be co-managers of the hotels. Anything less than standing as co-Masters of the House would be a national and racial humiliation for a country fond of congratulating itself on being good to its guests. Although Clement Chen was able to talk his Chinese partner into acquiescing, after an entire year of discussion, to hiring the Hong Kong-based Peninsula Group to manage the Jianguo, the Chinese partner in the Great Wall venture was not willing to follow the same course. The major international hotel chains wanted, the Chinese felt, too big a piece of the action; moreover, the Great Wall was too visible for the Chinese to accede to the symbolic humiliation of having foreigners in command. After lengthy negotiations, the American and Chinese partners agreed finally upon a compromise: appointment of a Chinese-American, Peter Sun, as general manager. With Sun in charge, the Chinese newspapers could proudly boast of his having "Chinese blood" and distant revolutionary ties to the motherland (Sun was a great-grand-nephew of Sun Yat-sen, the revered leader of the 1911 Revolution that toppled the last imperial dynasty). Under Peter Sun, the Great Wall Hotel's glories would belong, by proxy, to all Chinese.[15]

Unfortunately for Sun and his employers, the Great Wall Hotel got off to a terrible start. First, it bled financially from expensive delays in construction. Then, once completed and open, low room occupancy, thin patronage of restaurants and lounges, and poor service—as measured by international standards instead of domestic guesthouse standards—became the talk of the town. In July 1984 the hotel failed to pay the first installment due on its construction loan. Meanwhile, the Jianguo, under foreign management, sailed successfully out as soon as it cast off—its rooms and restaurants were filled, its service good. James Sterba, a reporter for the *Wall Street Journal,* recommended that American readers visit the hotel's Western restaurant, the best in town, with "waitresses who try so hard you want to kiss them and French tourists so ignorant about how far service has improved that you want to walk over and punch them in the mouth." Clement Chen began telling the press that the Jianguo was so profitable he expected to earn back his share of investment in just a few years.[16]

In the shadow of the immediate success of the Jianguo stood the brooding Great Wall, and also the Fragrant Hills Hotel, located in the Western suburbs of Beijing. It was wholly Chinese-owned and managed, and designed by the most famous living prodigal son of China himself, I. M. Pei. The Chinese government intended the hotel to stand as an inspirational testament to what the racial collectivity—the Chinese People—could achieve. Its unfortunate beginning was not wholly the fault of its management or staff, which could neither alter its hapless location far from the center of town nor secure for it steady sources of electricity and water. Pei's design, which unlike that of the other major new hotels sought to incorporate Chinese architectural traditions, produced an esthetically pleasing building. But the air conditioning and heating did not work, and water leaked through the ceilings.

Other matters were within the control, at least theoretically, of its management. The service staff, faithful to the honored traditions of the Chinese guesthouse, did not worry much about cleaning and earned for themselves a reputation for neglecting guests. In 1984 an American reporter wrote: "Within a few months of the hotel's opening last April, the Fragrant Hills came to resemble the vast majority of hotels in this country. Signs fell down, wastebaskets weren't emptied and toilet paper was missing. The carpets and dining-room tablecloths developed holes, and guests sat fuming while waiters chatted among themselves." Similar accounts circulated at the same time about other new, wholly Chinese-owned and managed hotels. At the Xiyuan, for example, a foreign guest complained that raw sewage backed up through his bathtub, and he could not find a member of the hotel staff to take care of the problem because they were taking their daily *xiuxi.* Word quickly got around the foreign community: Avoid the Chinese-managed hotels.[17]

Surveying its own dismal record and the equally disheartening plight of Chinese-managed hotels that were struggling on their own, the governing board of the Great Wall Hotel decided that it had to swallow its pride and hire a foreign hotel chain to assume managerial control. A chain, with its worldwide, computerized reservation system, would provide a steady source of guests, or so at least the Chinese liked to justify the decision, skirting the other issues concerning management and service standards. At a press conference called to announce that Sheraton had been chosen, a reporter asked John Kapioltas, the chairman of the hotel chain, whether the U.S.–based company's entry was like "the cavalry riding in." Kapioltas was polite and gently deflected the question by saying "I wouldn't say we see it quite like that." The Chinese officials who were on hand for the press conference were pointedly silent, which one reporter said was "as if they wished to convey the reluctance with which they entered into the Sheraton deal." If they seemed glum, it surely must have been because of the symbolic significance of the moment, reluctantly turning over control of what had been intended as the showpiece of Sino-American economic cooperation, the two partners participating as co-equals. But the foreign managers who were brought in there and elsewhere discovered that they were not necessarily the masters of the house, either.[18]

The number of expatriate managers in the new hotels was small compared to the far larger Chinese staff below them. Depending on the size of the hotel and the tolerance of the governing boards, expatriates usually ranged between 40 and 100, but they supervised a staff that was often 1,000 to 2,000 in number. The generally low productivity of Chinese staff members meant that an international hotel in China needed almost twice as many employees for a given number of guest rooms as a comparable hotel outside China. Yet the expatriates, small though their numbers were, cost more than the far larger Chinese staffs they oversaw. At the Jianguo, for example, the salaries and other benefits paid to the 45 expatriates cost about $1.5 million in 1985, when the total payroll for the 700 Chinese employees was only $1 million. Such paradoxes did not go unnoticed by the Chinese staff, which could not help but be aware of disparities in compensation and standard of living, because expatriate managers lived as well as worked in the hotel. Their off-duty personal lives were inseparable from their on-duty identities.[19]

A hidden cost of expatriates that the Chinese especially deplored was the wage inflation the joint-venture hotels set off even in the Chinese-owned hotels and enterprises, where managers saw how much foreigners earned and demanded raises. The Chinese press carefully tracked the expense of the expatriates, celebrating cases in which Chinese managers replaced foreigners, and condemning cases in which foreign exchange costs for salaries and imported supplies at some hotels actually exceeded receipts from foreign guests. The Chinese also scrutinized the expatriate managers to make sure they applied work rules consistently. The Sheraton, for example, was praised for promptly firing a foreign cook on the same day that he had struck a Chinese cook, while a similar incident at the Hilton International in Shanghai, involving a Hong Kong front-office manager who had argued with and slapped a Taiwanese guest, did not end with a firing. The Hilton was unusual because it was wholly foreign-owned and managed, and the hotel and local Chinese authorities publicly feuded over the proper disposition of the slapping incident and other matters. But the hotel, not beholden to any Chinese partner, was unrepentant. Rosa Lau, public relations manager for the hotel, said: "I think [the Chinese] envy us because we are free to manage in our own style."[20]

No one particular style of management was shared by all the new hotels, nor were all the expatriates in any one hotel necessarily of one mind about management approaches. Some prescribed give-no-quarter strictness; others, gentle sensitivity to "cultural differences." Even within the different nationalities—Hong Kong providing a majority of the expatriate staff members, with Singapore, the Philippines, Western Europe, Australia, and the United States supplying the others—differences could be seen that followed individual experiences and temperaments more than lines of nationality. Generally speaking, however, the expatriates all believed that improved training of the Chinese staff was the highest priority, and training was helped by starting with a clean slate and hiring only Chinese who had had no previous hotel work experience. Alex Tan, the personnel manager at China's largest hotel, the Garden in Canton, explained why he preferred to work with "raw material": "If people come to us from a locally run hotel, they might think that brushing their hair or standing on one leg in public is acceptable behavior, as it is in local hotels." Tan and his counterparts at the other hotels brought in all the apparatus used in training hotel employees in other foreign countries—training manuals, videotape courses, English teachers. The training not only covered specific skills, such as how to register a guest, clean a table, or open a bottle of wine, but also how to greet guests cheerfully—even how to smile. Joseph Roseman, the first general manager sent to the Great Wall after Sheraton took over, launched a hundred-day "smile campaign."[21]

The frustration the expatriates frequently expressed concerned a post-training problem: the failure of the intermediate layer of Chinese supervisors to admonish employees who did not adhere to standards. Eighty expatriates could not supervise the work of 1,600 employees alone, check the beds of 1,000 guest rooms or watch every plate that left ten kitchens. But Chinese supervisors, in the words of one expatriate general manager, "are reluctant to use their authority over their colleagues." The observed phenomenon—that the Chinese supervisors "would rather turn away from a problem than confront it"—was rooted in the nature of labor relations in post-Cultural Revolution China.[22]

When the Sheraton took over the Great Wall, the Chinese press acclaimed the philosophy of "mutual understanding" that would guide, it was said, its labor relations. A fictional problem was proposed: Suppose a Chinese worker frequently reported to work late. How would the supervisor solve the problem? The Sheraton system would direct the departmental supervisor to seek out the worker for a chat and approach the problem without accusations: "If you could solve the tardiness problem, that would be a big help to me." Later, the supervisor could have the trust of the employee and could work with him or her in analyzing the reasons for tardiness and discuss any personal difficulties. The Chinese press summed up the "special characteristic" of this Sheraton management philosophy in this way: "The manager should place him or herself in a position equal to that of the employee, and should proceed from understanding the other person's perspective." This was enthusiastically welcomed by the Chinese because it fit neatly with the fictional egalitarianism that dominated the rhetoric of the Chinese workplace—no one was to exercise authority over anyone else.[23]

This talk of managers-as-best-friends, however, was not heard for long. Not unlike Wang Xifeng in *The Dream of the Red Chamber,* the expatriates at the Great Wall Sheraton and all the other foreign-managed hotels instituted regulations that spelled out the individual responsibilities of each worker; the compliant were offered generous material incentives, the uncompliant, stiff punishment, or at least the threat of it. Even Chinese-managed hotels began to adopt similar systems. At the Jinling Hotel in Nanjing, which was wholly Chinese-owned and managed, but which had adopted the management system of a Hong Kong hotel where its managers had studied, Liu Binyan observed the minuteness of the details of rules that stipulated fines for minor infractions such as entering the hotel compound without showing one's identification, yawning, or not offering a polite greeting when meeting guests.

Appalled that Chinese still had to have disciplinary rules spelled out for such simple things, Liu read deeper significance into the apparent need for such rules, seeing them as a warning about the very state of

Chinese civilization. Consider the case of Japan, he said, where he had gone in 1940 and had noticed that even in the lowest class of hotels, the staff members had already internalized courtesies and habits of basic hygiene; the hotels by then no longer needed to stipulate that spitting carried a fine. Yet more than forty years later, here were the highest class hotels in China, whose service employees—picked as the crème de la crème of the work force and the beneficiaries of elaborate training—still had to be fined so that "they would not make a loud hubbub or pick their nose in public, who still had to be required to say 'hello' and 'excuse me' and the other Ten Polite Expressions that have become the standard phrases of the citizens of the advanced countries!" To Liu, such details signaled a dismal state of affairs for China as a nation.[24]

Liu even defended the controversial use of foreign furnishings and supplies in the new hotels, costly and symbolically humiliating though they were, because China simply did not make substitutes of adequate quality. The prosaic toilet was offered as an example. The foreign-made toilet was a wonder: It flushed cleanly, and it stopped when it was supposed to. On the other hand, Liu said disdainfully, Chinese toilets simply would not do: They always leaked. Liu continued:

> Do you want to know the reason? Of course it is not because Chinese people are stupid. But one cannot say that there is not a bit of laziness. Why laziness? Because there is no competition, no need to rack one's brain, to be original, to keep improving. So long as you met or exceeded the production value quota, the work was done.

Sardonically, he added, "Anyway, the state takes care of everything; it's a planned economy, isn't it?"[25]

Another Chinese, Zhang Xinsheng, an interpreter who accompanied foreign tourist groups, described his own change in feelings about the demanding standards of the new international hotels. In the old days of 1977, when he dropped off two American women at their room at the Nanjing Hotel, at the time the best one in town, he overheard them loudly exclaiming how filthy the room was. He had been surprised and had rushed into the bathroom to see what was the matter. It turned out there were a few water drops on the sink and some stains on the floor tiles. He had nodded politely but had thought how bourgeois these tourists were, finding things to complain about in such a splendid room. Ten years later, however, after he had a chance to visit the United States, he had discovered that American bathrooms were so clean that small rugs could be placed on the floor without mishap and one did not have to wear thongs to keep above the excreta on the latrine floor as one did in China. Most impressive of all to Zhang was that the cleanliness was not solely the result of the labor of exploited maids. "In many well-off families," Zhang told Chinese readers, "the housewife kneels on the floor and scrubs and cleans."[26]

These details were fascinating to Chinese because of the rarity in China of private bathrooms and the decline in the maintenance of public bathrooms. When state propaganda maintained that everyone was the Master of the House, then over time, after the fading of ideological exhortations to contribute to the public weal, no one had felt the responsibility to take much care of public space, leaving the disagreeable tasks such as care of the latrines to someone else—that is, to no one. The arrival of the joint-venture hotels and their high standards of cleanliness came as a jolt to a society that had become habituated to ignoring the filth outside the interior, private space of each family. In 1988, concerned that execrable conditions in the bathrooms in Beijing, including those in restaurants that catered to foreign guests, were leaving a terrible impression on visiting tourists, Bo Xicheng, director of the Beijing Tourism Administration (and a powerful figure by virtue of his father, Bo Yibo, a senior member of the Party Central Committee), launched a campaign for toilet hygiene, "the embodiment of a people's level of civilization."

Leading a "toilet patrol" of journalists on surprise inspections of restaurant bathrooms around town, Bo found that he was fighting entrenched acceptance of unclean toilets. Foreign reporters who tagged along on one patrol asked one Chinese man whether the bathroom at which they were standing seemed smelly to him. The man asked in reply, "Can a toilet really not smell?" Such attitudes made the introduction of international hotel standards to China significant because the new standards demanded a fundamental change in the way that public space was regarded. The Chinese had to be trained to recapture the attitude that had been present in their society in the 1950s but had subsequently been lost, that public space was to be regarded with the same concern and care as private.[27]

The tension in China that existed between managers, who wanted to exercise the prerogatives of their position, and their employees, who resented the empty rhetoric of their putative status as proletarian masters, not underlings, could be seen in virtually all places of work, regardless of whether the managers were foreign or Chinese. The problem of poor worker performance can be traced back to the late 1960s and early 1970s, when managers returned to their posts after the worst of the chaos of the Cultural Revolution had passed, but no longer had the means or the desire to enforce discipline. Thus began what Andrew Walder has called "indulgent patterns of authority," when Chinese managers turned a blind eye to tardiness, absenteeism, bogus claims for sick leave at full pay, theft of tools and materials, and work force problems. Most damaging was the slowing of the pace of work, which workers regarded, like the noonday nap, as another reason why socialism was superior to capitalism. Although the Maoists who had created the conditions in which these problems germinated were no longer in authority by the 1980s, the residual legacy was pervasive.[28]

Supervisors never fully regained authority over subordinates, who knew that ordinary workers were the unprivileged in a society rife with special privileges and who clung all the more tenaciously to the only thing they did possess, the old rhetoric of the proletariat standing as Masters of the House. Expatriates unknowingly collided with this political legacy of the past when they looked to Chinese middle managers to exercise supervision over the rank and file. Training in hotel skills could not quickly solve a deeper problem of political culture. As the largest employers of all foreign-managed ventures, international hotels exposed the tension most visibly. But other foreign managers in the broadest possible array of work sites, from the large operation of a 4,000 employee Jeep assembly plant in Beijing, to the three-person representative offices found in a number of major Chinese cities by the late 1980s, all inherited the problem of enforcing a post-indulgent regime of discipline.

No one prepared Irl Hicks for the lax work attitudes of the 3,600 Chinese employees who would be placed under his charge. Hicks, a mechanical engineer who had spent his career with Babcock and Wilcox, was asked in 1985 to go to Beijing to manage the company's new boiler-manufacturing joint venture. All he knew about China before his departure was its blurry remoteness: China was "somewhere on the other side of the map." He later recalled how little preparation he had been given from his company. "Basically all they said was, 'Go to China. Good luck.' " In contrast to the international hotels, which were built from the ground up, this venture, like many of the larger industrial operations set up as joint ventures, inherited plant, machinery, and work force from the Chinese partner. When Hicks arrived at the site and toured for the first time, he was taken aback by the presence of 600 beds scattered around the factory floor. "People were sleeping all over the place." In his estimation, only 1,200 of the 3,600 employees actually worked; the rest were "loafing."[29]

Hicks instituted a new regime: no sleeping, no drinking, no card-playing. The noonday break was trimmed back from the prevailing custom of three hours to forty-five minutes. Employees were required to wear identification badges. The work force was reduced from 3,600 to 2,200. Steep bonuses were offered to high-performing departments, but evaluations were determined in part by spot-checks by Hicks or the other expatriate managers, who roamed through the factory several times a day with a silver counter in hand, clicking only when they observed a worker visibly working. These measures helped Hicks reclaim authority and hold each employee responsible for placing factory interests above personal interests while on the job. It was a difficult process because of the beginning presumption of the workers that they, not the managers, were the Masters, at least in their own immediate workplace, the one area where they were not powerless. At one point, several hundred angry employees in a department that had received lower bonuses than others staged a wildcat strike and surrounded Hicks, shouting and brandishing bricks. Factory Party officials came to the rescue, but Hicks did not back down; the bonus system remained in place.[30]

Don St. Pierre, the president of Beijing Jeep, discovered the same resistance to managerial authority. In an interview published in 1986 in the *People's Daily,* St. Pierre was frank about his frustration in trying to get management decisions implemented. He was not accustomed to having to explain all assignments thoroughly and spending so much time on persuasion. He told the Chinese reporter: "In the United States, the words of the boss are orders—there is nothing for the worker to say." But in the Jeep factory, a decision made at the top would be passed down through the intermediate layers until it reached the lowest level, where workers obeyed or disobeyed, seemingly as they pleased. Chinese managers too were frustrated about their inability to move subordinates in desired directions, but they had become inured to their own weakness. Expatriate managers like St. Pierre, however, were not accustomed to this state of affairs and fought hard to exercise the powers managers took for granted in the United States. The Chinese authorities were sympathetic to the complaints but only up to a point; the St. Pierre interview was carried in the overseas edition of the newspaper, not in the domestic edition.[31]

If the frustration of these American factory managers seems to be the plaint of the notoriously impatient American archetype, the similar frustration of other expatriate managers suggests that this was not the case. The complaints were alike because they faced a common problem, ejecting Chinese workers as figurative occupants of the boss's office. The experience of Werner Gerich, a retired West German engineer appointed in 1984 as the first foreigner to manage a Chinese factory since the Communists had taken power, deserves mention. Gerich tried his best to transform a diesel engine factory in Wuhan into an efficient producer of reliable engines. Toward this end, he fired the incumbent chief engineer and the head of quality control, whose department Gerich described as a "home for the old and sick, a harbor for the lazy and a sanitarium for those who have good connections." He revamped the wage and bonus system in such a way that the completion of work tasks and the workers' own material self-interests were linked.

After one year, Gerich had implemented some 120 separate improvements in operations, but though a Chinese journal praised his instilling a greater sense of "urgency" in the work force, the cumulative effect of the change was barely noticeable. The factory was still overstaffed because though he had fired the two top employees, he did not have the power to go further and trim the work force of 2,100 down to the 1,400 he thought was actually needed. It still took three days to get done what would take only three hours in Germany. Most discouraging of all, when Gerich returned to the factory in 1986 after a two-month home leave in Germany, he discovered that workers had reclaimed their accustomed rights and gone back to their old ways: reading newspapers, napping, or sitting in apparent idleness when they were supposed to be working. Gerlich was demoralized. "After a year of fighting, I am tired."[32]

Race was also an issue when the Chinese were concerned about remaining in control of imported technology. Although joint ventures, by their very nature, suggested a sharing of power, in fact the Chinese partner was not willing to give up any prerogatives that it did not absolutely have to. And those were few because foreign supplicants were not averse to making compromises in China that would not be made elsewhere. Ying Price, the American commercial officer at the U.S. consulate in Canton, summarized the proposition that the Chinese offered to foreign guests in 1986:

> Basically, what China means by a joint venture is "You come to us. You bring us the capital. You bring us your most up-to-date, state-of-the-art technology. You even bring us the market that we can sell into. Then you teach us everything you know. And, after 15 or 20 years, after we've

> mastered your technology, we say goodbye. You leave and go back to where you came from. And then we take your product, which you taught us to make, and which we can now manufacture in our country cheaper than you can manufacture it in your own, and we compete with you in the international market."[33]

Chinese interest in technology was often saturated with nationalism and racism, with the conviction that China's greatness, though temporarily hidden, would eventually manifest itself and teach the condescending outside world who was who. All that was required was getting hold of the technology, the practical tools of the West that had attracted the Self-Strengtheners of the nineteenth century. Japan was a source of inspiration—doubly so because if the Japanese, the traditional targets of Chinese derision, could master Western technology, surely nothing would stop the Chinese from doing the same and going on to do even better. When one of the first Chinese reporters from the People's Republic came to the United States in 1978, he visited CBS studios and noticed that the color television sets were all Japanese made. The reporter, Wang Ruoshui, reasoned aloud in his report to readers back home that if Japanese television sets were superior to American ones, then China should be able to make sets better than both. "Why can't we accomplish what the Japanese can?" Wang asked rhetorically. It was less of a question than a call to action.[34]

China depicted its adult students who received foreign technical training as patriotic exemplars of studiousness, defying the expectations of foreigners by working twice as hard in their studies and succeeding twice as fast as anybody else. Even Liu Binyan could get caught up in the emotion of such stories; he proudly repeated the details of an inspiring tale of a group of Chinese hotel managers who went to Hong Kong and mastered in only forty days of dawn-to-midnight study a management course that usually took six months to complete. Such stories were not the creation of the Chinese imagination; real Chinese studied as hard as the stories said they did, and numerous American hosts corroborated the stories. But another set of impressions, which did not get much play in the American press and got absolutely none in the Chinese press, was that American managers and engineers, in the course of supervising and training ordinary Chinese workers, found that they were not noticeably eager, attentive learners. The Americans complained, in fact, that Chinese mechanics and the other skilled tradespeople who were assigned to learn the details of the operation and maintenance of imported equipment from the United States were perhaps the most unreceptive "know-it-alls" they had ever worked with.[35]

Many American technical personnel had previously worked in similar capacities as trainers in Saudi Arabia, and their comparisons of the Saudi Arabian workers and the Chinese were not flattering to the latter. The Americans were not necessarily looking for obsequiousness—certainly the Saudis were the equal of the Chinese in possessing a strong sense of self and nation—but the Americans were expecting that their advice would be listened to. In China, it was openly disregarded. Attitudes among individual technicians merely reflected the spirit of official policy. When Americans counseled incremental steps and the transfer of less complex technology, the Chinese demanded the state of the art. The government reasserted the maxim that the Chinese were their own masters, and no one else's advice mattered. Grab the satchel of tools and send the foreigners packing. How strikingly different were scenes taking place in Saudi Arabia at the same time, as Saudi engineers quietly replaced the last remaining expatriates, but without histrionic breast-beating about their Saudi superiority.[36]

The overweening pride of Chinese officials and managers was often costly. Foreign visitors could not help but see the hulks of tens of millions of dollars' worth of imported machinery and equipment—plastic molding machines, welding robots, machine tools, mainframe computers—gathering rust outside factories or dust inside, plainly unused from the moment they had arrived because of insufficient technical expertise on hand. American companies also discovered that it was difficult to convince Chinese factories to stock spare parts for imported equipment, or if they were willing, often only after rejecting a recommended list and drawing up their own. Penny-wise, pound-foolish stories about Chinese resistance to foreign advice circulated in endless variation within the expatriate communities in China, such as the case of the three-cent washer that had to be sent via air express from the United States. The ultimate moral of such mishaps, however, was that this was the cost when the Chinese refused to accede to any advice that would, in their eyes, erode the absoluteness of their control.[37]

The gentle voice of Ray Vander Weele, a professor of accounting at the University of Wisconsin who made several lecture trips to China, can stand as an example of the mildest form of friendly advice offered to the Chinese. Weele was teaching one winter in a factory in the early 1980s when the Chinese manager, speaking through an interpreter, boasted of his plans to place a dozen personal computers in the factory by the next year. Weele, who was teaching in a room that had ten broken windows and in which the students were huddled together to keep warm, did not praise the decision as the factory manager apparently expected. Instead he replied, in English, "What you really need before you buy computers is a good piece of chalk, some decent pencils, and someone who can buck the bureaucracy to get the windows fixed." But then Weele told his interpreter not to translate his reply because he did not want to "deflate the manager's expectations." The Japanese were more blunt and treated the Chinese as students. One could say that the Japanese turned the Chinese boast back on them. If the Chinese were indeed masters of their own house, then they should stop complaining and take more responsibility for the success or failure of their technology imports. As much as Americans may have wanted to express similar sentiments, for the most part they spared the Chinese such direct criticism, just as Ray Vander Weele instinctively pulled his punches, not wanting to risk offending his host. The ultimate effect of American reluctance to offer frank criticism, however, was to corroborate tacitly the exaggerated sense Chinese had of their own omniscience.[38]

Percival Darby was an American hotel manager who, while working as general manager for Chinese hotels, first in Shenzhen, later in Chongqing, butted heads with Chinese officials over the issue of who would be in command. The battles that would make him a cause célèbre in the Chinese press in 1988 can be seen, in retrospect, as originating a few years earlier in 1985, when he was manager of the Shenzhen International Hotel. He introduced a new incentive system, including an "employee of the month" award. He intended the award to be conferred on the basis of performance, a notion that clashed immediately with the ideas of the Chinese supervisors, who instead saw the award as a plum that could be promised, well in advance, to favored subordinates. Other problems concerned how seriously Chinese employees took the standard injunction used in hotel training for employees to treat the hotel as respectfully as they would their own home, reinforced by frequent references in the professional jargon to a hotel as "the house."

In many Third World countries, Western hotel managers found that this was initially difficult to get across, but not so in China. Chinese workers arrived with the idea that the hotel, like everything else in the People's Republic, was supposed to be theirs; it was plainly a lie that invited "hit-and-run" attempts to make good on the empty promises wherever opportunity presented itself. The well-known short life of the joint-venture agreements further reinforced the idea that hotels "belonged to China," hence the Chinese People and managers like Darby had to contend with the pathologies that resulted: extraordinarily high rates of theft of food, cutlery, linen—virtually anything of value that was not bolted down. Darby, a former professor of hotel administration in Florida, was taken aback by the apparent lack of compunction that should have moderated employee theft. Rat traps that he personally set around the hotel disappeared; even the decorative goldfish in the hotel pond did not last long.[39]

These complaints alone are not noteworthy. Other expatriate managers had their own sets of stories of employee pilferage, and so did the Chinese—managers of state enterprises had their own tales of brazen employee theft, and the employees had matching tales of official corruption and appropriation of state property for private use. What makes the Darby case of particular interest is the way it illuminates the hidden shapes of power and proprietorship upon which Western management systems transferred to China foundered. In 1986, when Darby moved to the position of general manager of the Chongqing Hotel, a joint venture that was preparing for its grand opening, he began with a new work force. The same conflicts followed. Darby put in a strict regime of fines and firings which held both the employees and their Chinese supervisors strictly responsible for performance. He made a conspicuous example of holding himself, and his wife Norma, who was the supervisor of the coffee shop, to the same standards. When he discovered, during one of his infamous impromptu inspection tours, that a napkin on one of the coffee shop tables had a hole, he fined the waitress 5 yuan [$1.35] for failing to notice it, and Norma 3 yuan for being partly responsible.[40]

Darby was not inhibited about making his displeasure public, and he told a reporter from the *Washington Post* of the vexations of managing a hotel where the Chinese managers were afraid to make strict demands on subordinates and did not know how to provide good service, where the chief housekeeper thought that getting hotel rooms "almost clean" was good enough. He fired more than 100 employees at the hotel during his first eighteen months as manager, which the Chinese press regarded as "probably a record for China since 1949." Darby, however, denied that he fired people: "They fire themselves. I make rules and penalties. You knowingly break a rule, you're out." But while enforcing his own rules, Darby broke several unwritten rules of the prevailing organizational culture in China, one of which was do not fire the sons and daughters of high-level officials. He himself was fired by the hotel's Chinese board of directors in early 1988.[41]

The announced reasons for his firing were so incredible that a Chinese newspaper dispatched an inquisitive investigative reporter, Jiang Yang, to look into the matter. When the hotel's board chairman told Jiang that Darby had been fired for his inexperience and lack of suitable qualifications, Jiang pointed out this was puzzling, because just a few months before Darby had been praised by the board for his strict and "scientific" management, for raising standards and increasing revenue. As for lack of qualifications, Jiang asked, how could a certified hotel administrator and former professor in the field be judged unqualified? The board chairman changed tack and said the real problem was that there were others who were simply better than Darby. After all, was it not the board's right to experiment constantly, to weed out the weaker candidates and select the stronger? Jiang allowed that this reasoning was plausible enough, but here did not seem credible because the general manager position at the hotel remained vacant after Darby's forced departure.[42]

One hotel official said that Darby had "slandered Chinese managers and hurt the feelings of the Chinese people" with the critical remarks that had appeared in the *Washington Post* story. But Jiang went back to the *Post* story and confessed that he could not find any passages that were slanderous or offensive. One by one, Jiang lobbed back each reason that he was given for Darby's dismissal. Darby was accused by his ex-employers of not understanding "the state of the nation"—this was the euphemistic catchphrase frequently used among Chinese for the deplorably backward conditions of China—but Jiang rejected the charge when applied to Darby. The principal Chinese condition that Darby did not "understand," Jiang said, was the Chinese partners in the joint venture throwing banquets and entertaining officials and their cronies, claiming that this was the only way to get things done. When Darby had ordered the accounting department to provide daily reports of income and expenditures, the Chinese staff, accustomed to preparing reports at more leisurely monthly intervals, complained that Darby did not "understand China." This cliché and its equally handy variant, "we don't do things that way here in China," were used to ward off changes that demanded more work.[43]

Darby, like all other foreigners in China, could always be told that his methods were inappropriate because foreigners did not, *could* not, truly understand a country as different as China. This reasoning depended on imagery that emphasized extreme differences, invoked only when it was convenient. Jiang, however, saw through the excuses and got to the heart of the Darby case by pointing out that ultimately it concerned a struggle over who was to run the hotel. Darby had not tolerated interference with his management decisions, as when the Chinese chairman of the board and others authorized expenditures on their own. Darby was quoted as having once told the board, "Let me drive this car [referring to the hotel]. As long as I'm driving, how it is driven is my responsibility. If while driving, you grab the steering wheel, and then another person comes along to grab it too, the car will flip over, and you'll say it's my responsibility." Darby wanted sole command of the wheel, or to change metaphors, Darby wanted to be the master of the house, and that proved intolerable.[44]

The board that had hired Darby had not gotten used to the idea that appointing a general manager meant delegating power. The Darby case was only one of a number discussed in the Chinese press as examples of mismanagement by the Chinese who headed the boards of directors of joint ventures. On those occasions when the authorities recognized it was a problem that endangered the success of joint ventures and China's campaign to attract foreign investment, they ascribed the problem to simple inexperience. The chairs were supposed to exercise their authority only by convening board meetings, not by taking on the mantle of operational manager and usurping the delegated powers of the general manager, such as ordering that certain individuals be hired. The chairs were known to bypass the foreign general manager entirely and give orders directly to the shadow structure of Chinese deputies that created a dual management system: the official one, whose chief of operations was the foreign general manager, and the unofficial one, whose de facto chief of operations was the Chinese board chair. By 1988, Beijing, Fujian, and several other places had begun to offer special training classes for board chairs and members, based on the premise that education would fix the problem.[45]

It could be argued, however, that the problem was less one of education than the deeper one of an inherited style of unbridled command at the top, which the arrival of foreign general managers in joint ventures undermined. Even though Western observers often explained to foreign businesspeople that China was a country in which decisions were made only by consensus, the most powerful individuals in any given Chinese organization exercised power far in excess of that of their Western counterparts. The Chinese organization contained the phenomenon of peremptory executive orders at the same time that routine decisions were openly challenged. Don St. Pierre of Beijing Jeep was frustrated because his Chinese subordinates did not accept his instructions, but this was because he was a foreigner managing Chinese. Chinese officials who managed a Chinese organization were not bound by strictly defined job descriptions that would circumscribe their powers; they had power over housing assignments, ration coupons, medical and welfare benefits, and other critical resources that governed the personal lives of employees and their dependents. If Americans like St. Pierre were fond of saying that the words of the boss were orders, the Chinese could say that they too had their own equivalent expression: "Whatever I say, goes."

One Hong Kong businessperson who talked with a number of Chinese officials about possible investment projects said the Chinese often tried to allay any uneasiness he had about investing in their localities by saying, "Rest assured that if you invest here, you are certain to make a lot of money because around here, 'Whatever I say, goes.' " These words did not have their desired effect on the Hong Kong investor. As soon as he heard them, he knew that he would be utterly dependent on the patronage of a single person and would have no assurance of local compliance with national policies and laws. But these words suggest that Chinese bureaucrats were accustomed to getting their own way. Within their own organizations, these Local Emperors, as they were derisively called by their unappreciative minions, ruled with virtually no effectual check on their powers, but their powers were exercised for personal gain, not for the furtherance of collective interests.[46]

As joint ventures brought Chinese partners together with Western, Chinese managers discovered as great a change in the accepted way of operations at the top of the organization as Chinese employees did at the bottom. It was extremely difficult, however, to set up what were in effect isolated islands of distinctly separate organizational cultures, where performance on the job was to matter more than preexisting networks of favors and personal connections. Liu Binyan saw this and lamented how even at the Jinling Hotel in Nanjing, which was entirely managed by Western-trained Chinese, the hotel's fragile "microclimate" was beset by constant intrusion from without. When members of the hotel staff, for example, finished their first day of work within an environment that prized courtesy and high standards of service and changed out of their uniforms back into street clothes, they were bursting "from head to toe with the spirit of a 'Jinling person.' " But then they left the hotel and headed home; outside, they encountered on the bus and at stores the sullen or rude patterns that were the antithesis of what they were told service should be in the hotel. When they returned to work the next day, Liu said, they had to "consciously work to regenerate the smile of the 'Jinling person.' "[47]

For Liu, the microclimate of the joint-venture hotels represented not just a vast improvement over the service offered outside, it also offered a model of strictly defined accountability he suggested the government would do well to emulate. What would it be like, Liu wondered aloud, if the promotion and demotion system of the Jinling Hotel were to be converted into an evaluation system for the Chinese government itself. Chinese officials at the various levels—department head, section head, bureau head—would be evaluated monthly and annually and would have to explain their concrete achievements for each period under review. These were not proper thoughts for a Communist Party member, or so at least said the Communist Party. Liu's essay, published in November 1986, got him in trouble with the authorities. It was not the first time, but it soon proved to be the beginning of the last.[48]

When student demonstrations for democracy erupted the next month and Liu lent his support, the Party expelled him. The student protests of December 1986 and January 1987 would turn out to be a prelude to the uprising in 1989, which came to overshadow all the smaller groundswells that had preceded it. But it should not be forgotten that at the time it appeared, Liu's essay about service standards in the new hotels raised questions about the status quo that made the authorities uncomfortable. As improbable as it may at first seem, Liu's discussion of coffee shop service in 1986 was seditious because it broached the revolutionary notion of accountability and extended it to the government itself. Although the ferment for change that appeared in the spring of 1989 grew most visibly in the microclimate of China's universities, in its own small way the microclimate of the joint venture contributed too.[49]

V

SPREADING CONSUMERISM

10.

THE MARKETING OF MARKETING

Like many best sellers of an earlier day, Carl Crow's *Four Hundred Million Customers* (1937) is today virtually forgotten. Blessed and cursed with a beguiling, if misleading, title, the book, if remembered at all, is referred to as a musty reminder of early unrealized dreams of the fantastic China market. But this is so only because it goes unread. The book, in fact, is an album of humorous sketches of Westerners and Chinese employing different cultural codes as they go about trying to conduct business with each other, often unsuccessfully. Carl Crow (1883–1945), born, raised, and educated in Missouri, had gone to Shanghai as a reporter in 1911 and spent most of the next few decades in Asia, including many years as owner of his own advertising agency in Shanghai. Prone to sentimentalizing the Chinese, whom he described as "interesting, exasperating, puzzling, and almost always lovable," but with a self-deprecating Midwestern style that mocked his own behavior and attitudes, Crow attempted in *Four Hundred Million Customers* to explain precisely how Chinese and Americans differed in their views of business. A reporter for the *Financial Times* would many years later say—apparently solely on the basis of the book's title—that Crow had "prematurely" touted the "marketing opportunities in China," but Crow had done nothing of the sort. Rather, he tried to explain why the opportunities in China were limited and would remain so. In a passage that could have served as well in describing China chic in the early 1980s as it did when it was written in the 1930s, he wrote: "It is really remarkable how much vanity there is in supposedly astute businessmen, or how much romance. It is either vanity or the romantic idea that business is like an adventure story that, in many cases, provides the urge to make them open expensive branch offices all over the world."[1]

Foreign offices, said Crow, "broke out in Shanghai like measles" in the period following World War I. He observed: "It is to be hoped that the manufacturers had a lot of fun out of their ventures, because they didn't make much money." The problem, he said, was not so much the difficulty of knowing how to market goods in China; instead, the very idea of marketing itself, of devoting attention to the processes of distribution and selling and of making plans accordingly, was foreign. With broad generalizations and what may seem to some to be an excessive fondness for the well-told anecdote, Crow was more raconteur than academic sociologist. But his interest in the subject of the transplanted sales representative in China, and the interest shown by his readers at the time—*Four Hundred Million Customers* quickly went through a number of printings both in the United States and in England—reveal antecedents of the interest in Willy Loman on the Beijing stage fifty years later.[2]

Americans and Chinese were a pair of opposites, according to Crow. On the one side of the Pacific, America had produced "the greatest race of salesmen the world has ever known" because the entire nation reveled in selling and being sold to. On the other side, China seemed not to have produced any salespeople, or at least none who were held in any honor. Chinese customers knew exactly what they wanted, Crow said, and were suspicious of "any form of eloquence that is designed to part them from their money." Salespeople were held in such low repute that Crow could not even imagine a convention of Chinese salespeople being held because "everyone would be ashamed to attend it." Chinese merchants went to great lengths to avoid any appearance of sales pressure: The most prosperous shops in Shanghai were ostentatiously shabby, windowless and dark, cluttered with boxes in the aisles that hid ancient display cases, as if to reassure customers that money had not been frittered away on interior decor. Chinese students who went abroad to attend college in the United States had returned to China with what Crow called "the plate glass and steel furniture complex and the idea that China's progress depended on the adoption of these window dressing methods." A few had convinced their fathers to change, but most had not.[3]

War intervened, with the Japanese invasion in 1937, then the civil war that followed the defeat of the Japanese in 1945. The founding of the People's Republic, and its subsequent isolation from the capitalist world, meant that many more years passed before China was next exposed to the American enthusiasm for marketing. By then, the years of strictures about capitalism should have left the Chinese even more wary than before of marketing, but by then the field of marketing had itself changed. The attention given to surface appearances—for Crow, flashy furniture, for Miller's Willy Loman, the "smile and a shoeshine"—had given way to an elaborate apparatus of survey research and statistical analysis designed to better understand consumer behavior. No longer ideologically tainted as capitalist chicanery, marketing was now a neutral "science," safe for application in the socialist world.

Marketing research in the United States impressed the Chinese with its thoroughness, documenting the frequency of headaches, or diaper changes, or other actions one ordinarily gave little thought to. One Chinese article said that Procter and Gamble had even conducted "secret studies" to determine whether toilet paper was folded when it was used. To Chinese observers, market research seemed socially useful because it helped companies better meet the demands of the market. A simple model was tacitly assumed: Producers were passive respondents to market signals. Questions were not raised about how companies helped to contribute to the psychology that they were supposedly responding to.[4]

Marketing professors from the West who went to China to lecture were surprised that their Chinese students responded so enthusiastically to the "marketing concept," even though the professors regarded it as "fuzzier" than other disciplines like accounting and finance. Initially their students had seemed uneasy, but in the end they imbibed the marketing ethos with enthusiasm. A 1987 survey of current and past students at the Chengdu Management Center showed that they regarded courses on marketing, new product development, and consumer behavior as the most useful they had taken, even more than courses on materials management, cost accounting, and economics. In 1987, James Livingstone, a British professor who lectured at the State Economic Commission Management Center in Beijing, came to the opposite conclusion about Chinese culture and marketing than that arrived at by Carl Crow fifty years earlier. Livingstone said that Chinese receptivity to marketing concepts was "virtually innate in the Chinese character."[5]

The quintessential statement of the American marketing ethos that was sent to China was the philosophy that joined the promotion of the salesperson's own interests with those of the wider society. "I am Number One," declared Chen Yaqiong, a Chinese-American businesswoman who was interviewed for a Chinese magazine. Her declaration was delivered without apology; it was given, and clearly received, as inspirational advice for all businesspeople in China. Chen's philosophy was inspired by an American automobile salesman whom she admired and who had sold more than 1,400 cars in one year. He himself lived by the "I Am Number One" dictum and by so doing, she said, had made it come true. In China, said Chen, the traditional habit is not to promote oneself, but successful sales demanded the opposite. One must always start by liking and believing in oneself, she said, delivering New Age nostrums to New China. She told Chinese readers some secrets of how to gain the confidence of potential customers, but the techniques were less significant than the underlying ethos embodied in her unapologetic proselytizing for looking after Number One. If such an ethos could be held up for praise, then no institution from the capitalist West, no matter how loathsome originally, could be barred.[6]

Receptivity to the marketing concept led ineluctably to the reintroduction of commercial advertising, the central totem of capitalist culture, whose reappearance in China preceded the reappearance of stock markets by several years and first forced the Chinese to reconsider the distinctions that formerly had been drawn between capitalist and socialist societies. For most of its history, the People's Republic had castigated advertising as the apotheosis of the capitalist religion of consumption. This was especially so in the late 1960s during the height of the Cultural Revolution. Afterward, few commercial billboards or newspaper advertisements interrupted the skein of relentlessly political messages that crossed public space. When advertising was reintroduced in 1979, and its sanctioned scope expanded beyond industrial goods, the state faced a daunting ideological task: rebuilding a case for advertising in a socialist system that had long defined itself as one that did not need commercial exhortation. In essence, it had to sell the legitimacy of selling.[7]

The first announcement of the return of advertising was made indirectly, in January 1979, when an editorial appeared in a Shanghai newspaper calling for "restoring the good name of advertising." The author, Ding Yunpeng, conceded that people commonly associated advertising with "pulling tricks" and "empty boasting," but he claimed that advertising in capitalist countries had contributed to their economic successes and deserved study in socialist countries too. For example, in China during a time-out in a sports program broadcast on television, viewers had no choice "other than to rest for a moment." Ding added, "I think this is an enormous waste of the screen. I have heard that in other countries the evening period between 7 and 9 P.M. is 'golden time' during which the viewing rate is highest. Inserting commercials into this time period obtains effective results and high prices." Advertising could be useful for earning revenue, and also for "expanding the horizons of the great masses" and "increasing foreign exchange receipts." But one benefit mentioned by Ding stands apart from the rest, at least to American eyes habituated to commercial blight: "Outstanding advertisements can be used to beautify the people's cities, pleasing both the eye and the mind," which in turn would make people appreciate "the socialist economy and culture." The mention of esthetics suggests that in China escaping a monochromatic landscape may have been as much a rationale for permitting advertising again as anything else.[8]

The restoration of advertising proposed in this January 1979 editorial was presented merely as one person's thoughts. But this was not airing one person's opinion so much as it was an announcement to the public of a policy decision that had already been made and was about to be made manifest. The curtain lifted in Shanghai's *Liberation Daily* on the first day of the Chinese New Year in 1979, when a four-day series of advertisements for both consumer and industrial products appeared. Other ads followed quickly in Canton, Tianjin, and Beijing. Shortly thereafter, foreign companies were informed that they could place advertisements on radio, television, and billboards, and in newspapers and magazines. A newly resuscitated Shanghai Advertising Corporation immediately pursued foreign clients with English-language advertisements: "Do You Want To Promote Your Business? Consult Us. We Are Ready To Offer Full & Efficient Services."[9]

The Chinese staff members in these advertising agencies were anxious to deemphasize both the newness of their profession and its connection with capitalism, so they spoke often of the ancient world origins of advertising and its seemingly omnipresent character, stripped of a capitalist setting and found at the beginning of recorded history. In a chronological list of "firsts" in the advertising industry that was assembled for readers of a new marketing magazine, the "earliest advertisement" was traced to ancient Egypt, circa 3000 B.C., testimony to its apparent universal nature.[10] The same beginning has frequently been cited in the West. British historian Raymond Williams observes:

> It is customary to begin even the shortest account of the history of advertising by recalling the three-thousand-year-old papyrus from Thebes, offering a reward for a runaway slave, and to go on to such recollections

> as the crier in the streets of Athens, the paintings of gladiators, with sentences urging attendance at their combats, in ruined Pompeii, and the flybills on the pillars of the Forum in Rome. This pleasant little ritual can be quickly performed, and as quickly forgotten.

Williams suggests that the modern institutionalized system of advertising is a very different phenomenon; in Britain, the modern system emerged in the half-century between 1880 and 1930 and sought not so much to supply the market as to organize it. He adds, if by advertising we simply mean giving notice of something, "some pleasant recollections from the Stone Age could be quite easily devised." The Chinese did not go quite so far back, but the new historians of advertising in China did reach back to the Warring States period (for "Earliest Banner for a Wine Shop") and the Sui-Tang periods (for "Earliest Printed Advertisement.") These milestones belonged in no particular historical or economic context; they were merely "firsts."[11]

Looking back on the Republican period in the 1930s, when advertising had reached its fullest development in China, Chinese historians in the 1980s ignored the political and economic contexts defined by Chiang Kai-shek and capitalism, and noted with apparent approval the Republican period's various "firsts" ("Earliest Interior Neon Signs"; "Earliest Commercial Radio Broadcast"; "Earliest Advertisement On A Vehicle"). They also reached into the past for advertising techniques. The 1931 Shanghai debut of Mei Lanfang, then unknown but soon to emerge as one of China's best-known Beijing opera stars, became, in 1987, a study of the "clever" way in which a theater owner created interest through newspaper advertisements. As the story is retold, the theater owner purchased the entire front page of a newspaper and placed on it only three very large characters: Mei Lan Fang. Readers were completely mystified but intrigued. The advertisement ran three days in a row, and only on the fourth, in small type, was information added that explained the upcoming scheduled performances. All the shows were subsequently sold out, and the lesson drawn from the story for today's application was clear: Learn to use "psychology."[12]

More than historical anecdotes were needed, however, to undo the official denunciations of advertising during the preceding years; the state had to provide positive reasons for readopting advertising. It was not easy because the task required embracing an institution that the state itself had long identified as representing all that was pernicious in capitalism. Officialdom also had to keep clear in the minds of the general public how advertising in socialist China would not be the same as advertising in capitalist societies, though the differences were not easy for Chinese theoreticians to identify.

The state offered a basic reason why advertising should be encouraged in China: Advertising transmitted important economic information that helped link producers and consumers. This function, the authorities said, was as important in socialist as it was in capitalist society. The consumer demand for product information, one Chinese defender of advertising noted, "will not disappear simply because he has arrived in a socialist society." Therefore, people in a socialist system "will still have demands for advertising." The more news about products and services that went out to potential purchasers, the better for all—consumers and enterprises alike. The state argued that advertising did nothing more than factory sales agents in China already did: pitch products to potential customers. Advertising merely diffused product information more efficiently. In a country of such vast size, advertising could reach hundreds of thousands in a fraction of the time it took agents to make personal calls on dozens of potential customers. Simple geography dictated the use of advertising; ideology had no bearing on the matter.[13]

The Soviets had pressed the Chinese to curb advertising in the 1950s. One thoughtful Chinese writer in the 1980s recalled how logical it seemed then to spend money only on the physical production of goods. Distribution would take care of itself. In a capitalist system, firms were forced to advertise in order to triumph amid fierce competition, but in a planned economy—if not due to the plan, at least due to the scarcity—it was not necessary to advertise. Forbidding advertising in China's socialist society had been viewed as a source of tremendous savings, though ironically the Soviet Union, its socialist mentor, was having second thoughts and had begun to encourage advertising and product differentiation in the late 1950s. China remained unaffected, steadfastly eschewing such revisionism.[14]

In the 1980s, however, huge savings were said to be achievable only by encouraging advertising, not suppressing it. For example, a Chinese author, Ji Lianggang, argued in 1985 that advertising could not only bring in foreign exchange, it could also eliminate waste and promote import substitution. Writing in a Shanxi academic journal, Ji said that in some places in China's socialist economy, demand for a given good far exceeded supply, while in others supply of the same far exceeded demand; the lack of what Ji called a "matchmaker," a little bird that could fly from place to place, transmitting economic information, led to waste of material and human resources. Advertising could serve as the matchmaker, disseminating needed economic information about surpluses and shortages, and saving resources. Ji played on patriotic sentiments in presenting his argument: With the help of advertising, for example, Chinese factories could purchase automatic lathes produced by previously unknown domestic manufacturers instead of importing them at six times the cost at which they could be produced domestically. Enormous savings for the nation would result.[15]

Similarly, when research in China discovered the ability of a new toothpaste to prevent and treat certain kinds of mouth sores, few people knew about it until advertising came to the rescue, bringing healthful benefits—economic and literal. The Chinese advertising community argued that the consumer needs "scientific guidance in a socialist system as well as in a capitalist system." If advertising were "scientific"—the attraction to "science" endured even when the attraction to Marxism-Leninism was fading—then it could fulfill the role of "scientific guide."[16]

The Chinese public was told again and again in the 1980s that China needed advertising to be scientific and modern, to operate the economy efficiently, to catch up with the capitalist countries. But Chinese writers and lecturers had difficulty maintaining that China's use of advertising would somehow catch up with capitalist practice yet at the same time remain significantly different. Some Chinese advocates seemed unaware that the arguments they used to defend advertising were precisely the ones critics in capitalist societies used to attack it. These Chinese writers cheered advertising's ability to "stimulate the consumers' desire to consume." By converting "latent demand" into actual buying behavior, advertising helped meet the socialist goal of "expanding the sales of commodities." One author in 1985 even argued that advertising would help the Chinese work harder: "When people see or hear an advertisement, they will think, 'If I have enough money, I can buy these products.' These material reasons will impel them to work hard." He drew the conclusion that "advertising consequently accelerates the expansion of production." Another writer, reporting on the successful advertising campaigns of a Shanghai cosmetics factory, forthrightly called upon advertisers to "create demand." At that point, however, the ostensible distinction between socialist advertising and its capitalist cousin disappeared.[17]

Western observers were no less sensitive to the ideological significance of advertising than Chinese Party theoreticians. As soon as advertising was reintroduced on the mainland, the *Christian Science Monitor* declared in the unequivocal terms echoed by other newspapers and magazines in the United States that advertising was "the very essence of competitive bourgeois capitalist society." Foreign reporters had relished the discovery made in the early 1970s during the Cultural Revolution that the People's Republic of China tolerated multi-million-dollar advertising campaigns in Hong Kong on behalf of PRC-owned enterprises and PRC exports. PRC advertisements could be found throughout the colony on radio and television, newspapers, magazines, billboards, and even media sympathetic to Taiwan. Compared to others, their advertising was described by American reporters as sober and restrained, but in 1976, in another instance of puzzling change well before the official beginning of the open-door policy in 1978, a Westernizing shift was observed. The old patriotic appeals to overseas Chinese were discarded in favor of new themes stressing quality and economy and featuring middle-class models. But the PRC-owned advertising agency in Hong Kong that directed these campaigns was "almost pathologically shy," in the words of the *Los Angeles Times,* and refused to discuss its work with foreign reporters, betraying continued ideological unease about the subject. Americans watched the growth of PRC spending on advertising in Hong Kong with great interest, waiting for the opportunity to take Madison Avenue institutions directly to Beijing.[18]

The opportunity came in the late 1970s, with the further opening of the door to international contacts and business. American advertising agencies wasted little time in heading for China, but they were aghast at how little the Chinese knew about advertising. In July 1979, three large American agencies sent representatives to Beijing and Shanghai on a trip that, in the words of a chatty *New York Times* columnist, would "impart the wisdom of the West in exchange for the dream of finding the riches of the East." Their Chinese hosts, however, evinced the most fascination with the Polaroid cameras and slide-show paraphernalia the representatives brought along. Before the Chinese talked about advertising, said a representative of one of the American agencies, they should first learn more about the preliminary steps of marketing, such as product development, pricing, and distribution. Instead of talking about how their firms could help the Chinese in promoting exports abroad, their visit, in the words of one representative, "turned out be a Marketing and Advertising 101 course."[19]

Still, the American advertisers were not displeased to have found themselves in the role of teacher. Their hosts had "hung on to every word," and other advertising executives from the United States were also pleased to discover an opportunity to transfer their excitement about their professional calling to novices. One Western advertising executive in China described himself as an "evangelist," spreading knowledge among people who were thirsty to learn; his colleagues spoke of the satisfaction of being present at the creation of history. The first contingents of advertising executives seemed oblivious to hyperbole, such as the case of one person who exulted that he had helped do "what had never been done before" upon the occasion of placing an advertisement for Lux soap on the front cover of a Chinese magazine.[20]

Evangelical enthusiasm also infused another group of Western marketing professionals who headed to China: specialists in public relations. The first PR office was opened in Beijing in 1985, and the Chinese were again credited with being "natural public relations people." They already seemed to be master arrangers: knowing how to make proper seating arrangements and organizing ceremonies and putting the best public face on things. It seemed to be a valuable business skill, one of the few visible in the People's Republic, and hence disproportionate praise was lavished upon it. In 1985, for example, Robert Leaf, an executive for the giant Burson-Marsteller agency, said that "with the thoughtfulness in how they do things, the Chinese could give lectures on the subject right now." The *Washington Post* declared that taking the public relations business to China was "like bringing chopsticks."[21]

The welcome extended to American PR firms was smoothed by the prior existence of Party propaganda departments in all state enterprises and offices; many of the old departments were reincarnated as public relations offices. Lucy Hobgood-Brown, a public relations executive hired in 1982 by the Great Wall Hotel to help it prepare for its public opening, was frequently met with the greeting, "Oh, so you work in propaganda." The Americans were amused, but they also began to see that their conception of public relations departed from that of their Chinese counterparts in at least one important aspect: Western conceptions of public relations, at least ideally, included the function of gathering and analyzing feedback from the public, a function Chinese PR departments were slow to adapt because of their earlier incarnation as propaganda departments whose function was to pass the official line downward, not public sentiment upward.[22]

Still, the Chinese seemed to be a "PR practitioner's dream," said Scott Seligman of Burson-Marsteller. Press conferences drew every newspaper invited, and baldly commercial press releases were usually printed, often verbatim, because Chinese media regarded mention of any item related to foreign trade to be newsworthy. Hotel openings, groundbreakings, ribbon cuttings, factory openings—no ceremony was too trivial to be ignored by a press that seemed to have an insatiable appetite for stories that depicted a China in the process of modernization. Ronald Cromie, who headed the Beijing office of Hill & Knowlton, said he was often surprised to receive money in the mail from Chinese editors for press releases that had been sent out and published. "We returned the payments and explained that a press release was free information, free to be used however they wanted," Cromie said. He also discovered that some editors in China, unfamiliar with the rules of the game, mistook press releases for advertisements and wanted to know how much advertising space the agency was buying.[23]

Americans were no less aware of the ideological significance of public relations than of advertising. In the words of *Business Week,* Chinese interest in public relations was a sign that China was "serious about capitalism." American PR practitioners were excited about their self-defined roles of pioneers, offering American clients an opportunity to write the desired corporate images on what Seligman called a "blank slate," far removed from the inherited images that could never be erased at home. The Chinese were such apt pupils that in the eyes of the Americans no limits appeared to circumscribe the realm of the possible for the imaginative PR professional. Hobgood-Brown helped Disney arrange for a party for high-level officials and their children as part of a promotional campaign for a cartoon show, which alone would have been noteworthy in the annals of public relations in China, but she also arranged to hold the party at the Great Hall of the People, which was rented out for the occasion, a first. But the greatest coup was that of Burson-Marsteller, which did not open a Beijing office of its own, as did its archrival, Hill & Knowlton. Instead, the firm signed an agreement with the Xinhua News Agency, the official state news monopoly, with 6,000 employees, to serve as its resident partner. When Robert Leaf announced the new agreement, he said that there was "nothing like it in the PR field," which in this instance was *not* hyperbole. Having the sole news agency of China represent Burson-Marsteller's clients was the ultimate expression of why China was indeed the "PR practitioner's dream."[24]

China's new advertising and public relations professionals were hungry to learn about the promotional techniques of the capitalist countries, and their own professional journals were remarkably free of ideological cant. The specialized advertising journals in China provided readers with feasts of images of billboards and signs and other examples of foreign advertising, often without any accompanying explanations, ideological or otherwise. For example, a sampling of American cheesecake art in the 1940s, drawn from "One Hundred Years of Coca-Cola Advertising," appeared simply as a gallery of Western advertisements in *Chinese Advertising,* China's principal magazine for advertising professionals. In one typical Coca-Cola advertisement, a beauty in a bathing suit reclines at the beach, smiling coquettishly at an outstretched arm that offers a priapic bottle of Coke; the accompanying copy consists solely of a succinct double entendre: "Yes." Other issues provided Chinese with pictures of a Taco Bell restaurant, the golden arches of McDonald's, a gigantic papier-mâché bull standing on top of a steak house, and other samples of outdoor advertising in America, all without a word of commentary. When a Chinese newspaper carried a story in 1984 on Levi Strauss's agreement with the U.S. Olympic Committee, which had arranged for America's Olympic athletes to wear outfits supplied by the company, no mention was made of the controversy surrounding commercialization of America's amateur athletics. The Chinese credited the company with shrewdness and blandly described the American Olympians as "living advertisements."[25]

Western critics had long decried the numbing assault upon the senses of constant commercial messages, but the Chinese were not so critical. In 1987 one contributor to *Chinese Advertising,* for example, noted that in the United States every person, every day, received some 1,600 commercial messages. This fact alone, however, was not of interest; it simply was accepted as a part of modernity. What was deemed significant was that psychologists said the average consumer could remember only some ten or so messages by bedtime. The conclusion drawn was that Chinese advertising agencies must recognize the importance of psychology and find ways to make their own client's advertising memorable.[26]

Instead of focusing on the stupefying quantity of Western advertising, the Chinese chose to focus on the sophistication of the artistic quality of American and other foreign advertising, which was viewed as exemplifying the subtlety the Chinese advertising industry would be wise to emulate. For example, when a Chinese reporter visiting New York came across a lifelike statue in a small park near the World Trade Center and was fooled into thinking for a moment that the figure sitting on a bench dressed in a suit and shoes was a real person, he discovered nearby a small metal sign that identified the foundry which had created the work. This impressed him as a wonderful example of advertising—ingenious, artistic, and effective. In his story about the experience for a Chinese newspaper, he drew the lesson that advertising lacking "any obvious signs of advertising" was the most successful.[27]

Similar praise of a subtle approach was heaped upon Lufthansa's advertising campaign in the United States. A Chinese newspaper carried a tribute to the "feeling of intimacy" that "allows readers to be carried away" when they encountered a Lufthansa advertisement such as one that had appeared in *Newsweek.* It featured a young girl holding hands with a female flight attendant; the copy stated simply, "Love at first flight." The Chinese commentator drew an invidious comparison with Chinese advertisements: "When our advertisements say 'Quality Is Number One,' or 'Our Customers Are Tops,' or 'Superior Technology,' or 'Popular Throughout the Nation,' even though these slogans may be correct factually, they still seem rather self-congratulatory." The writer criticized the design of Chinese display advertisements, crammed full with detailed explanations of a product or service—one "dense, black mass." The less cluttered, more subtle Lufthansa style, which relied upon implicit messages, was touted as more effective. The example came from America, but the lesson that consumers should be allowed to draw conclusions by themselves was one that Chinese could readily appreciate, the author said, for it was the same lesson that had been crystallized long before in a traditional Chinese expression, "Draw the bow without shooting; just indicate the motions."[28]

China's economic planners, as well as its advertising professionals, were eager to earn advertising revenue from foreign clients. In the minds of some Chinese planners and professors, the revenue that could be earned from the deep pockets of foreign companies would be an enormous sum—$400 million annually from American and Japanese advertisers alone, according to one hopeful calculation. But at the same time, some more conservative sections of the Communist Party and civil government did not want foreign advertising to become dominant. They deployed public letter-writing campaigns as a weapon in the intragovernment squabble, encouraging viewers and readers to express concern about foreign dominance of advertising to editors and television station officials. On a couple of occasions, the responsible ministries responded by slowing the permitted advance of foreign advertisers—ordering in 1985, for example, the replacement of a prominent Sony billboard in Beijing with a political one extolling socialism. But such instances were rare, and the disappearance of the Sony board reflected selective pressure placed on Japanese companies, not on others.[29]

Some Chinese critics of foreigners viewed foreign companies that advertised in China as predators against whom Chinese enterprises were poorly equipped to compete not because of the mismatch in size, but because of the Chinese failure to appreciate the strategic importance of advertising. In 1987, Fang Zhenxing of Shanghai University registered concern that Chinese enterprises still regarded advertising expenditures as superfluous; advertising was the first item individual enterprises cut to achieve savings. Fang warned that the developed countries were using advertising as a tactic to enter the Chinese market and were claiming the most prominent pages in the newspapers, the highest billboards, and the choicest time on television. Chinese enterprises needed to adopt the same aggressive use of advertising or be left behind.[30]

Foreign advertisers were fortunate because Chinese authorities initially were reluctant to impose restrictions on cigarette and liquor advertising. Foreign cigarette companies, for example, were warmly welcomed in 1979; these companies accounted for four of the first five advertising accounts for Chinese television. Two years later, even when the Chinese decided to ban foreign cigarette and liquor advertisements, as well as those for cosmetics, the authorities were reluctant to tell foreign advertisers. The ban took effect without official public announcement.[31]

The government's ban showed only a half-hearted concern with protecting the public from the physical harm caused by cigarette consumption. The foreign tobacco companies were free to take advantage of every possible opportunity to promote their products short of explicit advertising, and were permitted to sponsor sports events and display the company's name prominently in stadiums. Sponsorship of such events did not cost the companies much—in fact, they complained bitterly that these opportunities were too few to absorb the millions of dollars they wanted to spend on advertising in China. But at the same time, some Chinese criticized cigarette companies as examples of overzealous foreigners "thinking up various channels and ways to place advertisements that are forbidden in China."[32]

Few though the occasions were, these foreign-sponsored sports events, with the attention they drew to the healthful images of Chinese and foreign athletes juxtaposed with the unhealthful images of cigarettes, did make the public health agencies of the Chinese government uncomfortable. Eventually, the authorities decided that the problem was the outcome of overly lax restrictions on foreign advertising as a whole, and in 1987 the state issued "Draft Regulations for Greater Control over Sports Advertising." The regulations imposed mild controls, however, because the Chinese government (like so many others) was reluctant to relinquish the advertising revenues earned from the tobacco companies. The regulations prohibited the use of either the company name or the product name of cigarettes or liquor as the name of a sports contest championship; in addition, pictures of the products themselves could not be shown at the event. But the regulations still permitted sponsorship of events and officially sanctioned the display of company and product names on banners and signs in the stadium, on the equipment and scoreboard, on the record book, on promotional items, seemingly everywhere.[33]

Foreign advertisers also encountered some restrictions placed on the total quantity of advertising accepted for television, newspapers, and magazines. The limits applied to domestic advertisers as well as foreign, and indicated a concern that the most important media not be overwhelmed by commercialism. When China Central Television first announced that it would carry commercials, it stated its intention to restrict commercial time to only fifteen minutes each day, and it stuck by this policy. Other stations were not able to hold to limits so successfully. In southern China, where commercial impulses often were not contained by the administrative directives issued from Beijing, Guangdong Television began with the announced intention to restrain commercials to six minutes per hour, but soon relaxed the limit to ten minutes per hour. In all cases, the Chinese placed television commercials at the end or beginning of a program, and did not permit them to interrupt the program itself.[34]

Newspapers had similar limits imposed on the space devoted to advertising—the total amount of advertising was not to exceed one page in a four-page paper. For the *People's Daily,* the rule was strictly enforced; for newspapers in the south, it was not. One way that revenue-hungry newspapers skirted the limitation was to print six pages instead of four, and fill the extra space with advertising. Many more newspapers would have liked to add extra pages but could not, simply because of the nationwide shortage of newsprint.[35]

American firms that decided to go ahead and attempt an advertising campaign in China had to winnow advice about how their advertising should be adapted for the China market. Perhaps the most discussed change was removing the sexual imagery, an injunction issued by the Chinese and repeated again and again by Americans offering advice to

American firms. "Goodbye, Calvin Klein," said a number of American wags. Some companies did encounter Chinese resistance to advertising they sent over. Lever Brothers, for example, was forced to delay its Lux soap commercials because Shanghai authorities frowned on the samba dancers in the background who were dressed in skimpy outfits. Nonetheless, Americans took a certain pride in the fact that sex was a distinguishing characteristic of their own advertising. Philip Dougherty, the *New York Times* advertising industry columnist, jokingly predicted that of all the differences between America and China, it was the sexual restrictions in advertising that would most upset "the Western advertising mind." If the Chinese insisted on sexless advertising the American men would abide, but they seemed to take pleasure in repeating the Chinese restrictions, as if to highlight American virility (a silly competition—after all, by the same measure, the much more prurient European advertising cultures, like that of West Germany, made America's look puritanical in contrast, if American men dared to compare).[36]

Procter and Gamble's advertising in China shows clearly the company's desire to produce appropriate commercials. In an American version of a spot for its Tide detergent, a mother is shown folding towels, and in the Chinese version, shirts. The Chinese-American consultant who had advised the company about the change explained, "The Chinese don't take big baths, and don't use big bath towels, so they wouldn't know what the heck they were." This kind of small detail was seen by *International Advertiser* as "the difference between a commercial's success or failure in the China market."[37]

Yet at the same time that Procter and Gamble was fussing about towels versus shirts, it was also running on Chinese television a spot that depicted the American suburban ideal. In it, a Chinese boy was shown getting dirty playing baseball with his two white American friends on the grass lawn of his suburban home. When called inside by his mother, his cleaning routine included bathing with Ivory soap, brushing his teeth with Crest, and having his mother wash the stained clothing in Tide. The picture of the smiling boy being scrubbed in his family's own bathtub, however, even though filmed specifically for the China market, remained wildly fanciful in a country in which only a privileged minority of residents had such facilities. What it appeared to say subliminally to the Chinese audience was that the bath fixtures and tiles might be well beyond reach, but Ivory soap could mentally transport them into the American suburban tableau.[38]

Chinese researchers conducted surveys of audience reactions to advertising, particularly television commercials, but no clear pattern emerged. A 1983 survey of about 200 Beijing households appeared to indicate that a majority of television viewers were irritated by commercials—only one of every five respondents said he or she watched commercials with interest. Some viewers said that when commercials came on, they turned the sound off or switched channels. But a few years later, in 1987, another survey of Beijing residents painted a different picture of an audience enthralled by commercials. No less than 96 percent said that they enjoyed watching television commercials for almost any consumer product, from cosmetics and medicines to appliances and books; only industrial products were not of interest. The Associated Press reported that in China "TV ads have become paeans to the happiness that comes with material acquisition."[39]

The Chinese surveyed in the early 1980s did have some specific proposals for improving advertising. A large portion of the television audience was unhappy with commercials that extolled a product's features and did not mention price. This was a problem that could be readily solved, the Chinese researchers added. More difficult to solve, however, was another frequently reported problem—too much time reserved for commercials, which displaced regular programming. Here the researchers proposed that "commercials, as much as possible, should not exceed the viewers' tolerance." But the rider "as much as possible" betrayed tacit acknowledgment that commercials inherently would tax the patience of viewers, and that nevertheless the commercial show had to go on.[40]

The strongest attack on advertising was launched during the "anti-spiritual-pollution campaign" of 1983–84, which zeroed in on foreign influences in China's advertising industry. China's domestic advertising agencies were criticized for having taken the "profits-point-of-view" of their Western counterparts. Other charges against Chinese agencies on the bill of particulars included the following:

> Some, in order to earn foreign exchange, have no scruples about producing big propaganda on behalf of foreign businesses. Some place advertising for foreign businesses in overly prominent places. Some impugn the Chinese people's dignity. Some use every capitalist means possible to attract customers. . . .

To counter such criticism, advertising personnel had to declare their opposition to slavish copying of the foreigners. But they were careful to reaffirm the need to separate the essential Western things from the dross, and to blend the West's quintessence with China's to create "socialist advertisements" that reflected China's own "special character." This was a goal that all Chinese could support, and though the defining characteristics of a "socialist" advertising style remained vague, mere mention of the goal served to deflect criticism of undue Western influence.[41]

By 1986, *Chinese Advertising* was concerned that the advertising industry had lost sight of the difference between socialist and capitalist advertising. It warned: "If the advertising industry does not clearly grasp the special characteristics of advertising in a socialist system, a number of problems will arise that could have been avoided." China's *Economic Daily* attempted in 1987 to show the noncommercial importance of advertising in a socialist society, but used examples of what *should* be done (for example, promoting "healthy, uplifting recreational activities" and "a positive tone for studies") rather than what had been done.[42]

One distinguishing characteristic claimed for China's adaptation of foreign advertising practices was its insistence on the absolute truth in all advertising. The Chinese often mentioned that their own high standards for truth-in-advertising were a shock to foreign companies, which came to China without realizing that their advertisements would be held to the same standards. Chinese writers repeated on countless occasions the story of how Toyota had launched an advertising campaign based on an old Chinese proverb about having faith: "When you get to the foot of the mountain, a road will appear." Toyota had added "Wherever there is a road, there is a Toyota." A year after Toyota's slogan appeared on billboards, in newspapers, and on television, the Chinese authorities told Toyota that it constituted false advertising. Reasoned one official, "China has roads but there are not necessarily Toyotas on them. The roads in other countries do not necessarily have them either." Toyota had to drop the campaign temporarily, and thereafter the Chinese regarded the story as the embodiment of the crucial difference between the strict standards of socialist advertising and the lax standards of its capitalist counterpart.[43]

This was the outer face that China presented to Western businesspeople. The advertising of foreign companies was easy to supervise punctiliously, and the supervision satisfied a nationalistic interest as well. But Chinese authorities actually had their own hands full trying to control false advertising placed by domestic Chinese advertisers. The *Economic Daily* and other newspapers received what they described as a "continuous flow" of letters from readers who had been misled or cheated by domestic advertising. A story from Jiangsu in 1983 represents many similar cases: A factory had run advertisements for a solar stove, claiming that it could be used in winter and had many superior features. Only after a number of orders had been placed was it discovered that the stove's development was still at the test stage and no finished versions were available for purchase. The factory had placed the advertisements merely to test demand. At least in this case the product existed, even if it was not ready for sale. In other cases, however, the advertised product was a phantom. A widely quoted exposé of fraudulent advertising published in the *People's Daily* told of another Jiangsu factory which had advertised that its "products performed well and are beautifully made." But when a purchasing agent from Hubei had arrived to place an order, he could not find the factory at the stated address—it turned out not yet to have been built.[44]

The principal recourse for the unhappy consumer in China was to write a letter to the editor of the local paper and hope it would be published and embarrass the guilty firm to the point of offering proper restitution. Duan Pingyu, one such mail-order purchaser who wrote to the *People's Daily* in 1985, was one of the lucky ones whose tale of woe was published. He placed responsibility for the problem of fraud directly on the newspapers themselves, for publishing advertisements whose claims were not verified. As long as newspapers continued to accept advertising whose veracity was confirmed only by the word of the advertiser, then consumers would continue to be hurt and the newspapers' reputation damaged when products failed to live up to the advertised claims. "After time passes," Duan wrote, "people will come to regard advertisements as they do 'quack medicine sold on the riverbank,' with total disbelief.[45]

China's new advertising agencies also shared the blame for problems of reliability. By 1987 over 600 advertising agencies were operating in China, but as their domestic critics pointed out, few actually created advertisements. Most served merely as intermediaries, introducing advertisers to media, collecting commissions (which was legal), and sometimes paying kickbacks for the business (which was not). No specialized expertise seemed to be needed. As one critic sardonically put it: "Hang up a sign, casually bring together a few employees, and you'll be able to make a fortune." The trustworthiness of the agencies was not enhanced when the general public read of reports that advertising budgets were sometimes devoted to entertainment and junkets. It was estimated publicly that no less than 28 percent of the total sum spent on advertising in China in 1985 went to "facilitators" who performed no tangible service.[46]

To defend themselves against such criticism, the staff members of Chinese advertising agencies habitually offered self-criticism as propitiation, but their enthusiasm for such displays was obviously limited. Many in the advertising industry spoke out for the need of better "understanding" by the public of the service advertising performed. Yes, the industry said, some critics of advertising were concerned that it was purchasing the talents of some of China's finest artists, and were worried that this would lead to the commercialization and decline of art in China. But the concern was unnecessary, the industry replied, because the more artists who joined the ranks of the advertising world, the higher the artistic standards. Had not modern China's greatest writer, Lu Xun himself, written advertisements for book publishers? And yes, some critics had charged that China's advertising industry had shamelessly exploited images of attractive women in advertising campaigns. But here again the industry had a ready reply. Female images, it said, should not be equated automatically with "spiritual pollution." Those images that were "helpful in promoting a product should be permitted, and may even be necessary." The sole problem was to ensure that the artwork stressed "health and propriety."[47]

Occasionally, China's advertising industry discovered that its ties to the West, which were politically troublesome during times of conservative reaction, provided a compensating benefit: access to well-prepared defenses that their brethren in the advertising industry elsewhere had used when they faced criticism in their own countries. Much of the criticism in China was oddly similar to that in capitalist countries. Consequently, the advertising profession in China could feel a kinship to members of the industry in the West. In 1984 *Chinese Advertising* published a condensed translation of a pamphlet that a European advertising association had published, *Ten Questions About Advertising.* The European industry had had to contend with some of the same criticism: advertising increases the price of a product, causes the consumer to purchase unnecessary goods, is untruthful, is disdainful of women and children, and insults the intelligence of the general public. The pamphlet provided responses to each charge, explaining how advertising served to reduce the price of products (by enlarging sales, thus leading to gains in efficiency from large-scale production), how advertising could never compel consumers to buy unwanted products, and so on. Here and elsewhere, where the Chinese advertising industry turned to capitalist countries for guidance on how to defend itself, professional solidarity overrode the formal boundaries of ideology.[48]

In pursuit of expanding exports in the United States, the Chinese did their best to adapt to the standards of their targeted market. Earlier, in the 1970s, before authorities had restored advertising domestically, the People's Republic had encountered difficulties as it groped to find effective ways to reach potential buyers in the United States. One of its more promising export products was traditional Chinese patent medicines, which contained exotic ingredients that were hard to obtain in the United States. The U.S. Food and Drug Administration did not care whether American consumers ingested ground antlers, dried sea horses, rhinoceros horns, or even dried human placenta. But it did take issue with the curative claims that were made for the medicines. The "Sugar Coated Placenta Tablets," for example, claimed to "cure" both insomnia and lassitude. An FDA official warned the Chinese, "If you want to sell dried flies for people to eat, you can, but you can't say it cures the common cold unless you can prove it." Unfortunately for the Chinese exporters, many of their nostrums, FDA inspectors discovered, contained unlisted powerful drugs that required prescriptions for dispensing. The FDA confiscated tons of the medicines in the early 1970s, but its staff was overwhelmed by the quantities that were imported and could make only spot inspections to check for compliance with federal regulations. A decade later, in the early 1980s, after China had begun to develop its own advertising industry, the Chinese exporters agreed to compromise on the labeling of the patent medicine exports. They won FDA approval for a ginseng tonic that was marketed in the United States as a "health drink" but that had no specific medicinal claims on its label.[49]

The Chinese exporters had to learn that in some instances, such as when promoting their patent medicines, they had to tone down their claims, but that in other instances, such as when touting their Great Wall vodka, they had to cast caution to the wind and be extremely aggressive. In the mid-1970s, when Great Wall vodka was introduced to the United States, the Chinese faced stiff entrenched competition from the Soviet Union, whose Stolichnaya dominated the imported vodka market. Guided by their American distributor, the Chinese marketed their vodka as "the most expensive in the world," a claim substantiated by a letter from the usually restrained *The New Yorker.* Stolichnaya challenged the claim, and the absurd spectacle of the two largest socialist countries in the world vying for the claim of marketing the most expensive vodka in the richest luxury-goods market reached its climax when the dispute was taken to court and settled in 1977 by the New York Supreme Court, where the coveted title was signed over to the Chinese. Several years later, China's marketing efforts in the United States continued to enjoy the benefits of being regarded as those of the "good" Communists when the "bad" Communists of the Soviet Union invaded Afghanistan, and the American distributor of Great Wall vodka declared the opening of a new "vodka war" in the United States. Consumers and retailers made a game of smashing bottles of Stolichnaya, egged on, it was rumored, by the Soviets' international competitors.[50]

American importers who had purchased goods from the Chinese in the heyday of the Canton Trade Fair in the 1970s could understand, when China remained virtually closed to outside influences, the lack of familiarity with international quality standards and fashions. But in the 1980s American importers were puzzled by the lag in Chinese acquisition of what *Business Week* called "even the most basic fashion and marketing sense." If not specifically told to do otherwise, Chinese manufacturers would mix button sizes on a single shirt, or match a knit shirt with one shade of red with a skirt of another shade deemed "close enough." Most pathetic was the display as late as 1986 of a foot-pedal sewing machine called the Flying Dove that was offered in Canton for export. An American reporter was reminded of "grandma's old black Singer": The Chinese machine was decorated with gold curlicues, and even if electrified, stood little chance of competing against its computerized rivals in the home-machine market of the United States. The Flying Dove sold well domestically in China, but competition in the Chinese marketplace was still so protected from the winds of real international competition that domestically successful producers developed a false sense of confidence about the global competitiveness of their products.[51]

The catalogue of gaffes and blunders committed by untutored Chinese in export advertising was a long one. The Chinese attempted to sell their exports with English-language brand names that only drew derision: White Elephant brand batteries; Sea Cucumber brand shirts; Maxipuke playing cards (*pu ke,* pronounced as two syllables, was the Chinese transliteration of poker); and Pansy brand men's underwear. Chinese advertisers also showed little knowledge of foreign media, purchasing space in the *New York Times* for dried vegetables, and in the *London Times* for Snowflake brand surgical dressings. The Shanghai

Advertising Corporation showed better judgment when it placed an advertisement for Chinese furs in *Vogue,* but the advertisement was illustrated with simple line drawings of models. One American advertising critic heaped scorn on the advertisement's "wooden imperviousness to esthetics" as well as its failure to list an American address for interested buyers. "It is hard to imagine a Park Avenue hostess cabling the Shanghai Animal By-Products Branch of CHINATUHSU to price a box-shaped 'Golden Leaf'-brand 'real weasel fur' jacket." A plan to export rat skins abroad also stumbled, eliciting amused notice in American newspapers. Some Americans were more tolerant and declared that Chinese advertisements had a "refreshing, unpolished look." But for most Americans in the advertising industry, China's "unpolished" look needed much buffing.[52]

The persistent lack of "basic fashion and marketing sense" in the Chinese was not a genetic trait; it was the consequence of the incompleteness of China's economic reforms and the persistence of a seller's market in the domestic economy, where attention to fashion, marketing, and advertising was unnecessary. This made it all the more difficult for Chinese firms to catch up with their global rivals when products were promoted in foreign markets.[53]

Chinese-Americans did their best to tell Chinese producers that the marketing mentality necessary to be competitive in the United States required a thorough change in thinking. Chen Qing-jun, an American resident since childhood who held a Ph.D. in nutrition, said in an interview published in China in 1988 that when he visited the People's Republic on his frequent trips to lecture and do business, he was often told by local officials that wonderful locally produced items were ready for export. They wanted the American to advise them how they should proceed. In strong language that a non-ethnic-Chinese foreigner would never dare use, Chen reproached the Chinese for their "primitive and immature" thinking. Don't begin with the products, he said, begin with the market. In the United States, business people first determine what the market needs before they go after money, technology, and materials to fill it, and Chinese should do the same. Betty Bao Lord, the popular novelist and wife of the then U.S. ambassador to the People's Republic, offered similar criticism that pulled no punches. She walked with a Chinese reporter in tow through an unnamed store in Beijing that offered items intended for foreign tourists, pointing out the problems that could readily be seen in the tablecloths, pillow cases, and other items intended for export. Americans liked their bed sheets to be plain, not embroidered with flowers, she said. The question here and elsewhere was not one of quality; it was one of taste. If China were to gain greater foreign acceptance of its products, it had to pay more attention to what suited foreign tastes.[54]

Chinese students in the United States sent home letters to the editors of Chinese newspapers sounding the same message: Instead of trying to export whatever was already produced, Chinese producers first should learn what foreign customers wanted. Look at Japan's export of pianos to the United States, wrote one Chinese student whose letter was printed in 1987. Without any domestic tradition of piano production, Japan had conducted market research in the United States, shrewdly evaluated an opportunity to export pianos, and made the necessary investment to create a capacity to export an extremely competitive product to the United States. Not only were Chinese producers too passive, so were the Chinese representatives who were posted to the offices opened in the United States during the 1980s. A Chinese graduate student at Yale's management school urged the U.S. offices of Chinese enterprises to be more aggressive: "Instead of waiting for customers to call, as is now often the case, these organizations will need to go out and make things happen."[55]

Chinese students who went to the United States were appalled to discover how few PRC goods were to be found for sale. Even in local Chinatowns, the students often had to buy cooking oil, sauces, and other foodstuffs produced in Taiwan or elsewhere. The few goods from the mainland usually were close-outs found outside the stores on the sidewalk. Initially, students thought it might have been because of lingering hostility toward the Communists. When a curious Chinese student asked the owner of a large discount store that sold cheap merchandise why goods from Taiwan and Hong Kong were carried in abundance, but none from the mainland, the owner denied that it was politically motivated. She did not care where her merchandise came from, she said, as long as she could make money selling it. But no one had ever approached her to sell mainland goods.[56]

Greater aggressiveness unquestionably was needed. Students of history can observe that similar calls upon China were made early in the century when, for example, an American friend of China, Emil Scholz, publicly urged the Chinese in 1927 to advertise their wares to American consumers, who he said preferred Chinese goods over Japanese, but could not find them or did not know about them. Exactly sixty years later, in 1987, Li Yanning, the Washington correspondent for a Chinese business paper, repeated the same message, but in his exhortations showed how nationalism could transform sound advice into a misleading panacea. The imports from Taiwan, South Korea, and Hong Kong that he had found crowding the shelves of American stores were not so impressive, he wrote for readers back in China. Many of China's factories were capable of matching their standards, or could do so with a "little effort." China was shut out only because of poor marketing, a hasty conclusion that ignored real differences in production quality.[57]

Other Chinese agreed with Li, however; marketing would solve their problems. Chinese exhibitors at a trade fair in Beijing in the summer of 1988, for example, savored the surprise that registered on the faces of visiting Americans when the Chinese told them that Chinese factories were indeed capable of producing the impressive industrial equipment displayed in pictures adorning the booths. Out of hearing of the Americans, the Chinese representatives complained to a Chinese reporter that the principal obstacle that stood in the way of their exports to the United States was the scant "promotional work abroad" that had been done on their behalf. Chinese who complained about poor advertising, without talking about other problems, were selectively hearing only what they wished to hear from the foreign marketing professors. More advertising, more promotion, more attention, they believed, and the world would beat a path to their door.[58]

Americans were inclined to view China's tolerance of Western advertising as an indication that Chinese were becoming less alien, more "American." When Frankie Cadwell, of New York-based Cadwell Davis Partnership, returned in 1985 from a visit to China to lecture about advertising techniques, she declared: "I think they'll be just like Americans someday." A marketing culture was ascendant, and China seemed to have changed fundamentally. When an advertisement in China for a Chinese brandy showed a non-Chinese woman sipping from a snifter, Ronald Cromie of Hill & Knowlton said: "I thought it would be a long time before I saw foreigners portrayed in domestic Chinese advertisements." But Cromie was delighted: "It means they're beginning to think about what is effective." Americans savored Chinese testimonials to the effectiveness of advertising and marketing because they came from what the *New York Times* called "a rather unexpected quarter." The socialist country that had denounced American capitalism in the most emphatic terms only a few years before had finally come around. All the sweeter to American ears was China's song of praise to Madison Avenue.[59]

11.

COCA-COLONIZATION

Advertising, television, consumerism, and the Cold War got tangled together in China, in a way that Milton Moskowitz might be credited with foreseeing in 1979, right at the beginning of the reintroduction of advertising in China. Moskowitz, a business columnist writing with tongue only partly in cheek, spoke of advertising as a "weapon" and predicted that China would have to increase the number of television stations (it then had 40 compared to America's 700), once American advertisers "get their turn at the bat." He predicted:

> Everyone will lust for a TV set to see the commercials for Coke, Geritol, Crest, Efferdent, Ex-Lax, Anacin and Listerine. Advertising, the Chinese will soon find, is addictive. It's our secret weapon. Far better than hydrogen bombs and nuclear submarines.[1]

The military metaphor was not farfetched; the Cold War was still on, and the prospect of gaining access to a market of one billion consumers was freighted with much ideological opportunity. Moskowitz predicted a "lust" for televised images of consumer products, but the lust that Americans most wanted the Chinese to reveal was not for the images, but for the products themselves. If the Spartan proletarians of China manifested the same material addictions as did Americans, then the American celebration of materialism would be vindicated. The Chinese, by virtue of numbers and ideological distance traveled, could legitimize consumerism with a force that no single country within the capitalist world could ever accomplish on its own. Thus, the invasion of Western consumer culture in China, and how it was received, took on a significance that went beyond the visible business details.

The vigil that awaited Chinese Communist vindication of capitalist consumerism actually began earlier in the 1970s, when Americans closely monitored Chinese imports of expensive consumer goods. The total value of Japanese television sets and Swiss watches that were imported in 1977, for example, was estimated at a modest level of about $70 million, but it marked an 80 percent increase over the previous year. In 1978, foreign observers noted with satisfaction that Chinese authorities had begun to sell imported luxury goods in department stores open to the public. The prices were high—the after-tax price of a twenty-inch Japanese color television set was $1,600—and these goods were affordable only to a tiny, emergent "national bourgeoisie" consisting of high-level bureaucrats and professors or those with generous overseas relatives. Yet the fact that the goods were no longer hidden in special shops but were displayed for all to see meant the government had decided that the public should no longer be shielded from these formerly forbidden sights.[2]

The real excitement among foreign observers began at the end of the 1970s when the Chinese government permitted members of the general public to be actual participants in the pleasures of consumerism that hitherto had been reserved for the elite. Ordinary Chinese appeared dumbstruck when gazing for the first time upon the material baubles of another world. When Seiko opened a shop in Beijing's busiest shopping district, initially it served as a museum, where 5,000 "customers" lined up each day for a brief glimpse of the displays; the crowds were so large that store clerks were traffic managers, keeping the procession of visitors moving in a constant stream, in one door, out the other. The Chinese public's homely otherworldliness led *Advertising Age* to predict that they would not shed "Mao jackets for disco duds or trade their flat-soled shoes in for autographed sneakers for some time to come."[3]

One moment, the ordinary Chinese seemed to be gawkers. The next, the same Chinese embarked upon a conspicuous shopping spree that appeared at times to engage all of urban China in what the *Wall Street Journal* happily reported in a front-page story this way: "Chinese Learn the Joy of Shopping . . ." Beijing led the way. In 1979, virtually no household had much in the way of household appliances, but by 1983, for every 100 families there were 55 electric fans, 25 tape recorders, 16 washing machines, and 2 refrigerators. Color television sets that cost the equivalent of a year's salary sold at a brisk pace, testimony to the "addictive" attraction Moskowitz had spoken of. By 1986, expatriates noticed that they were no longer importuned by Chinese friends to buy basic items in short supply, such as cooking oil or beer. Instead, the requests of Chinese friends had escalated to reflect the increasingly sophisticated consumerism: from radios to four-speaker decks to televisions to refrigerators to videocassette recorders.[4]

The "joy of shopping" in China went far beyond consumer durables and other appliances. Americans catalogued the changes in Chinese fashion, adornment, and entertainment. Brighter clothing began to appear. Women and men went to the hairstylists for permanent waves. Blue jeans and Western-style suits and ties appeared. Crucifixes and sunglasses and sun visors imprinted with English inscriptions ("Ole Miss Rebels") and other new accessories went in and out of fashion. Americans were quick to ascribe this to the unstoppable force of "good fashion," which *Textile Industries* described as a "universal allure" that ignored geographic boundaries and in the modern age of rapid communications "instantly permeates all parts of the globe." The Chinese authorities, however, put their own twist on this explanation, pointing less to membership in thc fashion circles of the West than to the advent of higher living standards accomplished by socialism and the Communist Party. What foreigners regarded as ideologically threatening, the Party merely transformed into propaganda ammunition for its own.[5]

Seeing yellows, reds, pinks, greens, and purples on downtown streets, remarked a reporter for the *People's Daily,* "gives one the happy feeling that in recent years the people's living standards have really improved." As for the new hairstyles, "Now we see nothing wrong with every woman's wanting to look her best," said Liu Xitian, the male manager of a hair salon who could have said the same about Chinese men, too. Liu placed government authorities on the defensive by intimating that official interference with the pursuit of fashion would create antagonism with the Chinese populace. After all, Liu said, the new styles were "something the masses demanded."[6]

Fashion shows like Cardin's were staged by a Chinese "fashion demonstration team," a euphemism for fashion models that emphasized the collective over the individual. Requirements for employment as a team member were stringent: One had to have "attractive facial features and the body type required to show off clothing—wide shoulders and a narrow waist for men, a well-rounded figure and delicate hands for women." An article in the *People's Daily* that offered a justification for fashion shows was unintentionally revealing. It observed that "propaganda" for clothing helped to "accelerate consumption." Provided with an aura of desirability by display in a Chinese fashion show, clothing items that had formerly languished on store shelves immediately sold well. The author, realizing that this line of reasoning was leading straight to the world of fashion shows in the capitalist world, then tried to reverse direction and retreat to a defense of the distinguishing and uniquely praiseworthy attributes of fashion shows in socialist China. While the show in the West was produced for purely commercial reasons, that in China was an "artistic performance" as well as a commercial one. It was also claimed as an exercise in esthetics education in which Chinese consumers were led to "love beauty, understand beauty, and master beauty."[7]

Such lyrical praise could also have served to defend fashion shows in the West. It was the same song Western cosmetic and perfume companies were fond of singing, and they jumped at the opportunity to help Chinese women take greater "care" of their appearance. Max Factor began in 1979 with makeup demonstrations in selected cities; and in 1980 it set up counters in Friendship Stores and hotels. Avon tried, and failed, to gain permission to knock on household doors for sales, and settled for beginning with producing a facial cream with a Chinese partner. Fifty years earlier, Carl Crow had been pleased to point to the fact that cosmetics had been used in China 5,000 years ago, so when his advertising agency placed the first lipstick and vanishing cream advertisements, he viewed it less as a change brought from the outside than as promotion of native institutions. In the same way, foreign representatives of cosmetics companies in China defended their products as universally desirable. Avon, taking a leaf from the Chinese authorities' fondness for medical justification, argued that its facial moisturizing cream, which had the unusual medical name "Love Fragrance," was not as frivolous as it might have appeared and was a useful product in the dry Beijing winter.[8]

China's own cosmetics industry grew rapidly. By 1988, thousands of small cosmetics factories in China turned out lipstick, eyeshadow, rouge, nail polish, and other cosmetic lines. It was hard to sort out, however, to what degree this obvious enthusiasm for beauty products was confirmation of Western assertions about the universality of the appeal and what was simple reaction to the extreme asceticism that had been enforced during the Cultural Revolution. Advertising also played a role, promoting not only the products themselves, but also the idea that women were to be associated with beauty; the adorned, idealized female images that appeared in advertisements of unrelated industrial products, and on calendars and playing cards, represented a major ideological change in China.[9]

Western observers watched closely as Chinese consumers wandered ever further from traditional socialist orthodoxy and closer to Western tastes. The Chinese seemed eager to remake themselves into a more Western-like people, as foreign reporters wrote lengthy features about the plastic surgery clinics that opened in China in the early 1980s, offering Chinese women new eyelids, noses, dimples, and enlarged breasts. Matchmakers were quoted as saying that male clients demanded the new features in prospective marriage partners. The cost of the operations did not daunt; one woman who had had the eyelid procedure performed said, "For that money I can be beautiful for the rest of my life."[10]

The consumption of entertainment also headed in a Western direction. Rambo set off a craze when introduced to mass audiences in China in 1985, a craze that Western reporters, again, recorded in scrupulous detail. Their stories collectively constitute a separate tale of Western fascination with all signs of Chinese Westernization. Gazing at a theater poster of the bleeding, sweaty mass of brawn that was Sylvester Stallone's Rambo, clutching his machine gun, a young female Beijing law student was quoted gushing about how fantastic his body was, "so vigorous and graceful." Universal, Paramount, and MGM-United Artists joined together in selling some of the most popular older films in their vaults to the Chinese, sending over *Love Story* and *Spartacus* and others on generous terms, foregoing profits that would presumably come later. If China seemed temporarily mesmerized by Hollywood spectacle, Hollywood itself was mesmerized by the One-Billion spectacle of China. When Hu Yaobang, then head of the Communist Party, was quoted in the Western press in 1985 as having declared, "What's wrong with rock-and-roll? I'd learn how to dance rock-and-roll myself if I weren't so old," no boundaries seemed left to separate Us from Them. A few years earlier, when the first Chinese journalists visited Disneyland in 1978, Western reporters had said that the Chinese enjoyed the saccharine Disney anthem, "It's a Small World After All." In the 1980s, consumerism in China seemed to turn the anthem into reality at a breathtaking pace.[11]

The danger in this reporting was of exaggerating the extent of change in China. Appearances were partly deceiving because of the nature of

Western-Chinese interaction, which even at the freest moments tended to bring the most Westernized Chinese into most frequent contact with Westerners. Moreover, the sentiments of the 80 percent of the population who lived in the countryside, out of sight of all but a handful of foreigners, remained for the most part unknown. (Their sentiments could hardly be guessed from afar—poorly educated young people in rural Shanxi had the idea in 1988, for example, that "Western" sport jackets and suits were invented in China and borrowed by the West.) Conscientious reporters dutifully acknowledged from time to time that rural China remained poorly covered, but this did little to moderate the sensational tone pervading the stories of each successive consumer-related taboo that was crossed for the first time. In the foreign coverage of many firsts for China in the 1980s, which was really focused on the largest cities only, the emphasis was on recording novelty, not on gauging depth or representativeness.

The appearance of strong state support for the new consumer revolution was also deceiving because the constituent factions of the Communist Party leadership were not consistently of one mind about the desirability of the changes. Conflicting signals were periodically issued from on high. In early 1983 Wan Li, a high-ranking member of the reform faction, publicly advocated a switch to Western attire for men, calling for "diversification" in men's clothing and offering justifications appealing to esthetics ("Western clothing makes one look good") and comfort (the high collar on the Chinese-style dress jacket, Wan said, was "uncomfortable"). But in late 1983, the "antispiritual-pollution campaign" targeted the same Western attire as a pernicious influence. In response, the defenders of Western fashion rallied behind the personal examples set by Party leader Hu Yaobang and then-premier Zhao Ziyang, who had made a point of wearing Western suits and ties on recent trips abroad.[12]

Americans joined the debate and argued that China could never succeed in discouraging pursuit of fashion domestically while at the same time exporting large quantities of Western-designed textiles and apparel, one of its most important sources of foreign exchange. Chinese textile industry workers were exposed to the lure of fashion in the course of their work, reasoned one American journalist, so "it is difficult to see how fashion can be kept away from the populace for too long." Americans saw the spread of Western influence as inexorable, and pitied the blindness of Chinese leaders who could not recognize this elemental force.[13]

Conservative leaders remained unimpressed. During the "antispiritual-pollution campaign," the authorities told Chinese employees to avoid "bizarre dress" or face being sent home. Men had to shave off sideburns and mustaches; women were told not to wear heavy makeup or earrings or other "unhealthy ornaments." These new regulations were intended, said the *People's Daily*, to "preserve our habits of simplicity and bitter struggle," but their enforcement proved to be brief for the "antispiritual-pollution campaign" faded shortly after it was launched. Americans took this as proof of the inevitability of the acceptance of Western fashions, and gleefully quoted the new line taken by the *People's Daily* that sanctioned a renewed blooming of fashionable styles. The newspaper declared that "drabness is not a tradition and poverty is not a virtue." Xu Yongqian, a clothing designer who proudly told an American reporter that his city, Shanghai, was "the Paris of China," explained that fashion and politics occupied separate spheres: "Ideology is ideology, fashion is fashion. We've studied our documents and find no problem with people trying to look good."[14]

Ideology could not be overcome so easily, however. Even though the "antispiritual-pollution campaign" ended quickly, residual ideological concerns were still in the air. Defenders of Western fashions had to use the old idiom of Marxist orthodoxy to justify adoption of new styles from the West. When blue jeans appeared on Chinese streets in large numbers in 1984, shortly after the "antispiritual-pollution campaign" had sputtered to a stop, the new apparel still brought charges of "bourgeois." One Chinese writer tried to rescue jeans by pointing to their un-bourgeois origins in the United States, where jeans had been worn by "hard-working American cowboys who had little to do with the bourgeoisie." More commonly, Western fashions were defended in China not by searching for proletarian origins in the West, real or exaggerated, but by finding precedents in China's own history. Mid-length slacks for women, which became fashionable in China in the summer of 1984, were defended by alleging that the design had originated in a coastal area along the South China Sea and was "endowed with the beauty of simply-dressed hard-working people." Even bell-bottom trousers, which enjoyed a vogue in China and were often used by cartoonists as the dress of disreputable Chinese characters who worshipped all things Western, were justified by the discovery that similar trousers had been worn by some Chinese in the Tang Dynasty (618–907).[15]

Conservatives in the Party leadership who opposed the new emphasis on materialism knew that Marx could not serve as a helpful authority in the cause of countermaterialism, so they retreated beyond Marxism to a home-grown spiritualism. No less an authority than Yu Guangyuan, head of the highest state research institution devoted to the study of Marxism-Leninism-Mao Zedong Thought, turned away from the holy trinity when arguing against consumerism. In a speech given in Tokyo in 1981, Yu called for a refurbished Confucianism that emphasized proper relationships among people instead of the growing mass pursuit of materialist goods. Promoting mutual understanding, love, helpfulness, and democracy were virtues Yu said came more easily to Eastern countries like China and Japan—here, with a conspiratorial wink, Yu included Japan as a "spiritualist" country superior to the crassly materialist West. (This was a curious characterization of Japan, whose gross national product was then the second largest in the non-Communist world and whose consumer electronics products had come to be identified as among its best-known products worldwide.) As a Marxist, Yu said, he still believed that Marxist philosophy could be helpful in solving many problems of the present, but "at the same time, as a Chinese, and as a son of ancient Eastern countries, I also recognize that in splendid traditions of Eastern countries like China and Japan, there are many things that can be used in treating contemporary social ills."[16]

When China's official custodians of Marxism abandoned Marx in their drive to push consumerism back out of the country, reformers seized the opportunity to claim Marx for their own cause, as a champion of consumerism. Most comrades understand that without production there can be no consumption, said a Chinese newspaper in 1984. But many do not understand that "Marxist economics tells us that production without consumption lacks a goal." If an item of clothing sat unsold in a warehouse, it still did not exist technically as a "commodity"; it was consumers, the article said, who should be credited with "helping" production by creating demand for new products and for buying and using the fruits of the production process. A front-page *People's Daily* editorial took up the same theme, criticizing those who ignored the potential importance of consumption and the vast untapped domestic market. This line of reasoning led to the claim that consumers in China should be encouraged to spend their money as well as guided so that they spent it wisely. The traditional wisdom about keeping clothes for nine years or as long as possible—"new for three years, old for three years, then patched for three years"—was no longer appropriate. Go ahead, the newspapers said, if you've got money, don't be afraid: spend it.[17]

The news that the Chinese state was officially encouraging people to buy new clothes simply for newness was excitedly reported in the Western press as resembling the stance of a "Western chamber of commerce" and evidence that Party theoreticians had finally capitulated. This characterization was not wholly fair, however. It turned the position of reformist factions, temporarily ascendant, into the unanimous position of all leaders in the Party and the government. Moreover, the theoreticians were concerned about the macroeconomic problems of underconsumption which they believed China, as poor as it was, confronted in some sectors. A vice-premier reasoned that the traditional reluctance of an individual in China to buy new clothes until the old clothes could no longer be patched kept demand for Chinese cotton too low. "How are we going to develop our textile industry if everyone keeps wearing the same garment for nine years?" he said.[18]

Li Yining, the Beijing University economics professor who advocated expanded stock trading, also advocated popular acceptance of the notion that consumption was not shameful, as long as it did not exceed one's income. "Even if it is consumption for high-grade commodities," Li said, it "should not be regarded as extravagance." But when these officials and economists told Chinese consumers that greater spending helped the national economy, the populace was quick to see the happy congruence of official state interests and personal interests. A smiling Beijing taxi driver told an American reporter: "I am buying new clothes because they look good, of course, but I'm also doing it because it helps the economy, and by helping the economy, I am helping the country, and that's what the Party wants."[19]

Consumerism by its nature, however, demanded a shift in the center of gravity, a shift away from the interests of the state and toward those of the individual. Above all else, it was pursued for personal, not patriotic, reasons. The hedonistic appeal could not be fully hidden, even if the state pretended otherwise. As He Wenzhong, an official at Radio Peking, philosophized informally over a beer in 1986, "When you put money in the bank, you get nothing. When you spend it, you enjoy life." But enjoyment of life, though sanctioned by officialdom for the moment, undermined the traditional discourse between the state and the masses. The state had always hammered away at opposite themes: abnegation of personal interest, devotion to the collective and to the state, renunciation of "bourgeois" indulgences for the sake of simple pleasure. By temporarily softening, it relaxed the tethers that had kept the populace tied to a producer orientation—and to the state itself.[20]

Consumerism has two very dissimilar meanings: One refers to zealous pursuit of ever-increasing consumption, the other to the political movement to protect consumers from unsafe or shoddy merchandise, unfair charges, and other abuses that arise in an unregulated marketplace. In 1979, on the eve of the period when consumerism of the first type would spread through Chinese cities, Ralph Nader, America's best-known advocate of consumerism of the second type, paid a two-week visit to China at the invitation of the Chinese. Upon his return to the United States, he described China as a country blessed with certain advantages. Its automobile industry was as small as America's in 1910, and Nader had told the Chinese that if they installed seat belts in all cars now "they could save one million Chinese lives over the next 40 years and millions of serious injuries." He praised the Chinese approach to major problems affecting American consumers in sewage control and garbage recycling, pest control, and national health care, which was created, Nader sarcastically added, "without any help from the Harvard Business School."[21]

Similar tributes paid by foreign observers to China's health care system go back to the days of revolutionary tourism in the 1970s, and those paid to China's propensity to recycle material and create the impression that, as Nader said, "nothing is wasted," go back to much earlier visits a century before that. Nader's superficial appraisal was open to easy ridicule from the *Wall Street Journal,* which referred in an editorial to his recommendation that capitalism had much to learn from the Chinese conservation ethic: "If Mr. Nader doesn't mind, we'd just as soon stay home." But even from the perspective of Chinese consumers, Nader's praise of their institutions would have seemed fatuous. It was they who were familiar with egregious pollution of water, air, and soil; with the shortcomings of their underfunded health care system; with the enormous waste in their economy, of which one form was unsalable merchandise, which Chinese newspapers admitted occupied one-third of the total stock of some department stores.[22]

Moreover, Nader did not say a word about the adequacy of existing organizations in China to give voice to concerns of the country's otherwise unorganized consumers, the very area in which he had contributed so much in the United States. As Chinese consumers pursued consumerism of the first type, increased purchases, they soon began to give attention to consumerism of the second type and tried to organize to protect consumer interests. In so doing they revealed deep dissatisfaction with the status quo that had not been visible to short-term foreign visitors like Nader.

Unlike the official labor, women's, or "national minority" groups, the consumer groups in the People's Republic began from the bottom, not the top, and although the government tried to appropriate and control the movement for itself, a testy independence remained. The first consumer association in China was founded in rural Hebei in 1983, and others popped up around the country, some quasi-official, others fully official, such as the feeble Consumers Association that was set up by the State Council in 1985, charged with monitoring product quality and fair pricing but lacking any teeth. A new nationally distributed magazine, *Consumers,* which began publication in 1984, provided a feisty voice for consumers that was conspicuously independent of the government. Its masthead carried the motto: "Everyone is a consumer; consumers publish *Consumers.*"[23]

The Chinese looked to the United States for lessons to be learned from the tragedies produced by unsafe products, and for lessons in how a consumer movement could be organized. America's *Consumer Reports* seemed especially exemplary to Chinese consumer advocates. One newspaper introduced a summary of the magazine by alluding to the universal need for such a magazine: Where in China, it asked, was there a powerful voice to promote the interests of buyers and counterbalance advertising?[24]

Consumer advocates in China raised nettlesome ideological questions for the government. Theoretically, they said, consumers in a socialist country should be much better protected than those in a capitalist country; yet this was plainly not the case. Wang Renzhong, the head of the state-sponsored Consumers Association, pointed out in the *People's Daily* that the warranties offered to purchasers of consumer durables in the People's Republic did not even bear comparison with pre-Liberation China, when factories competed to offer good warranties to establish reputations of quality for their brands. "Socialist enterprises should do still better," Wang said.[25]

Others argued that Chinese consumers needed a fundamental consumer protection law and revised procedures for civil suits. Consumers who had been victimized had little incentive to seek redress in Chinese courts. Class action suits were not permitted; awards were not sufficient to compensate for the time and effort necessary for each aggrieved individual to see a case through to the end. It was not until 1987 that a Chinese consumer won a landmark suit against a manufacturer of a product that did not work—the case, involving a defective television set, took two years to litigate, and the plaintiff received no compensation beyond restitution for the amount originally paid for the set. The futility of going to court was demonstrated by peasant sit-ins in Shandong, pressing for more forceful action against the counterfeit fertilizers, pesticides, seeds, and other products that had flooded the market.[26]

One might have thought that the Chinese government, in its self-appointed role of "dictatorship of the proletariat," could have enforced protective legislation with ease; but even if it mustered the will, it lacked the means. The fiasco of the 1987 Shoddy Goods Exhibit brought national and international attention to the government's domestic impotence. A newly installed Minister of Light Industry, Zeng Xianlin, had no sooner started his job than he received a torrent of letters from consumers around the country outraged by the poor quality of the products they had bought. One that especially moved Zeng was from a man who wrote that he had always held Chinese-made goods in high esteem, defending them against those who maintained that foreign-made goods were superior, and that he had patriotically bought a Chinese washing machine—which broke down frequently. Upon his head had fallen the wrath of his family, who said that this was the predictable outcome of the foolhardy purchase of Chinese goods. Knowing that in the past the central government had repeatedly ordered that the quality of Chinese products be raised, to no apparent avail, Zeng thought a new tack should be tried: publicly embarrassing the producers of the shoddiest products with a "competition" to see which were the worst and place them on display in a public exhibition. As soon as the exhibition was announced, the ministry was swamped with letters and suggested submissions; a guarded warehouse was soon filled with malfunctioning washing machines, color television sets that did not display color, leaky batteries, and other candidates for the competition, whose identities were to be kept secret.[27]

A second unofficial competition began among the nation's manufacturers: to find out if their own products were among those in the warehouse, and if so, to use every imaginable wile to get them out and repair them before they were judged. Factory representatives flocked to Beijing, calling upon patrons in the bureaucracy to help them, and when a preliminary report from the exhibition's organizing committee was leaked and it became known that some of China's most famous brands were also rated among the shoddiest, other ministries called Zeng's office and urged that the Ministry of Light Industry be "prudent" lest it hurt

China's exports. Beset by lobbying from without, and dissension and leaks from within, the Ministry of Light Industry eventually surrendered and announced the "triumphant completion" of the exhibition, even though it was never publicly held that year as promised.[28]

The usually docile press was outraged and ran prominent editorials expressing dismay. These may have had some effect, because the next year the ministry tried again and managed to push the Shoddy Goods competition through to a publicly visible completion. The most credit for sounding an alarm about the scandal of the competition in its inaugural year should go to China's *Economic Daily,* whose story about the demise of the exhibition took up almost half of the front page. This was an unusually long story for the paper. At the end the reporter, Li Tiejing, drew a conclusion that revealed the fundamental challenge a consumer movement presented to the status quo. Li wrote that the exhibition and the forces mounted to oppose it represented a battle between two very different systems, one new, the other old, and that whenever new things emerged, entrenched interests and conservative powers would enter a fierce battle of self-defense.[29]

These words, proven true again and again, did not spell out exactly what the new order contained, but other advocates of consumer interests ventured to push for "freedom of choice" as a basic consumer right. Such a right would mean not just an end to uncompetitive sales practices, such as the hated "package deal" in which Chinese consumers were forced to buy unwanted goods in order to obtain one highly desired, and inevitably scarce and otherwise unavailable, product. It also would mean a much deeper change in the economic system itself, with the state encouraging competition and prohibiting oligopolistic control of the market by individual enterprises or cartels. Just as with financial reforms, so too with consumer protection, Chinese reformers proposed incremental changes that would mean changing the system itself in everything but name.

American companies were elated, needless to say, at the emergence of popular conspicuous consumption in China. Even though per capita income was low—the equivalent of $262 in 1984, compared to $8,777 in Mississippi, the United States's poorest state—and even though the nonconvertibility of the domestic currency presented difficulties, the mere emergence of a visible consumerism was itself sufficient to excite the imagination of many American consumer goods companies. When Beatrice launched a new snack foods and soft drink operation in China in 1984, its chairman, James Dutt, declared excitedly: "It's like being a child in a candy store."[30] CBS, which began sending China dozens of hours of American programs for commercial broadcast, was sanguine about the hold it would have over consumers. In 1985, when a CBS executive was asked how China's socialist revolution could coexist with the Tournament of Roses parade and made-for-television movies ("Quarterback Princess" and "Muggable Mary: Street Cop"), with commercials running through them all, he replied:

> At least for now, the current hierarchy seems to think that its "revolution" can live side by side with these Western influences, but my hunch is that at some point the Party may come to feel that the whole situation is getting away from it, and may want to put on the brakes. But the thing about TV is that once people start watching certain kinds of programs they get used to them. And when they reach that point you can do almost anything to them except take those programs away.[31]

This prediction recalls Moskowitz's earlier one about the addictiveness of televised advertising. A few years later, in 1988, another television executive saw potentially drastic changes following the invasion of American television programs and commercials. Michael Jay Solomon of Lorimar said: "China is the last bastion. But it's scary because we're going to change the way these people act and feel and think."[32]

Some American companies were not bashful at all about declaring their intention to change the tastes of Chinese consumers. General Foods, for example, hoped to convert the tea-drinking Chinese into coffee drinkers, just as American G.I.s had done to a certain extent in England during World War II. Nabisco opened a snack food factory in Beijing, producing Ritz and other crackers (but not Oreo cookies, whose appeal was tested by Chinese samplers prior to the factory's opening and found to be lacking because of their dark color.) Gillette set up a shaving blade factory in China, dreaming of the old arithmetic of One-Billion, modified for males: 350 million men over the age of 16 multiplied by ten or twenty blades purchased each year. Philip Hung, general manager for the Gillette venture, enthused: "The old idea of selling hundreds of millions of Chinese just one or two boxes of matches is finally becoming possible." Even though, Hung acknowledged, Chinese men commonly did not experience heavy growth of facial hair and had not developed the habit of shaving daily, he thought a marketing effort could overcome resistance. With education, Chinese men could learn that shaving was "an integral part of good grooming." Hung said it was an old marketing problem that had already been overcome in Hong Kong and Singapore.[33]

The American wheat industry took a close interest in teaching Chinese consumers the benefits of increased consumption of wheat-related food products. It was a promotional campaign as commercially motivated as the other American campaigns, but it stood apart from them because it was begun at the invitation of the Chinese government, which in 1978 had asked Bob Bergland, the U.S. Agriculture Secretary, for help in increasing China's industrial baking capacity. The Chinese government, for its part, promoted bread on the pages of the *People's Daily* and other newspapers, presenting it as a nutritious, ready-to-eat staple that was adapted "to the fast pace of modern life." U.S. Wheat Associates, an industry group partly funded by thirteen wheat-producing states eager to expand exports to China, oversaw the construction of an automated bread bakery, flour mill, and instant noodle factory in China. American observers could not resist calling attention to the themes suggested by bread-to-China, a modern-day reversal of Marco Polo's earlier promotion of noodles in the West. *Time* wondered whether many Chinese "will complain that they are hungry again an hour after eating a jelly doughnut."[34]

American wheat growers calculated the familiar mind-boggling numbers: "If each of China's 900 million people were to consume just one additional pound of grain a week," the resulting tonnage would equal the entire annual wheat crop in Canada, or the total annual consumption of wheat in the United States. American tobacco companies were even more excited by projections of a market of One Billion opening because, unlike the wheat industry, the tobacco industry was besieged at home and facing declining sales, and in China it did not have to create a taste for its product. Chinese smokers constituted the single largest market for cigarettes in the world. Foreign tobacco companies found, however, that Chinese authorities were ambivalent about their arrival, as noted in the earlier discussion of the return of advertising to China. The revenue from cigarette taxes was welcomed, and just like any loyal hometown paper in North Carolina, the newspaper in Xiamen, where an R. J. Reynolds cigarette factory was built, expounded at length about the contributions of the enterprise to state coffers. But other Chinese newspapers with no local interest in a thriving tobacco industry cast a more critical eye on the foreign tobacco companies, and noted that the percentage of smokers in the United States, Great Britain, and other developed countries had fallen recently, and yet sales of tobacco had not fallen nearly as fast. The reason: increased sales to developing countries. Some Chinese began to liken the invasion of Western cigarettes to a new Opium War.[35]

The resistance to the expanded presence of American cigarette companies, though not visibly effective, did symbolize a nascent internationalization of the consumer movement. Chinese consumer advocates were attentive when U.S. Surgeon General C. Everett Koop, when asked about the ethics of relying on foreign consumption of tobacco to balance America's unbalanced trade, replied: "I don't think that we as citizens can continue to tolerate exporting disease, disability, and death." Officially, the Chinese government intermittently declared war on smoking. In 1987, it called upon Karl Marx to serve as the inspirational example of a heavy smoker who had quit on the advice of his doctor. This campaign, like the rest, soon faltered, however. The antismoking cause was not helped when Deng Xiaoping told a visiting foreign dignitary that he attributed his good health partly to heavy smoking. For those smokers who remained concerned, the government promoted "healthful" cigarettes as a substitute. Still, in the face of this weak support at the top, consumer advocates below continued to raise voices of concern in the press.[36]

Reflecting the growing autonomy of Chinese consumerism, the *China Youth News* ran in 1988 a particularly hard-hitting piece against smoking, showing that the self-trumpeted tax contributions of the tobacco industry were surpassed by the less visible costs not only of the medical expenses from smoking-related diseases, and from fires, but also from the expenditure of foreign exchange on grain imports needed because tobacco cultivation in China took up scarce arable land. Humankind should not pursue economic growth that was based on "sacrificing health." Here we can see the duality of American exports to Chinese consumers: the cigarettes, promoted by private American interests, and the antismoking ammunition to resist them, provided by public interest lobbies in the United States, the World Health Organization of the United Nations, and others in an informal confederation of consumer advocacy.[37]

If global marketing theory and its predictions of the homogenization of global consumer preferences bore any relation to reality, American consumer goods companies should never have had to be concerned about teaching Chinese a taste for American products. The theory was an offshoot of the talk about global political and cultural convergence in the early 1960s, when the *Harvard Business Review* presented a "new World Customer," deracinated by the progress of expanded jet routes and mass communication, and represented by Brazilian Indians as an example, who had taken up smoking cigarettes and were beginning to wear jeans and shirts. Everyone around the globe seemed to be consuming the same goods, all in pursuit of "growth and progress," which were not defined in detail, but were pleasantly assumed to be "the only possible goals of life."[38]

Modernization around the Third World did not proceed as smoothly and unidirectionally toward the American sun as predicted, but twenty years later, in the early 1980s, Theodore Levitt took up the cause again in the *Harvard Business Review* with cheerful confidence that "the products and methods of the industrialized world play a single tune for all the world, and all the world eagerly dances to it." Levitt stressed that nothing was exempt and the nature of companies themselves was in the process of a thorough transformation: The multinational corporation, which adjusted its products and practices to the varying conditions in the many countries in which it operated, was being replaced, he said, by the "global corporation," which treated the world as a single entity, with homogenized tastes, "selling the same things in the same way everywhere."[39]

Levitt's global-marketing evangelism won many corporate converts, but the subsequent discovery that the global village had yet to arrive was profoundly disillusioning to the companies (Levitt remained steadfast in his faith). It turned out that the French still did not like orange juice for breakfast; that Middle Eastern peoples generally preferred spicy toothpaste; that a single global advertising campaign for Parker Pen, geared for an assumed single constituency worldwide, worked nowhere. McDonald's, a prime candidate for the "global corporation" philosophy, disavowed global marketing and pointed to international variations in its supplemental menu—the beer served in West Germany, the wine in France, the noodles in the Philippines. An obituary for global marketing theory published in 1988 quoted a Booz, Allen consultant who disposed of it with a sardonic question, "Nice fad, wasn't it?"[40]

The global marketing theory is certain never to go away completely, however. A tendency toward cultural homogenization is undeniable, no matter how foolish or premature the assumptions today that confuse a tendency with accomplished fact. As long as the tendency is visible, moreover, Americans will be interested in tracking its progress for reasons other than the design of marketing strategies. The proposition that the world's peoples are becoming one single market—and, not incidentally, a Westernized, and highly Americanized one at that—strikes deeply at feelings that concern national pride and anxiety about America's place in an uncertain future. Global marketing theory will not go away completely for still another reason: The size of the exceptions that do seem to support the theory—the worldwide popularity of American television programs, and the remarkable global appeal of Coca-Cola and Pepsi—keeps the idea of a quiet revolution of consumer homogenization alive.[41]

When China opened wider to the outside world, it was seen as an important test for global marketing theory, what *Advertising Age* referred to as the "people are people" theory, which was "to be tested as never before." China was of interest not only because of the size of the potential market, but also because of its position as our opposite: There the ultimate plebiscite for global marketing could be held, testing the limits of the universality of Western consumer tastes. In China's newly reopened marketplace, the fate of history's single most successful consumer product, Coca-Cola, drew the most interest both inside and outside China because of its totemic significance—and because of historical amnesia that blocked memory of Coca-Cola's sales in China's cities before 1949 (the Shanghai bottling plant had been one of the largest ones outside the United States before the Communists closed it). The announcement in December 1978 that Coca-Cola had reached an agreement to supply the People's Republic with its cola drink had the power to rival the other announcement that came a few days later, that the United States and China had agreed to restore diplomatic relations. The American press was suspicious about the timing of the two announcements and the well-known ties between Paul Austin, the head of Coca-Cola, and President Jimmy Carter. Murray Kempton wrote a humorous column about the American system of international relations, in which "the treaty follows the award of the soft-drink monopoly."[42]

The significance attributed to the arrival of Coke in the People's Republic was registered by virtually every political cartoonist in the United States, and also by newspaper editors who provided almost hour-by-hour coverage of the first shipment of Coca-Cola from Hong Kong to China. Two years later, when the first bottling plant in China was ready to open, the fanfare that the company arranged—it staged a gala at the Great Hall of the People for the occasion, with Aretha Franklin belting out through loudspeakers "Coke adds life"—impressed one American reporter as exceeding that which the announcement of diplomatic relations had gotten earlier. The chairman of Coca-Cola declared in Beijing that the opening of the bottling plant in the People's Republic "may be one of the most important days in the history of our company, and, in more ways than one, in the history of the world."[43]

The Chinese authorities, for their part, maintained that the fuss was unnecessary. Coca-Cola was being brought in only to accommodate the anticipated demand of foreign tourists. "As for us Chinese," said a Chinese official, "we prefer our green tea." An official spokesperson for the Ministry of Foreign Trade was condescending when he emphasized that Coke would only be sold at foreign tourist hotels because "Chinese people have no such habits." Coca-Cola executives, however, had bigger ambitions, but they were patient and did not force the issue. When the Chinese bottler was permitted in 1981 to begin selling Coke directly to the Chinese public, initial Chinese reactions appeared to confirm the earlier official pronouncements that Coke was an acquired taste. Mostly unrefrigerated, the first samples distributed on the streets outside the tourist hotels were dismissed by Chinese tasters as bitter and medicinal. Even a Chinese worker at the bottling plant, when asked by an inquisitive reporter what she thought of it, could manage only a diplomatic admission: "I'm getting used to it." The *Wall Street Journal* commented that the Chinese failure to take advantage of the opportunity to buy and drink Coke was "enough to give a marketing man nightmares." Yet once Coke was distributed in refrigerated form, the marketing nightmare turned into a dream come true: Popular demand grew so quickly that Coca-Cola was selling all it could bottle, and Pepsi, which had begun a canning operation in Shenzhen, ending Coke's short-lived "exclusive" franchise in China, also sold all it could produce. By 1989, Coke had eight bottling plants in operation, as well as a concentrate plant in Shanghai, and demand was so high in the summer months that long lines of customers waited to buy the drink at the door of the bottling plant.[44]

Lingering ideological reservations about the domestic incursion of American soft drinks flared up from time to time, betraying the difficulty for China of swallowing the symbolic significance of Coca-Cola and Pepsi—what a *People's Daily* article described as "capitalism concentrated in a bottle." Chinese authorities showed remarkable tolerance of the colas, especially when compared to other Third World countries that were usually placed within the American orbit; democratic India had forced Coca-Cola to leave in 1977 because the company would not divulge the closely held secret recipe of its concentrate, while Communist-ruled China and the Soviet Union imposed no such condition. Still, the Chinese Communist Party was uncertain about the proper degree of welcome that it should show. In its austere theoretical journal *Red Flag,* it began to allow advertisements in 1980 for all foreign products, except for cigarettes, liquor, cosmetics—and Coca-Cola.[45]

At times, the distinctive red-and-white Coke cans were stacked in small pyramids in front of officials seated at state banquets and plainly visible on the television news; at other times, the state loudly announced that it was dropping Coke at official functions. PepsiCo chairman Donald Kendall, who took his board of directors on a tour of China in 1986 that culminated in sipping Pepsi with Premier Zhao Ziyang, encountered residual hostility when his entourage stopped in Guangdong and met with the provincial governor, Ye Xuanping. Ye pointedly served the American guests tea. Kendall took a sip and said, "Someday we hope to convert you to serving Pepsi." Ye drily replied, "It will take you 2,000 years to reach that goal." An awkward silence followed, and not knowing what else to do, the PepsiCo directors applauded.[46]

American companies that had no connection to the soft drink industry watched closely as China modulated its official welcome to Coke and Pepsi. When an attack on Coke was published in a Chinese magazine in 1983, the wider American business community took offense. The article was critical of Coca-Cola's high caffeine content, high price, and impact on the country's foreign exchange reserves; Chinese who were associated with its distribution were described as "despicable" and "criminal." In the wake of the article, foreign business publications tried to fathom the extent of official backing, and quoted the reactions of panicky Westerners who read a larger meaning in the attacks on the sacred product: "How do you explain to foreign businessmen that you warmly welcome your guest to your home and slap him on the face the next day?"[47]

The Chinese ministries moved quickly to distance themselves from the offending article. The official press published rebuttals, responding to each separate charge leveled against Coke. Caffeine? Tea had much more. Outflow of foreign exchange? No, net inflow, because Coke earned far more foreign exchange from sales to foreign visitors in China than was spent in purchasing the syrup from the United States. The original attack on Coke had talked about it as a problem for the Chinese people involving "nationalistic sentiments." But a reporter for a Canton newspaper who rallied to the cause of Coca-Cola ended a spirited defense with a series of questions: "Why is it that when foreigners drink Chinese tea or *maotai* liquor or Qingdao beer, they don't have their own 'nationalistic sentiments' offended? When foreigners eat Chinese food, does that mean they do not love their own country?"[48]

One of Coca-Cola's American officials had another question for those who attacked his company's product: If drinking Coke was so unhealthy, then why had so many Chinese brands of cola drinks appeared? In 1982, Tianfu Cola was launched in Chongqing, beginning a wave of new domestic soft drinks that claimed to embody "Chinese characteristics." The Chinese backers of Ginseng Cola, pointing to ginseng's ability to enhance health in general and sexual potency in particular, had ambitions to break into the U.S. cola market; "851 Super-Nutrition Drink" took healthful claims one step further in its promised ability to "detect and kill cancer cells in less than 48 hours."[49]

The arguments that Chinese supporters and critics of American soft drinks exchanged, and the earnestness with which new domestic cola drinks were marketed as health tonics, show that the Chinese approached colas with a seriousness that was antithetical to the effervescence American soft drink companies touted when marketing their own products. Coca-Cola's Paul Austin was delighted to learn that the Chinese rendering of Coca-Cola—*Kekoukele,* literally, "Can-Be-Tasty-Can-Be-Happy"—conveyed the idea of refreshment, and Pepsi's president Wayne Calloway told the Chinese that his company was "selling refreshment," which he candidly admitted "is not the first thing that a country like China may need." On occasion, Donald Kendall too was embarrassed by the trivialness of his company's principal products, and in 1986 told a Chinese audience at Fudan University in Shanghai that "even I will admit that soft drinks are not a necessity of life, or a priority of international trade." For Kendall, they were merely a democratic form of pleasure, of "refreshment." The nature of the company's far-flung operations even emboldened him to think of himself as an emissary of world peace, whose soft drinks played a "critical role" in opening lines of communication among customers in 148 countries whose beliefs "span the entire ideological spectrum," yet who all belonged to one giant collectivity because of their shared taste in soft drinks.[50]

For the Chinese, however, membership in this consumer community was not the issue, nor was the intangible, "refreshment." In the Chinese view by the late 1980s, the colas were viewed as another statistical index of modernization. Long forgotten was the initial disdain. Chinese planners looked not to Chinese tea and tradition, but rather to international soft-drink consumption figures. When they compared the average annual per capita consumption in developed countries with that in China, all they saw was a wide disparity that a priori was assumed to be one China should strive to overcome. Soft drinks were even a major item on the Seventh Five-Year Plan, covering 1986–1990, joining steel tonnage and kilowatt production and the older staples of state-directed planning. China was determined to catch up with the West in all categories—bar none.[51]

When Coca-Cola made its postrevolutionary debut in China, American commentators and political cartoonists predicted that McDonald's golden arches would not be long in arriving. America's largest fast-food chain had indeed begun preliminary talks with the Chinese and its American competitors had followed, but none of the hamburger chains was happy about what they learned about China. Feasibility studies revealed disturbing variations in the fat content of beef, and other procurement problems; steep import duties of 360 percent would be levied on all kitchen equipment; rents suddenly escalated when it was learned that a foreign company would be the lessee; repatriation of profits seemed all but impossible. With daunting business problems such as these, little attention was devoted to the more interesting marketing question—would cheeseburgers and french fries delight the palates of Chinese in the People's Republic? In the end, it was Kentucky Fried Chicken that stepped into the role of fast-food pioneer in the socialist world. By accident its flagship outlet in China overlooked Tiananmen Square, where the demonstrations for democracy in spring 1989 and the bloody suppression that followed on June 4 brought into sharp relief the consequences of the changes that had made the presence of the restaurant in the People's Republic possible in the first place.[52]

Like the bread promotion campaign assisted by the American wheat industry, Kentucky Fried Chicken (KFC) got its start in China with an invitation from the Chinese government. Chicken offered the prospects of a smooth transition between Western fast food and Chinese tastes—some regional Chinese cuisines traditionally prepared a fried-chicken dish, while none had even a remote equivalent to the hamburger. KFC had long before made a disastrous foray into Hong Kong in the mid-1970s, and had failed so completely that it closed all its outlets there after only two years, leaving just as McDonald's arrived. It later returned to Hong Kong, and by the late 1980s the company was emboldened to consider ventures into the untried market of mainland China, especially after market research drew a response to samples that was the most encouraging KFC had ever gotten anywhere in similar surveys. No matter how often dismissed in rational analysis, the One Billion phantom reappeared and beckoned; the president of Kentucky Fried Chicken International gushed at the opening of the Beijing outlet in November 1987: "The long-term potential for stores in a country with one billion people is mind-boggling."[53]

The first restaurant, a joint venture between KFC and two Chinese partners, was opened at its Qianmen site, just off Tiananmen Square, after a number of alternative sites were evaluated and rejected. Chinese business folklore—"If the wine is good, it doesn't matter if the shop is on a back alley"—clashed with the three secrets of American small business success—"Location, Location, Location!"—and the Americans prevailed. One of the senior Chinese managers said: "In today's fast-paced life, people don't have the time to probe an alley that is off the beaten track. I'm afraid the old expression must be changed to 'Even if the wine is good, the shop can't be hidden on a back alley.'" The venture paid dearly for the privilege of being so near Tiananmen. The rent was a flat $1 million for a ten-year lease, originally due in advance in one lump payment, later negotiated as payable in three instalments.[54]

The wisdom of choosing that location was proved as soon as the three-storied palace opened and began breaking various KFC world records for sales. It was, KFC claimed, the largest fast-food restaurant in the world, with over 15,000 square feet and seating for more than 500. Western reporters recorded its auspicious beginning breathlessly. The arrival of fast food in China was described by one business magazine this way: "The impossible has happened." One reporter likened Kentucky Fried Chicken to a "cultural meteorite" that had landed in the historically most sensitive spot in China, within a stone's throw of the sarcophagus of Mao, whose once-famous sayings provided easy pickings for ironic quotation ("We must never relax our vigilance against the frenzied plots for revenge by the imperialists and their running dogs. . . .") The reporters should have taken a hint from the young Chinese intellectual who was asked, as he ate a chicken dinner at the restaurant, whether Chinese might not be offended by the placement so close to the symbolic center of Chinese communism of "this monument to American capitalism," as the restaurant was described. The Chinese replied simply, "Oh, who cares. Capitalism is no longer a bad word in China.[55]

Western reporters saw a Kentucky Fried Chicken that was identical in all visible features to its American progenitors. The same menu, the same uniforms, the same logo, the same plastic furniture—even the same prices. The only differences discernible were minor ones—the mashed potatoes, for example, were actually made directly from real potatoes, the only KFC outlet in the world where this was done. The interior decor had pictures of the Manhattan skyline and the Statue of Liberty, as well as a poster proclaiming "America—Catch the Spirit," decorations that later in 1989 would wanly overlook the Goddess of Liberty as it was briefly erected, then crushed, in the square several hundred yards away. Regardless of Kentucky Fried Chicken's apparent American origins and unchanged form after transplantation in China, it was viewed in fundamentally different ways by its Chinese customers. The lesson here, as with so many other American business transplants, is that seemingly unchanged institutions undergo *de facto* transformation when they are placed in a new context, seen in a different light, and put to novel uses. Kentucky Fried Chicken provides an instructive example.

First, many Chinese chose to see the restaurant as stripped of any country's identity, and purchase of a meal was not necessarily a vote of consumer solidarity for "America—Catch the Spirit"; it was a vote for a meal of chicken and potatoes and gravy. The restaurant loudly publicized the fact that it obtained its ingredients locally—everything but the packaging materials and spices—which also helped Sinicize the restaurant in the minds of customers. The two expatriate managers on site were both ethnic Chinese from Singapore, and a Chinese reporter undoubtedly spoke for others when he betrayed a racial delight in the discovery that Chinese "with black hair and yellow skin" were in charge of the restaurant, not blonde Caucasians. This too helped Sinicize it.[56]

Second, the Chinese viewed the restaurant's operations as a demonstration of "rational, scientific methods" which, the Chinese chairman of the KFC venture averred, should not be regarded as belonging to America or to any one country. By the calculations of one Chinese consumer magazine, which took to heart "the American scientist Franklin's famous saying, 'Time-is-money,' " a family feast prepared in a Chinese home required six person/hours spent purchasing ingredients and preparing the dishes; assigning a monetary value to the time and calculating the opportunity costs along with the costs of the ingredients, the magazine concluded that a large home-cooked meal actually cost the equivalent of 23 yuan (about US $6.00), a sum far larger than would have been guessed. The time spent preparing three meals a day, over the course of a lifetime, added up to the equivalent of decades of full-time labor. To save a portion of that time, "there is a need for a revolution," the magazine said in 1987, using "revolution" without self-consciousness to refer to the savings in time created by greater reliance on fast-food restaurants, or what was more formally dressed up as "the socialization of labor."[57]

How strange it was that thirty years after the Great Leap Forward forcibly communized rural kitchens under this banner, "the socialization of family labor," the phrase would be used again, but this time as part of a peaceful "revolution" of fast-food restaurants. But this "revolution" was not defined as the embodiment of everything Chairman Mao opposed. It represented a radical change in method, but not necessarily in ideology. Fast-food operations reduced the steps of food preparation to a numbingly simple system suited for the least-skilled segment of the American work force—teenagers lacking in work experience and prone to high turnover. The KFC operations manuals that were originally compiled in Louisville, Kentucky, transferred readily to China because the system they prescribed broke the requisite steps down so minutely that anyone, no matter how inexperienced, could operate his or her assigned station and be part of a highly productive system of food production. Like other "advances" that carried the alluring aura of science, this greatly appealed to the Chinese. KFC fit nicely into the old formulation—useful foreign techniques would be adopted, but China's own essence would remain undisturbed.

Third, and most important, Kentucky Fried Chicken was popular in China because it provided an oasis of friendly service and eating areas that were clean and quiet. Even the bathrooms, kept clean with the attention of a full-time attendant, uplifted the spirit. For Americans, fast-food restaurants were appealing because they were easy to reach in an automotive culture, and they were cheap. American customers usually did not linger. For Chinese patrons headed for the first KFC restaurant in Beijing, however, cars were not available to place it within convenient reach, and it was inexpensive only by comparison with the banquets that cost an entire month's salary. The motivation of Chinese patrons was one that Americans would not have thought of: pursuit of an attractive ambiance, where one *wanted* to linger. Comparing the KFC experience to the shortcomings of Chinese restaurants at the time, a Chinese reporter described his experience in almost rapturous terms that would seem ludicrous if read outside his own country: "This is not merely eating," he said, "this is a kind of psychological rest, relaxing the nerves, providing people with a place of peace and comfort amid the din of the city." In short, Kentucky Fried Chicken offered Chinese customers something that it would never think of claiming it offered American customers—refreshment. Unfortunately, the soft-drink behemoths had already appropriated the marketing of "refreshment" for themselves.[58]

Perhaps the managers of the KFC anticipated that a portion of their appeal would be this less tangible product of ambiance, or perhaps it was not anticipated. Curiously, on the landing of the stairway leading up to the seating area on the second floor hung a huge picture that departed from the Americana featured on the other walls. It showed the second floor eating area, devoid of patrons, beckoning with an expanse of pristine tables, seats, floor. Even banquet restaurants in China would have been hard pressed to compare favorably with this vision of immaculate (and people-less) perfection. Downstairs, in addition, the allure of friendly service in a society in which rudeness had become a new norm also proved to be enormously powerful. The fact that a simple smile in greeting from a clerk in a KFC uniform could produce an outpouring of gratitude from a customer (one happily pledged, "even if more expensive, I'd gladly pay") tells less about KFC than it does about the prevailing norms in commercial society in the People's Republic and the low expectations of consumers. (Later, in January 1990, when McDonald's opened its first restaurant in Moscow to large, appreciative crowds, the smiles and polite manner of the staff drew similar attention from the customers.)[59]

Kentucky Fried Chicken was the beneficiary of the failures of China's own service industry, and it did so well—setting a single-day KFC record, for example, of $22,400 in sales—that the Chinese chairman of the board was optimistically predicting the entire initial investment would be recouped in just one and a half years. The instant success of the first Beijing outlet led quickly to the opening of two smaller ones and dreams of big plans for the future: 25 outlets in Beijing alone by 1993. The question of how to repatriate profits was not a concern; the profits would be plowed back into further expansion. In late 1988, when other foreign companies in China were moving more cautiously in the wake of tightened import restrictions, rumors of currency devaluation, and other unfavorable policy changes, Kentucky Fried Chicken said it would be unaffected and intended to push on full speed with plans for expansion. But the main Qianmen restaurant, arguably the most successful of all the American business ventures in China established during the preceding decade, was literally engulfed by the drama of April, May, and June 1989 at Tiananmen. At one point, PLA troops occupied the restaurant for a week. When it reopened for business, the bright business prospects that had seemed so sure a month earlier were in doubt.[60]

In the wake of the June 4 massacre, the corporate headquarters of

KFC in the United States withdrew a television commercial that included footage filmed earlier at the main Beijing restaurant; the association with China, which only a historical moment before the company had proudly pointed to as a glorious story of success now was unseemly. Business revived quickly, and in August 1989 the Beijing restaurant set a new single-day record for sales. Still, predictions seemed foolhardy, and KFC, Coca-Cola, and other American companies with vested stakes in China's future found themselves groping, with uncertain step, in darkness.[61]

CONCLUSION:

SALESMAN REVISITED

The fate of Ying Ruocheng, the veteran actor and director who had played Willy Loman in the Beijing production of *Death of a Salesman,* encapsulates the changes and ambiguities in China's official posture toward the West. When *Salesman* debuted in 1983 its foreign provenance was controversial, and Ying had had to lobby hard to secure permission for the production and defend it from conservative attackers. Once staged, the play turned out to be a popular success and played to capacity houses for three months. Subsequently, as officials permitted the country to open up further to outside contacts, and as the public welcomed plays, books, and movies that brought in formerly heterodox ideas, the Chinese state was more tolerant of ideological experimentation. Ying was a gifted translator (of Shakespeare, among others) but his other talents were much in demand in films and the theater. He finally was seen in the United States in a dramatic leading role befitting his stature when he played the prison warden in the movie "The Last Emperor." Soon Ying was asked to serve the government as vice-minister of culture, under Wang Meng, the newly appointed minister, who himself was a distinguished novelist. Together, the two worked to push open the doors and windows of China to the outside world of literature and the arts, and Ying put into effect new policies that gave state-run theater companies more autonomy in choosing plays, hiring actors, and managing their own finances.[1]

After the brutal suppression of the democracy movement in June 1989, however, the official encouragement of openness was cast into doubt. Campaigns against "bourgeois liberalism" and the contaminating germs of Western "spiritual pollution" were resumed. Li Ruihuan, a Politburo member, explained the surge of gambling, pornography, and drugs in China as the intended result of a plot by "hostile overseas forces." America was once again portrayed as a center of depravity (sample headlines: "Gambling: Another Form of Pollution in the United States" and "The Forgotten Child Laborers of the United States"). The seditious power of Coca-Cola and Pepsi were indirectly acknowledged when the Chinese government banned canned beverages from all state functions and banquets. All officials were required to issue statements in support of the government's suppression of the students. Wang Meng conspicuously refused to do so and was dismissed from his post, apparently signaling an end to the openness in the arts that had prevailed during his tenure.[2]

Ying remained and publicly sided with the government position that intellectuals had nothing to fear so long as they did not participate in "counterrevolutionary" activities. Ying had long been identified with reform-minded intellectuals and himself had tested the state's willingness to experiment at the edges of ideological orthodoxy when *Salesman* played in Beijing, and also in early 1989 when the People's Republic staged the first exhibition of oil paintings featuring nude figures. But in the chill of the post-massacre crackdown in 1989, Ying openly distanced himself from many of his colleagues and from his own past. Loyal to the official Party line, he isolated himself from the reformers and busied himself in the fall of 1989 with a politically "correct" arts festival in Beijing that was explicitly intended to show the stability of the regime to a skeptical world.

Many of the flesh-and-blood Willy Lomans who had gone to China to do business and fled during the violence in June 1989 returned after the Chinese government welcomed them back. The authorities went to great lengths to reassure foreign businesspeople, as best it could, that basic policy had not changed, that China remained open for business as usual. A decade earlier, China's official pronouncements of welcome were instantly accepted as sincere, but in 1989 they were met with cautious, and often cynical, reception. A decade before, China was regarded by many foreign businesspeople as a special place; after the shootings around Tiananmen Square in June 1989, China was returned to the Third World fold. In August 1989 a Western diplomat based in Shanghai remarked: "It's not enough to say the open-door policy remains. Burma and Laos say the same thing, but who invests there?"

China no longer looked as large in the world, and by 1990 the star examples of what the *New York Times* called "cuddly Communism" were the democratizing countries of Eastern Europe. Business interest shifted accordingly, and a newly founded American Chamber of Commerce in Budapest reported a stampede of American companies interested in investing in Hungary: "It's like the gold rush."[3]

In curious ways, China's official post-crackdown stance in 1989 recalled the stance of fifteen years earlier, in the early and middle 1970s, when the country was first opening up. At that time, the end of the Cultural Revolution had yet to be declared, and international business was kept neatly separated from domestic politics. When the first wave of American businesspeople arrived at the Canton Trade Fairs, they were kept safely isolated from the denunciations of the imperialist West that still filled the Chinese press. Chinese trade officials reassured their foreign guests that "business is business" and that they were safe from the intrusion of politics. Then, American businesspeople accepted "business is business" as a sign of PRC pragmatism. In 1989, however, the same line was seen in a much less favorable light, as a government ruse to escape culpability for the violence that crushed the democracy movement. Scott Seligman, vice-president of Burson-Marsteller China Ltd., said in August 1989: "To multinationals, one of the more vexing consequences of the Tiananmen [shootings] has been the return of China business to the political realm from the purely commercial. More than a decade of hard work to normalize business relations seems to have been undone overnight." After 1989, Westerners refused to so easily accept China's official pronouncement that economics and politics would be kept separate. Foreigners observed that Party secretaries at the factory levels had been given increased power to overrule professional managers. Forward movement on price decontrols, sales of state enterprises, and other market-oriented reforms stopped. Foreigners also noticed the strong terms used by Chinese officials like Jiang Zemin, the new general secretary who had deposed Zhao Ziyang, to denounce capitalism before domestic audiences. Roger Sullivan, president of the U.S.–China Business Council, was not reassured by Jiang Zemin's first major speech, released in October 1989: "The best you can say about it is that he's trying to define a policy of openness to the outside world without reform. I don't think that's possible."[4]

Chinese apologists for the government's actions in 1989 used the capitalist idiom to make the case for business-is-business, just as the Chinese government had adroitly used it in earlier years whenever it suited its own purposes. When foreign business visitors had protested the high prices they were forced to pay in order to woo the Chinese, the Chinese had responded that their prices simply reflected the operation of the market. In 1989, the Chinese press—once the Party gerontocracy had recaptured control—again used capitalist rhetoric as apology for government actions. Observing that many foreign firms refused to make any public statement in the wake of the crackdown, the press quoted approvingly the apolitical philosophy "business-is-business" that it claimed was held by the foreign business community in China. Capitalist pragmatism, the Chinese government reassured the public, would keep foreign businesspeople committed to China. In fact, many business people were afflicted with conflicting emotions. Chris Morton, a Beijing manager for Joy Technologies, explained his company's decision to stay in China after the June 1989 shootings: "You're torn. You have a business obligation but you know what you have seen."[5]

To help capitalists come to their "pragmatic" senses, the government called upon the lure of the mist-enshrouded vastness of the China market, the old ploy it had used to such great effect in earlier years, when trade and investment ties between the United States and China were just beginning. In the decade preceding 1989, the mesmerizing One Billion had been artfully used to overcome Western resistance. Even after the 1989 crackdown, some American companies remained as enthralled with the vision as before: Kentucky Fried Chicken, for example, pushed on and opened a new restaurant in Shanghai. Coca-Cola's president of its international division, John Georgas, flew to China for the fortieth anniversary celebrations in the fall of 1989, and was welcomed by Jiang Zemin, who personally expressed his "appreciation" for the American company's "cooperation." Avon announced a new joint venture with the Chinese in February 1990, just as excited about the prospect of reaching the "500 million women" in China as ten years before.[6]

But the accretion of experiences in the interim had taught other foreign businesspeople that gaining access to the fabled One Billion had been slow and incomplete and had been fought every step of the way by various Chinese government officials and satraps who were protective of domestic producers and of the country's foreign exchange. The difficulties American companies had confronted in China once the initial honeymoon was over were not trivial: finding reliable sources of local materials and skilled and motivated workers was hard, gaining basic legal protection and avoiding crippling bureaucratic interference were harder still, and securing foreign exchange, hardest of all. These problems remained, and in some cases appeared to worsen in the wake of the violence and suppression of mid-1989.

June 1989 was seen as the watershed, but actually most of the problems experienced afterward were evident well before that spring. Quality standards in China's exports had been sliding for two years, leading many American importers to begin using the word "cheating" for the first time. In China, American businesspeople had encountered ever escalating demands for payoffs and kickbacks, which had become so common that many foreign executives had concluded that backdoor dealings had virtually eliminated legitimate competition. A Boston businessman, Garrison Rousseau, described his experience attempting to do business in China: "The difference between graft in China and other places is that in China, [you] can't get things done even when you've paid bribes." Add to this the central government's austerity measures, implemented in October 1988, which pinched domestic loans and subsidies, leaving many domestic buyers and export-oriented plants strapped for cash. The violence of June 1989 did not create these business problems; it merely drew attention to conditions that had been denied but had already existed.[7]

The Chinese authorities, however, did not acknowledge that the intervening historical experience had taught foreign investors to be much more wary. Chinese officials once again touted the domestic market, with its boundless if admittedly far from realized "potential." But the authorities did add a twist that got right to the heart of capitalist competition: If a foreign firm withdrew from China, the Chinese warned, the firm's competitors would simply move back in and have a free hand. Vice-Premier Tian Jiyun exploited this vulnerability when he addressed a group of British businesspeople in late June 1989: "If one country does not come, another one will." This was a reincarnation of the fear that had sent many American companies into China in the late 1970s and early 1980s. It was a threat that found a receptive audience in George Bush's brother Prescott, who visited Beijing on a business prospecting trip in September 1989. Responding a mite defensively to inquiries about the timing of his China visit, Bush said: "We aren't a bunch of carrion birds coming to pick the carcass. But there are big opportunities in China, and America can't afford to be shut out."[8]

Even after the crackdown in 1989, just as before, Americans dreaded most of all the aggressiveness of their Japanese competitors. Americans remembered the discovery of Japanese ahead of them during the sprints to exhibit areas at the Canton Trade Fairs of the 1970s, and later as Japanese companies began advertising consumer products in China even before being permitted to sell there. The same aggressiveness was evident in 1989 immediately after the crackdown, when Japanese companies resumed business relations and pressed forward with new investments with such unseemly haste that Japan's own foreign minister, Hiroshi Mitsuzuka, was moved to criticize the companies for creating an image of Japan as "trying to make money like a thief at a fire."[9]

To gain a perspective on the immediate crisis posed by the crackdown, American companies could look back on their experiences in China over the course of the preceding years and observe some patterns. Three in particular dominated. The first is the recurrent tension between the growth of imports into China and China's maintenance of national pride. The more China has allowed in that is visibly foreign—whether modern hotel towers or made-for-television movies or Coca-Cola—the more conservative elements in the government and in the populace have responded with reassertion of China's own domestic resourcefulness. Responding to conservative attacks, Ying Ruocheng had to justify the Beijing production of *Death of a Salesman* in 1983 by describing it as a stone that could help polish the precious "jade" of China's own culture. Other Chinese who sponsored imports from the West were also attentive to nationalistic sensitivities and minimized the significance of the imports as much as possible.

This tension between foreign imports and Chinese pride persisted throughout the 1970s and 1980s, in times when imports expanded as well as when they were restricted. It was revealed whenever Chinese purchasers insisted on making their own decisions about what spare parts to order for equipment bought from foreign firms, or whenever Chinese partners in joint ventures insisted on using a Chinese construction company, despite complaints from foreign partners that the local materials and workmanship did not yet meet international standards. The pride with which the Chinese spoke in their own press of Chinese-managed hotels and factories that were the equal of the Western-managed competition in China bespoke an urgent need to reclaim an imagined loss of national identity brought about by the intrusion of the West.

It was this same need to compete with, and best, the West that might explain a great deal of the appeal of Marxism in the early twentieth century: By embracing an ideology which offered a way of claiming a position that was more "advanced" than the capitalism of the West, Chinese Communists avoided having to play the perpetual game of catch-up that would be required if China followed the same route to modernization as the nations of the already developed capitalist West. Marxism offered a way of leapfrogging right over capitalism, and even after the hold of the ideology over the Chinese public had conspicuously disintegrated by the late 1980s, it still appealed to those in power, regardless of the problems that had been exposed in its practice. It not only served to justify their own rule, it also solved this basic underlying tension between reliance on things Western and national pride. Marxism was the one import from the West that was never injurious to the nation's self-image because the West had been slow to adopt Marxism for itself.

After the crackdown in 1989, official government ideologues felt so threatened by the destabilizing effect of Western influences that they launched their most strident attacks on Chinese critics who had dared to question not Marxism but an even more sacrosanct subject: the glorious heritage of Chinese culture itself. "River Elegy," a previously acclaimed six-part television series about Chinese culture which had been broadcast on national television on two occasions in 1988, became the focus of blistering attacks in the official media during the late summer of 1989. The Yellow River of the program title stood as the symbol of Chinese culture itself: stagnant, erratic, and at times violent. The program suggested that China's contemporary poverty was created not by its contacts with the West, but by a stagnant indigenous culture of China's own making, whose earlier achievements obscured its modern failings. In the wake of the crackdown, Su Xiaokang, the principal scriptwriter of "River Elegy," was the target of a nationwide manhunt before he escaped from the country. His persecutors claimed that Su's program had extolled the virtues of capitalist culture, but this attack was only for the sake of conforming to a pat ideological orthodoxy. Clearly what most enraged the state was Su's willingness to spit at the overweening pride of traditional Chinese nationalism. This was far more heretical than if he had spit on the grave of Marx.[10]

A second tension that has dominated the course of business relations between China and the United States concerns the question of whether China can choose to invite selectively designated imports, or isolated salespeople, without any accompanying baggage. The Chinese government has consistently maintained that imports from the West—or reforms inspired by the West—may be chosen or rejected case by case, while the foreigners have maintained with equal conviction that imports and reforms come as a package. In the early 1970s, the Chinese government began to expand technology imports from the West, and did so with relative equanimity, relying on the old formula inherited from the nineteenth-century Self-Strengtheners, who had proposed borrowing material tools from the West while keeping China's cultural essence unchanged. The opening wider to the West that Deng Xiaoping oversaw was also meant to be selective, with the emphasis on practical tools, producer goods, and tangible hardware that could make an easily understood contribution to China's future wealth and power.

The Chinese government was much less interested in consumer goods, or more intangible software or institutional reforms that would change the operating environment into which the imported machines were to be placed. But when joint ventures with Western partners were started and began to multiply in the 1980s, foreigners in China argued that if the ventures were to succeed, more substantial changes were needed. New hotels, for example, needed more than new physical facilities, they needed new management structures, new work attitudes, new incentive systems. Even Chinese enterprises that had no connections to foreign investors also came to realize that one reform led ineluctably to another. For example, enterprises that were made financially autonomous discovered that they had to find new sources of capital, which led to stock issues, then stock trading, and later stock exchanges, all necessary if they were to be successful in attracting the needed infusion of private investment. Any given step was always seen as isolated by the Chinese authorities, or alternatively as part of a larger process of necessary reforms by foreigners, who often spoke of a bicycle as a metaphor for reform: It had to keep moving forward, or it would fall over.

In 1989, after the crackdown, Deng Xiaoping again averred that economic reforms would go forward, unaffected by the political turmoil. The door to trade and investment would remain open, and the Western salesperson would be as welcome in Beijing as before. But he was to come alone, leaving the rest of the West behind. It was a position wholly consistent with Deng's past statements and belief in the separability of particular reforms. He believed that the Chinese government could choose how far the reforms would be permitted to proceed and what would come in from the West. And also as before, foreign observers of China disagreed, questioning the ultimate success of moderate changes in domestic economic policies that did not complete the process of transformation, and that promised economic reform without political reform. After the crackdown, the political stability of the regime, never regarded by prospective investors before as a matter of concern, was a new source of worry and made foreign salespeople newly attentive students of Chinese politics.

In retrospect, we can see that the very nomenclature used by the Chinese, both reformers and conservatives, and faithfully repeated by foreigners, disguised the significance of the economic policy changes that were set into motion during the 1980s. The bland, moderate noun—"reforms"—was ideologically safe and conveniently capacious, encompassing revolutionary changes as well as minor ones. It was used indiscriminately by everyone, with little thought to the cumulative significance of the many individual changes in the existing order. Perhaps the conscious awareness of competing ideological systems that had been so much in the minds of Chinese and Americans in the early years of the business encounters in the 1970s and early 1980s should be remembered. The ideological competition between two distinct systems was not a parlor game for ideologues. It was a conflict on a gargantuan—almost geological—scale.

When China and the United States came together to do business, two discrete ideological systems engaged in a grinding battle, like two enormous tectonic plates. By the late 1980s, business had developed and been routinized so far that this subterranean grinding was temporarily forgotten. But in June 1989 the government violence that attended the suppression of the democracy movement revealed the depth of basic contention that had been going on all along, with pressure apparently building as the socialist economy lost more and more ground in the ideological competition. The octogenarians who controlled the country post-crackdown were not simple despots holding onto power for power's sake. They were defenders, just as they said, of a system that was in much more serious trouble than was generally understood so long as everyone talked of "reforms." In a macabre way, Deng Xiaoping was correct: The democracy movement, just like the movement to further liberalize and privatize the economy, was headed in a definitely radical, that is "counterrevolutionary," direction. These ideological matters were deadly serious ones.

If Chinese authorities, after the crackdown, thought that the evils of "bourgeois liberalism" could be combatted by sacking Minister of Culture Wang Meng and reinstituting tighter controls on cultural performances and publications, and on the often wayward thinking of university professors, they missed the less obvious but potentially seditious impact of seemingly innocuous consumer goods and services brought in from the West. We can speculate that in their own modest way the unleashing of foreign consumer goods—the onslaught of color television sets, perfume and makeup, gold jewelry and other adornments, Coca-Cola and Pepsi—and the advertising and promotion that accompanied the goods themselves, contributed in unpredictable ways to destabilizing the status quo by creating new hungers for a better life, hungers that expanded to the realm of political change. It was not inevitable, and it would be easy to overstate the case—one does not want to argue that the history of consumerism in modern China is a Madison Avenue fairy tale in which one day the Chinese tasted Coke, and the next day they filled Tiananmen Square demanding democracy. But we cannot ignore the intuitive suspicion that in some ways, still poorly understood, the enormous changes in the sights and sounds and tastes of urban life in modern China during the eventful decade of 1979 to 1989 all played some role in the amazing display of popular unhappiness with the established order briefly witnessed in the late spring of 1989.

Somewhere in the decade bracketed on one end by the fuss over the Pierre Cardin fashion shows and the opening of the first Seiko watch outlet in Beijing, and on the other by the opening of the three-story Kentucky Fried Chicken outlet just off Tiananmen Square, in the heart of the capital, were changes that helped shape the *Zeitgeist.* To suggest a connection runs the risk of trivializing the democracy movement and deemphasizing the movement's own explicit targets of corruption and an unresponsive bureaucracy. The gravity of popular dissatisfaction with the political status quo, however, need not be diminished by the minor suggestion that great change in one sphere of individuals' personal lives—the economic—may well have contributed to dissatisfactions in other spheres, both personal and political. Many urban residents had begun to supplement their meager salaries in factories, stores, or government offices with entrepreneurial activities; had developed an individualist ethos and concrete economic interests that were politically unprotected. Many others had the same ethos, and the lines separating the economic and political, the public and the private, were blurred. Wuer Kaixi, the youthful student leader of the democracy movement who escaped to the West after the crackdown, spoke retrospectively of the growing awareness among China's youth of the importance of sexuality and personal expression as significant aspects of the inner life of the student uprising. "You might find it strange, but I do not," said Wuer at a conference in New York in October 1989, "that one aspect of our movement was the student who stood naked on top of a university building shouting, 'I am what I am.' "[11]

The third major pattern in the business encounters between Americans and Chinese is that of the often self-serving constructions Americans have tended to put on the Chinese, and the equally self-serving constructions the Chinese have placed on Americans. When Americans first went to China as "revolutionary tourists" in the early 1970s, they were entranced by the exotic: the neatly organized social order, the *frisson* of revolutionary rhetoric, the delight in gaining access to a country that friends at home had never had the opportunity of visiting. American department stores like Bloomingdale's commercialized the exotic and further accelerated the phenomenon of China chic, giving the allure of high fashion to the plebeian work clothes of Chinese peasants. American businesspeople proved no less immune to the excitement about gaining access to China than anybody else and, led by the major oil companies, poured into China, seeing and hearing whatever positive signs they wanted to. James Stepanek, an experienced Beijing expatriate, looked back from 1989 and said: "After nearly five years living in Beijing, I still cannot comprehend the ease with which the Chinese side extracted the extra discount, the extra week of negotiations, the extra favor." Stepanek concluded, "When it came to China, people threw away the book."[12]

The Chinese hosts of American businesspeople also had their own overlay of meanings that they placed upon their foreign guests and China's relationship with the United States. Just as Americans tended to sentimentalize the Chinese as a people blessed with especially appealing attributes, the Chinese sentimentalized Americans, telling them that Americans were more honest, easier to do business with, compared to foreign partners such as the Japanese. Americans were flattered and wished that the "special relationship" the Chinese often spoke of would result in the completion of more business deals.

The perceptions of one people in the eyes of the other could also change abruptly, which suggests to what a great degree the relationship was dominated by subjective influences. Before Nixon's and Mao's initiative to move the two countries toward a restoration of economic and diplomatic relations, the Chinese were viewed in the popular American mind as the threatening Blue Ants last encountered directly in the Korean war; after Nixon's visit to China, the Chinese became overnight the lovable Communists, now clearly distinguished from their less lovable cousins to the north. In China, popular perceptions of Americans varied according to the shifts in official policy. In the late 1970s, America was still depicted as a dark hell in which the social ills of a disintegrating capitalism were evident on every street corner; then, abruptly, an unrecognizably new America began to be reported in Chinese newspapers, a country rich and full of technological marvels. During the 1980s, depending upon the needs of the moment, the Chinese authorities carefully calibrated the relative weight of positive and negative elements in the picture they created of the United States. But the tension created by the different pictures that each side had of the other was mostly produced by the natural inclination of both to see on the other side of the Pacific whatever accorded best with their own inclinations. When Deng Xiaoping visited the United States in 1979, touring the Ford assembly plant in Georgia and donning cowboy garb at the barbecue in Texas, Americans were inclined to see a penitent Communist leader ready to imbibe American ways, despite the ambiguity of the evidence when it was sifted objectively.

Were the Chinese becoming more like us? When we look closely at specific instances when American influence would seem to have been undeniably significant during the past decade, we find complications. The transplanting of MBA programs to China, for example, reveals that a certain body of concepts and analytical techniques traveled there without apparent damage, but the MBA's tools were seen by incumbents in Chinese organizations in a much different light, or were ignored altogether. Consequently, the impact of Western-trained MBAs was limited. Even in the case of Kentucky Fried Chicken, which enjoyed success from its opening day, the success did not necessarily reflect a populist affirmation of American culture. Despite the superficially identical nature of the food, Chinese patrons perceived the attractions of the restaurant in fundamentally different ways than most American patrons, so the experiences in one country should not be too hastily interchanged with those in the other.

Yet after duly noting the dangers of glib assumptions that the Chinese were actually becoming more like us, the enigma of the democracy movement of 1989 still lingers. The ability of the 1989 movement to gather wide support beyond the Beijing campuses where it began, support that brought literally millions of sympathizers into the streets, astonished American viewers, who were transfixed by the images on their television sets of the drama unfolding halfway around the globe. But not only Americans were surprised; so were the movement's own youthful leaders, who themselves had not anticipated the extent of the popular support they received.

Until the government crackdown, the movement was able to give expression to collective yearnings for a more democratic administration, for freedom of the press and the right to assemble and other rights that Americans know well from the catechism recited in American civics classes. The yearning for democracy—for one shining moment in 1989—revealed itself with poignant universality. Admittedly, from the beginning of China's unsteady experiments with reform during the previous decade, Americans have been tempted at various points to see the Chinese as becoming more like ourselves with every passing day. If the impulse was premature before 1989, in the spring of 1989 it seemed to be coming to pass with the undeniable force of the millions of protesters and supporters in the streets of Beijing and other major cities. Later in 1989, the dramatic surge of reform movements in Poland and Hungary, then in East Germany, Czechoslovakia, Romania, and many Soviet republics, shocked the West with their speed and power. Most dramatic of all was the case of East Germany, the wealthiest country among the Warsaw Pact nations, yet whose economic and political system collapsed with unmatched speed.

The triumph of the West in the Cold War appeared to have been ratified by an unofficial referendum in all of these countries. Still, in the case of the preceding events in China, at least, some doubts linger about interpreting the democracy movement as the logical culmination of the eventful decade of Western influences that had preceded. We should be suspicious of any historical determinism that reduces events to an overly tidy formula. The 1989 democracy movement in China had predecessors that did *not* gain wide social support. The "democracy spring" of 1979 and the short-lived student demonstrations of late 1986 and early 1987 were both suppressed rather easily by the government. The 1989 movement began as a small student movement and seemed destined to remain so, until tactical decisions made by the leaders—such as the hunger strike and the erection of the Goddess of Liberty—helped to galvanize support far beyond the movement's original base. If we were to look back at the fluctuating fortunes of the 1989 democracy movement in China day by day, we would get a much different picture, and hold much less conviction that its growth—and also its eventual suppression—were historically inevitable.

The Goddess of Liberty was the most touching evidence of the Chinese protesters' drawing inspiration from an American model. But in the wake of the suppression of the movement and the destruction of the statue, we have no way of knowing what ordinary Chinese would say today, if suddenly given the opportunity to shape a thorough overhaul of China's political and economic systems. Would the public wish simply to take up where the democracy movement left off? Would rural residents agree with urban, or those in the north with those in the south? If the current regime were to collapse, would any portion of the public get a chance to express its will at all?

After 1989, despite a decade of emotionally intense involvement in China's opening to the outside world, Americans were left, as they had started, with American Willy Lomans uncertainly facing their Chinese customers and suppliers, confronting a country around which an opaque veil had descended again. Arthur Miller had wondered what Chinese "in their heart of hearts" had made of *Death of a Salesman.* One might ask about the larger verdict that the Chinese people "in their heart of hearts" would reach, in the end, about all the other ideas, institutions, and products introduced by Americans during the 1980s. The intense engagement of the American public with the news coverage of China in 1989 reflected a new level of emotional investment in the fate of the people of the People's Republic. Americans undoubtedly will listen closely when future political changes in China make it possible to learn more fully what verdict the Chinese people have rendered about things American.

ABBREVIATIONS

AWS *Asian Wall Street Journal* [weekly edition]
BJRB *Beijing ribao* [*Beijing Daily*]
CBR *China Business Review*
CSM *Christian Science Monitor*
GMRB *Guangming ribao* [*Guangming Daily*]
GRFL Gerald R. Ford Library, Ann Arbor, Michigan. Papers of the National Council for U.S.–China Trade.
JJRB *Jingji ribao* [*Economic Daily*]
LAT *Los Angeles Times*
NYT *New York Times*
QNB *Zhongguo qingnian bao* [*China Youth News*]
Renda Zhongguo renmin daxue (People's University). *Fuyin baokan ziliao* [*Periodical Reprint*] series.
RMRB *Renmin ribao* [*People's Daily*]
WP *Washington Post*
WSJ *Wall Street Journal*

NOTES

INTRODUCTION

1. "Weile renmin de youyi" [For the friendship of the people], *GMRB,* 7 May 1983; Arthur Miller, *Salesman in Beijing* (New York: Viking Press, 1984), vii–viii.
2. Miller, *Salesman in Beijing,* vii–viii; "Arthur Miller Says Chinese Understand His 'Salesman'," *WP,* 1 May 1983.
3. Miller, *Salesman in Beijing,* 8.
4. Miller, *Salesman in Beijing,* 54–55.
5. Miller, *Salesman in Beijing,* 14–15; "Willy Loman Gets China Territory," *NYT,* 7 May 1983.
6. Miller, *Salesman in Beijing,* 196; "Arthur Miller," *WP.*
7. " 'Salesman' Opens Door to Hearts of Peking Audience," *LAT,* 8 May 1983.
8. Miller, *Salesman in Beijing,* 5, 229–231.
9. Miller, *Salesman in Beijing,* 233.
10. Miller, *Salesman in Beijing,* 254.
11. "Yishen weise de 'Tuixiaoyuan de si' ['Death of a Salesman'—Deep But Difficult], *RMRB,* 28 June 1983.
12. " 'Salesman' Opens Door," *LAT.*
13. " 'Salesman' Opens Door," *LAT;* "Willy Loman," *NYT;* Yuan Henian, " 'Death of a Salesman' in Beijing," *Chinese Literature,* October 1983, 104; Miller, *Salesman in Beijing,* 131.
14. "China's Idea of Success Has Changed," *LAT,* 11 November 1984; "Arthur Miller," *WP;* Miller, *Salesman in Beijing,* 131; Arthur Miller, *Timebends: A Life* (New York: Grove Press, 1987), 184–185.
15. Ying Ruocheng, "Xiang, yao xiangde shen" [Think, think deeply], *BJRB,* 4 June 1983.

CHAPTER 1: THE CANTON FAIR

1. "Nixon Eases China Trade Embargo to Allow Nonstrategic Exports; Chou Says 'New Page' Has Opened," *NYT,* 15 April 1971.
2. "Trade Fair Reflecting Chinese Difficulties," *NYT,* 15 May 1976.

3. "U.S. Businessmen Find Haggling with Chinese Is Exhausting Work," *WSJ,* 2 November 1972.
4. Robert Hoffman, "U-M Grad Writes Home During His Visit to the Trade Fair in Canton, China," *Michigan Alumnus,* December 1974, 15; "To China and Back—A Shopping Trip Leads to Pleasure," *NYT,* 18 May 1972.
5. "Canton Trade Fair Prices Found High By U.S. Buyers," *NYT,* 13 November 1972; "Kwangchow Diary—Spring 1975," *U.S.–China Business Review,* May–June 1975, 48; Letter, no salutation, "Friday Morn," date stamped (in DC) 13 May 1975, folder "*CBR* vol.2, no.4, Background (3)," Box 188, GRFL.
6. "U.S. Businessmen," *WSJ.*
7. "Shrewd Chinese Bargainers in No Rush to 'Buy American'," *Industry Week,* 21 May 1973, 15; "China Traders May Be in for Some Surprises," *Purchasing,* 23 July 1974, 11.
8. "Shrewd Chinese Bargainers," *Industry Week,* 15; Letter, "Dear Nick," date stamped (in DC) 13 November 1975, folder "Importer Services Trade Fairs, Canton Fair, Fall 1975, Reports (1)," Box 73, GRFL.
9. Letter, "Greetings All," date stamped (in DC) 28 October 1975, folder "*CBR* vol. 2, no. 6, Canton Fair," Box 189, GRFL.
10. Letter, "Greetings All," GRFL.
11. "Canton 43—New Flexibility, New Era?," *CBR,* May–June 1978, 38; "Buying From the Chinese Is a Tricky Business," *Purchasing,* 18 February 1975, 14–15.
12. Stanley Marcus, "Marcus Polo at China Trade Fair," *NYT,* 4 June 1972; "U.S. Businessmen," *WSJ.*
13. Letter, "Dear Nick," 5 May 1975, folder "*CBR* vol. 2, no. 4, Background (4)," Box 188, GRFL; "Kwangchow Diary—Spring 1975," *U.S.–China Business Review,* 48.
14. "Kwangchou Diary—Spring 1975," *U.S.–China Business Review,* 44; Letter, "Dear Nick," 5 May 1975. GRFL.
15. "Canton Trade Fair Prices," *NYT;* Letter, "Dear Nick," date stamped (in DC) 3 November 1975, folder "*CBR* vol. 2, no. 6, Canton Fair," Box 189, GRFL; Notes, "Pacific Seaborne" on top page of sheaf, folder "*CBR* vol. 2, no. 6, Importer's Notes," Box 189, GRFL.
16. "U.S. Businessmen," *WSJ;* Stanley Lubman, "Misconceptions Abound on All Sides," *Financial Times,* 9 December 1985.
17. "U.S. Businessmen," *WSJ.*
18. "Shrewd Chinese Bargainers," *Industry Week,* 15–16; "Buying from the Chinese," *Purchasing,* 11.
19. "China Traders," *Purchasing,* 11.
20. Memorandum, [X] to All Staff, 2 January 1975, folder "Staff NL, Tung Fang Club," Box 176, GRFL. The curious reader can examine the original document in the archives and discover all of the particulars, but here decorum compels me to use an "[X]" to protect the identity of the author.
21. "Shrewd Chinese Bargainers," *Industry Week,* 16.
22. "Kwangchow Diary—Spring 1975," *U.S.–China Business Review,* 48.
23. "U.S. Businessmen," *WSJ;* John Kamm, "A Touch of Euphoria: Report on the Spring 1977 CECF," *CBR,* May–June 1977, 22.
24. Notes, "Importer's Notes," folder "*CBR* vol. 2, no. 6, Importer's Notes," Box 189, GRFL.
25. Notes, "Importer's Notes"; Letter, "Hello Everyone!," 10 November 1974, folder "Importer Services, Trade Fairs, Canton Fair—Fall 1974, Reports," Box 73. GRFL.

26. Report, "Compiled Responses to the Light Industrial Consumer Goods/Handicraft Questionnaire," 17 February 1978, folder "Importer Services—Questionnaire—Compiled Responses," Box 58; Notes, "Please Save All Notes" on top page of sheaf, n.d., and "Visit to Dept. of Commerce" on top page of sheaf, n.d., folder *"CBR* vol. 2, no. 6, Importer's Notes," Box 189; Letter, [X] to Sobin, 14 March 1977 [one of two letters in folder with same date and addressed to Sobin], folder "Importer Services—Trade Fair, Canton Fair Briefing April 1977 (2)," Box 71, GRFL.
27. Letter, [X] to Sobin, 14 March 1977; Notes, "Importer's Notes"; Report, "Compiled Responses," GRFL.
28. Letter, "Dear Nick," 27 October 1975, and Notes, "Visit to Dept. of Commerce" on top page of sheaf, n.d., folder *"CBR* vol. 2, no. 6, Importer's Notes," Box 189, GRFL.
29. Minutes, "Pre-Canton Fair Briefing," 5 April 1977, folder "Importer Services: Trade Fairs, Canton Fair Briefing, April 1977 (2)," Box 71, GRFL.
30. Notes, "Visit to Dept. of Commerce"; [X] (Jewelry) on top page of sheaf, folder *"CBR* vol. 2, no. 6, Importer's Notes," Box 189, GRFL.
31. Notes, "Visit to Dept. of Commerce," GRFL.
32. Notes, "Visit to Dept. of Commerce," GRFL.
33. Letter, "Greetings All,"; Letter, "Friday Morn," date stamped (in DC) 13 May 1975, folder *"CBR* vol. 2, no. 4, Background (3)," Box 188, GRFL.
34. Report, Christopher H. Phillips, "The First Annual Report of the National Council for U.S.–China Trade," folder "Council Publications, Annual Reports," Box 177; Letter, "Greetings All," GRFL.
35. Letter, "Hello Everyone!," GRFL.
36. Letter, "Dear Nick," 3 November 1975, GRFL.
37. "Kwangchow Diary—Spring 1975," *U.S.-China Business Review,* 49. Direct quotation from Mr. Zhang originally appeared in *China's Foreign Trade.*
38. Wallace Chaykin, "The China Trade: An Unfulfilled Promise," *Columbia Journal of World Business* 8, no. 1 (Spring 1973): 84; Letter, "Dear Nick," 3 November 1975, GRFL.
39. "Shrewd Chinese Bargainers," *Industry Week,* 16; Letter, "Greetings All," GRFL.
40. "China: The Payoff Starts for U.S. Traders," *Business Week,* 7 April 1973, 38; "Frustrations at the Canton Fair," *NYT,* 3 December 1972.
41. Letter, "Friday Morn," GRFL.
42. "Frustrations," *NYT.*

CHAPTER 2: OPENING WIDER

1. Kenneth Lieberthal and Michel Oksenberg, *Policy Making in China: Leaders, Structures, and Processes* (Princeton, NJ: Princeton University Press, 1988), 194–198.
2. Harry Harding, *China's Second Revolution: Reform after Mao* (Washington, DC: The Brookings Institution, 1987), 131; Nicholas Lardy, *China's Entry into the World Economy: Implications for Northeast Asia and the United States* (Lanham, MD: University Press of America, 1987), 3–4; James T. H. Tsao, *China's Development Strategies and Foreign Trade* (Lexington, MA: Lexington Books, 1987), 91–92.
3. Ann Fenwick, "Chinese Foreign Trade Policy and the Campaign against Deng Xiaoping," in Thomas Fingar and the Stanford Journal of International Studies,

eds., *China's Quest for Independence: Policy Evolution in the 1970s* (Boulder, CO: Westview, 1980), 204, 207.

4. Deng Xiaoping, "Some Comments on Industrial Development," in *Selected Works of Deng Xiaoping* (Beijing: Foreign Languages Press, 1984), 44.
5. Joseph R. Levenson, *Confucian China and Its Modern Fate: A Trilogy* (Berkeley and Los Angeles: University of California Press, 1968), 1:60. For a panoramic view of Chinese fascination with American technology over the course of a century and a half, and of earlier historical precedents for Chinese views of American society as a land of extreme economic inequities, see R. David Arkush and Leo O. Lee, eds., *Land Without Ghosts: Chinese Impressions of America from the Mid-Nineteenth Century to the Present* (Berkeley and Los Angeles: University of California Press, 1989).
6. Kuo Chi, "Foreign Trade: Why the 'Gang Of Four' Created Confusion," *Peking Review,* 25 February 1977, 17; Jing Shi, "Cong Zhang Zhidong ban gongchan kan yangnu zhexue de pochan" [A look at the blind worship of everything foreign in the factories of Zhang Zhidong], *GMRB,* 22 July 1976.
7. Jing, "Cong Zhang Zhidong."
8. "Chairman of Delegation of People's Republic of China Teng Hsiao-ping's Speech at Special Session of U.N. General Assembly," *Peking Review,* 12 April 1974, supplement p. 4.
9. Fenwick, "Chinese Foreign Trade Policy," 215, 218.
10. "China Earth Station," *RCA Relay,* March–April 1972, 2–7.
11. Notes, "RCA Interview," 14 October 1976, folder "*CBR* vol. 4, no. 1, U.S. Technicians in China, Company Interviews," Box 190, GRFL.
12. Stephanie R. Green, "China's American Residents: US Company Technical Personnel In China," *CBR,* January–February 1977, 28–29; Notes, Wabco, 23 September 1976, folder "*CBR* vol. 4, no. 1, U.S. Technicians in China, Company Interviews (1)," Box 190, GRFL.
13. Walter M. Buryn, "Pullman Kellogg: A Case Study," in David C. Buxbaum, Cassondra E. Joseph, and Paul D. Reynolds, eds., *China Trade: Prospects and Perspectives* (New York: Praeger, 1982), 288–291.
14. Stephanie R. Green, "Chinese Technicians in the United States," *CBR,* November–December 1977, 27–29.
15. Green, "Chinese Technicians in the United States," 29; Notes, n.d., "Stewart & Stevenson," folder "*CBR* vol. 4, no. 6, Chinese Technicians In U.S.," Box 191, GRFL.
16. Green, "China's American Residents," 31.
17. Green, "China's American Residents," 31.
18. "Kwangchow Diary—Spring 1975," *U.S.–China Business Review,* May–June 1975, 45.
19. Letter, "Greetings Everyone," n.d., folder "*CBR* vol. 2, no. 6, Canton Fair," Box 189, GRFL.
20. Robert Hoffman, "U-M Grad Writes Home during His Visit to the Trade Fair in Canton, China," *Michigan Alumnus,* December 1974, 19; "Shrewd Chinese Bargainers in No Rush to 'Buy American'," *Industry Week,* 21 May 1973, 16.
21. Letter, "Friday Morn," date stamped (in DC) 13 May 1975, and letter, "The Second Chapter of the Great Kwangchow Novel," n.d., in folder "*CBR* vol. 2, no. 4, Background (3)," Box 188, GRFL; John T. Kamm, "Down to Business, Cordially," *CBR,* November–December 1977, 35.

22. Letter, "Dear Nick," date stamped (in DC) 3 November 1975, folder "*CBR* vol. 2, no. 6, Canton Fair," Box 189, GRFL; John Kamm, "A Touch of Euphoria . . . Report on the Spring 1977 CECF," *CBR,* May–June 1977, 23.
23. Kamm, "A Touch of Euphoria," 23.
24. Kamm, "A Touch of Euphoria," 23; Kamm, "Down to Business," 38–39; "Canton 43—New Flexibility, New Era?," *CBR,* May–June 1978, 37.
25. Kamm, "Down to Business," 35; "U.S. Businessmen Flood Canton Fair," *WP,* 18 November 1977.
26. Report, John Kamm, "Piece of the Action," attached cover letter dated 23 November 1978, folder "Importer Services Trade Fair, Canton Fair, Fall 1978 Report," Box 76, GRFL; "Canton 43," *CBR,* 33.
27. "Niuyue de liangge shijie" [The two worlds of New York], *RMRB,* 10 July 1978; "Ziben zhuyi shijie de dufeng" [The gambling frenzy in the capitalist world], *RMRB,* 7 August 1978.
28. Wang Ruoshui, "Meiguo yipie—yi" [A glance at the United States, Part I], *RMRB,* 17 October 1978.
29. Wang Ruoshui, "Meiguo yipie—yi"; Wang, "Meiguo yipie—san" [A glance at the United States—Part III], *RMRB,* 19 October 1978; "Chinese Publish Rave Reviews of U.S.," *LAT,* 6 November 1978.
30. Wang Ruoshui, "Meiguo yipie—yi."
31. Wang Ruoshui, "Meiguo yipie—yi"; Li Yanning, "Minhang, tielu he neihe hangyun: Meiguo jiaotong jianwen zhiyi" [Air, rail, and river transport: some impressions of transportation in the United States], *RMRB,* 1 November 1978; Li Yanning, "Meiguo de qiche he gonglu" [Automobiles and highways in the United States], *RMRB,* 3 November 1978.
32. Wang Ruoshui, "Meiguo yipie—san."
33. "U.S. Gives Soviet Glittering Show" and "The Two Worlds: A Day-Long Debate," *NYT,* 25 July 1959; Richard M. Nixon, *Six Crises* (Garden City, NY: Doubleday, 1962), 254.
34. "The Two Worlds," *NYT;* Nixon, *Six Crises,* 262–263; "Premier Calls His First Hot Dog a World-Beater," *NYT,* 23 September 1959.
35. "Pickets Battle Police Near U.N.," *NYT,* 19 September 1959; "The Scramble Is on for Tickets to the Gala," *WP,* 26 January 1979; "The Chinese Visitors' Mao Tai Farewell," *WP,* 1 February 1979; "Teng Takes Quest for U.S. Technology to Atlanta," *NYT,* 2 February 1979.
36. "Texas Greets Teng with Band, Backlash and Rain," *NYT,* 3 February 1979; "Teng Speaks Of Plans for Imports in Billions," *NYT,* 4 February 1979.
37. "Reporter's Notebook: For Teng, Only Oblique Vision of America," *NYT,* 2 February 1979; "Reporter's Notebook: 'Inscrutable' Is a Two-Way Street," *NYT,* 6 February 1979.
38. "Reporter's Notebook: For Teng," *NYT.*
39. Untitled typescript, folder "Deng Visit, Atlanta, GA," in Box 18, Presidential Papers of Jimmy Carter, Staff Offices, Press (Advance), Office File, Carter Presidential Library; Orville Schell, *Watch Out For the Foreign Guests: China Encounters the West* (New York: Pantheon, 1980), 86.
40. Ryosei Kokubun, "The Politics of Foreign Economic Policy-Making in China: The Case of Plant Cancellations with Japan," *China Quarterly,* no. 105 (March 1986), 39; "After Taking Capital by Storm, Mr. Teng Marches On Sun Belt," *WSJ,* 2 February 1979; "Teng Visits Atlanta Car Plant to Learn," *LAT,* 2 February 1978; Schell, *Watch Out for the Foreign Guests,* 88.

41. Fox Butterfield, *China: Alive in the Bitter Sea* (New York: Bantam, 1983), 446–447.
42. Schell, *Watch Out for the Foreign Guests,* 124; "Barbecue, Bulls and Stagecoach Help Teng Get Flavor of Texas," *NYT,* 4 February 1979.
43. Schell, *Watch Out for the Foreign Guests,* 117–119; Mao Tsetung [Mao Zedong], *Selected Works of Mao Tsetung* (Peking: Foreign Languages Press, 1977), 5:410.
44. "After Taking Capital by Storm," *WSJ;* "Stages of Growth," *NYT,* 7 February 1979.

CHAPTER 3: CHINA CHIC

1. "China: It's The Latest American Thing," *NYT,* 16 February 1972; *Ladies Home Journal,* February 1972.
2. Committee of Concerned Asian Scholars, *China! Inside the People's Republic* (New York: Bantam, 1972).
3. Hans Magnus Enzensburger, "Tourists of the Revolution," in *The Consciousness Industry: On Literature, Politics and the Media,* Michael Roloff, ed. (New York: The Seabury Press, 1974), 129–157; Paul Hollander, *Political Pilgrims: Travels of Western Intellectuals to the Soviet Union, China, and Cuba, 1928–1978* (New York: Oxford University Press, 1981); Jonathan Mirsky, "Message from Mao," *New York Review of Books,* 16 February 1989, 17.
4. David Rockefeller, "From a China Traveler," *NYT,* 10 August 1973.
5. "China Asks West How to Turn Off Its 'No Vacancy' Sign," *CSM,* 19 March 1979; "Fazhan luyouye, jiedai gengduo luyouzhe lai woguo guanguang" [Develop the tourist industry so even more tourists will come to China for sightseeing], *RMRB,* 28 August 1978; "Travel Agents Use Ingenuity to Book Tourists for China," *WSJ,* 1 August 1978.
6. "Tour Trickle in China Now Like a Torrent," *CSM,* 31 August 1978.
7. Marilyn Bender, [untitled essay on op-ed page], *NYT,* 9 November 1978.
8. Bender, *NYT,* 9 November 1978; cf. " '78 Chic: Americans in China," *San Francisco Chronicle,* 1 September 1978, an earlier, and slightly different, version of the Bender essay.
9. "Hot and Sour Coolies," *New Republic,* 13 February 1984, 4, 42.
10. "How Bloomingdale's Is Selling China," *NYT,* 7 September 1980; "Archetype Capitalist Linkletter to Peddle Goods from Peking," *LAT,* 2 May 1972; "China Chic Blooms in N.Y.," *Advertising Age,* 22 September 1980; "China: New Opening to the East Side," *NYT,* 21 September 1980; "Bloomingdale's Embraces China!" *Stores,* August 1980, 42.
11. "How Bloomingdale's Is Selling China," and "China: New Opening," *NYT.*
12. "Bloomingdale's Embraces China!" *Stores;* "A Look At China Wares," *NYT,* 25 September 1980.
13. "U.S. Firms Are Given Key to China Trade; It's Called Friendship," *WSJ,* 4 April 1980.
14. "Zusun xiaotan Zhongguo hang" [Grandson smiles and talks about his China trip], *Jingji cankao,* 22 June 1988.
15. Carol S. Goldsmith, "Sister-State Relations," *CBR,* July–August 1980, 44–46; "U.S. Governors Flocking to China," *LAT,* 11 October 1985; Goldsmith, "Sister Relations," *CBR,* May–June 1984, 8; "U.S. States, Chinese Provinces Starting 'Sister' Relationships," *AWS,* 13 September 1982; "Blanchard Signs Trade Agreement; It's Not First for Chinese Province," *Grand Rapids Press,* 12 June 1984. In Chinese these arrangements were called "friendship" agreements to

avoid the use of *jiemei* (sisterly), which literally means elder sister/younger sister and presents the question of which partner would assume which role.

16. "Selling Washington Apples to China: Two-Way Trade Gets Down to the Core," *CSM,* 19 October 1982; "State to Province, City to City," *CBR*, September–October 1979, 23; "Ohio's 'China Connection,' " *CSM,* 3 April 1980.
17. "China Pacts: Show and Snow?" *Chicago Tribune,* 24 March 1985; "Chinese In Maryland on Trade Mission," *NYT,* 11 September 1979.
18. "Boston Seeks China Connection," *CSM,* 17 June 1982.
19. "Selling Washington Apples," *CSM;* "China Pacts," *Chicago Tribune;* Goldsmith, "Sister Relations," 10.
20. Goldsmith, "Sister Relations," 10; "Boston Seeks China Connection," *CSM;* "Feinstein Answers Trip Critics," *San Francisco Chronicle,* 17 June 1979.
21. "China Pacts," *Chicago Tribune;* "U.S. Governors Flocking," *LAT.*
22. "U.S. States, Chinese Provinces," *AWS;* Paul E. Shroeder, "The Ohio-Hubei Agreement: Clues to Chinese Negotiating Practices," *China Quarterly,* September 1982, 482; "Bradley Looking to Cash in on China Ties," *LAT,* 13 December 1982; "Fujian Business Pact Produces Few Deals," *Oregonian,* 11 May 1986; "Selling Washington Apples," *CSM.*
23. "China Travelers Hope Good Trip Will Result in Good Business," *Minneapolis Tribune,* 7 October 1979.
24. "Tackling the China Challenge," *Industry Week,* 28 May 1979, 39; "Firms Doing Business in China Are Stymied by Costs and Hassles," *WSJ,* 17 July 1986.
25. "China after Marx: Open for Business?" *Fortune,* 18 February 1985, 29; "Traveling to Peking for Business? Leave Those Gifts at Home," *WSJ,* 26 September 1980; "Chinese Policy Shift Unleashes Scramble for Foreign Business," *AWS,* 12 November 1984.
26. "U.S. Firms Hunt a China Connection," *WP,* 7 January 1979.
27. "Counsel from an Old China Hand," *Fortune,* 26 March 1979, 67; "U.S. Companies Assert the Time Is Ripe to Rush Through China's Open Door," *AWS,* 15 April 1985.
28. "U.S. Companies Assert," *AWS;* "Counsel from an Old China Hand," *Fortune,* 67.
29. "China: Trying the Market Way," *Fortune,* 31 December 1979, 54.
30. "A Primer for Doing Business in China," *NYT,* 11 April 1982; "Socialism Is a Failure, Occidental Chief Says," *LAT,* 5 April 1982; "Occidental Petroleum Hasn't Always Thrived from East Bloc Deals," *WSJ,* 30 August 1984; Armand Hammer, with Neil Lyndon, *Hammer* (New York: Putnam, 1987), 456.
31. Hammer, *Hammer,* 456–458.
32. Hammer, *Hammer,* 458–459, 464.
33. "Occidental Petroleum," *WSJ.*
34. "The Cartel's New Competitor," *Newsweek,* 29 September 1975, 69.
35. Kenneth Lieberthal and Michel Oksenberg, *Policy Making in China: Leaders, Structures, and Processes* (Princeton, NJ: Princeton University Press, 1988), 220, 266; "China Faces Tough Demands for Better Offshore Contracts," *AWS,* 3 June 1985; "Offshore Oil: No One Is Getting Rich Quick," *Business Week,* 17 September 1984.
36. Lieberthal and Oksenberg, *Policy Making in China,* 220.
37. "China Business Brief," *AWS,* 6 January 1986; "China's Oil Bubble May Burst for West," *AWS,* 19 March 1984; Lieberthal and Oksenberg, *Policy Making in China,* 234–236.
38. Lieberthal and Oksenberg, *Policy Making in China,* 219, 239.

39. "China's Oil Bubble," *AWS;* "The X Factor: Is Chinese Oil Worth China's Price," *Business Week,* 19 March 1984, 94; "China Offshore Oil 'Boom' a Bust, Western Firms Find," *LAT,* 17 November 1985; "China Looks for Help to Keep Its Oil Flowing," *NYT,* 16 May 1988; Lieberthal and Oksenberg, *Policy Making in China,* 241.
40. "Mobil, After Three Years Without a Contract, Is Closing China Office," *WSJ,* 17 February 1984; "China Trade," *Barron's,* 24 October 1983, 52, 72–73.
41. "China Offshore Oil," *LAT;* "China Faces Tough Demands," *AWS;* "The X Factor," *Business Week;* "Falling Oil Prices Lead China to Reassess Major Offshore Gas Project with Arco," *AWS,* 6 October 1986.
42. "Geosource Inc. Ships Armadillos to Peking Zoo," *WSJ,* 5 December 1980; "China Offshore Oil," *LAT;* "China Looks for Help," *NYT.*
43. Lieberthal and Oksenberg, *Policy Making in China,* 260–261; "China after Marx," *Fortune,* 30–31.
44. "How to Dicker with the Chinese," *Time,* 19 February 1979, 53; "China Trade Small, Coverage Large," *LAT,* 30 January 1977.
45. "China Trade Small," *LAT.*
46. "China Trade Small," *LAT.*
47. "How a Teenager from New Jersey Broke into the China Trade," *NYT,* 1 July 1984; "China Deal," *NYT,* 2 December 1984.
48. Robert F. Roth, "There's More Gold in Enchiladas Than in Fortune Cookies," *Industrial Marketing,* November 1979, 76–77; "A 'Coals to Newcastle' Prospect for Trade in the Pacific," *CSM,* 27 July 1979.
49. "The China Bubble Bursts," *Business Week,* 6 July 1987, 89.

CHAPTER 4: BUMPS

1. Nicholas Lardy, *China's Entry into the World Economy: Implications for Northeast Asia and the United States* (Lanham, MD: The Asia Society, 1987), 21; Harry Harding, *China's Second Revolution: Reform after Mao* (Washington, DC: The Brookings Institution, 1987), 137–138.
2. National Council for U.S.–China Trade, *U.S.–China Trade Statistics 1981,* Special Report Number 28, May 1982, 6; Harding, *China's Second Revolution,* 149.
3. "After Hectic Months, China Slows Its Talks with Western Firms," *WSJ,* 5 March 1979; "How Companies Can Respond to China's Slowdown," *CBR,* May–June 1979, 37; "China, U.S. Steel Sign Contract for $1 Billion Plant," *WP,* 6 January 1979; "How Chase Group Scored Peking Victory in Race for Huge Trade Center Contract," *WSJ,* 10 April 1979; "A Slow Road to U.S.–China Trade," *San Francisco Examiner,* 14 September 1980.
4. "Problems Building Big Steel Mill Reflect Failure of China's Modernization Drive," *WSJ,* 2 September 1981; Ryosei Kokuban, "The Politics of Foreign Economic Policy-making in China: The Case of Plant Cancellations with Japan," *China Quarterly,* no. 105 (March 1986), 20; "How Companies React to Peking's Decision to Cancel Contracts," *Business China,* 11 February 1981, 18.
5. "Analysts Voice Optimism about U.S.–China Trade," *AWS,* 28 December 1981; "China on Our Minds," *Industrial Marketing,* November 1979, 69.
6. "China's Hopes for Joint Ventures with Foreign Companies Are Fading Fast," *LAT,* 24 November 1980.
7. "New Wariness over China Deals," *NYT,* 1 October 1980; "China's Hopes for Joint Ventures," *LAT.*
8. "Analysts Voice Optimism," *AWS;* "A New Burst of Business Enthusiasm over

China," *Business Week,* 30 April 1984, 37; "The China Bubble Bursts," *Fortune,* 6 July 1987, 86.

9. Wu Dakun, "Meiguo de jingji he shehui: chongfang Meiguo yougan" [The U.S. economy and society: Thoughts after another visit to America], *Shijie zhishi,* no. 13, 1980, 7.
10. "China Document Shows Lingering Distrust of U.S.," *LAT,* 1 April 1980; Wang Ruoshui, "Meiguo yipie—san" [A glance at the United States—Part III], *RMRB,* 19 October 1978; Fox Butterfield, *China: Alive in the Bitter Sea* (New York: Bantam, 1982), 37–38; "Chinese Cooking," *WSJ,* 2 April 1980.
11. "China's Views on Exploitation May Discourage Joint Ventures," *AWS,* 7 April 1980; "China Foreign Trade Drive Hindered by Ideological Rifts," *AWS,* 30 November 1981.
12. "China Foreign Trade Drive," *AWS.*
13. "Chinese Keep Watch on U.S. to Find Out What Makes It Tick," *WSJ,* 28 October 1980.
14. "Chinese Keep Watch," *WSJ.*
15. "The Bob Hope Show That Startled Beijing," *San Francisco Chronicle,* 5 July 1979; "Bob Hope Finds China Full of Comedians," *San Francisco Chronicle,* 3 July 1979.
16. William Hewitt, "China Diary," *JD Journal* 3, no. 2 (1974): 17; Notes, WABCO, 23 September 1976, folder "*CBR* vol. 4, no. 1, U.S. Technicians in China, Company Interviews (1)," Box 190, GRFL; Edward Gorman, "A Visit to China," typescript, 1978, Box 12, Bentley Historical Museum.
17. "Communist Giants Are Too Burdened at Home to Lead Much Abroad," *WSJ,* 6 February 1989; " '78 Chic: Americans in China," *San Francisco Chronicle,* 1 September 1978; "Bringing S.F. a Little Bit of China," *San Francisco Chronicle,* 10 September 1980; Gorman, "A Visit to China."
18. "China's Views on Exploitation," *AWS.*
19. "China Signals That the Welcome Mat's Still Out," *LAT,* 7 June 1985.
20. "China Signals," *LAT.*
21. Letter, "The Second Chapter of the Great Kwangchow Novel," dated 9 May 1975 by DC office, folder "*CBR* vol. 2, no. 4, Background (3)," Box 188, GRFL; "Prices Soaring in China—But Just for Foreigners," *LAT,* 24 May 1980.
22. "Currency-Starved Chinese Charge Visitors Whatever Market Will Bear for Services," *WSJ,* 25 July 1980.
23. "Prices Soaring," *LAT.*
24. "China after Marx: Open for Business?" *Fortune,* 18 February 1985, 32; "When Doing Business in China, Expect the Unexpected," *Mini-Micro Systems,* March 1985, 60; "Cost of Doing Business in China Keeps Soaring," *LAT,* 22 March 1985; "The China Bubble Bursts," *Fortune.*
25. "Currency-Starved Chinese," *WSJ;* "Prices Soaring," *LAT;* "Why Investors Are Sour on China," *NYT,* 8 June 1986.
26. Butterfield, *China,* 36; "Pricing Policy Costing China Friends," *AWS,* 5 July 1982.
27. "U.S. Businessmen Getting Disillusioned Dealing with China," *San Francisco Examiner,* 8 February 1982; Stephen FitzGerald, " 'Genuine Friendship, Genuine Frankness': Some Frank Comments on Our Friendly Economic Relations," in John Finchner and Pan Cheng-lieh, eds., *In Business with China: Planning and Managing Sino-Australian Economic Cooperation* (Canberra: Contemporary China Centre, Australian National University, 1986), 121.
28. "Prices Soaring," *LAT;* "Price Hikes and the Foreign Business Community,"

CBR, March–April 1986, 52; "Foreigners Feel the Pinch in Peking," *South China Morning Post,* 20 December 1984.
29. "Pricing Policy Costing China Friends," *AWS;* Jerome Alan Cohen and Stuart J. Valentine, "Foreign Direct Investment in the People's Republic of China: Progress, Problems and Proposals," *Journal of Chinese Law* 1, no. 2 (1987): 199.
30. "Pricing Policy Costing China Friends," *AWS.*
31. "Motto of China Today: Make Foreigners Pay," *U.S. News & World Report,* 11 February 1985, 34.
32. "Pricing Policy Costing China Friends," *AWS;* "Cost of Doing Business," *LAT.*
33. "Prices Soaring," *LAT.*
34. "Our New China Traders Must Learn Patience" [letter to the editor], *NYT,* 12 January 1988.
35. Lardy, *China's Entry into the World Economy,* 21–23.
36. Lardy, *China's Entry into the World Economy,* 25–26.
37. "The Chinese Gulliver Stirs, and Has a Shock for Us," *LAT,* 9 September 1985.
38. "Shultz Visit: Simply Going There May Have Been Best Boost," *Business China,* 9 February 1983, 17–19; "Shultz Snaps at U.S. Businessmen in Peking," *NYT,* 4 February 1983.
39. Cohen and Valentine, "Foreign Direct Investment," 195; "China: Trying the Market Way," *Fortune,* 31 December 1979, 54.
40. FitzGerald, " 'Genuine Friendship, Genuine Frankness,' " 114.

CHAPTER 5: NEGOTIATIONS

1. Alexis de Tocqueville, *Democracy in America,* J. P. Mayer, trans. (Garden City, NY: Doubleday, 1969), 565–567.
2. Scott Seligman, "A Shirtsleeves Guide to Chinese Corporate Etiquette," *CBR,* January–February 1983, 9; "Why Nolan Wasn't at the Dinner," *Star Tribune Newspaper of the Twin Cities,* 19 May 1988. For a later, greatly expanded version of Seligman's "Shirtsleeves Guide," see his *Dealing with the Chinese: A Practical Guide to Business Etiquette in the People's Republic Today* (New York: Warner Books, 1989).
3. Seligman, "A Shirtsleeves Guide," 10; "How To Dicker with the Chinese," *Time,* 19 February 1979, 52.
4. Seligman, "A Shirtsleeves Guide," 11.
5. "Yu waibin xiangchu shi ying zhuyi na xie shi?" [What should we pay attention to when with foreign guests?], *Gongren ribao,* 14 March 1981.
6. "Yu waibin xiangchu," *Gongren ribao.*
7. "Yu waibin xiangchu," *Gongren ribao.*
8. Lucian Pye, *Chinese Commercial Negotiating Style* (Cambridge, MA: Oelgeschlager, Gunn & Hain, 1982), 28.
9. "Making It Look Easy: High Voltage Engineering Corp. Makes Sale of High Energy Physics Equipment To China," *CBR,* November–December 1978, 6; Pye, *Chinese Commercial Negotiating,* 30.
10. Wang Yihe, Xu E, and Zhou Jianping, *Zhongwai hezi jingying qiye* [The management of Sino-foreign joint ventures] (Shanghai: Shanghai shehui kexueyuan, 1984), 343–345; Stanley B. Lubman, "Negotiations in China: Observations of a Lawyer," in *Communicating with China,* Robert A. Kapp, ed. (Chicago: Intercultural Press, 1983), 68; Pye, *Chinese Commercial Negotiating,* 55.

11. Clark T. Randt, Jr., "Negotiating Strategy and Tactics," in *U.S.–China Trade: Problems and Prospects,* Eugene K. Lawson, ed. (New York: Praeger, 1988), 272–273; John Frankenstein, "Trends in Chinese Business Practice: Changes in the Beijing Wind," *California Management Review,* Fall 1986, 152.
12. Pye, *Chinese Commercial Negotiating,* 26–27.
13. Pye, *Chinese Commercial Negotiating,* 55, 79; "AMF in the China Market: Part II, Making Rubber Balls Snowball," *Business China,* 24 November 1982, 169–170; Lubman, "Negotiations in China," 62.
14. "Shizhang bu hai 'hongyan bing,' waishang jinguan lai zhuanqian" [Mayor won't get 'Red-eye Disease,' even if foreign business people earn profits], *Jingji cankao,* 22 June 1988; Pye, *Chinese Commercial Negotiating,* 23.
15. Pye, *Chinese Commercial Negotiating,* 11; "Negotiating Strategy, Chinese Style," *AWS,* 27 December 1982; Business International, *Business Strategies for the PRC* (Hong Kong: Business International, 1980), 296.
16. Wang Yihe et al., *Zhongwai heze,* 336; "Legal Maze Still Confounds Foreign Investors in China," *AWS,* 16 March 1986.
17. Xun Jun, "Liaojie waishang dixi cai buzhi shangdang chikui: Waiguo xuezhe de zhonggao" [Learn everything about foreign business people to avoid being taken advantage of: Sincere advice from foreign scholars], *Waiguo jingji guanli,* no. 1, 1983, 60.
18. "Wei Yuan yu 'shi yi zhi changji yi zhi yi' " [Wei Yuan and 'Mastering the superior technology of the barbarians to control the barbarians'], *GMRB,* 27 July 1983; Wang Yihe et al., *Zhongwai heze,* 339–340; Ye Zhijie, "Lun Zhongwai hezi qiye de tanpan celüe" [Negotiating tactics for Sino-foreign joint ventures], *Jingying yu guanli,* January 1986, reprinted in Renda, *Gongye qiye guanli,* March 1986, 76–78.
19. Pye, *Chinese Commercial Negotiating,* 35; Stanley Lubman, "Misconceptions Abound on All Sides," *Financial Times,* 9 December 1985; "Ventures in the China Trade," *New York Times Magazine,* 3 April 1983, 32.
20. Walter M. Buryn, "Pullman Kellogg: A Case Study," in David C. Buxbaum, Cassondra E. Joseph, and Paul D. Reynolds, eds., *China Trade: Prospects and Perspectives* (New York: Praeger, 1982), 297; "China's Inscrutable Paper Play," *Fortune,* 6 October 1980, 75; "How to Dicker," *Time,* 52.
21. Stephen FitzGerald, " 'Genuine Friendship, Genuine Frankness': Some Frank Comments on Our Friendly Economic Relations," in John Finchner and Pan Cheng-lieh, eds., *In Business with China: Planning and Managing Sino-Australian Economic Cooperation* (Canberra: Contemporary China Centre, Australian National University, 1986), 117, 122.
22. "China on Our Minds," *Industrial Marketing,* November 1979, 70; Jerome Alan Cohen and Stuart J. Valentine, "Foreign Direct Investment in the People's Republic of China: Progress, Problems and Proposals," *Journal of Chinese Law* 1, no. 2 (1987): 199.
23. Victor H. Li, *Law Without Lawyers: A Comparative View of Law in China and the United States* (Stanford, CA: Stanford Alumni Association, 1977), 95–99.
24. "China Earth Station," *RCA Relay,* March–April 1972, 4–5; Notes, "Boeing Interview," n.d., folder "*CBR* vol. 4, no. 1, U.S. Technicians in China, Company Interviews," Box 190, GRFL.
25. "Ventures in the China Trade," *New York Times Magazine,* 37; Notes, WABCO, 23 September 1976, folder "*CBR* vol. 4, no. 1, U.S. Technicians in China, Company Interviews (1)," Box 190, GRFL.

26. Cohen and Valentine, "Foreign Direct Investment," 195, 201; Wang Yihe et al., *Zhongwai heze,* 343.
27. FitzGerald, "Genuine Frankness," 118–119; Cohen and Valentine, "Foreign Direct Investment," 202; "Negotiating Strategy, Chinese Style," *AWS.*
28. "Ventures in the China Trade," *New York Times Magazine,* 34.
29. FitzGerald, "Genuine Frankness," 116–117; Jerome Alan Cohen, "Improving China's Investment Environment," talk delivered to the World Affairs Council, San Francisco, 6 October 1987.
30. Cohen, "Improving China's Investment Environment"; Frankenstein, "Trends in Chinese Business Practice," 158.
31. Ye Zhijie, "Lun Zhongwai hezi," 76; Dong Hongqi, "Geguo shangren de butong tanpan fengge" [Differing styles of negotiation among various nationalities of business people], *Zhongguo qiyejia,* no. 10, 1987, 60–61.
32. "Doing Business with China," *WSJ,* 31 August 1979; Dong Hongqi, "Geguo shangren," 60–61.
33. Dong Hongqi, "Geguo shangren," 60–61.
34. Randt, "Negotiating Strategy and Tactics," 277; "Making It Look Easy," *CBR,* 6; "China's Narrow Door to the West," *Fortune,* 26 March 1979, 69; "Ventures in the China Trade," *New York Times Magazine,* 36.
35. Ye Zhijie, "Lun Zhongwai hezi," 75.
36. Wang Yihe et al., *Zhongwai heze,* 339; "U.S. Businessmen Lack Asian Savvy," *AWS,* 2 April 1984; Frankenstein, "Trends in Chinese Business Practice," 154; "Our New China Traders Must Learn Patience" [Letter to the editor], *NYT,* 12 January 1988.
37. "Cashing in on the China Trade," *Dun's Review,* November 1978, 107; "How to Dicker," *Time,* 53.
38. "China Opens the Door to U.S. Electronics Firms," *Electronic Business,* 15 March 1986, 107.
39. Pye, *Chinese Commercial Negotiating,* 56–57.
40. "China Opens the Door," *Electronic Business,* 115.
41. "China Opens the Door," *Electronic Business,* 108.
42. Pye, *Chinese Commercial Negotiating,* 36.
43. Working in China Conference, held in Beijing, September 1984, unpublished transcript, Stanford East Asia National Resource Center.
44. "China Opens the Door," *Electronic Business,* 115.
45. Pye, *Chinese Commercial Negotiating,* 40, 56–57.

CHAPTER 6: EXPATRIATES

1. "Modern Times," *WP,* 3 January 1979; "Americans in China—Both Sides Adjust," *LAT,* 24 January 1979.
2. "Missionary's Son Helps Smooth Way for Trade with Mainland China," *WSJ,* 7 November 1975.
3. "The China Trade Lags, But Consultants Hawk 'Expertise' to Hopefuls," *WSJ,* 24 February 1972.
4. "China Trade Lags," *WSJ.*
5. "China Trade Small, Coverage Large," *LAT,* 30 January 1977; "China Trade Lags," *WSJ;* "Hong Kong-Based Middlemen Make Trade Matches for China," *AWS,* 27 August 1984; "Making the Right Contacts in China," *NYT,* 30 May 1988.
6. "The P. T. Barnum of China Trade," *Fortune,* 5 May 1980, 186–187.
7. "P. T. Barnum," *Fortune,* 186.

8. "Need Help in China? Call Gen Lin," *San Francisco Examiner,* 26 May 1985.
9. "Need Help In China?" *San Francisco Examiner.*
10. "Missionary's Son," *WSJ;* "China Trade Lags," *WSJ.*
11. Phillip M. Perry, *China Business Directory: A Practical Guide to Trading with the People's Republic of China* (Westport, CT: Technomic Publishing, 1980), unpaginated introduction; "Beware of China Traders Peddling Books," *AWS,* 23 March 1981.
12. "Beware of China Traders," *AWS.*
13. "The New China Traders," *Savvy,* October 1986, 64.
14. "New China Traders," *Savvy,* 64.
15. "China Card," *Forbes,* 4 June 1984, 206–207; "Brokering Deals Between East and West," *NYT,* 13 January 1985; "New China Traders," *Savvy,* 66.
16. "WJS Inc.: Cutting Deals in the New China," *Business Week,* 22 July 1985, 88; "Coddling the Chinese," *Venture,* March 1983, 79; "Enterprising U.S. Women Discover How to Succeed in the China Trade," *AWS,* 21 February 1983; "Mrs. China Trade," *NYT,* 14 November 1976; "Finding a New Career in Old Chinese Treasures," *San Francisco Chronicle,* 29 November 1979.
17. "A Chinese Millionaire Leads Peking's Search for Foreign Investors," *WSJ,* 14 November 1979; "Some Ex-Capitalists Find Home in China," *LAT,* 17 February 1980; "Millionaire—A Capitalist Tool in China," *LAT,* 5 March 1980; "A Former Capitalist Emerges as China's Top Dealmaker," *NYT,* 9 February 1986; "China's Mister Right," *Fortune,* 5 January 1987, 109; "Rong Yiren bangshang youming" [Rong Yiren, on the rolls of the famous], *Jingji cankao,* 11 January 1987; "Chinese Bank Is an Anomaly," *NYT,* 4 May 1987.
18. "Enthusiastic Consultants Up to Their Ears in Trade," *CSM,* 28 March 1979; Working in China Conference held in Beijing, September 1984, unpublished transcript, Stanford East Asia National Resource Center. Anonymity of the participants is intentionally protected here and elsewhere when cited.
19. Working in China Conference; Roderick Macleod, *China, Inc.: How to Do Business with the Chinese* (New York: Bantam, 1988), 54–55.
20. Working in China Conference.
21. "The Rewards of China Duty," *CBR,* November–December 1985, 18–19; "In Search of Experts on Chinese Business," *AWS,* 11 March 1985.
22. Working in China Conference; "Lonely Expat Workers in China Get Princely Pay for Their Pain," *AWS,* 19 May 1986; Organization Resources Counselors, Inc., *Multinationals in China: Human Resources Practices and Issues in the PRC* (New York: Organization Resources Counselors, 1986), 191–203.
23. "Trading on Youth in China," *Dallas Morning News,* 31 March 1986; "Go East, Young Woman: China Offers Opportunities for the Imaginative," *AWS,* 31 March 1986; "Young Turks Take Over," *China Trade Report,* November 1985, 11.
24. "Trading on Youth," *Dallas Morning News;* Working in China Conference.
25. Graeme Browning, *If Everybody Bought One Shoe: American Capitalism in Communist China* (New York: Hill and Wang, 1989), 127; "New China Traders," *Savvy,* 71.
26. Working In China Conference; "New China Traders," *Savvy,* 71.
27. "New China Traders," *Savvy,* 66.
28. Margery Wolf, *Revolution Postponed: Women in Contemporary China,* (Stanford, CA: Stanford University Press, 1985); Emily Honig and Gail Hershatter, *Personal Voices: Chinese Women in the 1980's* (Stanford, CA: Stanford University Press, 1988).

29. "Making the Right Contacts," *NYT;* "New China Traders," *Savvy,* 71.
30. Working in China Conference.
31. Walter E. Hoadley, "The People's Republic of China: A Refreshing Sense of Reality," *Dun's Review,* June 1979, 11; Tom Hayden, "Our Language, Learning Gap in the Pacific," *LAT,* 4 October 1985.
32. Stephen J. Kobrin, *International Expertise in American Business* (New York: Institute of International Education, 1984), 29; "Training Expats To Manage in China," *AWS,* 26 August 1985.
33. Jan Carol Berris, "The Art of Interpreting," in Robert A. Kapp, ed., *Communicating with China* (Chicago: Intercultural Press, 1983), 56–57; Nigel Campbell, *China Strategies: The Inside Story* (University of Manchester/University of Hong Kong, 1986), 40, 42, 123.
34. "If You're Simulating a Duck, Don't Look Like an Airplane," *WSJ,* 23 May 1980.
35. Berris, "The Art of Interpreting," 42–43; G. B. Trudeau, *An Especially Tricky People* (New York: Holt, Rinehart and Winston, 1977), unpaginated.
36. Working in China Conference.
37. "Enterprising U.S. Women," *AWS;* Working in China Conference.
38. Working in China Conference.
39. Berris, "The Art of Interpreting," 55.
40. Working in China Conference.
41. "Chinese-Americans Help U.S. Employers Bridge the Language Gap in China Trade," *WSJ,* 3 July 1979; "When RCA Executive Speaks, Chinese Listen—And Understand," *AWS,* 20 April 1981; "Building Bridges for Americans on China's Capitalist Road," *NYT,* 4 December 1988.
42. "Coddling the Chinese," *Venture,* 80.
43. "Problems with Sino-U.S. Trade," *San Francisco Examiner,* 30 April 1984; "Building Bridges for Americans," *NYT.*
44. "Chinese-Americans Help," *WSJ.*
45. Joel Kotkin, "The New Yankee Traders," *Inc.,* March 1986, 26; "Building Bridges for America," *NYT.*
46. Kotkin, "The New Yankee Traders," 25.

CHAPTER 7: WORK AND PLAY

1. "Moving In, in China: A Puzzled Isolation," *NYT,* 26 March 1981; "U.S. Youngsters Discover Peking Is 'Big League,'" *WP,* 9 November 1979.
2. "The Quick Red Taxi," *WP,* 2 January 1979.
3. Organization Resources Counselors, Inc., *Multinationals in China: Human Resources Practices and Issues in the PRC* (New York: Organization Resources Counselors, 1986), 93–94; "Where Mao Danced, Capitalists Now Deal (If They Plan Ahead)," *WSJ,* 3 December 1979.
4. "For Wisconsinites, China Isn't 'Just Like Home,'" *Milwaukee Journal,* 19 January 1985.
5. "Foreigners Are Finding Life in Peking More Palatable, If Still Somewhat Poky," *AWS,* 15 August 1982.
6. "Frustrations of Expatriate Life in Peking," *AWS,* 18 January 1982.
7. "Americans in China—Both Sides Adjust," *WP,* 24 January 1979.
8. Working in China Conference held in Beijing, September 1984, unpublished transcript, Stanford East Asia National Resource Center.

9. "Opening A Peking Office: A Look at Some Other Parts of the Picture," *Business China,* 13 July 1983, 96; Organization Resources Counselors, Inc., *Multinationals in China,* 108.
10. Working in China Conference; Organization Resources Counselors, Inc., *Multinationals in China,* 30.
11. Working in China Conference.
12. Working in China Conference; "The New China Traders," *Savvy,* October 1986, 66; "Where Mao Danced," *WSJ.*
13. Organization Resources Counselors, Inc., *Multinationals in China,* 20, 113; "The Rewards of China Duty," *CBR,* November–December 1985, 21; John Frankenstein, "The Quality of Life," *CBR,* November–December 1985, 22.
14. Working in China Conference; "U.S. Youngsters," *WP;* Organization Resources Counselors, Inc., *Multinationals in China,* 116.
15. Frankenstein, "The Quality of Life," 22; "Boredom Is a Problem of Socialist Life, So China Revives the Waltz and Tango," *WSJ,* 28 August 1984.
16. Organization Resources Counselors, Inc., *Multinationals in China,* 95.
17. " 'Not Since Marco Polo . . .' " *Forbes,* 3 January 1983, 280.
18. " 'Not Since Marco Polo . . .' " *Forbes,* 281.
19. "Rewards of China Duty," *CBR,* 20; Frankenstein, "The Quality of Life," 23; Organization Resources Counselors, Inc., *Multinationals in China,* 144; "Lonely Expat Workers in China Get Princely Pay for Their Pain," *AWS,* 19 May 1986; "Moving In," *NYT.*
20. "China Finds a Sure Bet in Capitalists' Gamble," *San Jose Mercury News,* 11 March 1989; "Trendy Mart Colors China Yule Western," *Miami Herald,* 24 December 1984.
21. "Foreigners Are Finding," *AWS.*
22. "Golf Course Tees Off Some Chinese," *Chicago Tribune,* 3 May 1985; Orville Schell, *Discos and Democracy: China in the Throes of Reform* (New York: Pantheon, 1988), 55–63; "At Bush's Beijing Villa, Marxists Pursue Profit," *NYT,* 26 February 1989.
23. Organization Resources Counselors, Inc., *Multinationals in China,* 114, 130.
24. Rosalie L. Tung, "Corporate Executives and Their Families in China: The Need for Cross-Cultural Understanding in Business," *Columbia Journal of World Business,* Spring 1986, 24; "China Finds a Sure Bet," *San Jose Mercury News;* Organization Resources Counselors, Inc., *Multinationals in China,* 141.
25. "Ta zong shi xiang duo wei Zhongguo zuo yidian shiqing" [She always wants to do a little more for China], *GMRB,* 14 June 1985; "Shou ren zunjing de dongfang nüxing: Ji Meiji huaren Zhang Wen nüshi [An Eastern woman who is respected: A visit with Ms. Zhang Wen, a Chinese-American], *BJRB,* 13 December 1986; "Jiaqi Zhong Mei qiyejia xianghu lijie de qiaoliang" [Building bridges of mutual understanding between Chinese and American businesspeople], *JJRB,* 6 December 1986.
26. "Building Bridges for Americans on China's Capitalist Road," *NYT,* 4 December 1988.
27. "Building Bridges for Americans," *NYT.*
28. "Building Bridges for Americans," *NYT.*
29. Elizabeth Mueller Gross, "Staffing Your Beijing Office," *CBR,* March–April 1984, 30; "Foreign Firms Are Frustrated by Beijing Agency's Control of Local Work Force," *AWS,* 11 January 1988.

30. "Peking's Foreign Bankers Are Skittish about an Ex-Red Guard in Their Midst," *AWS,* 27 January 1986.
31. "China Discriminates Against Its Own," *AWS,* 17 February 1986; "Foreigners in China Emerge as a Privileged Class," *WP,* 9 March 1980.
32. "Buyao wangji Zhongguoren" [Don't forget the Chinese], *Guoji shangbao,* 28 March 1987.
33. "China Discriminates," *AWS;* " 'Dishi' wenti mianmian guan" [A look at the various sides of the taxi problem], *BJRB,* 23 June 1988.
34. "China Discriminates," *AWS.*
35. "China Discriminates," *AWS;* "In China, Foreigners Are More Equal Than Others," *NYT,* 10 March 1979.
36. "Foreigners in China," *WP.*
37. "AIDS: Will It Spread in China?" *Beijing Review,* 10 August 1987, 7.
38. "Streetwalkers, Dance Hall Hookers Return to Beijing," *LAT,* 15 June 1979.
39. "Beijing Expels Businessman Found in Bed with Girl," *South China Morning Post,* 24 August 1987; "Beijing Denies Man Was Ousted Over Sex," *South China Morning Post,* 27 August 1987; "China's Campaign to Arrest Immorality Corners Prostitutes and Their Patrons," *AWS,* 19 December 1983.
40. "Beijing Expels Businessman," *South China Morning Post;* Jerome Alan Cohen, "Sex, Chinese Law, and the Foreigner," *Hong Kong Law Journal* 18, no. 1 (1988): 102-110.
41. "China Trial Hears American's Plea," *LAT,* 24 July 1985; "Final Pleas Are Heard in Trial of American Businessman in China," *NYT,* 24 July 1986.
42. Stanley B. Lubman and Gregory C. Wajnowski, "Criminal Justice and the Foreigner," *CBR,* November–December 1985, 27–30; "Trial Offers Rare Look at China Justice," *LAT,* 28 July 1985.
43. "China Trial," *LAT;* Lubman and Wajnowski, "Criminal Justice," 30.
44. "From Prison to Palace: U.S. Businessman Jailed in Hotel Fire Returns to Beijing," *AWS,* 16 November 1987.

CHAPTER 8: MANAGERIALISM

1. "China Is Emerging As a Source of Capital in the World Markets," *WSJ,* 3 February 1984.
2. "China Is Emerging," *WSJ.*
3. "China's Business Woes in U.S.," *NYT,* 7 May 1983.
4. "China Seeks to Learn Management Skills of Capitalism in New Hampshire Town," *AWS,* 11 July 1983; Carroll R. Bogert, "America's Open Door," *CBR,* September–October 1984, 43; "Santec Ends Talks with Chinese Firm on Forming Venture," *WSJ,* 27 February 1985; "Beijing's Bitter Lesson in Capitalism," *Business Week,* 16 July 1984, 44.
5. Bogert, "America's Open Door," 43.
6. "China Gets a Lesson in U.S. Capitalism: Let Buyer Beware," *WSJ,* 20 June 1988. Eventually, the Chinese company changed the name of the project from Chinaberry Lakes to Lantana Lakes in order to divert attention from the company's nationality. See "Chinese Quietly Entering the U.S. Housing Market," *NYT,* 30 July 1989. Another Chinese company, which took over a steel plant in Delaware, was assailed by the United Steelworkers of America for its treatment of the American workers. The union charged that the Chinese managers acted "just like the worst capitalists." See "Union Takes on China-Owned Factory," *NYT,* 6 September 1989; and "Chinese-Owned Steel Plant Is Accused of Bias in Hiring," *NYT,* 28 November 1989.

7. James J. Flink, *The Car Culture* (Cambridge, MA: The MIT Press, 1975), 71–72; Kendall E. Bailes, *Technology and Society under Lenin and Stalin: Origins of the Soviet Technical Intelligentsia, 1917–1941* (Princeton, NJ: Princeton University Press, 1978), 50; Bailes, "Alexei Gastev and the Soviet Controversy over Taylorism," *Soviet Studies* 24, no. 3 (July 1977): 373–394; Harry Braverman, *Labor and Monopoly Capital: The Degradation of Work in the Twentieth Century* (New York: Monthly Review Press, 1974), 12; Mark R. Beissinger, *Scientific Management, Socialist Discipline, and Soviet Power* (Cambridge, MA: Harvard University Press, 1988), 5, 23.
8. Deng Zhongwen, " 'Tai-le zhi' dui tigao qiye guanli shuiping de xianshi yiyi" [The contemporary significance of Taylorism for raising the standards of enterprise management], *Gongye jingji guanli congkan,* no. 2, 1981, 61–66, reprinted in Renda, *Gongye qiye guanli,* March 1981, 3–6.
9. Pan Chenglie, "Zhongguo gudai de guanli sixiang" [Management thought in ancient China], *Qiye guanli,* no. 9, 1984, 58; Deng Zhongwen, " 'Tai-le zhi,' " 8; "Tai-le zhi' shi shenme?" [What is 'Taylorism'?], *RMRB,* 26 September 1986.
10. Zhou Shulian, "Tantan dui guowai qiye guanli de yanjiu" [The study of foreign enterprise management], *Waiguo jingji guanli,* no. 5, 1981, 60; D. Eleanor Westney, *Imitation and Innovation: The Transfer of Western Organizational Patterns to Meiji Japan* (Cambridge, MA: Harvard University Press, 1987), 18–24.
11. Xiang Min, "Meiguo 'Jun qiyejia' " [American 'Intrapreneurs'], *Shijie zhishi,* no. 2, 1985, 28; "Qiye neibu de qiyejia" [Entrepreneurs within the organization], *Zhongguo qiyejia,* no. 10, 1986, 57; Meng Xiangsheng, " 'Yifenzhong' guanli faze" [The rules of 'one-minute' management], *Qiyejia tiandi,* no. 8, 1986, 23; "Yifenzhong jingli" [The one-minute manager], *Qiye guanli,* no. 7, 1983, 41–44, 48; Jia Yu, "Xiang duzhe tuijian 'Yifenzhong jingli' " [I commend to readers 'The one-minute manager'], *Qiyejia yuekan,* no. 6, 1985, 40–41; "Qiyejia, qing zhuyi ni de chuanzhuo" [Managers, please pay attention to your dress], *Qiyejia yuekan,* no. 1, 1987, 41; "Chinese Have Long Way to Go," *San Francisco Chronicle,* 22 January 1981.
12. Cui Kene, "Woguo qiye guanli zhong xishou guowai jingyan wenti" [The problem of the absorption of foreign experience in Chinese enterprise management], *Jixu jingji yu guanli yanjiu,* no. 2, 1981, 18–22, reprinted in Renda, *Gongye qiye guanli,* August 1981, 15–19; "Ziben zhuyi de jingying guanli fangfa yao bu yao xue? Zenyang xue?" [Should capitalist management methods be studied? How should they be studied?], *GMRB,* 15 November 1984; Zhou Shulian, "Cong Xifang qiye guanli jingyan zhong keyi xuexi shenme" [What can be studied from the management experience of Western enterprises?], *Hongqi,* no. 16, 1982, 43–45; Wu Jiapei, "Guanli xiandaihua yao you Zhongguo tese" [The modernization of management should have Chinese characteristics], *Jingji guanli,* no. 11, 1983, 2–5, reprinted in Renda, *Gongye qiye guanli,* December 1983, 55–58.
13. Pan Chenglie, "Zhongguo gudai de guanli," 58–59.
14. Yang Xianju, "Sun Wu de zhanlüe sixiang" [The strategic thinking of Sun Wu], in He Qi, et al., eds., *Zhongguo gudai guanli sixiang* [The management thought of ancient China] (Beijing: Qiye guanli chuban she, 1986), 33–40; "Sunzi bingfa yu jingying guanli" [Sunzi's *The Art of War* and management], *Shijie jingji daobao,* 24 January 1983; "You guowai de 'Sanguo re' xiangdao de" [Some thoughts leading from the 'Three Kingdoms' fever raging abroad], *JJRB,* 29 August 1986.

15. Quan Li, "Rang 'bing shi jiang yi' " [Let 'the troops know the intentions of the general'], *Qiyejia yuekan,* no. 1, 1987, 19; Pan Chenglie, "Zhongguo gudai de guanli," 61; "Chinese MBA Students in Buffalo Compare U.S. and Chinese Industry," *Business America,* 7 December 1987, 15; Meng Jie, "Zai xiandai guanli zhong zenyang yingyong chuantong wenhua" [How to use traditional culture in modern management], *Guoneiwai jingji guanli,* no. 2, 1987, 30–31; Yang Xianju, "Sun Wu de zhanlüe sixiang," 37; "An Overrated Ancient Chinese Guide to War," *WSJ,* 18 April 1983.
16. Pan Chenglie, "Wang Xifeng de guanli" [The management of Wang Xifeng], *Qiye guanli,* no. 11, 1984, 42–43; Hua Zhuang, "Wang Xifeng yu xitong guanli" [Wang Xifeng and systems management], *Zhonghua qiyejia,* no. 3, 1985, 59; Tan Luofei, " 'Hong lou meng' zhong de jingying guanli sixiang" [The management philosophy in 'The Dream of the Red Chamber'], *Guoneiwai jingji guanli,* no. 18, 1987, 23, 27–30. *The Dream of the Red Chamber* is perhaps the best-known translation of the title *Hong lou meng,* but readers who seek the best English translation available should consult the magnificent work by David Hawke, who uses another title, *The Story of the Stone* (Suffolk, England: Penguin Books, 5 volumes). See Chapters 13 and 14 in Volume One for the Wang Xifeng episode discussed here.
17. Zhou Shulian, "Tantan dui guowai qiye guanli," 60–63; Ruth L. Wang, "Transferring American Management Know-How to the People's Republic of China," *S.A.M. Advanced Management Journal* 51, no. 3 (Summer 1986): 4.
18. Cui Kene, "Woguo qiye guanli," 15.
19. William A. Fischer, "The Management Center in Dalian," *China Exchange News,* June 1983, 12–14; "Bu chuguo de liuxue" [Studying abroad without leaving the country], *RMRB,* 28 November 1986.
20. "Chinese Get Latest Word on U.S. Management Skills," *NYT,* 17 August 1982; "Students Earn American Degrees in China," *Beijing Review,* 21 November 1988, 37–39; Leo A. Orleans, "Chinese Students and Technology Transfer," *Journal of Northeast Asian Studies* 4, no. 4 (Winter 1985): 8.
21. Beth Keck, "China's Managers Look West," *CBR,* May–June 1985, 37; Lisa Jacobson Treacy, "The Managerial Elite," *CBR,* November–December 1988, 38; "Chinese Learning How to Profit from Wheeling, Dealing," *LAT,* 5 May 1983; Cindy P. Lindsay and Bobby L. Dempsey, "Ten Painfully Learned Lessons about Working in China: The Insights of Two American Behavioral Scientists," *Journal of Applied Behavioral Science* 19, no. 3 (1983): 265–276.
22. "China: Three Perspectives," *Coopers & Lybrand Newsletter,* April 1981, 3; Keck, "China's Managers," 37; "U.S. Executives School Chinese on Capitalism," *Journal of Commerce,* 18 August 1988; Tom Peters, "Doubting Thomas," *Inc.,* April 1989, 92; "East Meets West Via Internships," *San Francisco Chronicle,* 5 September 1986.
23. "Chinese Students Learn Western-Style Management in Buffalo," *NYT,* 29 March 1987; Richard Holton, in foreword to Peter Kwok, *Managing Enterprises in the People's Republic of China* (Berkeley: Institute of Business Research and Economic Research, University of California, Berkeley, 1981), i–ii; "From Red Guard to MBA Student—How to Get Ahead in China," *CSM,* 18 June 1985.
24. "U.S. Experts Train Chinese in Modern Managerial Skills," *San Francisco Examiner,* 17 May 1987; "Teaching Management to Marxists," *Fortune,* 23 March 1981, 102–103; "China Joins with U.S. Universities in Effort to Teach High-Level Managerial Skills," *Chronicle of Higher Education,* 23 January 1985, 35–36.

25. "U.S.-Backed MBA Program Under Way in China," *Mainichi Daily News,* 2 June 1985.
26. "Executives of China's State-Owned Firms Learn to Do Business the American Way," *WSJ,* 19 February 1987; "U.S.-Backed MBA Program Under Way," *Mainichi Daily News.*
27. "China Joins with U.S. Universities," *Chronicle of Higher Education;* "Training the New Managers," *Newsweek,* 10 December 1984, 14; Richard W. H. Lee, "Training Ground for a New Breed of Professionals," *CBR,* May–June 1985, 39–42.
28. "Mingyun beiwang lu" [A record of their fate], *QNB,* 2 December 1987. A slightly abridged version was also published in *Jiushi niandai,* January 1988, 52–57.
29. "Mingyun beiwang lu," *QNB.*
30. "Gaige ganbu renshi zhidu pozai meijie" [Reform of the cadre assignment system is extremely pressing], *QNB,* 8 December 1987; "Shehui zhongshi rencai, rencai xianshen shehui" [Society takes proper care of the talented, and the talented devote themselves to society], *QNB,* 15 December 1987; "Guanyu 'Mingyun beiwang lu' de duihua" [A dialogue about 'A record of their fate'], *QNB,* 19 December and 25 December 1987 [identical headlines both days but entirely different contents]; "For Chinese, A Mismatch of Job Skills," *NYT,* 27 December 1987.
31. Joseph Alutto, "The Status of Management Education in China: Lessons for the Future," [SUNY-Buffalo] *Reporter,* 18 February 1988.
32. "Mingyun beiwang lu," *QNB;* "For Chinese, A Mismatch," *NYT.*
33. "China's Expensively Trained M.B.A. Graduates Are Stuck in Jobs That Don't Tap Their Skills," *AWS,* 30 May 1988.
34. M. W. Searls, Jr., "Managers of Future," *NYT,* 12 January 1988; "Mingyun beiwang lu," *QNB.*
35. "Mingyun beiwang lu" and "Guanyu 'Mingyun beiwang lu' de duihua," *QNB.*
36. "Gaige ganbu renshi zhidu," *QNB;* Telegram from Shenyang, "Complaints by Dalian MBA's Underscore Problems in Northeast China," January 1988, U.S. Department of State; "Students Earn American Degrees," *Beijing Review,* 39; Treacy, "The Managerial Elite," 40.
37. Donald M. Kendall, "The Four Simple Truths of Management," *Vital Speeches* 52, no. 15 (15 May 1986): 475–478.
38. "American Executive[s] Are Aggressive," *St. Louis Countian,* 11 July 1987; Sheng Zongshen, " 'Guanjun' de youshi shi zhanshi de" [The top position of the 'champion' is only temporary], *Zhongguo qiyejia,* no. 3, 1987, 35; Li Cong, "Duiwai kaifang yu qiye guanli" [The opening to the outside and enterprise management], *Qiyejia yuekan,* no. 4, 1987, 29.
39. Liang Shenghu, "Zhongwai qiye guanli zhexue de chayi" [Differences in the philosophies of Chinese and Western enterprise management], *Qiyejia tiandi,* no. 4, 1986, 21–22.
40. "China Revives Law to Permit Children to Inherit Property," *WSJ,* 18 December 1979; "Chinese Companies Show More Interest in Leasing to Save Funds, Cut Red Tape," *WSJ,* 3 December 1982; "Socialism Grabs a Stick: Bankruptcy in China," *NYT,* 7 March 1988; "Free Markets and Chapter 11—Can This Really Be China?" *Business Week,* 9 May 1988, 60–62; "China Revives Another Piece from Its Capitalist Past," *Asian Wall Street Journal* [daily edition], 10 June 1988; "Insuring Interests," *CBR,* March–April 1988, 4–5; "You Gotta Give 'Em Credit," *CBR,* September–October 1987, 5; "One

State-Run Company Buys Another in China's Latest Economic Experiment," *WSJ,* 1 September 1987.

41. "Playing Monopoly," *San Francisco Chronicle,* 28 April 1980; "Playing for Keeps," *CBR,* January–February 1989, 4–5; "China's Would-Be Monopolists Are Lords of the Game Boards," *AWS,* 10 October 1988.

42. "Guanyu xuexi he jiejian Xifang guanli jingyan de jige wenti" [Some problems in studying and drawing lessons from Western management experience], *Waiguo jingji guanli,* no. 6, 1984, 1–3, reprinted in Renda, *Gongye qiye guanli,* no. 1, 1985, 127–129.

43. "Quanguo zhaiquan gupiao faxing'e yi da 900 yi yuan" [The total value of stocks and bonds sold in China has already reached 90 billion yuan], *RMRB,* 14 September 1988; "China Experiments with Stock Issues to Raise Funds for Growing Firms," *LAT,* 14 October 1984; "Stock Markets' Role Grows in Chinese Economy," *NYT,* 10 April 1989; Nancy Dunnan, "Yuan to Invest," *New York Times Magazine,* 29 November 1987, The Business World Supplement, 28, 34; "China, Seeking More Efficiency, Looks to a Stock Market System," *NYT,* 5 December 1988.

44. "China Stock Owners Aren't Exactly Sure What Stock Is For," *WSJ,* 9 February 1988; "Stock Markets' Role Grows" and "Yuan to Invest," *NYT.* The alacrity with which Chinese investors purchased stocks contrasts sharply with the reluctance that Hungarian investors displayed in participating in a new stock exchange established in Budapest in 1987. More than two years later, the low volume gave the impression that the Hungarian exchange was "more like a student pilot project than a functioning financial market." See "Lonely Days for Traders at Budapest Exchange," *NYT,* 20 February 1990.

45. "School at China's People's Bank Trains New Generation of Financial Whiz Kids," *WSJ,* 18 November 1986.

46. "Huaerjie lüeying" [Impressions of Wall Street], *RMRB,* 28 May 1983; "Chinese Interns Beat Gorbachev to NYSE," *Journal of Commerce,* 8 December 1988; "Selling China on a 'Public' Privatization," *NYT,* 8 January 1989; "China, Seeking More Efficiency," *NYT.*

47. Dunnan, "Yuan to Invest"; "Meiguo de fengxian touziye" [America's venture capital industry], *JJRB,* 6 January 1987; "Canguan Niuyue zhengquan jiaoyi suo" [Visiting the New York Stock Exchange], *Banyue tan,* no. 8, 1987, 58–59; "Meiguo dagongsi yanglai Niuyue gupiao jiaoyi suo" [America's largest companies depend on the New York Stock Exchange], *JJRB,* 3 October 1985; "Toying with Capitalism Themselves, Communists Soft-Pedal Market's Woes," *WSJ,* 28 October 1987.

48. "Woguo suoyouzhi gaige de shexiang" [Some tentative ideas about reforming the ownership system in China], *RMRB,* 29 September 1986; Peter F. Drucker, *The Unseen Revolution: How Pension Fund Socialism Came to America* (New York: Harper and Row, 1976), 1–2.

49. "Zhongnanhai gou gupiao" [Buying stocks in Zhongnanhai], *RMRB,* 11 September 1988; "Zhongyao gengzheng" [Important correction], *RMRB* 15 September 1988; "Zhongguo yi dati jubei tuixing gufenzhi tiaojian" [China has already largely completed preparations for implementing a system of stocks], *RMRB,* 20 September 1988; "Long March to Free Markets," *The Economist,* 19 November 1988, 76.

50. "Chinese Get Wall St. Guide to Capitalist Road," *NYT,* 12 November 1986.

51. "Reluctant Rebel Joins Students' Cause," *NYT,* 28 May 1989. A year after the Tiananmen massacre, Gao Xiqing had resumed working toward establishing

a national stock exchange in Beijing. He was quoted as saying: "This is like rowing a boat upstream. You can't stand still. You have to go ahead or you go backwards." See "Calls for Economic Changes Rise Among Chinese Officials," *NYT,* 30 July 1990, and "Renewed Call for Chinese Stock Market," *NYT,* 20 August 1990.

CHAPTER 9: MASTERS OF THE HOUSE

1. Liu Binyan, "Sanshiqi cenglou shang de Zhongguo" [On the thirty-seventh floor of China], *Renmin wenxue,* no. 8, 1986, 45.
2. Liu Binyan, "Sanshiqi cenglou," 45.
3. Liu Binyan, "Sanshiqi cenglou," 45.
4. "China Rests on Tradition," *LAT,* 28 July 1980; Fox Butterfield, *China: Alive in the Bitter Sea* (New York: Bantam, 1982), 272.
5. "China Rests on Tradition," *LAT.*
6. "China Rests on Tradition," *LAT.* By 1984, the state had changed its mind and decided that encouragement of the noonday *xiuxi* was not such a good idea after all. But the tone of righteousness that had been used earlier when defending the institution meant that the authorities had to tread carefully when explaining the official reversal. For a sample letter to the editor that was used in the later unsuccessful campaign to eliminate *xiuxi,* see "Xiuxi shijian shaole hui yingxiang jiankang ma?" [Will reducing nap time hurt one's health?], *RMRB,* 26 December 1984.
7. Solveig Jansson, "Getting a Foot in China's Door," *Institutional Investor,* March 1986, 122; "Peking's New American-Style Hotel," *CSM,* 2 November 1982; "China Hotel Management Loaded with Frustrations," *Hotel & Motel Management,* 13 October 1986, 3; "A New Team Checks In at the Great Wall Hotel," *NYT,* 24 March 1985.
8. Chris Urago, letter to editor, "Craftsmanship in China," *Honolulu Star-Bulletin,* 27 June 1984.
9. Claire Bentley, "Changing the Face of China," *Asian Hotelkeeper and Catering Times,* September–October 1984, 15; "Zhong Xi hebi, gujin huicui" [A good blend of Chinese and Western elements, a gathering together of past and present], *Wenhui bao,* 17 June 1984; "Western Opulence in East," *Dallas Times Herald,* 29 April 1984; "Peking Communists Get a Taste of the High Life," *South China Morning Post,* 24 June 1984; "An Oasis of Privilege in China," *NYT,* 27 November 1983.
10. Liu Binyan, "Sanshiqi cenglou," 42.
11. "Beijing fandian jianchi zhua fanfushi jiaoyu" [The Peking Hotel maintains its anti-corruption education program] and "Jiaoyu zhigong zengqiang mianyili" [Staff are taught how to strengthen their immunity], *BJRB,* 26 May 1981.
12. "An Oasis of Privilege in China," *NYT.*
13. "A Home-made, Showpiece Joint Venture," *Asia Magazine,* 8 April 1984.
14. " 'Changcheng' neiwai" [Inside and outside the 'Great Wall Hotel'], *QNB,* 14 September 1987; "Fang Hou Xijiu" [A visit with Hou Xijiu], *Shijie jingji daobao,* 29 October 1984.
15. Jansson, "Getting a Foot in China's Door"; "A Home-made, Showpiece Joint Venture," *Asia Magazine;* "Hotel Bosses Have Room for Change," *South China Morning Post,* 25 June 1984; "A New Team, *NYT;* "Zhong Xi hebi," *Wenhui bao.*
16. "A New Team," *NYT;* "Reqing, yange er kexue de guanli" [Caring, strictness, and scientific management], *Zhongguo qiyejia,* no. 12, 1985, 24–25; "China's

New Hoteliers Find Tourists Frown on 'Eating from Same Pot,' " *WP,* 5 December 1984; "A 'Big Nose' Finds a Bed," *WSJ,* 4 December 1985; "San Franciscan, Shanghai-Born, Designs a Trailblazing Hotel for China," *LAT,* 25 April 1982.

17. "China's Large Tourist Hotels Struggle to Learn the Ways of Inscrutable West," *AWS,* 19 March 1984; "China's New Hoteliers," *WP.*
18. "A New Team," *NYT.*
19. "Zhongguo da jiudian" [The China Hotel], *Taigang yu haiwai,* January 1985, 30–31, reprinted in Renda, *Shangye jingji, shangye qiye guanli,* January 1985, 115–116; "Under Peninsula's Management, Jianguo Hotel Succeeds," *Hotels & Restaurants International,* 19 October 1985, 31.
20. "Pingqing guoji fandian jituan guanli de daijia" [The price paid for hiring an international hotel chain as managers], *Wenhui bao,* 17 July 1987; " 'Changcheng,' " *QNB;* "At China Hilton, Subject Was Butter," *NYT,* 15 December 1988.
21. "China's Large Tourist Hotels Struggle," *AWS;* "China Hotel Management," *Hotel & Motel Management,* 84–85.
22. "China Hotel Management," *Hotel & Motel Management,* 84.
23. "Reqing, yange," *Zhongguo qiyejia.* 24–25.
24. Liu Binyan, "Sanshiqi cenglou," 51.
25. Liu Binyan, "Sanshiqi cenglou," 43.
26. Liu Binyan, "Sanshiqi cenglou," 43–44.
27. "China's Toilet Patrol Embarks On a Smelly But Virtuous Task," *AWS,* 11 July 1988.
28. Andrew G. Walder, *Communist Neo-Traditionalism: Work and Authority in Chinese Industry* (Berkeley and Los Angeles: University of California Press, 1986), 205–219.
29. "Riding China's Capitalist Road," *NYT,* 10 May 1987.
30. "Riding China's Capitalist Road," *NYT.*
31. " 'Qie-nuo-ji' de qiangda qudong li" [The enormous power of the 'Cherokee'], *RMRB* [Overseas edition], 18 December 1986.
32. "Pinqing waiguo zhuanjia zhichang" [Hiring a foreign expert to manage the factory], *Jingji tizhi gaige,* no. 2, 1985, 36–37; "West German Engineer Tries to Bring Efficiency to China," *WP,* 25 December 1985; "Gerich Sums Up His Experience in China," *China Daily,* 25 January 1986.
33. "China Opens the Door to U.S. Electronics Firms," *Electronic Business,* 15 March 1986, 108.
34. Wang Ruoshui, "Meiguo yipie—san" [A glance at the United States—Part III], *RMRB,* 19 October 1978. Wang's later outspokenness in criticizing Mao's personality cult and in promoting what Wang calls "socialist humanism" led to his dismissal from the *People's Daily.* See Geremie Barmé and John Minford, eds., *Seeds of Fire: Chinese Voices of Conscience* (New York: Noonday Press, 1989), 150–152, 470.
35. Liu Binyan, "Sanshiqi cenglou," 44.
36. "Successors Ready, U.S. Oilmen Bow Out of Their Saudi Empire," *NYT,* 1 April 1989.
37. "For Chinese, A Mismatch of Job Skills," *NYT,* 27 December 1987.
38. Ray Vander Weele, "Catching China Fever: A Management Accountant's Perspective," *Management Accounting,* October 1985, 74; Han Guiwu, "Guanyu jishu yinjin tanpan" [On technology import negotiations], *Xiandai qiyejia,* October 1985, reprinted in Renda, *Gongye qiye guanli,* December 1985, 73–74.

39. "Strangers in a Strange Land: The Plight of Western Managers Based in China," *Baltimore Sun,* 1 October 1985.
40. "Chinese Inn's No Holiday for U.S. Manager," *WP,* 2 August 1987.
41. "Chinese Inn's No Holiday," *WP;* "Why A U.S. Manager Was Fired," *Beijing Review,* 6 June 1988, 38.
42. "Yang jingli weishenme bei citui?" [Why was the Western manager dismissed?], *JJRB,* 2 May 1988.
43. "Yang jingli," *JJRB.*
44. "Yang jingli" *JJRB.*
45. "Yao xuehui dang dongshizhang" [One should study how to be a board chairperson], *BJRB,* 20 June 1988. The public had some fun with Chinese homonyms and said that the board directors, *dongshi,* did not know what they were doing, *bu dongshi.*
46. "Yiwei waifang jingli de ku yu le" [An outside manager's troubles and pleasures], *Guoji shangbao,* 17 March 1987.
47. Liu Binyan, "Sanshiqi cenglou," 49.
48. Liu Binyan, "Sanshiqi cenglou," 47.
49. "Hu's Resignation Clouds Outlook for Reforms in China," *AWS,* 19 January 1987. For Liu's reflections about his political life, see his autobiography *A Higher Kind of Loyalty* (New York: Pantheon, 1990).

CHAPTER 10: THE MARKETING OF MARKETING

1. Carl Crow, *Four Hundred Million Customers* (London: Hamish Hamilton, 1937), 13, 286; "China: What's In It for Investors?" *Financial World,* 1 February 1979, 15.
2. Crow, *Four Hundred,* 286.
3. Crow, *Four Hundred,* 56–59, 84–85.
4. Yang Dongsong, "Meiguo de xiaofeizhe diaocha" [American consumer surveys], *Waiguo jingji guanli,* no. 4, 1987, 60; "Meiguo shangren zhongshi shichang diaocha" [American merchants emphasize market studies], *JJRB,* 11 November 1986.
5. James M. Livingstone, "The Marketing Concept in China—A Qualified Acceptance," in Malcolm Warner, ed., *Management Reforms in China* (New York: St. Martin's Press, 1987), 89, 93; Dong Yuguo, "A Window on the World," *Beijing Review,* 28 December 1987, 41.
6. Xiao Tan, "Wo shi diyi" [I am number one], *Zhonguo qiyejia,* no. 3, 1988, 58.
7. For a survey of the vicissitudes of official treatment of commercial advertising in the PRC before 1979, see Xu Bai-yi, "The Role of Advertising in China," University of Illinois, Department of Advertising, Working Paper no. 24, 15 November 1989, 19–20.
8. Ding Yunpeng, "Wei guanggao zhengming" [Restoring the good name of advertising], *Wenhuibao,* 14 January 1979.
9. "Chinese Will Permit Foreign Companies to Advertise Wares," *WSJ,* 28 February 1979; advertisement in *Beijing Review,* 9 March 1979, 32.
10. "Qutan guanggao de zui" [Some interesting talk about advertising], *Shichang yishu,* no. 3, 1988, 33.
11. "Qutan guanggao de zui," *Shichang yishu,* 33; Raymond Williams, "Advertising: The Magic System," in *Problems in Materialism and Culture: Selected Essays* (London: NLB, 1980), 170, 177–178.

12. "Qutan guanggao de zui," *Shichang yishu,* 33; Yang Xianju, "Guanggao de xinli yixu erze" [Two examples of psychological techniques for advertising], *Zhongguo qiyejia,* no. 4, 1987, 32.
13. Jin Huisheng and Li Enjing, "Zhenshi, shi guanggao de shengming" [Truth is the lifeblood of advertising], *Jiangxi caijing xueyuan xuebao,* January 1986, reprinted in Renda, *Shangye jingji, shangye qiye guanli,* July 1986, 107–110; Yu Guangyuan, "Tantan guanggao" [Talking about advertising], *Zhongguo guanggao,* no. 2, 1986, 2; Wang Zhongming, "Jianchi shehui zhuyi fangxiang" [Maintain a socialist direction], *Zhongguo guanggao,* no. 1, 1984, 2–3.
14. Yu Guangyuan, "Tantan guanggao," 2; Marshall I. Goldman, "Product Differentiation and Advertising: Some Lessons from Soviet Experience," *Journal of Political Economy* 68, no. 4 (August 1960): 346–357.
15. Ji Lianggang, "Guanyu shangye guanggao jige wenti de tantao" [An exploration of some problems in commercial advertising], *Shanxi caijing xueyuan xuebao,* March 1985, 91–94, reprinted in Renda, *Shangye jingji, shangye qiye guanli,* December 1985, 94–97.
16. Jin Huisheng and Li Enjing, "Zhenshi, shi guanggao de shengming," 108; Yu Guangyuan, "Tantan guanggao," 2.
17. Jin Huisheng and Li Enjing, "Zhenshi, shi guanggao de shengming, 108; Ji Lianggang, "Guanyu shangye guanggao," 95; Shun Tu, "Zhidao xiaofei, chuangzao xuqiu" [Guide consumption, create demand], *Zhongguo guanggao,* no. 3, 1987, 17–19.
18. "Peddling in China: Madison Avenue Style," *CSM,* 30 December 1980; "China Tries On Gray Flannel Suit for Size," *LAT,* 4 November 1974; " 'Capitalist Road' of Madison Avenue Lures China in Bid to Sell Wares Abroad," *WSJ,* 29 November 1976.
19. "Three Agencies Take Pitch to China," *NYT,* 28 June 1979.
20. "Three Shops Bring Ad Story to China," *Advertising Age,* 2 July 1979; "Chinese Are Given Lessons on the Lore of Madison Avenue," *WSJ,* 10 July 1979; "Three Big Ad Agencies Visit China," *LAT,* 7 August 1979; Carol S. Goldsmith, "China's U.S. Sales Strategy: The First Steps," *CBR,* November–December 1980, 28; "Advertising in China," *Asian Advertising & Marketing,* February 1988, 30, 35, 37.
21. "U.S. Firms Exporting Expertise in Public Relations to China," *WP,* 8 September 1985.
22. Scott D. Seligman, "Corporate and Product Promotion," *CBR,* May–June 1986, 13; "The Woman Who Brought PR across the Great Wall," *San Francisco Examiner,* 17 June 1987; "From Propaganda to PR," *China Trade Report,* November 1985, 7.
23. Seligman, "Corporate and Product Promotion"; "China A Sleeping Giant for Two PR Shops," *Advertising Age,* 26 November 1984; "Newest U.S. Export to China: PR," *San Francisco Examiner,* 14 April 1985.
24. "China Is Plunging into Public Relations," *Business Week,* 23 September 1985, 73; Seligman, "Corporate and Product Promotion," 13; "The Woman Who Brought PR," *San Francisco Examiner.*
25. " 'Kekou kele bainian guanggao' futu" [Illustrations from 'One hundred years of Coca-cola advertising'], *Zhongguo guanggao,* no. 3, 1986, unpaginated; "Meiguo huwai guanggao" [Outdoor advertising in America], *Zhongguo guanggao,* no. 1, 1985, 37, 41; "Cong Aoyunhui Meiguo yundongdui fuzhuang kan Meiguo fuzhuangshang de shengyijing" [The shrewd business sense of the American apparel business, as seen in the clothing of the U.S. Olympic athletes], *JJRB,* 28 July 1984.

26. Fang Zhenxing, "Guanggaojie jixu jiejue de ruogan wenti zhi wojian" [My views on some pressing problems needing attention in the advertising world], *Zhongguo guanggao,* no. 3, 1987, 7.
27. "Niuyue jietou yige chenggong de guanggao" [A successful advertisement on the streets of New York], *JJRB,* 10 November 1985.
28. "Guanggao de xuewen" [Advertising knowledge], *Jiefang ribao,* 26 June 1984. The phrase used by the author is *yin er bu fa, yue ru ye.*
29. Fang Zhenxing, "Guanggaojie," 6; "New Issue in China: Truth in Advertising," *NYT,* 4 March 1981; "China Likely to Curb Foreign Products' Ads," *Advertising Age,* 12 July 1982, 24; "China Market Hot Despite Setbacks," *Advertising Age,* 9 June 1986, 59. The actual percentage of foreign advertising in China's total advertising expenditures was never large during the period in which it became controversial in the early 1980s. In 1982, foreign advertising was estimated to constitute only about 10 percent of the total, or about $7.7 million; in 1984, only 6 percent. A survey of advertising sponsors during a week in October 1985 revealed that of 154 advertisements heard on the national and Beijing radio stations during the course of the week, not one was for a foreign product or service. See Scott D. Seligman, "China's Fledgling Advertising Industry: The Start of Something Big?" *CBR,* January–February 1984, 13; Xie Yuanzhen, "Waishang zai Zhongguo tuixiao chanpin juxian hezai" [What are the limits on foreigners selling products in China?], *Bai Xing* [Hong Kong], 16 July 1985, 3; Sally Stewart and Nigel Campbell, "Advertising in Mainland China: A Preliminary Study," *International Journal of Advertising* 5, no. 4 (1986): 317–323.
30. Fang Zhenxing, "Guanggaojie," 6.
31. *Advertising and Marketing in China: Past, Present, and Future* (Hong Kong: The Asia Letter, 1985), 159, 176–177; Michael H. Anderson, *Madison Avenue in Asia: Politics and Transnational Advertising* (Rutherford, NJ: Fairleigh Dickinson University Press, 1984), 280; Seligman, "Corporate and Product Promotion," 12.
32. *Advertising and Marketing in China,* 198; "The Impact Grows," *China Trade Report,* August 1987, 10; Ren Yunhui, "Cong wailai guanggao xianqi de . . ." [Some thoughts provoked by foreigners' advertisements], *Shichang yishu,* no. 3, 1987, 20–21.
33. "Jiaqiang tiyu guanggao guanli de xin guiding" [New regulations to strengthen control over sports advertising], *Zhongguo guanggao,* no. 3, 1987, 48. In 1987, the ban on explicit tobacco product advertising was formalized. See "New Regulations Ban Tobacco Ads, Redefine Content Prohibitions," *Business China,* 30 November 1987, 169–171.
34. *Advertising and Marketing in China,* 198.
35. *Advertising and Marketing in China,* 224; Xie Yuanzhen, "Waishang zai Zhongguo," 4.
36. "Shanghai Agency Taking Its Own Great Leap Forward," *Advertising Age,* 11 November 1985, 43–48; "Selling American in China," *NYT,* 12 November 1980; "Laying the Foundation for the Great Mall of China," *Business Week,* 25 January 1988, 69.
37. "The Appeal of China TV," *International Advertiser,* June 1986, 41.
38. "The Appeal of China TV," *International Advertiser,* 37.
39. Beijing shangxueyuan shangye jingjixi [Beijing College of Business, Department of Business Economics], "Beijingshi dianshi guanggao xuanchuan de diaocha" [A survey of television advertising in Beijing], *Zhongguo guanggao,* no. 5, 1983, 42; "Commercials Are Big Hits on Chinese TV," *San Jose Mercury News,* 9 January 1988; Richard W. Pollay, David K. Tse, and Zheng-yuan Wang, "Advertising,

Propaganda, and Value Change in Economic Development: The New Cultural Revolution in China and Attitudes Toward Advertising," *Journal of Business Research,* March 1990, 83–95. For an analysis of the weaknesses in Chinese survey research in the early 1980s, see Stanley Rosen, "Survey Research in the People's Republic of China: Some Methodological Problems," *Canadian and International Education* 16, no. 1 (1987): 190–197. For the first Western studies of Chinese reactions to advertising, see Richard J. Semenik, Nan Zhou, and William L. Moore, "Chinese Managers' Attitudes Toward Advertising in China," *Journal of Advertising* 15, no. 4 (1986): 56–62; Suk-ching Ho and Yat-ming Sin, "Advertising in China: Looking Back at Looking Forward," *International Journal of Advertising* 5, no. 4 (1986): 307–315.

40. Beijing shangxueyuan shangye jingjixi, "Beijingshi dianshi guanggao," 42.
41. Beijing shangxueyuan shangye jingjixi, "Beijingshi dianshi guanggao," 42.
42. Yu Guangyuan, "Tantan guanggao," 2; Jin Huisheng and Li Enjing, "Zhenshi, shi guanggao de shengming," 108; Pei Minhui, "Guanggao xuanchuan ying zhuyi shehui xiaoyi" [Advertising persuasion should emphasize social benefits], *JJRB,* 1 March 1987. For a defense of Chinese adaptation of the personals in their newspapers, see Wang Jihong, "Zhenghun guanggao de shehui zuoyong" [The social function of marriage proposal advertisements], *Zhongguo guanggao,* no. 3, 1987, 47–48.
43. *Advertising and Marketing in China,* 176; Wang Zhongming, "Jianchi shehui zhuyi fangxiang," 2.
44. "Guanggao xuanchuan zhong de hunluan xianxiang jixu jiuzheng" [Confusion in advertising promotion must be corrected], *JJRB,* 22 August 1983; "Guanggao de shengming zai yu zhenshi" [Truth is the life of advertising], *RMRB,* 31 January 1981.
45. "Kandeng guanggao ye ying yange shencha" [There should be strict investigation before publication of advertisements], *RMRB,* 18 May 1985.
46. Tang Zhongpu, "Shilun woguo guanggaoye fazhan de heli quxiang" [Some exploratory thoughts about proper directions for the expansion of China's advertising], *Zhongguo guanggao* no. 2, 1987, 4–6; Jin Huisheng and Li Enjing, "Zhenshi, shi guanggao de shengming," 110; Wang Zhongming, "Jianchi shehui zhuyi fangxiang," 3.
47. "Qingchu jingshen wuran, banhao shehui zhuyi guanggao" [Eliminate spiritual pollution, do socialist advertising well], *Zhongguo guanggao,* no. 5, 1983, 2.
48. Zhu Xuehai, trans., "Dui guanggao kanfa de jidian jieda" [Some answers concerning advertising], *Zhongguo guanggao,* no. 2, 1984, 44.
49. "The Chinese Claim They Have Remedies for Nearly Every Ill," *WSJ,* 29 March 1974; Chris Brown, "Pharmaceuticals," *CBR,* September–October 1982, 34.
50. "China Opens U.S. Liquor Market Push," *LAT,* 24 March 1980; Letter, Lucking to Keating, 11 October 1977, folder "*CBR* vol. 4, no. 6, Background," Box 191, GRFL; "The Sino-Soviet Vodka Dispute," *CBR,* November–December 1977, 50; "International Politics Invades Vodka Market—The Results Are Mixed," *LAT,* 22 June 1980.
51. "China's Push for Exports Is Turning into a Long March," *Business Week,* 15 September 1986, 66–68.
52. Scott D. Seligman, "China's Fledgling Advertising Industry: The Start of Something Big?" *CBR,* January–February 1984, 15; "Selling Design to the Shanghai Mandarins," *The Director,* January 1984, 38; "Open Channels, New Ideas," *CBR,* March–April 1980, 51; "China Takes Big Loss in Rat Skins," *San*

Francisco Chronicle, 8 November 1983; "Peddling in China: Madison Avenue Style," *CSM,* 30 December 1980.

53. "China's Push for Exports," *Business Week,* 66.
54. Wang Xiaoping, "Shichang yu guannian" [The market and the concept], *Zhongguo qiyejia,* no. 5, 1988, 46; "Bao Baiyi nüshi tan Xifang xiaofeizhe de 'kouwei' " [Ms. Bao Baiyi discusses the 'tastes' of Western consumers], *JJRB,* 10 December 1986.
55. " 'Ni xuyao shenme wo jiu chukou shenme' yu 'wo you shenme jiu chukou shenme' " ['I'll export whatever you need' and 'I'll export whatever I happen to have'], *Guoji shangbao,* 16 April 1987; Guo Jinghong, "Learning the Ropes," *CBR,* September–October 1987, 41.
56. " 'Ni xuyao shenme,' " *Guoji shangbao.*
57. Emil Maurice Scholz, "Advertising for China," *Chinese Students' Monthly,* November 1922, 22–23; "Dui Mei chukou dayou kewei" [Exports to the United States have tremendous potential], *Jingji cankao,* 12 November 1987.
58. "Shiwu de Meiguoren zai dating" [Practical Americans make inquiries], *Jingji cankao,* 22 June 1988.
59. "U.S. Advertisers Selling Their Image on TV to Crack the China Market," *AWS,* 11 March 1985; "China's Commercialism Sparks Advertising Boom," *Dallas Morning News,* 8 September 1986; "Chinese Praise for Television," *NYT,* 3 June 1986.

CHAPTER 11: COCA-COLONIZATION

1. "Madison Avenue in China," *San Francisco Chronicle,* 25 March 1979.
2. "Luxury Goods from West Are Proving to Be Big Hit in China," *LAT,* 20 August 1978.
3. "Foreign Consumer Goods for Man-in-the-Street," *Business China,* 28 May 1980, 73; "Chinese Ad Unit Determines Society's Needs, Not Wants," *Advertising Age,* 20 August 1979, S13.
4. "Chinese Learn the Joy of Shopping as Leaders Stress Consumer Goods," *WSJ,* 26 October 1983; "Buy, Enjoy Is New Ethic for Chinese," *LAT,* 26 November 1986.
5. "Chinese Flirt with Western Fashions," *AWS,* 18 July 1983; "China's Closet Consumerism Thriving," *AWS,* 22 February 1982; "Will Fashion Triumph Inside China?" *Textile Industries,* February 1984, 70.
6. "Curls Making a Comeback in China," *LAT,* 7 May 1979; "Chinese Flirt," *AWS.*
7. "China, Receptive to Fashion, Chooses First Models," *NYT,* 10 April 1984; "Woguo fuzhuang biaoyan riqu huoyue" [China's fashion demonstrations are gradually flourishing], *RMRB,* 26 December 1984.
8. "Curls Making a Comeback," *LAT;* "China Gets Touch of Glamour as Max Factor Opens Shop," *LAT,* 21 February 1980; "Peking Factory Making Avon Cream for Chinese," *NYT,* 23 September 1982; Carl Crow, *Four Hundred Million Customers* (London: Hamish Hamilton, 1937), 32–36.
9. "Cosmetic Changes," *CBR,* March–April 1988, 4; Emily Honig and Gail Hershatter, *Personal Voices: Chinese Women in the 1980's* (Stanford, CA: Stanford University Press, 1988), 42–43; Orville Schell, "Serving The People with Advertising," *Whole Earth Review,* Spring 1987, 88–93.
10. "In China, Beauty Is in the Eye of the One Who Is Beheld," *LAT,* 16 December 1982; "In People's Republic, Western Eyes Have It," *LAT,* 2 May 1982.

11. "Rambo Is Taking China's Box Offices by Storm," *AWS,* 21 October 1985; "Rambo Busts Through China's 'Open Door,' " *CSM,* 15 October 1985; "Bringing Hollywood Hits to China's Moviegoers," *NYT,* 27 December 1987; "Rock Music Finally Cracks China's Cultural Wall," *NYT,* 26 February 1985; "Chinese Publish Rave Reviews of U.S.," *LAT,* 6 November 1978.
12. "Uniform-Weary Chinese Throng to Fashion Show to See 'Bourgeois' Satins, Styled Hair," *CSM,* 17 May 1983; "Chinese Flirt," *AWS.*
13. "Will Fashion Triumph," *Textile Industries.*
14. "Peking's Fashion Code Leans Toward the Don't's," *NYT,* 18 October 1983; "Shanghai Chic: China Discovers Fashion," *WP,* 9 February 1984.
15. "Jeans Get Approval from Chinese Women," *San Jose Mercury News,* 6 October 1984; "How Backward Glances May Hinder Progress in China," *China Daily,* 30 September 1984.
16. Yu Guangyuan, "Shehui zhuyi jianshe yu shenghuo fangshi, jiazhiguan he ren de chengzhang" [Socialist construction and life styles, value systems, and maturing], *Zhongguo shehui kexue,* no. 4, 1981, 9–10.
17. "Yindao xiaofei, meihua shenghuo" [Guide consumption, beautify life], *GMRB,* 13 October 1984; "Zhongshi shenghuo fangshi de biange" [Emphasize changes in life-styles], *RMRB,* 12 October 1984.
18. "Chinese Rulers Exhort Citizens to Go Shopping," *Newsday,* 22 October 1984.
19. "Buy, Enjoy Is New Ethic," *LAT.*
20. "Buy, Enjoy," *LAT.*
21. "Nader Back from China," *NYT,* 12 March 1979; "China Asks Nader's Advice," *Newsday,* 23 March 1979.
22. "China Asks Nader's Advice," *Newsday;* "Nader Watch," *WSJ,* 6 April 1979; "Chinese Learn the Joy," *WSJ.*
23. "1983–1987—Zhongguo xiaofeizhe yundong jilüe" [1983–1987—A short account of China's consumer movement], *Xiaofeizhe,* no. 2, 1988, 2–5; "Xiaofeizhe xiehui yao wei xiaofeizhe mou liyi" [Consumers Association will work for the interests of consumers], *RMRB,* 18 February 1985.
24. "Meiguo xiaofeizhe yundong shi hua" [Talks about the history of the consumer movement in the United States], *Xiaofeizhe,* no. 3, 1987, 8; "Consumer Protection 101 for Chinese," *NYT,* 12 September 1988; "Xian kan 'Xiaofeizhe baogao,' zai qu mai dongxi" [First read 'Consumer Reports,' then go shopping], *Guoji shangbao,* 28 November 1987.
25. Ye Kuntong, "Yi woguo baohu xiaofeizhe de lifa" [On laws to protect China's consumers], *Xiaofeizhe,* no. 1, 1988, 3; "Xiaofeizhe xiehui," *RMRB.*
26. Ye Kuntong, "Yi woguo," 2; "Jianlun xiaofeizhe quanli" [A brief discussion of the rights of consumers] *Fujian luntan: jingji shehui ban,* no. 1, 1987, 59; "1983–1987," *Xiaofeizhe,* 4; "Calling for Quality," *CBR,* March–April 1989, 4.
27. "Hua bu liao juhao de Qinggong 'Lie zhan' " (Can't put an end to the Ministry of Light Industry's 'Shoddy Goods Exhibition'], *JJRB,* 19 December 1987; "China Display of the Shoddy Breaks Down," *NYT,* 20 December 1987.
28. " 'Liezhan' jihua wei shenme gaibian le" [Why was the Shoddy Goods Exhibition Changed?], *JJRB,* 16 December 1987; "Hua bu liao juhao," *JJRB;* "China Display of the Shoddy," *NYT.*
29. "Hua bu liao juhao," *JJRB;* "Jianlun xiaofeizhe," *Fujian luntan: Jingji shehui ban,* 59–60.
30. "Playing the China Card," *Forbes,* 7 April 1986, 107; "Why Beijing Is Hungry for U.S. Food Companies," *Business Week,* 24 December 1984, 43.

31. "Prime Time in Peking," *New Yorker,* 1 April 1985, 30–31.
32. "China's Appetite for U.S. TV Shows Is Increasing," *NYT,* 28 May 1988.
33. "Why Beijing Is Hungry," *Business Week,* 43; Jim Mann, *Beijing Jeep: The Short Unhappy Romance of American Business in China* (New York: Simon and Schuster, 1989), 97; "A Tobaccoville in China," *Winston-Salem Sentinel,* 16 January 1985.
34. "China Wants U.S. Help on Sliced Bread," *San Francisco Chronicle,* 12 November 1978; "New Peking Motto—Let Them Eat Bread," *San Francisco Chronicle,* 4 December 1978; "PRC Fancy for Cakes, Cookies, Bread Means Sales Chances for Firms," *Business China,* 8 December 1982, 181; "A U.S. Effort to Shift China To Wheat," *San Francisco Chronicle,* 17 August 1985; "Speeding Noodles to China's Tables with US Technology," *CSM,* 20 October 1982; "Bread for China," *Time,* 1 September 1980, 49.
35. "Bread for China," *Time,* 49; "R.J. Reynolds Unit to Begin Selling Cigarets in China," *WSJ,* 25 April 1979; "Marlboro Men Wined and Dined in Canton," *San Francisco Chronicle,* 10 November 1980; "Yi zuo 'Jinqiao' jiaqi" [A 'Golden Bridge' has been built], *Xiamen ribao,* 27 October 1988; " 'Yangyan' maimai li jihe" [What exactly are the benefits in the 'Western cigarette' trade?], *GMRB,* 3 July 1988.
36. "Pushing Cigarettes Overseas," *New York Times Magazine,* 10 July 1988, 18; "Battlefield for the Tobacco War," *Journal of the American Medical Association,* 6 January 1989, 29; "China Is Invoking Marx in Its War on Smoking," *AWS,* 4 May 1987; "New Prices, Old Vices," *CBR,* March–April 1989, 4–5.
37. "Yi bai qishi yi yuan bubai" [Now, We Get 17 Billion Yuan], *QNB,* 6 January 1988.
38. Ernest Dichter, "The World Customer," *Harvard Business Review,* July–August 1962, 122.
39. Theodore Levitt, "The Globalization of Markets," *Harvard Business Review,* May–June 1983, 92–93.
40. "Marketers Turn Sour on Global Sales Pitch Harvard Guru Makes," *WSJ,* 12 May 1988.
41. For a perceptive and entertaining report on the state of American cultural influence in Asia in the mid-1980s, see Pico Iyer, *Video Night in Kathmandu* (New York: Knopf, 1988).
42. "Spreading the Capitalist Tool," *Advertising Age,* 30 September 1985, 16; "Cold Drinks War Hots Up," *China Trade Report,* April 1985, 13; "Coca-Cola to Go on Sale in China as U.S. and Peking Expand Ties," *NYT,* 20 December 1978; "Coca-Cola Scores Its Own Breakthrough," *WSJ,* 20 December 1978; "Soda-Pop Politics, At Home & Abroad," *New York Post,* 26 December 1978.
43. "20,000 Cases of Coca-Cola Going to China," *San Francisco Chronicle,* 23 January 1979; [Photo captioned:] "First Shipment of Coca-Cola to China," *NYT,* 24 January 1979; "Coca-Cola's Back in China, Just in Time for New Year's Party," *LAT,* 24 January 1979; "Coke Brings 'Tasty Happiness' to China," *NYT,* 16 April 1981.
44. "Can Coke Add Life to Overseas Markets?" *Chicago Sun-Times,* 24 December 1978; Orville Schell, *Watch Out for the Foreign Guests: China Encounters the West* (New York: Pantheon, 1980), 150; "How 'Western' Will Chinese Become?" *CSM,* 9 April 1979; "Easy Access to Spur Coke Sales," *Advertising Age,* 14 December 1981, p. S11; "For Some Chinese, Coke Isn't Their Cup of

Tea," *AWS,* 22 June 1981; "Coke Comes to China," *San Francisco Chronicle,* 3 January 1981; "The China Syndrome," *WSJ,* 8 May 1980; "Coke and Pepsi Carve Tiny Niche in Huge Market," *Advertising Age,* 9 June 1986, 56; "In Patient Pursuit of China: Coca-Cola China Limited," *Journey: The Magazine of the Coca-Cola Company,* February 1989, 4–5.

45. "Kekoukele faji shi" [A history of the rise to power of Coca-Cola], *RMRB,* 20 June 1982; "PepsiCo Accepts Tough Conditions for the Right to Sell Cola In India," *WSJ,* 20 September 1988; "Ad Space Offered in Red Flag Journal—Of All Places," *Business China,* 23 January 1980, 11–12.
46. "Coke Snubbed in Peking," *LAT,* 12 July 1986; "Pepsi's Pitch to Quench Chinese Thirsts," *Fortune,* 17 March 1986, 60.
47. "Weibi 'Kekou' geng bu 'kele' " [It is not necessarily good-tasting, or refreshing], *Xinguancha,* no. 11, 1983, 23; "Big Fizz over Coke Erupts in China Press as New Plant Opens," *AWS,* 20 June 1983; "Consumerism in Peking," *WSJ,* 7 July 1983.
48. "Fang Beijing 'Kekoukele' chejian" [A visit to the Beijing 'Coca-Cola' plant], *Yangcheng wanbao,* 27 July 1983; "Guangzhou Kekoukele yinliao chang jianwen" [Sights and sounds at the Guangzhou Coca-Cola Beverage Factory], *Yangcheng wanbao,* 28 July 1983.
49. "Big Fizz Bubbles Up," *AWS;* "Coca-Cola's Chinese Rival," *China Reconstructs,* August 1987, 42; "Chinese-Style Drinks Success," *China Economic Weekly,* 24 August 1987, 3; "Ginseng Cola Hopes for Sweet Success," *Atlanta Journal and Constitution,* 12 July 1987; "Anti-Cancer Drink," *China Daily,* 11 August 1988.
50. "Coca-Cola Scores Its Own Breakthrough," *WSJ;* "Pepsi's Pitch," *Fortune,* 58; Donald M. Kendall, "The Four Simple Truths of Management," *Vital Speeches,* 15 May 1986, 477; "Coca-Cola's Chinese Rival," *China Reconstructs,* 42.
51. "China's Soft-Drink Industry," *Beijing Review,* 7 December 1987, 34.
52. "Kentucky Hatches Its Chickens in Beijing," *Asian Business,* February 1988, 17. It was many years later—only in 1990—that serious discussion of American hamburgers in China resumed, and the occasion was when Fast Lane Burgers, a tiny two-restaurant "chain" based in Phoenix, announced its plans to open a restaurant just off Tiananmen Square, "making history in the burger world." See "Small U.S. Chain Takes Hamburgers to China," Reuters, 24 January 1990.
53. Ellen F. Chen and Christopher G. Oechsli, "A Fast Food Frontier?" *CBR,* November–December 1988, 30; "Kentucky Hatches," *Asian Business,* 17–18; "Capitalist Chicken Goes to Beijing," *WP,* 13 November 1987.
54. Zhao Xiuyun, "Xinjueqi de Meishi kuaicanting" [A newly risen, American-style fast food restaurant], *Zhongguo qiyejia,* no. 5, 1988, 17; "Kentucky Hatches," *Asian Business,* 19.
55. "Kentucky Fried Chicken Titillates Tastebuds in Beijing," *China Reconstructs,* February 1989, 54–55; "Kentucky Hatches," *Asian Business,* 17; "A Kentucky Colonel in the Heart of Beijing," *San Jose Mercury News,* 13 November 1987; "Capitalist Chicken," *WP.*
56. Zhao Xiuyun, "Xinjueqi de Meishi kuaicanting," 18.
57. "Kentucky Fried Chicken Titillates," *China Reconstructs,* 55; Liu Yan, "Xiaofei yu shijian" [Consumption and time], *Xiaofeizhe,* no. 5, 1987, 11.
58. Zhao Xiuyun, "Xinjueqi de Meishi kuaicanting," 16.
59. Zhao Xiuyun, "Xinjueqi de Meishi kuaicanting," 16; "Russian Milkshakes and Human Kindness," *NYT,* 1 February 1990; "Muscovites Queue Up At American Icon," *WSJ,* 1 February 1990.

60. "Colonel Sanders Greeting More Chinese Customers," Xinhua General Overseas News Service, 11 November 1988; "Foreign Companies in China Devising Plans to Weather Sudden Policy Shifts," *AWS,* 14 November 1988.
61. "Wariness about Business in China Persists," *AWS,* 15 June 1989; "Ad Set in China Is Withdrawn," *NYT,* 7 June 1989; "Despite Hard Times, Chinese Show Passion for Foreign-Style Fast Food," *Chicago Tribune,* 14 January 1990.

CONCLUSION: SALESMAN REVISITED

1. "An Actor Gives New Direction To China's Stage," *NYT,* 10 January 1988.
2. "China Fires Up Propaganda Machine To Halt Inroads of Western Influence," *AWS,* 27 August 1990; "America, Unbeautiful, As Portrayed by China," *NYT,* 12 April 1990; "Continental Can Finds Business in China Requires Reading of Political Tea Leaves," *WSJ,* 9 January 1990; Arthur Miller, "Death in Tiananmen," *NYT,* 10 September 1989; "Deng Is Silent, And the Chinese Can't Tell Where the Power Is," *NYT,* 17 September 1989; "Nude Art Photos at Beijing Bookstands Still Controversial," Xinhua General Overseas News Service, 9 April 1989; "Art Festival Shows Stability of China," Xinhua General Overseas News Service, 11 September 1989. Miller wrote erroneously that Ying Ruocheng had been dismissed along with Wang Meng; see Michael Gasster's correcting letter to the editor, "China Culture Official Remains in Favor," *NYT,* 2 October 1989. Regarding the politics of soft drinks in the United States, Pepsi counterattacked in its own fashion in late 1989 when it ran television commercials that superimposed "Peace on Earth" and the Pepsi logo over an image of an East German soldier putting a flower in a buttonhole on his uniform. See "Blurred and Shaky Images That Burn in the Mind," *NYT,* 14 January 1990.
3. "Who's Minding the Store In China?" *Business Week,* 14 August 1989, 58; "A Beijing Campaign to Lure Back Businesses Swings Into High Gear," *NYT,* 21 June 1989; "Beijing Increasing Pressure on Foreign Firms to Return," *WSJ,* 19 June 1989; "As Foreign Investment in China Dwindles, Firms That Remain Shift Their Strategies," *AWS,* 25 June 1990; "Suddenly, China Looks Smaller in the World," *NYT,* 27 March 1990; "Business Stakes East Bloc Claims And a 'Gold Rush' Hits Hungary," *NYT,* 17 March 1990.
4. "Foreign Firms Shun Spotlight as Business Regains Normalcy," *AWS,* 21 August 1989; "China's Factories Again Toe Party Line," *WSJ,* 28 December 1989; "China's Economic Reform Program Enters Hibernation," *WSJ,* 26 September 1989; "China's Economic Reforms Stall As Leaders Push Conservative Line," *AWS,* 2 October 1989; "Beijing Is Reasserting Centralized Control," *WSJ,* 28 November 1989; "Beijing's Course: A Fractured Party Spinning in Circles Without Direction," *NYT,* 1 November 1989; "Jiang Zemin zong shuji de jianghua" [A speech by General Secretary Jiang Zemin], *RMRB,* 30 September 1989; "Foreign Firms Wary of China, Says Official," *LAT,* 2 October 1989.
5. " 'Shengyi zong shi yao zuode,' " ['There is always business to be done'], *JJRB,* 1 July 1989; "China Campaigns to Woo Back Foreign Business," *WP,* 19 June 1989; "Wariness About Business in China Persists," *WSJ,* 15 June 1989; "Business in China Adjusts to the Party Line," *NYT,* 25 September 1989; A. J. Robinson, "Will Business Ever Get Back to Usual in China?" *WSJ,* 19 June 1989; Robert Kleinberg, letter to the editor [responding to the Robinson article], "China Isn't Investment Oriented," *WSJ,* 28 July 1989.
6. "First Kentucky Fried Chicken Bar Opens in Shanghai," Xinhua General Overseas News Service, 9 December 1989; "Jiang Zemin Meets U.S. Coca-Cola

President," Xinhua General Overseas News Service, 2 October 1989; "Avon Calling—In China," *WSJ,* 1 February 1990.

7. Judith Lubman, "Quality of Exports Decline," *China Daily,* 28 April 1989; "Chinese Corruption Spurs Some Investors To Consider Moving Business Elsewhere," *AWS,* 17 July 1989; "Foreign Companies Brace for Plunge in Trade With China," *AWS,* 9 October 1989; "China's Austerity Program Puts Squeeze on Many Foreign-Backed Joint Ventures," *WSJ,* 29 December 1989; "After Tiananmen, Ominous Signs on Road to China," *WP,* 5 November 1989; "Headaches in China for Investors," *NYT,* 5 February 1990; "Developers in China Hit Hard Times," *NYT,* 6 August 1990.
8. "You yuanjian de waiguoren," [Farsighted foreigners], *JJRB,* 3 July 1989; "Bush's Brother and Other Americans Testing the Business Climate in China," *AWS,* 25 September 1989.
9. "Companies Hesitating On China," *NYT,* 3 July 1989; "China's Repression Has Japan's Leaders Divided About What Response Is Proper," *WSJ,* 26 June 1989.
10. Yi Jiayan, " 'Heshang' xuanyang le shenme?" [What exactly is 'River Elegy' advocating?], *JJRB,* 19 July 1989; "China Now Condemns Acclaimed TV Series," *NYT,* 2 October 1989. For a translated excerpt from the program, see Han Minzhu, ed., *Cries for Democracy: Writings and Speeches from the 1989 Chinese Democracy Movement* (Princeton NJ: Princeton University Press, 1990), 21–22.
11. "Retracing the Road to Tiananmen," *NYT,* 7 October 1989. In exile, Wuer Kaixi undermined his existential philosophy with materialist and carnal exploits that embarrassed his former supporters. See Joseph F. Kahn, "Better Fed Than Red," *Esquire,* September 1990, 186–197.
12. "China Gets Back to Business as Unusual," *WSJ,* 30 August 1989.

INDEX